WISDEN
ON INDIA

WISDEN

ON INDIA

AN ANTHOLOGY

Jonathan Rice

EDITED BY
Jonathan Rice

WITH A FOREWORD BY
Ravi Shastri

Published in the UK in 2011 by
John Wisden & Co
An imprint of Bloomsbury Publishing Ltd
36 Soho Square, London W1D 3QY
www.bloomsbury.com
www.wisden.com

ISBN 978 1 4081 2674 5

A CIP catalogue record for this book is available from the British Library.

Commissioned by Charlotte Atyeo
Edited by Rebecca Senior
Designed by Joc Lucas

Cover photograph © Getty Images

Picture credits: Images on pages 61, 171, 180, 194, 213, 305 © Patrick Eagar; viii, 14, 43 © Getty Images; 85, 128, 140, 320 © PA Images, 72 courtesy of MCC Library, 253, 271, 309 © Graham Morris, 83 © Central Press, 102 © Yorkshire Post 237 courtesy of Bob Thomas/ Popperfoto; 315 Global Ventures/BCCI/Getty Images. The portrait on page 48 has been detailed from photographs by the Sport and General Press Agency, Photopress, Mora (Brighton) and Mr R. V. Bishop (Guiseley). The portrait on page 57 has been detailed from photographs by Chandler (Southampton), Ramsden (Leicester), Central News, Sport and General Press Agency and Bassano.

This book is produced using paper that is made from wood grown in managed, sustainable forests. It is natural, renewable and recyclable. The logging and manufacturing processes conform to the environmental regulations of the country of origin.

Typeset in 10.5 Minion by Saxon Graphics Ltd, Derby
Printed and bound in Great Britain by Martins the Printers

CONTENTS

ACKNOWLEDGEMENTS

In putting together this anthology, I have had a great deal of help, both direct and indirect, from a number of people. To begin at the beginning, I should mention my father, whose love for India and its peoples rubbed off on me from the first time we went there, when I was eight. I remember the pungent bustle of Calcutta (as it then was) and staying at the Maidens Hotel in New Delhi, swimming in the pool and talking cricket with my brothers. On every subsequent visit to India, I have always found many people to talk cricket with.

Before I began work on *Wisden On India*, I read Ramachandra Guha's brilliant book, *A Corner Of A Foreign Field*, in my view by far the best national cricket history yet published anywhere in the world. This gave me a clear guideline as to who and what was significant in Indian cricket, even if *Wisden* did not necessarily recognise it at the time. I have been told that the four most important things to Indians today are God, family, cricket and Bollywood, in that order. In Sachin Tendulkar, at least three of those four important things are combined.

At Bloomsbury, I must thank Jill Coleman and Charlotte Atyeo, for a very pleasant lunch at which the idea of *Wisden On India* arose, and for all their help during its gestation period. Christopher Lane, as ever, has chipped in with words of wisdom when needed, and Becky Senior has edited the book superbly as always. Ravi Shastri has provided the perfect Foreword, for which I am honoured and grateful.

Lastly, I wish to thank my wife Jan, for putting up with me and my chaotic distribution of *Wisdens*, Post-it notes, page proofs and coffee cups all around the house as the anthology took shape.

All these people contributed, but any mistakes (and coffee stains) are mine.

Jonathan Rice
March 2011

Foreword by Ravi Shastri

Wisden Cricketers' Almanack is said to be cricket's bible. Not without reason. It delights its faithful devotees (fans), practitioners (cricketers) and clergy (administrators). And, for the less ardent follower, even local village games sometimes find a mention.

A copy of the latest edition tucked under your arm can give a sense of empowerment. This has been true for me, as it must have been for generations in the past – and will be for those yet to come.

Players' achievements acquire sanctity if recorded in *Wisden*. As you rise through the ranks, you have a burning desire to be one of *Wisden*'s Five Cricketers of the Year. And when old, you see many a withering frame with fading eyesight running their doddering fingers over an old copy to prove they once belonged.

The secret of its success is its authenticity. It pores over details, and then crystallises them in the briefest manner possible. Appreciation rarely goes overboard; criticism is hardly ever scathing. There is a moderation that often comes from wisdom. I guess wisdom and *Wisden* go hand in hand.

I have never appreciated *Wisden* more than since joining the media circuit two decades ago. Now, while voices behind mikes are shrill and pens spew mud and blood without a second thought, there is the example of *Wisden*. It never puts commercialism before the respect it gives to cricket or the joy it provides the game's devotees and practitioners. It never went looking for respect, but earned it through following a sincere and narrow path, year after year, decade after decade.

Interestingly, geographical boundaries haven't mattered. *Wisden* has the same aura and respect in India as it has in England. The same can be said for Pakistan, Sri Lanka and all the other Test-playing countries – or even in Associate nations who only now are beginning their formal association with the game.

I never became a *Wisden* Cricketer of the Year, though I like to think I came close once or twice. But when I look at the names of the 15 Indians that have been chosen in the last 77 years, I understand why. From C. K. Nayudu and the Nawab of Pataudi to Sunil Gavaskar and Kapil Dev, and then to Anil Kumble and Sachin Tendulkar, *Wisden* has enshrined the most prized legends of Indian cricket.

Today, as I move from one commentary box to another, a copy of *Wisden* is never far away. Wherever there is cricket, there will always be a *Wisden*.

Ravi Shastri played for India in 80 Tests and 150 one-day internationals between 1981 and 1992. He took 151 Test wickets as a left-arm spinner, and scored 11 Test centuries, including 206 against Australia at Sydney in 1992.

INTRODUCTION

When *Wisden* began publishing, in 1864, the Indian Mutiny, as British history books describe it, was less than a decade in the past. The power of the East India Company was only broken in 1858, when the British government took over the direct rule of the jewel in the Empire's Crown, British India. India changed in the minds of Victorians from being a remote outpost where men became rich or sick or both, to being the jewel in the crown of the British Empire, literally so in the case of the Koh-I-Noor Diamond, which had been acquired as spoils of war in 1850 and presented to Queen Victoria, the first Empress of India, a title first assumed in 1877.

Wisden from the outset looked beyond cricket played in England, so that even in that first edition the full scores of The English Eleven versus The Victoria Eighteen were published. The second edition, in 1865, included a report of George Parr's tour to Australia in 1863–64, and from then on, regular reports of cricket in Australia filled the early years of *Wisden*. Indian cricket took a little longer to reach the attention of *Wisden's* editors, but with cricket panjandrums such as Lord Harris and Lord Hawke becoming heavily involved in cricket on the sub-continent, by the end of the 19th century, cricket in India was beginning to be recognised as being worth reading about. The fourth Baron Harris was not only captain, president and secretary of Kent County Cricket Club (sometimes all three posts in the same year) and occasionally captain of the England side: he was not only President of M.C.C. in 1895, but also Under-Secretary of State for India in the 1880s and Governor of Bombay from 1890 to 1895. It is said that he spent most of his time in India playing cricket rather than governing, and that most of his cricket was among the Europeans in India rather than with or against the native population, but all the same, there is little doubt that he had a strong influence on the development of the game in India. If nothing else, Harris's presence in India gave greater publicity to the game there, and his perceived snub of the local Parsees, Hindu and Muslim players would have only spurred them on to greater determination to defeat the colonial power at cricket, if not in battle.

Lord Hawke, the Lord High Everything Else of Yorkshire. M.C.C. and England, was also a keen advocate of spreading the influence of cricket around the world. He took teams to New Zealand, South Africa, West Indies, Canada, the United States, and Argentina as well as India, where his sides toured in 1890 and 1892/93. They played a number of good-quality matches but *Wisden* concluded that the 1890 tour, captained by George Vernon, was rather a disappointment. "Considering the number of English-born residents in Calcutta, Bombay and other centres of population", wrote *Wisden*, "the small amount of progress made with cricket in India is a little surprising, and no doubt the visit of Mr. Vernon's team will arouse a greater amount of public interest, and give a much-needed stimulus to the game."

Whether it was the stimulus of visits by English sides, or whether it was the work of Brits and other expatriates based in India, cricket took hold in India, especially around Bombay (Mumbai) and Delhi, and Lahore in what is now Pakistan. It reached its highest early standard in the annual tournament held in Bombay, which began in the 1870s with an annual match between the Europeans and the Parsees. The 1892 match between the two sides is usually treated as the first first-class match played between two India-based sides, a match that the Parsees won.

In 1907, the Hindus joined in and the Triangular Tournament was born. Five years later, the Muslims were invited to put forward a team, and the Quadrangular Tournament became the highlight of each season, until in 1937 a team called The Rest (made up of Christians, Jews and the occasional Buddhist or Singhalese) made the tournament a Pentangular one. This was perhaps the final straw in breaking the support for what was increasingly seen as a divisive competition which only served to accentuate the differences between the communities. The tournament was discontinued in 1946, by which time the Ranji Trophy, instituted in 1934 with teams chosen on a geographical basis rather than along religious or community lines, had already taken over as the premier cricket tournament of India.

It is hard to work out exactly why cricket took such a hold in India. It may simply be an overwhelming desire among the citizens of former countries of the British Empire to show the colonial power that they are not always top dog, and cricket is one way of proving it, but that is merely the gloss on the satisfaction of playing the game, and surely not the main reason. Of course, the local people would have seen the English playing this strange game almost from the moment the first adventurers arrived on the sub-continent, but that does not explain why they took to it so willingly right across the social and cultural spectrum - Hindus, Muslims, Parsees and don't knows. The same question has to be posed in other countries too, especially the West Indies, where the local population quickly took to the game with enthusiasm, flair and no little skill. One could say that cricket appeals in so many ways to the Indian personality and way of life, but then it also does to the West Indian personality and way of life. Yet there are so few similarities between the life and culture of, say, a Bajan and a native of New Delhi, that we must conclude that cricket, a simple game that originated on English farmlands some three hundred and fifty years ago, is so multi-faceted that it can and does appeal to anybody, whatever his or her cultural baggage.

Cricket has the power to engage equally an Old Etonian, a Nottinghamshire miner's son, the son of Irish immigrants to Australia or New Zealand, a schoolteacher in Kingston Jamaica, an Indian prince and an untouchable, a Muslim farmer in the Swat Valley and a fisherman in Sri Lanka. To each there may be different aspects of the game that make it particularly attractive, and to analyse the appeal would be fruitless, but all we can say for sure is that when cricket took root in India in the late 19th and early 20th centuries, it took root very firmly indeed.

By the time that India attained its independence in 1947, the national side had been playing Test cricket for a decade and a half, but they had yet to win a Test. They had some very fine individual players, from Palwankar Baloo at the beginning of the century, C.K. Nayudu, Vijay Merchant and Vinoo Mankad, but they could not put together a side strong enough to overcome international opposition. Their first Test win came against England in February 1952 (a match that was the first and only match in which England have been captained by a Derbyshire player – Donald Carr – and which was held up for a day when King George VI died) and from that moment India seemed to gain a belief in her own skills that led, slowly at first, to the time when India took their place among the strong Test-playing countries of the world. *Wisden's* report of India's first Test wins over each Test match opponent is included in this anthology.

The true moment of change from the old to the new was when India, against all the odds, won the World Cup in 1983. Suddenly limited overs cricket took hold, cricketers became superstars and the money men began to rub their hands at the prospect of rich pickings. Over the next 25 years, the centre of cricket's universe moved from Marylebone to Mumbai, and now even English county cricket's internal workings are affected by Indian cricket, the IPL, its money and its administrators. Nobody, not even Kerry Packer, has had such an influence on cricket in the past fifty years, as Jagmohan Dalmiya, who was Treasurer of the Board of Control for Cricket in India (BCCI) when India won the World Cup in 1983, and went on to become President of the BCCI and Chairman of the International Cricket Council. In his time he revolutionised the finances of both organisations, and while opinions on him as a man tend to be polarized, there can be no doubting the changes he has wrought.

In particular, the growth of cricket in India over the past thirty years has brought home to those of us raised on the English roots of cricket – the village green – that international cricket is no longer a rural game. In India it has probably always been an urban sport, with pick-up matches being played on the *maidans* of Delhi, Kolkata and Mumbai rather than in the villages far away from the dirt and the noise and the skyscrapers of the great subcontinental cities. From the earliest days in India, cricket was espoused by the nobility – the Jam Sahibs, Nawabs and Maharajahs of the days of empire, who built cricket grounds and cricket teams just as the lords and landed gentry had done in England a century or more earlier. But the Indian princes held power in the cities they and their ancestors had built, rather than on rolling hills and sheep-filled fields of the English developers of cricket. When independence came and the Jam Sahibs were Jam Sahibs no longer, the responsibility for keeping cricket alive passed, willingly or unwillingly, to the big commercial organizations, such as the Railways, the banks, the armed forces and the airlines. In every case, the influence has come from the cities, not the villages. The Indian national team is made up of men from the cities. They are few boys from the local equivalent of Bowral or Pudsey or Unity Village, Guyana – M.S. Dhoni being the exception that proves the rule. The starting point for Indian first-class cricket was an annual tournament between the different cultural communities, held in Bombay, rather than a county cricket championship played on dozens of small grounds all around the country, and in which, until very recently, money has not been the deciding factor in creating success. The way the game is now staged, marketed and sold in India is entirely a metropolitan phenomenon: yes, there are state sides drawing on players over a wide catchment area, but in effect they are city teams. The IPL does not even pretend to spread its wings outside the biggest cities. This is surely the way all cricket will go in the future, just as football did a century ago. In India, football is not yet significant as a locally played sport, but as Indian money begins to buy up Premier League teams in England, and interest in football grows around India, will the position of cricket as the most popular sport, the passion of the nation, be challenged?

As this book was being completed, India won the 2011 World Cup on home soil, and thereby became the only nation to have won world cricket titles in the 60 over, 50 over and 20 over formats. They are also currently (April 2011) ranked as the number one Test nation. The only forms of the sport they do not dominate seem to be Kwik Kricket and Table Cricket. The women's team have still some way to go to match their male counterparts, but don't bet against them over the next decade or so.

The 2011 World Cup was far too long, of course, but it was superbly organised and produced some memorable matches, not least the Final between India and Sri Lanka, which was won by the Indian captain, Mahendra Singh Dhoni, hitting a six into the crowd to win by six wickets with ten balls remaining. How this will affect India's attitude to other forms of cricket remains to be seen, but it will certainly mean that players like Dhoni, Yuvraj Singh, Zaheer Khan, Virender Sehwag and even the demigod Sachin Tendulkar will be placed on even higher pedestals of popularity than before. And their bank balances will not be harmed either. Cricket is thriving in India more than anywhere else in the world. In India, cricket is the richest sport, so it attracts the best of the best out of over one billion inhabitants. India could well be top cricketing dog for a generation or more.

In times past, *Wisden* reported on matches and cricketers (and the occasional umpire) when dealing with Indian cricket. Now, as *Wisden* approaches 150 years of publication, articles are just as likely to be about finance, the Laws, Mahatma Gandhi, terrorist actions or illegal gambling rings as they are to be about the majesty of a Tendulkar innings or the brilliance of a quick, fizzing Kumble leg-break. This is perhaps a pity, but it reflects modern society: cricket reports from any other part of the world are likely to deal with many of these issues as well.

Wisden, of course, is not trying to be a social or anthropological history text book, and you will find few deliberate philosophical gems in its pages. Even more unlikely is political reporting. In India's case, it almost wilfully ignored the civil strife of the inter-war years and stuck to descriptions of the cricket matches, but between the lines we can trace the changing view of Indian cricket from a deeply paternalistic beginning to a somewhat overwhelmed present, when not only does India seem to have most of the world's greatest cricketers, but also most of the cricket world's money. Over a century and a half, cricket in India, and *Wisden's* reporting of Indian cricket around the world, have changed radically.

We are now at a crucial point in the history of international cricket (a claim that I must admit has been made down the years in *Wisden's* pages more than once), at a moment when the future of Test cricket is threatened by the rise and rise of the Twenty20 format. Is Test cricket alive or dead in India? Will cricket split into two separate sports, like Rugby Union and Rugby League? Will Test cricket still be played in twenty years' time? We do not know the answers: in fact, we do not even know that these are the right questions, but whatever the future holds for cricket, it will surely be shaped by events and decisions made in India.

Wisden on India is not a history of Indian cricket. It is a pot of trinkets, to be dipped into and enjoyed as a reflection on the way that cricket's greatest publication has looked at cricket's greatest conquest, India.

CHAPTER 1
THE FORMATIVE YEARS: 1864–1911

Wisden *did not pay very much attention to the progress of cricket in India in the early years, especially after the first tours by Parsees proved disappointing, both in terms of skill and in public interest. Until the first tour by an all-India side, in 1911, the main focus of interest as far as* Wisden *was concerned, was the glorious career of K. S. Ranjitsinhji, who for about a decade was the most brilliant player of the Golden Age of English cricket.*

The first mention in Wisden *of India was not in a cricketing context. The first edition of 'The Cricketer's Almanack for the year 1864, being Bissextile or Leap Year, and the 28th year of the reign of Her Majesty Queen Victoria' (who was not yet also Empress of India) is altogether more military. On the very first page of the Almanack, under the listings for January 1864, and only five days after the anniversary of the birth of Israel Haggis, of Cambridge, in 1811, comes the pithy single line, '28, Thurs. The Sikhs defeated at Aliwal by Sir Harry Smith, 1846.'*

This battle, the turning point in the first Anglo-Sikh War, earned Sir Harry Smith the grateful thanks of parliament and the Duke of Wellington, and allowed him to style himself 'Sir Harry Smith of Aliwal' thereafter. His wife, Juana Maria de los Dolores de Leon Smith, is better known today as the original Lady Smith, after whom was named the town in KwaZulu-Natal which was besieged for 118 days during the Second Boer War, but where first-class cricket is now regularly played.

Further entries in the Almanack section of that first Wisden *included, for March: '31, Thurs. Interest due on India bonds,' a fact that is repeated six months later, on 30 September, a Friday. The final mention of Indian events in that first Almanack revisits the Sikh Wars with the information that the Battle of Ferozeshah was fought on 22 December 1848. The concept of cricket on the subcontinent seems not to have entered the editors' minds.*

It was not until 1887 that there was any proper mention of Indian cricket.

WISDEN – 1887

THE TOUR OF THE PARSEES, 1886

From a cricket point of view the tour of the Parsees was a failure, and we have not thought it worthwhile to print any of the scores. In arranging the fixtures, the powers of the players had been much overrated, and in the whole series of matches, the Parsees only gained one victory. Despite their ill-success, however, they thoroughly enjoyed the trip, and returned home with the pleasantest remembrances of English cricket and English hospitality. We append the averages in batting and bowling of the most successful cricketers in the team.

Batting Averages

	Innings	Runs	Most in an innings	Times not out	Average
P. Dustur	33	587	89	1	18.11
A. Major	43	646	97	2	15.31
D. Patel	35	423	55*	7	15.3
J. Morenas	38	516	55	3	14.26

Dustur and Patel on account of hurt fingers had to retire from several matches.

Bowling Averages

	Overs	Maidens	Runs	Wickets	Average
S. Bhedwar	587	169	1,178	59	19.57
D. Khambatta	719	176	1,724	75	22.74
D. Patel	212	66	388	16	24.4
M. Framjee	973	289	2,110	79	26.56
A. Major	503	115	1,330	42	31.28

WISDEN – 1889

PARSEE TOUR

After an interval of two years this country was visited by the second team of Parsee cricketers. We are unable, through want of space, to give more than a brief reference to the tour, but it may be stated that the team proved stronger at all points, and achieved a greater amount of success, than their predecessors. Perhaps the most notable feature of the tour was the wonderfully successful bowling of Mr Pavri, who took 170 wickets at a cost of under 12 runs each.

Summary of all matches: 31 matches played, 8 won, 11 lost, 12 drawn.

Mr M. E. Pavri bowled 5,178 balls (as overs were not necessarily all of four balls), with 581 maidens, and took 170 wickets for 1983 runs, at an average of 11.11.

The only name that features in the averages for both tours is J. Morenas: clearly there was a major selectorial rethink between 1886 and 1888.

WISDEN — 1891

In 1891, a tour by an English team to India was first reported in Wisden, *and while these matches were not of first-class status, it showed that cricketers in England were taking serious note of what was happening in India.*

THE ENGLISH TEAM IN INDIA

Though in a great measure partaking of the nature of a pleasure trip, the tour in India of the side under the command of Mr G. F. Vernon was interesting as being the first visit to that country of a band of English cricketers. The team that left London in the autumn of 1890 was composed entirely of gentlemen players, and though by no means representative of amateur cricket in England, proved far too powerful at all points for most of the elevens that were encountered.

Two games were played in Ceylon and eleven in India, and of these the Englishmen won no fewer than ten, drew two and lost one. All the matches were eleven a side, but on several occasions the team might with advantage have met odds, as of the ten victories, six were gained in a single innings. The solitary defeat was sustained at the hands of the Parsees, and in a small-scoring match. The game aroused the greatest interest, and the success of the home eleven by four wickets was highly creditable.

Judging by the several heavy scores that were made by Mr Vernon's men, the Indian bowling for the most part was very moderate, but among the elevens were several batsmen of more than average ability, and some of whom were formerly well known in English cricket circles.

Owing to illness Lord Hawke was unable to take his place in the field as captain until the tour was more than half over, but in the few matches he played he did extremely well and came out at the head of the batting averages. The chief honours, however, belonged to the two Middlesex batsmen, Mr Vernon and Mr J. G. Walker, both of whom were seen to brilliant advantage on several occasions, and Mr Gibson and Mr Philipson also did themselves justice. A complete record of the bowling was not kept, and this was somewhat unfortunate, as Mr Hornsby, Mr Gibson, and Mr De Little, who did most of the work, must have had somewhat exceptional averages.

Considering the number of English-born residents in Calcutta, Bombay and other centres of population, the small amount of progress made with cricket in India is a little surprising, and no doubt the visit of Mr Vernon's team will arouse a greater amount of public interest, and give a much-needed stimulus to the game. Apart from the fact that one or two members of the side were somewhat affected by the climate, the trip was of the most pleasant description, and everywhere the Englishmen were received with the greatest cordiality and hospitality. We gather that Mr Vernon was thoroughly satisfied with the success of the visit from the fact that he has hopes of taking out a second team to India in the autumn of 1891.

Wisden *only prints the scorecards in full for the English scores, but to judge from the names of the people who took wickets against the tourists, there were very few Indians playing, except in the Parsee side, which was the one match Mr Vernon's team lost.*

Mr Vernon was not able, in the event, to take another team in the autumn of 1891.

WISDEN — 1893

CRICKET IN INDIA

We have been favoured by Lord Harris with the following statistics of the doings last season of the Government House eleven at Bombay. Out of 13 matches played, the eleven won nine, lost only one, and left three unfinished. All the matches but one were played on matting wickets. It may be mentioned that Mr Framjee Patell's team was composed of eight of the Parsee eleven and three good men of other nationalities. From the fact that he scored 327 runs, with an average of 46, it is pretty clear that the cares of office have not caused Lord Harris to lose his batting.

The one game lost was to Poona Gymkhana, but the Government House eleven got its revenge in the return match. Captain Poore, who was Lord Harris's ADC and who in 1899 would score 304 for Hampshire against Somerset, was the most prolific batsman with 647 runs at an average of 80.7, while Corporal Sharpe led the bowling averages with 60 wickets at 7.38 apiece.

WISDEN — 1894

LORD HAWKE'S TEAM IN INDIA

After an interval of three years a second band of amateurs visited India during the winter of 1892–93, and had a most successful tour. Three games were played in Ceylon on the way out, and 20 in India, and of these 15 were won, two lost and six drawn. The Englishmen lost the first match with the Parsees, who had beaten the previous team, and the second defeat was inflicted by the Behar Wanderers. In the latter case the local players had the assistance of one of the English team, Mr A. E. Gibson, who largely contributed to the result by scoring 33 and 55, and taking eleven wickets for 67 runs. The matches were eleven-a-side, and though in several cases the home teams were quite outplayed there was no doubt that a better class of cricketers was encountered than in 1889.

English Team v Parsees
Played at Bombay, December 22, 23, 24, 1892

By some capital all-round cricket, the Parsees gained a creditable victory by 109 runs. Hill took eight Parsee wickets for 53 runs, while for the home team Pavri accomplished a precisely similar feat. In the Englishmen's first innings Bapasola took four wickets for 37 runs; and in the second, M. Kanga 4-32.

English Team v Parsees
Played at Bombay, December 29, 30, 31, 1892

After a splendid contest, the Englishmen won the return match with the Parsees by seven runs. For their success they were greatly indebted to Hornsby, who took 15 wickets for 86 runs.

In 1893, the first great Indian cricketer made his first-class debut, winning his Blue for Cambridge, and playing several fine innings.

THE UNIVERSITIES — CAMBRIDGE

After Jackson, the best batting in the team was shown by J. Douglas and the young Indian cricketer Ranjitsinhji… Ranjitsinhji's introduction to the eleven was abundantly justified. Though he failed against Oxford, he played a number of good innings in other matches, and his fielding at slip was quite exceptional in its smartness. Not even the captain worked more keenly for the well-being of the side. At Cambridge the young Indian made himself highly popular, and he is not likely to forget the receptions accorded him by the public when he played in London.

WISDEN — 1896

SUSSEX

Probably never in the history of Sussex cricket has the county been able to put into the field such a powerful batting side as was the case last summer, the team being enormously strengthened by the presence of the young Indian, K. S. Ranjitsinhji, who appeared under the residential qualification…

Ranjitsinhji's appearance in the team took most people by surprise, as the fact of his qualifying for Sussex was practically unknown until the early part of May. However, he accomplished a remarkable performance in his first match for the county, making 77 not out and 150 against the Marylebone Club at Lord's, and scarcely ever looking back from his brilliant start, he quickly accustomed himself to the strange surroundings of county cricket, and scored heavily against all classes of bowling, his wonderful placing on the leg side quite disheartening many of the leading professionals, who were unaccustomed to see perhaps their best ball turned to the boundary for four.

For a time he was successful on all sorts of wickets, making over 100 on a fiery ground against Middlesex at Lord's, and exceeding three figures against Notts when the wicket had by no means recovered itself from the effects of heavy rain. Later in the season, however, he, like most prominent batsmen, suffered from the rain, and had his period of failure. He always maintained a high position in the first-class averages, and there can be no doubt that his presence in the Sussex team inspired the other members of the side with great confidence.

Ranjitsinhji finished the season in fourth place in the batting averages, behind L. H. Gwynn, A. C. MacLaren and W. G. Grace, with 1,775 runs at 49.11, with four centuries. Much greater things were yet to come.

WISDEN – 1897

SUSSEX

Ranjitsinhji's batting was so extraordinary that it makes it difficult to realise that he was playing for the team that came out last among the leading counties. He had a most brilliant year in 1895, scoring 1,364 runs in the county competition, with an average of just over 41, but last summer he put this record quite into the shade, making only two short of 1,700 runs with an average of more than 58 per innings…

In purely Sussex cricket he scored seven separate innings of over 100 as well as making 171 not out in the match against Oxford University, which was, of course, outside the county programme. He made a number of other fine scores, very rarely failing entirely. His crowning achievement was the making of two hundreds against Yorkshire when he took his place with Mr W. G. Grace, Mr A. E. Stoddart, Mr George Brann and William Storer – the only batsmen who have ever accomplished a similar feat in first-class cricket.

England v Australia
Played at Manchester, July 16, 17, 18, 1896

The second of the three great Test matches was in many ways one of the most remarkable matches of the season, for though the Englishmen were defeated at the finish, the two best performances of the game were accomplished for them, Ranjitsinhji playing perhaps the greatest innings of his career, and Richardson bowling in a style he has seldom approached.

… Much depended upon Ranjitsinhji, and the famous young Indian fairly rose to the occasion, playing an innings that could, without exaggeration, be fairly described as marvellous. He very quickly got set again, and punished the Australian bowlers in a style that, up to that period of the season, no other English batsman had approached. He repeatedly brought off his wonderful strokes on the leg side, and for a while had the Australian bowlers quite at his mercy. Could the other English batsmen have rendered him any material assistance, there is no saying to what extent the English total might have been increased, but as it was, there was no other score on the Saturday morning higher than 19. Ranjitsinhji's remarkable batting, and the prospect of the Englishmen after all running their opponents close, worked the spectators up to a high pitch of excitement, and the scene of enthusiasm was something to be remembered when the Indian cricketer completed the first hundred hit against the Australians last season.

MacLaren, Lilley and Hearne all tried hard to keep up their wickets for Ranjitsinhji, but Briggs after making 16, could not resist the temptation of jumping out to try and drive a slow ball from McKibbin. The innings came to an end for 305, Ranjitsinhji carrying his bat for 154. It is safe to say that a finer or more finished display had never been seen on a great occasion, for he never gave anything like a chance, and during his long stay the worst that could be urged against him was that he made a couple of lucky snicks. He was at the wickets for three hours ten minutes, and among his hits were 23 fours, five threes and nine twos.

Australia 412 (Iredale 108, Giffen 80; Richardson 7-168) **and 125-7** (Richardson 6-76). **England 231** (Lilley 65 not out, Ranjitsinhji 62) **and 305** (Ranjitsinhji 154 not out). Australia won by three wickets.

CRICKETERS OF THE YEAR 1897

K. S. RANJITSINHJI

Perhaps the prevailing feelings of the age were reflected in the comment that Ranji missed a Blue in 1892 because the authorities at Cambridge 'found it hard to believe that an Indian could be a first-rate cricketer'. Even after all his success Ranji was seen as the exception that proved the rule: the only colonials who could play cricket were the Australians.

Kumar Shri Ranjitsinhji, the young Indian batsman who has in the course of four seasons risen to the highest point of success and popular favour, was born on September 10, 1872. When he first began to be talked about, the statement gained currency that he knew nothing whatever of cricket before coming to England to complete his education, but on this point Ranjitsinhji has himself put the world right. It is true that when he went up to Cambridge he had nearly everything of the real science to learn, but he had played the game in his school days in India, and was by no means such an entire novice as has sometimes been represented.

It was in 1892 that the English public first heard his name, and there is little doubt that he ought that year to have been included in the Cambridge eleven. Naturally he was not then the great batsman he has since become, but he made lots of runs in college matches, and was already a brilliant field. The authorities at Cambridge perhaps found it hard to believe that an Indian could be a first-rate cricketer, and at the complimentary dinner given to Ranjitsinhji at Cambridge on September 29 – when his health was proposed by the Master of Trinity – Mr F. S. Jackson frankly acknowledged he had never made so great a mistake in his life as when he underestimated the young batsman's powers.

However, Ranjitsinhji's opportunity came in 1893 when, in his last year at the University, he, to his great delight, gained a place in the Cambridge eleven. It was not his good fortune to do much against Oxford at Lord's – getting out for nine in the first innings, and without a run in the second – but on the whole he batted very well, scoring 386 runs with an average of 29 and coming out third in the Cambridge averages. Moreover, he had the honour of being chosen for the South of England against the Australians at The Oval, and though his real greatness as a batsman was as yet scarcely suspected, he made himself a very popular figure in the cricket world, his free finished batting and brilliant work in the field earning him recognition wherever he went.

Having left Cambridge, and not being yet qualified for Sussex, his opportunities in 1894 were very limited, and in first-class matches he only played 16 innings. Still he did well, averaging 32 with an aggregate of 387 runs. For the immense advance he showed in 1895, it is safe to say that very few people were prepared. Qualified by this time for Sussex, he made a truly sensational first appearance for the county against the MCC at Lord's, scoring 77 not out, and 150, and almost winning a match in which Sussex had to get 405 in the last innings. From this time forward, he went on from success to success, proving beyond all question that he was now one of the finest of living batsmen. In the first-class averages for the year, he ran a desperately close race with A. C. MacLaren and W. G. Grace, scoring 1,775 runs with the splendid average of 49. Of these 1,775 runs all but nine were obtained for Sussex, his energies being so entirely devoted to the county that, rather than stand out of the Sussex and Hampshire match, he declined the invitation of the MCC committee to appear for the Gentlemen at Lord's.

What Ranjitsinhji did last season is set forth in full detail on another page of *Wisden's Almanack*, and there is no need to go twice over the same ground. It will be sufficient to say that he scored more runs in first-class matches than had ever been obtained by any batsman in one season, beating Mr Grace's remarkable aggregate of 2,739 in 1871. While giving the Indian player, however, every credit for his extraordinary record, it must always be borne in mind that while he averaged 57 last season, Mr Grace's average in 1871 was 78.

As a batsman Ranjitsinhji is himself alone, being quite individual and distinctive in his style of play. He can scarcely be pointed to as a safe model for young and aspiring batsmen, his peculiar and almost unique skill depending in large measure on extreme keenness of eye, combined with great power and flexibility of wrist. For any ordinary player to attempt to turn good length balls off the middle stump as he does, would be futile and disastrous. To Ranjitsinhji on a fast wicket, however, everything seems possible, and if the somewhat too-freely-used word genius can with any propriety be employed in connection with cricket, it surely applies to the young Indian's batting.

WISDEN – 1898

The county review for Sussex again implied the county's batting revolved around Ranji.

SUSSEX

Ranjitsinhji accomplished several remarkable performances, but could not approach his phenomenal doings of 1896, being towards the end of the summer severely handicapped by frequent attacks of asthma… As a memento of the county's capital record, Ranjitsinhji, before his departure for Australia, presented every regular member of the team with a very handsome gold medal, bearing on one side the arms of Sussex in dark blue enamel, and on the other side the name of the player; also the inscription, 'From K. S. R.'

MCC and Ground v Sussex
Played at Lord's, May 13, 14, 15, 1897

When Ranjitsinhji eclipsed all his previous performances in first-class cricket by scoring a superb innings of 260 for Sussex against the MCC, a victory for the club seemed almost out of the question, and yet, thanks to their careless fielding in the final stages, the county eleven were actually beaten after all.

It was a match of great scoring throughout although, of course, Ranjitsinhji's innings overshadowed everything else. He was batting for four hours and 10 minutes and after the first three-quarters of an hour or so, was always master of the situation. While his leg placing was as remarkable as ever, his driving was far more powerful than usual, and the fact that he hit a six, 36 fours, 14 threes and 17 twos and kept up an average of about 60 an hour from his own bat, sufficiently indicates the general character of his cricket. Despite his wonderful success, the side only made 418.

WISDEN – 1899

Ranji's first overseas tour with England proved a personal success but a team disaster.

ENGLAND IN AUSTRALIA 1897–98

To speak the plain truth there has not for a very long time been anything so disappointing in connection with English cricket, as the tour of Mr Stoddart's team in Australia last winter. The team left England in September 1897, full of hope that the triumph of three years before would be repeated, but came home a thoroughly beaten side.

Following the precedent of the previous tour, five test matches were played against the full strength of Australia, and of these the Englishmen only won the first, severe defeats being suffered in all the other four... One cannot believe that the Englishmen played up to their home form. MacLaren and Ranjitsinjhi batted magnificently; Storer and Hayward played many fine innings; and J. T. Hearne bowled with a steadiness beyond all praise; but the men as an eleven never got really to their best, as their best is understood in this country... Ranjitsinhji, though he made so many runs, suffered a great deal from bad health.

English Team v Australia
Played at Sydney, December 13, 14, 15, 16, 17, 1897

A very unpleasant incident, which gave rise to almost endless discussion, preceded the first Test match, the trustees of the Sydney ground taking it upon themselves to postpone the commencement of the game without consulting the captains of the sides. Heavy rain had fallen, but it was not thought by the players on Thursday – the match being fixed to start on the following morning – that any postponement would be necessary. As it happened, the ground on Saturday, after heavy rain for several hours, was under water, and it thus came about that the anxiously expected game did not begin until Monday December 13.

The delay had one happy result for the Englishmen, Ranjitsinhji, who had been very ill, recovering sufficiently to take his place in the team and playing finer cricket than on any other occasion during the trip. Considering his physical condition – he was quite exhausted after scoring 39 not out, on the first evening – his innings of 175 was a marvellous piece of batting. Before resuming play on the second morning he was in the hands of the doctor. He hit 24 fours, and was batting in all three hours and 35 minutes.

English Team 551 (K. S. Ranjitsinhji 175, A. C. MacLaren 109) **and 96-1.**
Australia 237 (H. Trumble 70; J. T. Hearne 5-42) **and 408** (J. Darling 101, C. Hill 86; J. T. Hearne 4-9). The English Team won by nine wickets.

WISDEN — 1900

At this time, references to Indian cricket within the pages of Wisden *were few and far between. Apart from a report on the visit of Ranjitsinhji's team to America at the end of 1899, a team that was entirely un-Indian apart from its leader, the only mention of cricket in India came from an essay on one of the Five Cricketers of the Year.*

Major Robert M. Poore, beyond a doubt the most sensational batsman of the season of 1899 was born on March 20, 1866, and is thus in his 34th year. To find any close parallel to his sudden jump to fame in the cricket world would be very difficult, for before the public became familiar with his name he had passed the age at which a good many of our amateurs give up first-class cricket for more serious occupations.

Major Poore was, as regards cricket, the victim of circumstances, his military duties in India and South Africa keeping him out of this country at the time, when, had he not been in the Army, he would have been making his name. He was, however, later than most men in taking seriously to the game, and in an interview with him, which appeared in *Cricket* during the autumn, it was stated that in order to make up for lost time he studied the *Badminton Book* as thoroughly as though he had had to get it up for an examination. While he was thus learning the theory of the game in all its branches he was getting plenty of practical experience on Indian cricket grounds.

WISDEN — 1901

Ranji continued his astonishing form for Sussex, who came third in the Championship, largely as a result of the runs compiled by Ranji and his colleague and good friend, C. B. Fry. In all matches, Ranji scored 3,065 runs at an average of 87.57, his average being 26 runs higher than the next man in the lists, C. B. Fry. Ranji was perhaps the first Indian to be affected by 'the cold weather in May', but he would not be the last.

There was a development in the 1901 edition when Indian cricket began to be mentioned in the obituaries of men who played there.

The county possessed a number of dependable run-getters, but Ranjitsinhji and Fry did such extraordinary things as to reduce all the other players to insignificance. It may be questioned whether two batsmen on the same side have ever kept in finer form during the whole of a long season. Between them, they scored in county matches alone 4,393 runs, Ranjitsinhji making 2,563 with an average of 85 and Fry 1,830 with an average of 63…

Ranjitsinhji, when once he had shaken off a slight lameness, due probably to the cold weather in May, distanced all the batsmen of the year… among his long innings being 275 against Leicestershire at Leicester, 220 against Kent at Brighton, 202 against Middlesex at Brighton, and 192 not out against Kent at Tonbridge...

It would be impossible to praise the two batsmen beyond their deserts. They made the Sussex team so great in run-getting power that every match, whatever the strength of the opposing county, could be entered upon with the hope of an even fight. The misfortune was that, despite all Tate's good work as a bowler, there was seldom much prospect of actual victory.

OBITUARIES

Prince, Christian Victor, who died of fever in Pretoria, in October 1900, was a capable cricketer while at Wellington College, and would very likely have got into the eleven at Oxford if a new wicketkeeper had been required while he was in residence. After going into the Army he made lots of runs in military cricket, and was one of the few men who ever played an innings of over 200 in India, scoring 205 for the King's Royal Rifles v the Devonshire Regiment, at Rawul Pindee, in 1893.

The Maharajah of Patiala, who died in November, was a great supporter of cricket in India, and had, during several winters, engaged W. Brockwell and J. T. Hearne to coach and play for his eleven.

WISDEN – 1902

Ranji's successes at Sussex continued.

As in the two previous summers, Ranjitsinhji scored over 2,000 runs for Sussex in championship matches, and the fact that his having done so attracted so little notice was in itself striking testimony to his abilities. Such marvellous batting triumphs have been achieved by the Sussex captain that followers of the game accept hundreds from him as in the ordinary course of things. Last summer he reached three figures on seven separate occasions. Three of these innings amounted to over 200, and one of them – his 285 not out against Somerset at Taunton – is the highest score he has ever made in first-class cricket...

The Sussex captain, it should be added, became more and more a driving player. Opposing teams endeavoured to cramp his game by putting on additional short legs, but, without abandoning his delightful strokes on that side of the wicket, or his beautifully timed cuts, he probably got the majority of his runs by drives – a notable change, indeed, from his early years as a great cricketer.

WISDEN – 1903

Ranji's Sussex career was not as all-conquering as before; other matters, in India as well as in England, were taking up his time and concentration. He still finished the season second in the first-class batting averages, behind only Arthur Shrewsbury, but never played Test cricket again.

Ranjitsinhji only took part in 11 of the 24 county matches… For some reason which was not allowed to become public Ranjitsinhji dropped out of the team altogether during the last few weeks of the county season, finishing up with the Australian match at the beginning of August. Rumours were freely circulated as to his having had difference with one or more of the professionals, but on this point, in the absence of definite information, one can say nothing.

The fact remains, however, that, for the time at least, the great cricketer withdrew himself from the team with which his fame has been so closely associated. Ranjitsinhji was not last season half such a dependable batsman as in previous years… In a word, he became for the first time in his career an uncertain batsman. Brilliant as ever at his best, he could no longer be looked to with confidence for a big score. His falling off was not limited to his efforts for Sussex, as in the three Test matches in which he took part he failed dismally.

WISDEN – 1904

The 'Oxford University Authentics in India', a tour that lasted from mid-November 1902 until mid-February 1903, is given two pages in Wisden, one page summarising the results of all 19 matches (Won 12, Lost 2, Drawn 5), but there are no details of individual achievements in the games. The second page is given to the Authentics' averages, but no mention of any opposition cricketer is made.

The tour ranged from Lahore to Calcutta, Bombay, Madras, Peshawar, Lucknow and Cawnpore, from Bangalore to Allahabad and Aligarh, an exhausting three-month itinerary. The two matches lost were against the Bombay Presidency (by 46 runs, the first match of the tour) and against the Parsees, also in Bombay. The Parsees' victory, by eight wickets, came in the third match of the tour, and after that the Authentics were unbeaten.

WISDEN – 1905

1904 was to prove Ranji's final season for Sussex for some time. He had handed over the captaincy to C. B. Fry, but his batting was as sublime as ever.

Unfortunately, Ranjitsinhji did not give so much time to the game as in 1903, only taking part in 16 county matches as against 21. Still, instead of being overshadowed by Fry as in the previous year, he fairly divided honours with him...

Among Ranjitsinhji's many fine innings, the best by general consent was the 207 not out, with which he saved his side against Lancashire at Brighton, in August. From the first ball to the last in that superb display he was at his highest pitch of excellence, and beyond that the art of batting cannot go.

OBITUARY

Col. C. A. Liardet, one of the greatest supporters there has ever been of Indian Cricket, died at Ootacamund (Madras Presidency), early in March. He took part in the first Inter-Presidency match – played 40 years ago – arranged in India, when a Madras team went up to Calcutta.

WISDEN – 1907

OBITUARIES

Mr H. Pogson, who was well known as a cricketer in Bombay, died in India in March. He twice played for the Presidency against the Parsees, and was a member of the Rajkote CC.

Mr S. B. Spencer, a well-known Parsee cricketer, died at Calcutta on January 30, aged 46. He was one of the chief supporters of the Elphinstone CC at Bombay, and in recent years he took Parsee teams to Madras, Hyderabad, Nagpore, etc. His portrait appeared in Mr M. E. Pavri's work entitled Parsi Cricket.

WISDEN – 1909

The 1909 Wisden devoted six pages of statistics to the career to date of Ranjitsinhji. In summary, it showed that Ranji had scored 23,415 runs in 466 innings, 60 not out, for an average of 57.67. He had to that time scored 68 centuries and 104 fifties.

HIS HIGHNESS MAHARAJAH JAM SAHIB OF NAWANAGAR (KUMAR SHRI RANJITSINHJI) IN FIRST-CLASS CRICKET, compiled by A. C. Denham

With Ranjitsinhji back in England after an absence of three years the brightest hopes were indulged in when the season began, and up to a certain point, the eleven got on splendidly... Ranjitsinhji played in ten matches as against Fry's eight, and though not quite the dazzling batsman of former years was still on occasions very great. It was only when judged by the standard he had set up for himself that he proved in a measure disappointing.

In point of style and general mastery over the bowling nothing could have been better than his 153 not out against Middlesex at Lord's, and his 200 against Surrey at The Oval. Even in those two splendid innings, however, he played what might be described as an orthodox game, being very sparing with the daring strokes on the leg side which at one time drove even the best bowlers to despair. His defence was as perfect as ever, but after the loss of three seasons he could not trust himself to run the old risks with good length bowling. Had a new batsman played as he did everyone would have been lost in admiration, but the recollection of past achievements was too strong.

Once during the season the spectators saw the old Ranjitsinhji, but that was at the Scarborough Festival when the Sussex matches were over. It is a strange thing to say, but it seems quite possible, judging from the results in May, that Sussex would have had a better season if their two great batsmen had not played at all. Playing in some matches and standing out of others Ranjitsinhji and Fry might be compared to the stars of an opera company. They did brilliant things themselves but did not help the ensemble.

Note: Ranjitsinhji headed the English Batting Averages in 1896, 1900 and 1904.

Ranjitsinhji headed the Sussex Batting Averages in 1895, 1896, 1897, 1899, 1900, 1901, 1902 and 1908.

OBITUARY

Commander H. F. Philbrick, who was well known in Indian cricketing circles, died in September. He captained the Bombay Gymkhana team in 1907 and also kept wicket for the Presidency.

WISDEN – 1910

Mr C. B. Fry having gone over to Hampshire, with which county all his interests are now associated, and Ranjitsinhji being in India, Sussex were without the two batsmen who had made so many thousands of runs for them, and yet, as one ventured to hint a year ago, they had a more cohesive side than in any recent season.

WISDEN – 1911

For the first time, the Almanack, which would be to hand when the first All-India team toured England in 1911, included a brief review of the Bombay Tournament, the premier Indian cricket tournament of the time. It took up half of page 522 in a 532-page book.

THE BOMBAY TOURNAMENT

For the second year in succession the Triangular Contest in Bombay between the Hindus, Parsus [sic] and Presidency was seriously interfered with by rain.

1st Match – Hindus v Parsus
Played at Bombay, September 16 and 17, 1910, and left drawn

The Parsus scored 80 and 90 for five wickets, innings declared closed (R. P. Meherhomji 31 and 51), and the Hindus 77 and 50 for no wicket. P. Balu, of the Hindus, took ten wickets for 70, and scored 0 and 38 not out.

2nd Match – Hindus v Presidency
Played at Bombay, September 20, 21 and 22, 1910, and left drawn

The Presidency made 234 (F. R. R. Brooke 81) and 55 for three wickets, innings declared closed, and the Hindus 112 and 112 for seven wickets (K. A. Date 37). P. Balu, for the Hindus, took ten wickets for 108 runs.

In 1907, the first year in which it was held, the Triangular Contest was won by the Parsus, and in the following year by the Presidency. In 1909 the first match was finished, the Parsus beating the Hindus by four wickets, but in September last it was not found possible to complete either game.

CHAPTER 2

THE GAME TAKES HOLD: 1911–1932

For the first 35 years of Wisden's *publication, Indian cricket was little more than a peripheral subject, always excepting Ranji's extraordinary feats. But these feats were performed in England, for Sussex in the County Championship, or for England, as the first, but by no means last, India-born England cricketer.*

In 1911, the first All-India side toured England, and although they achieved little on the pitch, it was the beginning of Wisden, *and by extension, the wider English cricket community, taking a greater interest in what was happening half a world away.*

The political situation in India between the wars meant that there was reference to India in the newspapers on an almost daily basis, but Wisden *followed its well-established policy of not bringing politics into cricket. This position finally became untenable in the late 1960s, during and beyond the D'Oliveira crisis and the issue of apartheid in South Africa, but in the 1920s and 1930s, whatever was going on in India was for the front pages of the newspapers, and not to be mentioned in* Wisden.

During these years, cricket in India became more organised, less caste-ridden and of a generally far higher quality. By the early 1930s, India was ready for Test match cricket.

WISDEN – 1912

THE ALL-INDIAN TOUR, 1911

The tour of the Indian cricketers was a complete disappointment. It was clear from the start that far too ambitious a programme had been arranged, and a succession of defeats destroyed any chance of public interest in the fixtures. The team suffered from having been indiscreetly praised in advance. English cricketers had been told that the side would be strong enough to make a good fight with most of the counties and that, whatever their inequalities, the Indians would reveal exceptional capacity in fielding.

The tour will no doubt have a beneficial effect on Indian cricket in the future, but there is no disguising the fact that it fell very flat indeed. Not till the season was far advanced did a victory over Leicestershire check the long run of disasters, and by that time it was far too late to rouse the public from indifference.

A better result might have been obtained if Mistri – unquestionably a high-class batsman – had been able to play right through the summer, but his duties kept him in close attendance on the Maharajah of Patiala, and he only took part in three matches. His innings at Lord's against the MCC, however, was sufficient in itself to establish his reputation. For the rest the bowling was often fairly good, and from time to time good individual scores were obtained, but the fielding never came within measurable distance of what had been expected. Of their 14 first-class matches, the Indians won only two and lost ten.

The edition did feature accounts of the tour matches from which the following comments about the players are taken.

v Oxford University: On the first afternoon, Balu, left-hand medium pace, with an action not unlike that of Llewellyn, bowled admirably, and never lost his length during the hour and a half he was kept on. (P. Balu 31-4-87-5.)

v South Wales: Meherhomji (75) and Mulla (98) batted in fine resolute style, but no one else did anything of note.

v MCC: Major Mistri gave a brilliant display of hitting, scoring his 78 out of 106 in 80 minutes, but no one else could make much headway against the fine bowling of J. T. Hearne and Tarrant.

v Cambridge University: The Indians found the bowling of Lockhart and Falcon too much for them, and apart from Major Mistri no one met with any great measure of success.
Balu's bowling, 29.5-6-103-8 in an innings of 434, is not mentioned.

v Warwickshire: On the Friday, Shivram batted with marked skill for three hours, hitting one five and ten fours, but the Indians could not recover their lost ground.

v Lancashire: *Balu's 18-1-83-7 gets no mention.*

v Staffordshire: *S. F. Barnes takes 15.5-9-14-5 and 12.3-6-15-9 as Staffs win by five wickets on a poor pitch, and Balu in reply has figures of 19.4-3-35-6 and 13-1-23-2.*

v Surrey: In the Indians' first innings Kanga and Jaya Ram batted in attractive style, putting on 122 together for the second partnership. Jaya Ram cut crisply and hit well to leg, and Kanga, whose figures included nine fours, was especially strong on the leg side. Meherhomji also gave an admirable display.

v Leicestershire: at Leicester, Thursday, Friday, Saturday, July 13, 14, 15, 1911. In beating Leicestershire by seven wickets, the Indians gained their first victory. From first to last they completely outplayed the county, their batting being more resolute than in any previous match, and their bowling and fielding alike excellent. Kanga and Meherhomji laid the foundation of the fine total put together by the Indians, scoring 178 together in two hours and 20 minutes for the first wicket. In playing the first three-figure innings for the side, Kanga drove with great power, and cut superbly, among his figures being 23 fours. Meherhomji made his runs by stylish strokes on the off side, and Shivram and Salamudin played dashing cricket.

Balu's 11 wickets for 185 again pass without mention.

v Somerset: at Taunton Monday, Tuesday, Wednesday, July 17, 18, 19, 1911. After a very exciting finish the Indians defeated Somerset by one wicket. Thanks to a splendid innings by Bajana [who hit 108 out of 196], who, always picking out the right ball, hit very hard, the Indians gained a lead on the first innings of 39.

The Indians were left with 265 to get to win, and thanks almost entirely to Shivram [113*] and Balu [55], both of whom batted finely, they accomplished the task.

v Sussex: In the first innings of the Indians, Mulla batted in capital style, hitting up 54 out of 58 in 17 minutes by clean, powerful driving.

v Gloucestershire: In gaining a lead on the first innings the Indians were mainly indebted to Meherhomji, Shivram, Salamudin, and Kanga. All played bright attractive cricket, their hitting being hard and clean. Kanga and Meherhomji put on 113 in 80 minutes, and Shivram and Salamudin 135 in two hours.

In the final first-class averages, Major K. M. Mistri topped the batting averages with 188 runs at 31.33. R. P. Meherhomji scored most runs – 684 at 24.42, and P. Shivram (631 at 28.68) and Dr H. D. Kanga (617 at 28.04) were the only others to exceed 500 runs.

P. Balu topped the bowling averages with 75 wickets at 20.12, with J. S. Warden second with 44 wickets at 25.59. A. Salamudin (32 at 32.81) and M. D. Bulsara (23 at 28.30) were the only other bowlers to take ten wickets.

In all matches, Meherhomji scored 1,227 runs at 28.53, and Balu took 114 wickets at 18.86.

THE BOMBAY TOURNAMENT

Although lacking the services of Meherhomji in the first match, and of Pai in both, the Parsees experienced little difficulty in winning the tournament. Warden obtained 21 wickets for 188 runs, and Bulsara 13 for 164.

1st Match – Parsees v Hindus: Played at Bombay on September 21 and 22, 1911, and won by the Parsees by nine wickets. The Hindus scored 82 and 121 (P. Vithal 62 not out) and the Parsees 184 (S. M. Chothia 58) and 20 for one wicket.

2nd Match – Parsees v Presidency: Played at Bombay on September 25 and 26, 1911, and won by the Parsees by eight wickets. The Presidency scored 104 and 85, and the Parsees 170 and 22 for two wickets. The Parsees won the toss and sent the Presidency in.

OBITUARIES

H. H. The Maharajah of Cooch Behar died at Bexhill on September 18, after an illness of some weeks. He was born on October 4, 1862, and was therefore in his 49th year at the time of his death. A fair cricketer, he was also a great supporter of the game in India. One of his sons, Prince Narayan, has been seen in the Somerset eleven.

Col. John Pennycuick, CSI, who died at Camberley on March 9, was born on January 15, 1841, at Poona. He did not obtain his colours at Cheltenham, but in India, where the greater part of his life was spent, he did much for the game, especially in promoting and encouraging it among the natives. In all matches during his career he scored over 12,000 runs and took considerably over 2,000 wickets.

WISDEN – 1913

Ranjitsinhji played a few matches for Sussex, at the age of 40. While at Oxford University, another noble Indian cricketer, the Gaekwad of Baroda, was hoping to make his mark as Ranji had done two decades earlier. Injury unhappily curtailed his career.

Sussex, while improving on their wretched record of 1911, did not do nearly so well as might have been expected, seeing that on several occasions they had the invaluable assistance of the Jam Sahib of Nawanagar, better known to the world as Ranjitsinhji...

Unfortunately, the Jam Sahib was unable to play as frequently as he would have wished last summer owing to a sprained wrist. This weakness handicapped him considerably even in the games in which he did take part, for he was unable to bat with his old freedom, and many a ball that would in the old days have been hit to the boundary had to be left severely alone.

Still, he scored 554 runs in 11 innings and played the highest individual innings for the side – 176 against Lancashire – and easily earned the foremost place in the batting table.

Sussex v Lancashire
Played at Brighton, July 22, 23, 24, 1912

The superb batting of John Tyldesley and the Jam Sahib formed the outstanding feature of the match… Ranjitsinhji put together 176 in five hours and 50 minutes. The Jam Sahib played the ball on to his wicket when 71 and made two or three unfortunate strokes but did not give an actual chance. His hits, like those of Tyldesley, included 23 fours.

The Seniors' Match
Played at Oxford, May 6, 7, 8, 1912

In the opening stage of the match the Gaekwad of Baroda, who unhappily met with a bad accident a few weeks later, batted with delightful ease and freedom.

Mr G. E. V. Crutchley's Side 292 (H. H. the Gaekwad of Baroda 92, G. D. Forrester 92) **and 47-3. Mr A. L. Hosie's Side 83** (G. D. Wood 6-23) and **348-7 declared** (F. H. Knott 109). Match drawn.

Oxford University v South Africans
Played at Oxford, May 20, 21, 22, 1912

Rain restricting play on Wednesday to little more than two hours, this match was left drawn. The honours, however, clearly belonged to the University, for whom Evans played two splendid innings, and bowled in fine form. The Baroda of Gaekwad played in very attractive fashion. Nourse, showing much skill and judgment, saved his side from complete failure. The South Africans bowled wretchedly.

Oxford University 278 (H. H. the Gaekwad of Baroda 62, A. J. Evans 56) **and 244-5 declared** (Evans 109, F. H. Knott 70). **South Africans 179** (Nourse 94; Evans 5-73) **and 138-3**. Match drawn.

THE BOMBAY TOURNAMENT

Played at Bombay, September 9–16, and won by the Parsis. For the first time the Mohommedans [sic] took part in the tournament, which was quadrangular, instead of triangular as formerly.

1st Match – Hindus v Parsees: Hindus 64 and 79; Parsis 183 (J. S. Warden, 115 not out). The Parsis won by an innings and 40 runs.

2nd Match – Presidency v Mohommedans: Presidency 101 and 140; Mohommedans 131 and 75 for three wickets. The Mohommedans won by seven wickets.

3rd Match – Parsees v Mohommedans: Parsees 333 (Dr H. D. Kanga 150, J. S. Warden 85). Mohommedans 86 and 70. The Parsees won by an innings and 177 runs. M. D. Parekh took 11 wickets for 76 runs.

OBITUARY

The Rt Hon. Beilby Lawley, 3rd Lord Wenlock, was born on May 12, 1849, and died at Portland Place, London, on January 15. Although an enthusiastic cricketer, he was not in the eleven at Eton or Cambridge, but in 1870 he became a member of the MCC and 15 years later was President of the Club. Whilst Governor of Madras, he and Lord Harris (then Governor of Bombay) more than once opened the innings together, especially for Ganeshkhind, whose ground had been made by the latter.

WISDEN – 1914

This piece comes from the Records section:

Two Separate Hundreds in One Match: In India, in February 1904, Mr Lionel P. Collins, the Old Marlburian, three times made two separate hundreds in a match within a space of ten days, scoring quite without parallel in the history of the game. He made his runs whilst on tour with the Gurkha Brigade.

THE BOMBAY TOURNAMENT

The Quadrangular Tournament was played at Bombay, September 8–17, the matches resulting as follows:

1st Match – Mohommedans v Parsis: Mohommedans [sic] 75 and 138 (J. S. Warden 4-15 and 5-50). Parsis 94 and 101. Mohommedans won by 18 runs.

2nd Match – Bombay Presidency v Hindus: Bombay Presidency 119 and 111; Hindus 171 and 62 for three wickets. Hindus won by seven wickets.

3rd Match – Hindus v Mohommedans: Hindus 167 and 254 for eight wickets; Mohommedans 162 and 174 for five wickets. Match drawn.

OBITUARY

Mr Dorab E. Mody, a well-known Parsi cricketer, died suddenly in May at the early age of 39. He was a useful, painstaking batsman and an energetic field.

WISDEN – 1915

During the years of the Great War, the reports of Indian cricket were minimal, but India continued to feature regularly in the Obituaries section.

CRICKET IN INDIA

In December 1913, a Triangular Tournament was played in Calcutta, Rangoon and Ceylon being the visiting teams. The results worked out thus:
Calcutta drew with Ceylon and beat Rangoon;
Ceylon drew with Calcutta and beat Rangoon;
Rangoon lost to both Calcutta and Ceylon.

OBITUARY

Lieut. Arthur Edward Jeune Collins, of the Royal Engineers, who was killed in action on November 11, came suddenly into note by scoring 628 not out for Clarke's House v North Town, in a junior house match at Clifton College, in June 1899, when only 13 years old. During the six hours and 50 minutes he was in he hit a six, four fives, 31 fours, 33 threes, and 146 twos, carrying his bat through the innings, and Clarke's, who scored 836, won by an innings and 688 runs. Collins also obtained 11 wickets in the match, seven in the first innings and four in the second, and in partnership with Redfern (13) put on as many as 183 for the last wicket... He was born in India in 1885.

WISDEN – 1916

OBITUARY

Lieut. Col. George Henry Neale (3rd Middlesex Regt), born at Reigate on January 31, 1869, was killed in France on September 28. He was an excellent batsman with strong back play and a very good off-drive… He played much Army cricket and in India especially made many large scores. At Peshawar in January 1903, he made 55 and 124 not out for Peshawar v Oxford University Authentics, in the second innings going in first and carrying out his bat, and on the same ground a month later contributed 267 to the total of 607 scored by Queen's Regiment v Gordon Highlanders.

WISDEN – 1918

OBITUARY

Sesha Chari, Mr Kilvidi, born in Madras, January 2, 1875; died of pneumonia, at Calcutta, January 25. Best wicketkeeper India ever produced. Came to England with the All-India team in 1911.

WISDEN – 1919

OBITUARY

Patel, Mr J. M. Framji, one of the staunchest supporters of Indian cricket, died in Bombay on October 11. He was the author of a very interesting book on the history of the game in India.

WISDEN – 1920

THE QUADRANGULAR TOURNAMENT

At Bombay in December 1919, the Hindus won the annual Quadrangular Tournament. The matches resulted as follows:

Parsees v Hindus: Parsees (167 and 164); Hindus (119 and 213 for four wickets). Hindus won by six wickets.

Mahommedans v Europeans: Mahommedans (194 and 126); Europeans (156 and 130). Mahommedans won by 34 runs.

Mahommedans v Hindus: Mahommedans (149 and 97); Hindus (252). Hindus won by an innings and six runs. P. Vithal scored 108.

OBITUARY

Baroda, The Gaekwad of (Maharaj Kumar Shivaji Rao), second son of the Maharajah of Baroda, was born on August 31, 1890, and died in India on December 5. He was a very promising batsman at Oxford and could keep wicket. For the

University in 1911 he made 51 not out v Kent, and in 1912, after scoring 92 in the Seniors' Match, made 62 and 0 v South Africans and 17 and 12 v Australians. When it seemed possible he might obtain his Blue, he met with an accident, which resulted in concussion of the brain. For All-India v Surrey in 1911 he scored 24 and 25, this being his best performance in London.

WISDEN – 1921

Ranji played four innings for Sussex in 1920, totalling 39 runs at an average of 9.75. His highest score was 16.

SUSSEX

For sentimental reasons the reappearance in two matches of Ranjitsinhji was very welcome, but it would be idle to pretend that the once unapproachable batsman gave much suggestion of his old power.

OBITUARIES

Narayan Singh, Prince Kumar Hitendra, who died of influenza at Darjeeling on November 7, aged 30, was brother of the Maharajah of Cooch Behar, and was educated at Eton and Cambridge and played a few times for Somerset. He was a good batsman and in 1908 made several large scores for Somerset Stragglers, among them 104 and 103 not out v Devon Dumplings at Taunton and 99 and 91 v Incogniti on the same ground.

Plowden, Sir Henry Meredyth, died at Ascot in January in his 80th year, having for some time been in failing health. He was born in Bengal on September 26, 1840. Sir Henry appeared in first-class cricket so long ago, and went out to India so early in his life, that his career belonged to a very distant part, but in his day he was a prominent figure at Fenner's and at Lord's.

Taking his BA at Cambridge in 1863 he was called to the Bar in 1866 and not long afterwards he went to India. He was Government Advocate at Lahore from 1870 to 1877 and Judge of the Chief Court in the Punjab from 1877 to 1894.

WISDEN – 1922

THE BOMBAY TOURNAMENT

1920: Presidency (171 and 298) lost on first innings to Parsis (293 and 105 for five wickets). Hindus (313 and 176 for six wickets, innings declared closed) won on first innings against Mohammedans (268 and 89 for two wickets). Hindus (428) drew with Parsis (214 and 190 for nine wickets) in the final, which, by the Rules governing the Competition, cannot be decided on the first innings.

1921: Presidency (347) beat Hindus (139 and 100) by an innings and 108 runs. Mohammedans (168 and 161) lost by two wickets to Parsis (161 and 171 for eight wickets). Presidency (482 for eight wickets, innings declared closed) beat Parsis (102 and 83) by an innings and 297 runs.

WISDEN — 1924

It seems that for this edition Wisden *had finally decided that Indian cricket deserved a little more space, and some background information about cricket in India was published.*

In the Public Schools Cricket section, a new star was beginning to emerge, and H. S. Altham was strong in his praise for one Cheltenham schoolboy.

Duleepsinhji was distinctly less successful with the ball than in 1922, his captures dropping from 50 to 35, and the cost of each rising from 13.50 to 18.50: his value as a bowler was nevertheless great, and he may easily be successful in better cricket where the genuinely slow spin bowler is becoming something of a rarity: perhaps he is apt to toss the ball a little too high, but he has the great virtue of inviting the batsman to come and hit him, and of not presenting him with many balls short of a length.

In batting I feel strongly disposed to waive all qualifications and write him down frankly as the best of the year. In natural gifts of eye, wrist and footwork he is certainly blest far above the ordinary measure: this year his defence seems to have improved considerably, without this costing him any of his strokes.

Watching him bat against Haileybury I was most struck by his cutting and by his power of forcing the ball, whether short or overpitched, to the on-side. This latter he may be inclined to overdo, and I very much hope he will not allow it to impair his off-driving, but there is no doubt about the judgement and certainty with which he takes toll of straight balls of anything but the most immaculate length. His late cutting is quite beautiful, and there is a certain ease and maturity about all his batting methods that stamps him as of a different class from the ordinary school batsman. As he is also a fine fielder, with a good cricket brain which made his captaincy a real asset to his side, his future career will be watched with close interest.

Lord's Schools v The Rest
Played at Lord's, August 6, 7, 1923.

The Lord's Schools proved altogether too strong for The Rest, and at half-past four on the second afternoon they won in the easiest fashion by nine wickets. Duleepsinhji, of Cheltenham, was the hero of the game. He played a beautiful innings of 108, completing his hundred in an hour and three-quarters, and in the follow-on by The Rest he bowled high-tossed leg-breaks with surprising success, taking five wickets for 41 runs.

THE QUADRANGULAR TOURNAMENT

Beginning in the 1912 season the Quadrangular Cricket Tournament between sides representing the Europeans, Hindus, Mohammedans and Parsis respectively, drawn from Bombay and its vicinity, has been played each year, even during the war period, either in Bombay or Poona. The 12th such tournament was concluded at Bombay during the first fortnight of December 1923, the matches being as follows:

1st Match – Europeans v Parsis: Europeans 278 (J. B. Higgins 56, G. C. Phillips 55, R. L. O. Wodehouse 52); and 171 (S. E. West 66). Parsis 224 (D. K. Kapadia 83); and 160 for nine wickets (A. W. Pocock taking five wickets for 66 runs). Europeans beat Parsis by 54 runs on the first innings.

2nd Match – Hindus v Mohammedans: Hindus 294 (K. J. Pardeshi 69, P. Vithal 64; C. A. Murad six wickets for 71 runs); Mohammedans 76 (M. Joshi six wickets for 43) and 82. Hindus beat Mohammedans by an innings and 136 runs.

Final Match between the two winning sides – Europeans v Hindus: Europeans 481 (F. G. Travers 107, G. C. Phillips 93, C. Rubie 84, A. L. Hosie 75) and 153 (Joshi seven wickets for 39 runs). Hindus 475 (P. Vithal 101, D. B. Deodhar 78, C. K. Naidu [sic] 76, S. M. Joshi 50) and 161 for one wicket (C. K. Naidu 74, K. J. Pardeshi 71 not out). Hindus beat Europeans by nine wickets.

The 1923 final match is a record of high scoring in the tournament.

OBITUARIES

Bapasola, Nasarvanji Cawasji, born in April 1867, died at Meerut in June, aged 56. He was a member of the Parsi team which visited England in 1888, when he scored 584 runs with an average of 12.32 and took 24 wickets at a cost of 18.10 runs each. He was chosen for the first Presidency match in 1892 and for All-India against Lord Hawke's team. From first to last he played for over 30 years.

Cooch Behar, The Maharajah of (Raj Rajendra Narayan), died in London on December 20, 1922, his 36th birthday. He was a keen supporter of the game in India.

WISDEN — 1926

Just five years after his uncle Ranji finally retired from first-class cricket, Duleep took his place in the top flight, and evoked immediate comparisons with his uncle.

CAMBRIDGE UNIVERSITY

Duleepsinhji had a place awaiting him and quickly realised the expectations raised by his doings at Cheltenham in 1923. Watching the ball carefully and playing forward a lot he seemed to induce bowlers to pitch short and then his power of placing to the on came out as the best feature of his batting. An injured arm limited his skill in cutting or Duleepsinhji might have approached more nearly to the exceptional standard of his uncle, K. S. Ranjitsinhji.

The Freshmen's Match
Played at Cambridge, May 2, 4, 1925

Duleepsinhji had most to do with Enthoven's side winning by nine wickets. The one batsman in the match to rise superior to difficult conditions, he scored 139 runs for once out. At his first opportunity he fulfilled the high promise shown at Cheltenham, and practically made himself sure of his 'Blue'. Not only did he score off all the bowlers on the leg side with delightful ease but his forcing strokes, drives and leg hits were all well timed, and he never seemed at fault when playing forward to the good length ball on a rather soft pitch.

WISDEN — 1927

After a two-year hiatus, Wisden *once again included details of cricket in India, while Duleepsinhji's exploits continued to be covered in detail.*

SUSSEX

K. S. Duleepsinhji, becoming qualified, came into the team after the University Match and, opening with scores of 97 against Leicestershire and 115 against Hampshire, at once firmly established himself. Up to the return match with Leicestershire at Hastings he did very well indeed, but he finished the season rather moderately.

THE BOMBAY TOURNAMENT

The annual Quadrangular Tournament, played at Poona last September, was interfered with so much by rain that the sides which qualified for the final did so by leading on the first innings. The Hindus, who had won through their batting in 1925, had their bowlers to thank for being successful again.

Brief particulars of the three matches are appended:

1st Match – Parsis v Europeans: Played on September 13, 14, 15, 1926. Parsis, 55 and 142, lost to Europeans, 127 and 46 for five wickets, on the first innings. B. Howlett's bowling figures were 4-18 and 4-37; O. B. Graham's 4-12 and 3-39. For the Parsis R. J. Jamsetji's first innings analysis was 6-46.

2nd Match – Hindus v Mahommedans: Played on September 16, 17, 18, 1926. Hindus 111, beat Mahommedans, 102, on the first innings. Abdus Salam took seven Hindu wickets for 28 runs, and Chandarana six of the Mahommedans' for 54.

3rd Match – Europeans v Hindus: Played on September 20, 21, 22, 1926. Hindus, 97 and 178 (D. B. Deodhar, 49), beat Europeans, 159 and 105, by 11 runs. B. Howlett took nine wickets in the match for 79 runs, and R. J. O. Meyer 7-103. For the Hindus, L. Ramji obtained 9-104 and Chandurana [sic], in the second innings 5-52.

Results: When the tournament was inaugurated, in 1907, it was Triangular, but since the admission of the Mahommedans in 1912, it has been Quadrangular. The winners have been:

1907	Parsis	1917	Drawn
1908	Europeans	1918+	Europeans
1909	Drawn	1919	Hindus
1910	Drawn	1920	Drawn
1911	Parsis	1921	Europeans
1912	Parsis	1922+	Parsis
1913	Drawn	1923	Hindus
1914	Drawn	1924	Mahommedans
1915+	Europeans	1925	Hindus
1916	Drawn	1926+	Hindus

+ Those marked thus were played at Poona, the others took place at Bombay.

For a definite result to be reached, the final must be played out, a lead on the first innings in that match going for nothing.

OBITUARY

Dastur, Mr M. P., one of the most gifted of Parsi cricketers, was killed in a motorcycle accident at Karachi on November 2, aged 30. Only a few days before he had appeared in a couple of matches against the MCC Team, scoring 32 and 38 for Parsis and Muslims, and 1 and 61 for All-Karachi. In representative Parsi games he had made 157 not out v The Rest, at Karachi, in 1920, and 142 v The Europeans, at Nagpur, two years later.

WISDEN – 1928

In the winter of 1926–27, MCC sent a team to India, of higher quality than any side that had visited India in the past. The touring party consisted of: A. E. R. Gilligan (capt.), W. E. Astill, G. S. Boyes, A. Brown, Major R. C. Chichester-Constable, P. T. Eckersley, G. F. Earle, G. Geary, M. L. Hill, J. Mercer, J. H. Parsons, A. Sandham, M. W. Tate, and R. E. S. Wyatt. A. Dolphin, M. Leyland and the Maharajah of Patiala also played for the MCC team during the tour.

But, perhaps of greater significance, was the illness that struck down Duleepsinhji during the early part of the English season.

THE UNIVERSITIES – CAMBRIDGE

Greatly as Cambridge distinguished themselves in run-getting, it is only reasonable to assume that, but for the illness which overtook Duleepsinhji, they would have proved an even more difficult side to dismiss. The accomplished young batsman had headed the averages in the previous summer and, showing at the start of last season increased variety of stroke, he scored 101 against Yorkshire and 254 not out – a record for the University ground – against Middlesex.

Everything suggested that he would become one of the leading cricketers of the year, when in the middle of May he caught a chill, and such a severe attack of pneumonia developed, that at one time his life was in serious danger. Happily he recovered, and was able to get about some weeks later, but the doctors decided he must play no more cricket last summer. Everybody will hope that he has wintered well, and that in the coming season he may renew the brilliant career so unhappily interrupted last year. As it was, although taking part in only three matches, he scored 434 runs with an average of 108.

MCC TEAM IN INDIA, 1926–27

The MCC team captained by A. E. R. Gilligan found the extreme heat very trying at times, but they went through an arduous tour without suffering defeat. It was found necessary to send for Mercer to strengthen the bowling, and when injuries incapacitated Brown and Hill, the two wicketkeepers, Dolphin proved a valuable recruit. Leyland – like Dolphin engaged as coach by the Maharajah of Patiala – played in a few matches. Defeat by All-India was averted narrowly at Bombay, but at Calcutta the MCC won by four wickets, and victory came in seven of the nine engagements to which three days were allotted, but a large proportion of the other games ended without definite result. Sandham, Wyatt and Parsons batted extremely well, and Tate, scoring 1,249 runs and taking 128 wickets, enjoyed great success.

Results of all matches: Matches played 34, Won 11, Lost 0, Drawn 23
Three-day matches: Matches played 9, Won 7, Lost 0, Drawn 2

MCC Team v Hindus
Played at Bombay, November 30, December 1, 1926

The 45,000 people who assembled on the two days found compensation for the lack of a definite result in the brilliant hitting of Earle and Naidu. Five wickets had fallen for 124 when Earle and Tate added 154 runs in 65 minutes. At one period Earle obtained 26 off five successive balls, and he hit eight sixes and eleven fours in a dazzling display. Fast as Earle scored, Naidu drove with even greater power, 11 sixes and 13 fours being included in his 153 – made out of 187 in just over 100 minutes. He was, however, missed when 33. Mercer made his first appearance for the MCC.

MCC 363 (Earle 130; Godambe 4-80) **and 74-one. Hindus 356** (Naidu 153; Astill 5-75). Match drawn.

MCC Team v All-India (Indians)
Played at Bombay, December 16, 17, 18, 1926

At the end of a drawn game, MCC were badly placed, their lead with five men out in the second innings amounting to only 22. All-India lost seven wickets for 278, but then Mistri and Deodhar put on 88 by attractive cricket, and the home side eventually led by 75. Deodhar played a great game after giving a chance before reaching double figures. Besides driving well to the off, he showed admirable defence during a stay of four hours and a quarter.

MCC 362 (Wyatt 83; Nazir Ali 4-114) **and 97-5** (Ramji 4-32). **All-India 437** (Deodhar 148). Match drawn.

THE QUADRANGULAR TOURNAMENT

By defeating the Hindus, the holders, in the preliminary round, and the Mahommedans in the final, the Europeans won the tournament for the first time since 1921. A feature of the games was the bowling of R. J. O. Meyer, who obtained as many as 28 wickets in the two matches. In the third game the Europeans also owed much to W. J. Cullen, who scored 79 in his first innings and 120 in his second.

1st Match – Europeans v Hindus: Played at Bombay on November 28, 29, 30, 1927, and won by the Europeans by 54 runs. **Europeans 268** (F. G. Travers 70, A. L. Hosie 52; L. Ramji 6-92) **and 101** (L. Ramji 7-41). **Hindus 219** (R. J. O. Meyer 5-94) **and 96** (R. J. O. Meyer 7-44).

2nd Match – Mahommedans v Parsis: Played at Bombay on December 1, 2, 3, 1927, and left drawn. The Mahommedans led on the first innings. **Mahommedans 390** (Wazir Ali 105, S. G. Rasool 74 not out, M. H. Khan 50; H. J. Vajifdar 5-131) **and 241 for six wickets declared** (Mahommed Hussain 75, Rasool 65). **Parsis 259** (S. N. Ghandy 76, H. J. Vajifdar 55) **and 121 for four wickets**.

3rd Match – Europeans v Mahommedans: Played at Bombay on December 5, 6, 7, 8, 1927, and won by the Europeans by four wickets. **Mahommedans 59** (R. J. O. Meyer 7-28) **and 437** (Abdus Salaam 111, M. H. Vishram 75 not out, S. G. Rasool 54, Wazir Ali 53; Meyer 9-160). **Europeans 217** (W. J. Cullen 79; Abdus Salaam 5-72) **and 280 for six wickets** (Cullen 120; R. J. O. Meyer 50).

WISDEN – 1929

Politics and other non-cricketing issues were beginning to interfere in Indian cricket by 1927, while in England in 1928 things returned to normal when Duleepsinhji returned to the cricket field.

CAMBRIDGE UNIVERSITY

Unbeaten during the previous summer, when illness kept Duleepsinhji and injury M. J. Turnbull out of the field, Cambridge, with every reason to believe the services of these two fine batsmen would be available, entered upon the season of 1928 in very promising circumstances.

Duleepsinhji and Turnbull duly turned out – the former as soon as the weather became at all genial – and as six members of the 1927 eleven were still in residence, the old blues available numbered eight in all… Duleepsinhji missed the first four matches and was not quite at his best until the latter part of the season when Sussex enjoyed the benefit of his services, but his play was full of skill and increased variety of stroke and in view of the dangerous illness he had passed through 12 months earlier, he performed wonderfully well.

SUSSEX

Happily restored to health, and able to take the place awaiting him in the Cambridge eleven, Duleepsinhji, after the University Match, did splendid service for Sussex. He started for the county by hitting up 121 in 80 minutes against

Glamorgan, and getting five more centuries, scored 1,082 runs with an average of over 60. Driving harder than hitherto, and more sure in his forcing strokes to the off, Duleepsinhji developed quite to the extent anticipated, and, with increased physical strength, he must become a great power in the eleven.

THE SIND TOURNAMENT AT KARACHI

Owing to real or fancied grievances the Parsis decided not to take part in the Tournament, which in consequence suffered in interest. The differences in opinion culminated in the Committee of the Sind Cricket Association suspending the Karachi Parsi Institute 'until such time as they, the Karachi Parsi Institute, do show satisfactory cause why the said suspension should be removed'.

The Hindus, after being successful in the first two matches, lost to the Mohammedans in the final by two wickets.

Hindus v Mohammedans: November 10, 11, 12, 1927. **Hindus 117** (Gulam Mahomed six for 37) **and 127. Mohammedans 146 and 101 for eight wickets**. Mohammedans won by two wickets.

THE BOMBAY TOURNAMENT

The Parsis, after having the better of the play against the Hindus in the opening match, beat the Europeans in great style in the final.

Parsis v Europeans: December 8, 9, 10, 11, 1927. **Parsis 316** (S. N. Ghandy 113, S. H. M. Colah 69, Palia 50 not out; Behrend 5-40, taken whilst 9 were being taken off him) **and 246. Europeans 278** (Lieut. I. W. A. Stephenson 135) **and 150** (R. J. Jamshedji took 10-100 – 4-66 and 6-34). Parsis won by 134 runs.

OBITUARIES

Dhatigara, Mr Sarab M., who died On June 18, aged 38, was a well-known Parsi batsman who had played in the Sind Tournaments at Karachi. He could cut particularly well and was a good field at third man.

Kanga, Mr Pestonji D., born in Bombay on June 2, 1859 died earlier in the year, aged 68. He captained the Parsi team which visited England in 1888, and was an all-rounder player – a free bat, a fast underhand bowler with a puzzling delivery, and a good field. During the tour he scored 655 runs with an average of 12 and took 71 wickets for 12.33 runs each. Against the Gentlemen of Northants, he had an analysis of seven for 16.

Mehta, Mr Dhanji S., who died on June 2, aged 63, toured England with the Parsi team of 1888. He was regarded as the best batsman in the side, but his form here was most disappointing.

Warden Mr Jehangir Sorabji, one of the best all-round cricketers the Parsis ever had, was born at Bombay on January 13, 1885, and died there on January 16, aged 43. He came to the front as a slow left-handed bowler with a big break, and he developed into quite a good bat. In 1911 he toured England with the All-India team making 928 runs with an average of 22.09 and taking 94 wickets for 20.42 runs each. In the game with Northumberland at Newcastle-upon-Tyne, which the county won by one wicket, he scored 116 and 11 and had analyses of 3-85 and 8-88.

In the Quadrangular Tournaments in Bombay he invariably made his presence felt with bat or ball, if not with both, and in such cricket he made 528 runs with an average of 40.61 and took 48 wickets for 12.25 apiece. When he carried out his bat for 115 against the Hindus in 1912, the next highest score in the total of 183 was only 15; and when he made 85 v Mahommedans in 1912, he and H. D. Kanga (150) added 209 together for the third wicket. For Jorah Bajan v Customs, at Calcutta, in 1920, he took five wickets with the first five balls of the match. He was the author of *Knotty Cricket Problems Solved*.

Kilner, Roy, born at Low Valley, Wombwell, near Barnsley, on October 17, 1890, died of enteric in the Barnsley Fever Hospital on April 5, aged 37... During the last winter in which he accepted an engagement in India, he played an innings of 283 not out for Rajendra Gymkhana v Gurgaon at Delhi, in November, 1927, hitting six sixes and 40 fours.

WISDEN – 1930

In 1929, yet another Indian prince made his mark in English cricket.

Oxford v Cambridge
Played at Lord's, July 8, 9, 10, 1929

Exceptional batting performances by J. T. Morgan and the Nawab of Pataudi rendered the match memorable... When Oxford, who, after an interval of five seasons, found themselves with serious cause for apprehension, the Nawab of Pataudi – new to the encounter – distinguished himself by accomplishing more than either K. S. Ranjitsinhji or K. S. Duleepsinhji had achieved for Cambridge. The one Indian who has scored a century in the great match at Lord's, Pataudi showed himself a versatile batsman – able to save a situation by stubborn defence and then to flog bowling he had worn down. He came near achieving what would have been the unique distinction of scoring two hundreds in the same University contest, his play for this reason maintaining interest in the game for an hour after a draw had become certain.

Cambridge University 377 (Morgan 149, Kemp-Welch 57; Wellings 5-118) **and 220-4 declared** (Block 55, Valentine 52). **Oxford University 246** (Nawab of Pataudi 106) **and 202-3** (Nawab of Pataudi 84, Crawley 83). Match drawn.

THE BOMBAY TOURNAMENT

In December 1929, the Hindus, after winning easily against the Mohammedans, beat the Parsis in the final.

Hindus v Mohammedans: December 1, 2, 1929. **Hindus 291. Mohammedans 123 and 154** (Dilawar Hussein 72). Hindus won by an innings and 14 runs.

Europeans v Parsis: December 3, 4, 5, 1929. **Europeans 141** (B. K. Kalapesi 5-45) **and 314 for seven wickets declared** (A. L. Hosie 104 not out, R. J. O. Meyer 85, R. E. H. Hudson 51). **Parsis 186** (T. C. Longfield 5-48, R. J. O. Meyer 5-56) **and 168 for eight wickets**. Parsis qualified for the final through leading on the first innings.

Parsis v Hindus: December 7, 8, 9, 1929. **Parsis 282** (N. D. Marshall 63; S. R. Godambe 4-42) **and 64** (Godambe 6-32). **Hindus 244** (C. K. Naidu 75; H. J. Vajifdar 6-74) **and 103 for five wickets**. Hindus won by five wickets.

CRICKETERS OF THE YEAR 1930

K. S. DULEEPSINHJI

Thirty-three years after his uncle became the first Indian to be honoured as a Cricketer of the Year, Duleep gained entry into Wisden's *hall of fame. Like Ranji, Duleep was never part of India's cricket or its development, which was gaining pace as the 1930s began.*

Kumar Shri Duleepsinhji, if not so famous as his renowned uncle, the Jam Sahib of Nawanagar (K. S. Ranjitsinhji), has already accomplished enough in cricket to be regarded as one of the great batsmen of the younger generation.

Born in India on June 13, 1905, he came to England and at Cheltenham made his mark as a schoolboy cricketer almost at once. In 1921, his first year in the College eleven, he had a batting average of 31 and took 39 wickets for just over 17 runs apiece. The next season his batting average was 26 and, with his very slow bowling, he obtained 50 wickets for under 14 runs each, while in his third and last year at Cheltenham he came out at the top of the batting table with an average of over 52 and was probably the best schoolboy bat of the year.

Playing later on for Lord's Schools v The Rest he enjoyed a great personal triumph, scoring 108 and, in the second innings, taking five wickets for 41 runs. His bowling figures that season for Cheltenham came out at 35 wickets at a cost of over 18 runs each.

Duleepsinhji did not proceed to Cambridge until after the cricket season of 1924, but his performances for his school had clearly stamped him as a remarkable batsman and, stepping into the Cambridge eleven in 1925, he scored 932 runs for the Light Blues, made two hundreds – 130 against Somerset at Bath and 128 against the Army at Cambridge – and finished up second in batting with an average of just over 49.

The University Match that year was left drawn, but Duleepsinhji had the satisfaction, as a Freshman, of scoring 75. In 1926 his average was not so high – just under 35 – but he headed the table and played the only three-figure innings for Cambridge – 118 against the Free Foresters.

Qualified by this time for Sussex, he attained the further distinction of finishing at the top of the county batting with an aggregate of 696 runs and an average of nearly 35. He scored 132 against Middlesex and 115 against Hampshire and narrowly missed equalling the triumph of his uncle (who in his first match for the county had made 150), by putting together 97 against Leicestershire on his opening appearance for Sussex.

The following year he seemed destined for wonderful things, starting with 101 against Yorkshire at Cambridge and, in the next match, against Middlesex, scoring 43 and not out 254. Soon afterwards, however, he was stricken by a serious illness and, subsequent to the end of May, played no more cricket that season.

A winter in Switzerland effected a great improvement in his health, but in 1928 he had to go very quietly for some time, missing the first four matches at Cambridge but playing delightfully in scoring 52 and 37 against Oxford at Lord's. Completely restored to health, Duleepsinhji assisted Sussex regularly to the end of the season and, in 19 innings, actually scored 1,082 runs, once more heading the batting with an average of just over 60. Starting off with 121 in 80 minutes against Glamorgan he subsequently hit up five more scores of over 100.

Last season he was again in brilliant form, seven times exceeding the hundred, with 246 and 202 as his best scores, and, with an aggregate of 2,028 in 36 innings, once more coming out at the top of the batting with an average of over 56. His most startling performance was in the match against Kent at Hastings in August when he followed 115 in the first innings with 246 in the second. Only on four previous occasions in first-class cricket had a player in one match made a score of 100 in one innings and over 200 in another.

He took part in the first Test match against the South Africans at Birmingham but failed and, unwisely as many people thought, the Selection Committee did not

~ MR K.S. DULEEPSINHJI ~

pick him again. To the surprise of nearly everybody he was not chosen for the Gentlemen at Lord's.

Since his school days he has not been considered as a bowler although on occasion he has taken a wicket or two. All his energies have been directed towards batting and it can be said that at present time he stands as a wonderfully well-equipped run-getter. Like his uncle, he possesses a remarkable eye and a pair of most supple wrists.

At one time he had his limitations as an off-side player but this one weakness in his batting is now overcome and few other cricketers can drive on either side of the wicket so hard and with such beautiful direction. Good footwork makes him the complete batsman.

In addition, he is a splendid slip fielder and might be even better if he did not sometimes stand in too close. At the end of last season he visited New Zealand as a member of the MCC team touring there.

WISDEN – 1931

Duleepsinhji followed his uncle into the England side, the second Indian to play for England, but not the second Indian-born player to represent England. D. R. Jardine, born near Mumbai, was one who had already won a Test cap – and, of course, there were more to follow, including two England captains, Colin Cowdrey and Nasser Hussain.

Back in England the following summer, Duleep continued his successes, starting with 173 on his debut against Australia at Lord's. He also hit 333 for Sussex against Northamptonshire at Hove; the first first-class triple century by an Indian player.

MCC TEAM IN NEW ZEALAND, 1929–30

The great run-getter of the team was Duleepsinhji who, playing a lot of delightful cricket, registered 1,421 runs with an average of 59, had 242 at Hawkes Bay as his highest score and, with an innings of 117 in the Auckland Test match, obtained 358 runs in those games.

New Zealand v England
Third Test, played at Auckland, February 14, 15, 17, 1930

Bowley and Duleepsinhji each gave a masterly display. The professional did not make a mistake and hit a six and 11 fours but in a brilliant stand was eclipsed by his partner. Duleepsinhji played dazzling cricket, surpassing anything seen in New Zealand of recent years. His footwork, timing and placing of the ball were perfect and not until after completing his century was he in the least trouble with the bowling. His beautiful strokes all round the wicket included a six and 11 fours.

England v Australia
Second Test, played at Lord's, June 27, 28, 30, July 1, 1930

Chapman again won the toss and England, batting for five hours and 50 minutes, scored on the first day 405 runs for nine wickets… Duleepsinhji and Hendren obtained the first real mastery over the attack, adding 104 runs in 90 minutes. The batting of these two after lunch was delightful, Duleepsinhji driving with fine power and Hendren scoring by cleverly executed strokes to the on… Duleepsinhji seemed certain to play out time after he had lost Robins at 363 but at quarter past six, with the score at 387, he was caught at long-off.

It seems ungracious to say it, but Duleepsinhji was guilty of a bad error of judgement. He had twice driven Grimmett to the boundary in glorious fashion and in the same over lashed out wildly. Batting for four hours and three-quarters he gave a magnificent display. When the occasion demanded it he exercised restraint and at other times hit beautifully all round the wicket, having 21 fours among his strokes. His innings was not faultless, for at 65 he was missed at short-leg by Woodfull from a very simple chance, while at 98 he was let off by Wall at third slip. Had Duleepsinhji been patient and stayed in until the close of play there is no telling what would have been the subsequent course of events.

Sussex v Northamptonshire
Played at Brighton, May 7, 8, 9, 1930

To Duleepsinhji this match brought the great distinction of beating the Sussex record made by his uncle, K. S. Ranjitsinhji, at Taunton in 1901. Going in with one run on the board, Duleepsinhji scored 333 out of 520 and, when seventh out was taking many risks. Batting for five hours and a half, he hit a six and 34 fours, his strokeplay all round the wicket being magnificent.

Sussex 521-7 declared (Duleepsinhji 333, Tate 111).
Northamptonshire 187 (Wensley 4-45) **and 125** (Tate 7-45).
Sussex won by an innings and 205 runs.

CRICKET IN INDIA, 1930

Owing to the unrest in India, the proposed visit of an MCC team in 1930–31 was postponed and the Quadrangular Tournament in Bombay was abandoned.

WISDEN – 1932

The 1931 University Match was a memorable one for a number of reasons. A. T. Ratcliffe of Cambridge scored 201, a record for the fixture, as Cambridge compiled 385 in their first innings. In Oxford's first innings the Nawab of Pataudi established a record that was to stand for 74 years.

Oxford v Cambridge
Played at Lord's, July 6, 7, 8, 1931

Beating Cambridge by eight wickets, Oxford not only registered their first victory over the Light Blues for eight years but, considering the circumstances in which the win was attained, accomplished by far the finest performance credited to either University since the War…

While Ratcliffe's big innings would… have rendered the match memorable, that batsman's score was not allowed to stand as a record for the University Match for 24 hours. Next day, the Nawab of Pataudi not only equalled Ratcliffe's total in 80 minutes less than that player had been at the wickets but went on to raise his figures to 238, and was still unbeaten when Melville declared. Batting altogether for nearly five hours, without giving an absolute chance, Pataudi made runs all round the wicket in masterly fashion. His 238 not out, it may be added, was his fifth hundred in the course of the last six innings he had played and – for those innings – brought his aggregate to 892 and his average to 223. In addition to making the record score in the University Match, Pataudi joined that very selected band of cricketers who have put together two separate hundreds in that encounter.

Pataudi stands alone among undergraduates in getting four consecutive centuries. The fact, moreover, should not be forgotten that in 1929 he came very near to making two separate centuries in the University Match. As a Freshman in 1928 he failed to find his Cheltenham form and did not get his Blue but in three games against Cambridge his scores have been 106, 84, 5, 20, 238 not out and 4 – a total of 457 with an average of 91. By these several distinctions Pataudi reached a unique position among University batsmen. In grace of style, technique, methods of strokeplay or aggressive supremacy he may have been excelled by Ranjitsinhji, A. G. Steel, C. T. Studd, R. E. Foster, Stanley Jackson and G. L. Jessop in their respective types of excellence, but none of these great batsmen scored in such a wonderful way as Pataudi has done while at University.

Duleep's final Test appearance for England also came in 1931, the year before India toured England as a Test-playing nation for the first time. He ended his 12-match Test career with 995 runs at an average of 58.52.

The Third and last Test match, at Old Trafford, proved a most depressing affair, no play being possible until after three o'clock on the last afternoon. Then, Lowry, having won the toss, put England in to bat and on a soft pitch 224 runs were scored for three wickets before the game came to an end in a hopeless draw. Only by the extraordinarily persistent efforts of the ground staff was even this little period of play possible, for rain fell so heavily day after day that there were occasions when water lay in great pools all over the field. On the first two afternoons the efforts of the groundsmen were neutralised by further rain but on the last day the sun shone at times and the downpour had at last ceased so that the few spectators who came into the ground in the end had some slight reward...

Paynter met with no success, being out with only eight runs on the board, but then came a splendid stand by Sutcliffe and Duleepsinhji who, once they had become set, punished the bowling in fine style. Altogether they were associated for an hour and 50 minutes and added 126 runs. Duleepsinhji's innings was not faultless for he gave a chance at second slip when 10, while Sutcliffe, at 53, was dropped in the long field. Hammond hit out rather rashly but Sutcliffe went on batting well and when stumps were pulled up he had scored 109 out of 224. Apart from his one chance Sutcliffe made no other mistake and driving, pulling and placing well to leg, he hit a six and nine fours.

England 224-3 (Sutcliffe 109 not out, Duleepsinhji 63)

CRICKETERS OF THE YEAR 1923

THE NAWAB OF PATAUDI

The third Indian cricketer to play for England (and also subsequently for India) was the Nawab of Pataudi, who was a very different cricketer and man from his two predecessors. As Wisden *noted, 'Possessed, like most men of his race, of a wonderful eye and quick footwork, Pataudi resembles neither Duleepsinhji nor the latter's famous uncle in his methods.'*

Nawab Iftikhar Ali of Pataudi, the third Indian cricketer to make a great name for himself as a batsman in this country, was born at Pataudi, in the Punjab, on March 16, 1910. Educated at the Chiefs' College, Lahore, he received his early coaching in cricket from M. G. Salter, the old Oxford Blue, and in 1926 came to England for the purpose of going up to Oxford.

When preparing for his University career he lived at Tonbridge and while there received further coaching from Frank Woolley during the winters of 1926, 1927, 1928 and 1929. Woolley very quickly came to the conclusion that he had under his charge a batsman of considerable promise and great possibilities. It is not untrue to say that in many quarters Woolley's praise of the young Indian was received a little doubtfully, but the famous Kent professional has lived to see his faith in Pataudi more than justified.

Pataudi went up to Oxford in October 1927 but, while he played fairly well on occasion, he did not get his Blue until 1929. He also appeared against Cambridge in the two following years. Over and above his skill as a batsman he showed himself to be a fine hockey player, being in the Oxford teams of 1930 and 1931, while at billiards he represented Oxford against Cambridge for three years from 1929.

The Nawab of Pataudi.

In the season in which he secured a place in the Dark Blues' team, he did little of consequence before appearing at Lord's but on that occasion accomplished two remarkably fine performances. Although most of his colleagues failed, he with a score of 106 saved the side from having to follow-on, and later on went very close to making another hundred with an innings of 84.

At his first attempt his skill in defence to begin with was extremely good and, having taken the measure of the bowling and to some extent worn it down, he hit brilliantly. He came out third in the Oxford batting figures with an average of 36.

The following season he was again third, averaging nearly 44 but he did very little against Cambridge, scoring only 5 and 20. For all that he played quite well in the earlier Oxford matches, being in excellent form against Gloucestershire, Yorkshire and Lancashire, while immediately before the University Match he hit up 167 not out at Eastbourne.

He reached the height of his fame last summer when, despite the wet wickets so generally prevalent, he actually scored 1,307 runs in 16 innings and came out at the head of the Oxford batting with an average of over 93. His form, to say the least, was amazing.

In the latter part of June in successive innings he made scores of 183 not out against The Army at Folkestone, 165 and 100 against Surrey at The Oval, 138 and 68 against Leveson Gower's XI, at Eastbourne, to wind up with 238 not out against Cambridge at Lord's. This was the highest individual score ever obtained in the University Match, and singularly enough it followed on the heels of A. T. Ratcliffe's 201 for Cambridge earlier in the contest. Thus, in one game between Oxford and Cambridge, the record of 172 not out held since 1904 by J. F. Marsh, of Cambridge, was twice beaten.

Honoured by being chosen to represent the Gentlemen against the Players at Lord's he was dismissed for scores of 2 and 19, and, taking part in a few other games, he did nothing of note.

Possessed, like most men of his race, of a wonderful eye and quick footwork, Pataudi resembles neither Duleepsinhji nor the latter's famous uncle in his methods. One great feature about the majority of his big innings has been the manner in which he has shown sound restraint while mastering the bowling and, when set, exceptional ease and confidence in asserting himself as a run-getter.

As the particular ball demanded he was able to use the drive, cut, leg-hit or pull and, last season, he brought to something like perfection practically every stroke in the game. Moreover he possessed the temperament for the big occasion.

It was announced towards the end of the summer that he would qualify for Worcestershire, so that if this idea is carried into effect much more should be seen of him in English cricket outside the rather limited circle with which he has hitherto been associated.

CRICKET IN INDIA, 1931

Owing to political unrest, the proposed MCC tour through India did not take place and the Bombay Tournament was abandoned.

OBITUARY

Henderson, Robert, a member of the Surrey eleven during the great years of the side when led by Mr John Shuter, first played for the county in 1883 at the age of 18. He was an excellent batsman, generally able to give of his best when most was required of him, a useful slow bowler in his early years of first-class cricket and a thoroughly sound, if scarcely brilliant, fieldsman... During one winter he went to India to coach the Parsees, was paid great honours on his departure, and on his return was given – by his Surrey colleagues – the name of 'Framjee'.

CHAPTER 3
THE RUNS BEGIN TO FLOW:
1933–1953

The first visit to England by a Test-playing team representing All-India took place in 1932. Twenty-one years after the only previous tour by an All-India side, a tour which did not include Test matches and which was described as a 'complete disappointment', the tourists of 1932 'acquitted themselves with great credit'. There was still a great deal of social distinction within the team, it being considered unthinkable that a representative Indian side could be led by anybody ranking below a Maharajah. Unfortunately, neither Duleepsinhji nor the Nawab of Pataudi was available for selection, so the captain – off the field at least – was the Maharajah of Porbandar, who had the tact to allow the side's best cricketer, C. K. Nayudu, to lead the side in the only Test match. The Maharajah finished the tour with two first-class runs to his name, average 0.66.

During the 1930s and 1940s, India was going through major social unrest as the sun was going down on the British Empire, even though the politicians in London kept trying to assert it was still British Summer Time. Cricket, the most intrinsically English of games, somewhat counter-intuitively, took real hold in India during this period, and certainly within the annual Quadrangular Tournament in Bombay, it was an expression of the Indian determination to defeat their British colonial masters. A sporting victory would have to do until political victory became inevitable.

In those years between the first Test-playing tour of England in 1932 and the third in 1946, when India was still, for one more year, a part of the British Empire, domestic cricket reached new heights, in run-scoring terms at least. Players such as Merchant, Hazare and Umrigar scored very heavily in domestic cricket. India finally achieved independence in 1947, but still had to wait for that elusive first Test victory, something that they did not achieve against any opposition until they beat England in February 1952, a game during which – with an overdose of political and sporting significance – King George VI died and the second Elizabethan age began.

WISDEN – 1933

THE ALL-INDIA TEAM IN ENGLAND 1932, by S. J. Southerton

Although they suffered defeat in their one representative match against the full strength of England, the team of Indian cricketers, who toured this country last summer under the captaincy of the Maharajah of Porbandar, acquitted themselves on the whole, if not with marked distinction, at any rate with great credit.

It can be said at once that those who came last season exceeded anticipations. Some little difficulty was experienced with regard to the captaincy, and after one or two disappointments the choice fell upon the Maharajah of Porbandar who had with him as vice-captain K. S. Ganshyamsinhji of Limbdi. For reasons apart from cricket the necessity existed of having a person of distinction and importance in India at the head of affairs, and it was almost entirely because of this that Porbandar led the team. No injustice is being done to him, therefore, by saying that admirably fitted as he was in many respects for the task, his abilities as a cricketer were not commensurate with the position he occupied.

Only those, however, with intimate knowledge of the many little difficulties arising in the command of a body of men of mixed creeds, habits and thoughts, can appreciate the tact and firmness required in maintaining that comradeship and united endeavour so essential to the success of a team on the field and the harmonious collaboration of its various units in other respects. Except for his limitations as a cricketer, the Maharajah of Porbandar enjoyed in full measure the attributes necessary to his position, and he certainly created in the team an excellent spirit. Wherever they went the tourists made friends, not only by the fine regard they had for the traditions of the game, but by their modest and correct demeanour at all times.

Fortunately for the side they possessed in C. K. Nayudu – easily their best batsman – a man of high character and directness of purpose who, in the absence of the two above him, was able to take over the duties of captaincy with skill and no small measure of success. He led the team in the Test match at Lord's and, although on the losing side, earned commendation for the manner in which he managed his bowling and placed his field ….

Still, they had no reason to be dissatisfied with their record, for of the 26 first-class engagements in which they took part nine were won, eight lost and nine drawn. Outside these, they played 12 other games, and in all matches they won 13, lost nine, and drew 14 while two were abandoned without a ball being bowled. As they opened their tour at the end of April and did not finish until 9 September, they came through a very trying season extremely well.

In one important particular they were fortunate, the weather after being cold and cheerless for the first month turning bright and fine and at certain periods almost as hot as in their own country. Mostly, therefore, they had hard wickets on which to bat but, all the same, the conditions generally were not quite like those under which they play in India. To two of the team this made little difference, Nayudu and Nazir Ali having had considerable experience of cricket in this country. Had it been possible for Duleepsinhji and the Nawab of Pataudi to assist, the side must have been very strong indeed, for these two cricketers would have given that stability to the batting which on several occasions was noticeably absent.

Their batsmen, for the most part, managed very well against our fast bowling and ordinary spin bowlers, but on their own confession they found considerable difficulty in dealing with googly bowling, and with Freeman of Kent in particular. There are practically no googly bowlers in India and this type of attack frankly puzzled them, for they could not be sure of spotting the wrong 'un, as it is colloquially called...

Mention of fielding immediately brings to mind the fact that in this respect the team as a whole attained to a high standard. No hit was too hard for them to attempt to stop, while the throwing-in was a model of power and accuracy. Colah and Jeoomal stood out by themselves in the manner in which they returned the ball to the wicketkeeper. No English cricketer, with the exception, possibly, of Voce, threw in so beautifully as Colah. In Navle, the team had a first-rate wicketkeeper, very quick in all that he did.

The tour proved of immense value to the Indians themselves who, about the middle of the summer, were 50 per cent better than when they arrived, and the lessons they learned will no doubt be passed on to the Indian cricketers of the future. The manager of the team was Major E. W. C. Ricketts, who, from his knowledge of the language gained while he was serving in the Indian Army and his courtesy on all occasions, proved an ideal man for a somewhat difficult position.

England v India

Test, played at Lord's, June 25, 27, 28, 1932

England, in their first representative match in this country with India, gained a fine victory shortly after four o'clock on the third afternoon by 158 runs. Before that result had been achieved, however, the home side, particularly on the first day, experienced some anxious moments. Actually, on the Saturday, they cut a very poor figure. Indeed, the manner in which they began called to mind the all too frequent failures in recent years of England at the beginning of a match against Australia.

England began in such disastrous fashion that in 20 minutes they lost their first three men for 19 runs and were all disposed of in another four hours for a total of 259.

As India in a poor light made 30 runs without loss at the end of the day – play being stopped for a quarter of an hour and finally ending at six o'clock – the visitors may be said to have had the best of matters. India failed to drive home this

ENGLAND	1st Innings	2nd Innings
P. Holmes b Nissar.	6	– b Jahangir Khan 11
H. Sutcliffe b Nissar	3	– c Nayudu b Amar Singh 19
F. E. Woolley run out	9	– c Colah b Jahangir Khan. 21
W. R. Hammond b Amar Singh	35	– b Jahangir Khan 12
*D. R. Jardine c Navle b Nayudu	79	– not out. 85
E. Paynter lbw b Nayudu	4	– b Jahangir Khan 54
†L. E. G. Ames b Nissar	65	– b Amar Singh 6
R. W. V. Robins c Lall Singh b Nissar	21	– c Jahangir Khan b Nissar 30
F. R. Brown c Amar Singh b Nissar	1	– c Colah b Naoomal Jaoomal. 29
W. Voce not out	4	– not out. 0
W. E. Bowes c Nissar b Amar Singh	7	
Extras (b 3, l-b 9, n-b 3).	15	Extras (b 2, l-b 6). 8

1-8 2-11 3-19 4-101 5-149 6-166 7-229   259   1-30 2-34 3-54 4-67   (8 wickets declared) 275
8-231 9-252 10-259   5-156 6-169 7-222 8-271

First innings – Nissar 26–3–93–5; Amar Singh 31.1–10–75–2; Jahangir Khan 17–7–26–0;
Nayudu 24–8–40–2; Palia 4–3–2–0; Naoomal Jaoomal 3–0–8–0; Wazir Ali 1–0–9–0
Second innings – Nissar 18–5–42–1; Amar Singh 41–13–84–2; Jahangir Khan 30–12–60–4;
Nayudu 9–0–21–0; Palia 3–0–11–0; Naoomal Jaoomal 8–0–40–1

INDIA	1st Innings	2nd Innings
†J. G. Navle b Bowes.	12	– lbw b Robins 13
Naoomal Jaoomal lbw b Robins	33	– b Brown 25
S. Wazir Ali lbw b Brown	31	– c Hammond b Voce 39
*C. K. Nayudu c Robins b Voce	40	– b Bowes 10
S. H. M. Colah c Robins b Bowes.	22	– b Brown 4
S. Nazir Ali b Bowes	13	– c Jardine b Bowes. 6
P. E. Palia b Voce.	1	– not out 1
Lall Singh c Jardine b Bowes	15	– b Hammond 29
M. Jahangir Khan b Robins	1	– b Voce 0
L. Amar Singh c Robins b Voce	5	– c & b Hammond 51
M. Nissar not out	1	– b Hammond 0
Extras (b 5, lb 7, w 1, nb 2)	15	Extras (b 5, lb 2, nb 2) 9

1-39 2-63 3-110 4-139 5-160 6-165 7-181   189   1-41 2-41 3-52 4-65 5-83 6-108 7-108   187
8-182 9-188 10-189   8-182 9-182 10-187

First innings – Bowes 30–13–49–4; Voce 17–6–23–3; Brown 25–7–48–1; Robins 17–4–39–2;
Hammond 4–0–15–0
Second innings – Bowes 14–5–30–2; Voce 12–3–28–2; Brown 14–1–54–2; Robins 14–5–57–1;
Hammond 5.3–3–9–3

England won by 158 runs.

initial advantage and were 70 runs behind when an innings had been completed on each side, and, although the early English batsmen again gave a poor display in the second innings, India never really got on top and, left to make 346 to win, were disposed of for 187.

The turning point in the game came after four wickets had gone down for 67 in the second innings of England. Then Jardine, who had batted uncommonly well in the first innings, and Paynter added 74 runs, and on the last morning carried their partnership to 89. That stand definitely gave England a commanding position which followed up by useful bowling enabled the home country to triumph.

Duleep and the Nawab of Pataudi declined to play for India, but Duleep played for Sussex against his compatriots. He scored only seven. Duleep captained Sussex in 1932, but his health was once again in decline. Sadly, he did not play first-class cricket again.

Most unhappily for Sussex, when the challenge to Yorkshire's supremacy was at its height, Duleepsinhji broke down so badly in health that he played no more cricket last summer... While again showing himself one of the greatest batsmen of the day and putting together quite a number of delightful innings, Duleepsinhji accomplished some of his best work in matches other than those in the County Championship... One of the first choices for the team the MCC sent to Australia in the autumn, he had, under medical advice, to decline that honour and wintered in Switzerland with every hope of being able to lead Sussex again in the forthcoming season.

Gentlemen v Players
The Lord's Match, played at Lord's, July 13, 14, 15, 1932

The Gentlemen, when bad light stopped the game shortly after six o'clock, had scored 17 for the loss of Wyatt's wicket and next day Hazlerigg, batting steadily, helped Duleepsinhji to raise the total to 73. Then came some delightful cricket by Duleepsinhji and Pataudi who put on 161 for the amateurs' third wicket. Duleepsinhji, who had gone in overnight, was at pains to play himself in but, having succeeded in that endeavour, appeared to marked advantage in putting together his fifth hundred of the season. When 24 he might have been caught from Freeman's bowling by Tate at mid-off and after passing his hundred he had a narrow escape at slip but for the most part he batted in almost faultless fashion. Driving and pulling a lot he hit 17 fours.

Pataudi took nearly two hours to reach 50, the Players' attack being nearly always maintained at a high level, and he had been at the wickets three hours and a half when he completed his hundred. Afterwards he travelled so fast that he registered his last 64 in 35 minutes. While occasionally, with a drive attempted, the ball went away in the slips, he gave no chance and had 21 fours among his strokes. He and Jardine put on 160 for the fourth wicket in a hundred minutes.

CRICKET IN INDIA, 1932

Owing to the political situation, there was no Quadrangular Tournament in India in 1931–32, but a series of trial matches was played at Lahore and Patiala to assist the Indian selectors in choosing the All-India team for England.

2nd Match – All-India v Rest of India (12-a-side): Played at Lahore. All-India 287 for ten wickets (innings declared closed), (Sheikh Dina 60, J. G. Navle 50, Jahangir Khan 6-41) and 238 (Nawab of Pataudi 80, Naoomal Jeoomal 5-33). Rest of India 299 (Wazir Ali 107 not out, Naoomal Jeoomal 49, C. K. Nayudu 47, Mahomed Nissar 6-54) and 73 (P. E. Palia 3-16, Mahomed Nissar 3-23). All-India won by 153 runs.

CRICKETERS OF THE YEAR 1933
C. K. NAYUDU

The first touring Indian to be included in the Five, C. K. Nayudu was the giant of India's developing years.

Cottari Kankaiya Nayudu, easily the outstanding batsman of the All-India team who toured England last season, was born at Nagpur, on October 31, 1895.

As quite a small boy he played cricket for the Hislop Collegiate High School, Nagpur, and in course of time captained the school and college at cricket. He did not confine his activities, however, entirely to this game, for he was very useful at athletics generally and achieved distinction at hockey and Association football. While still at the High School, he assisted the Modi Cricket Club and became captain of it. During these early days he received useful coaching from R. Rajanna, who played against the Oxford University Authentics team in India.

From 1916 onwards he played in the Quadrangular matches in Bombay; he represented the Central Provinces in 1919 and Madras in 1920.

Everyone who saw him last season could not fail to be struck by the fact that he seemed rather more comfortable on English wickets than most of his colleagues. This was no doubt due to the fact that he had been over here during the previous summer and had played fairly regularly for the Indian Gymkhana. So from personal experience and from what he had been told by his father and uncle, who were at Cambridge in Ranjitsinhji's time, he was to some extent conversant with the conditions for cricket which obtain in this country.

C. K. Nayudu.

Tall and well-proportioned, Nayudu is eminently fitted by nature to be a good cricketer and his doings for the Indian team fully bore out the good accounts of him that had come to us by reason of his excellent performances in his own land. Above all else he was a very strong player in front of the wicket, his driving both to the off and on being an outstanding feature of his batting.

For a first-class man he had one little peculiarity in that he conveyed the impression of being rather late in making up his mind to drive. This, however, did not detract in any way from his skill or effectiveness. Possessed of supple and powerful wrists and a very good eye, he hit the ball tremendously hard but, unlike the modern Australian batsmen, he lifted it a fair amount.

In the course of the tour he played six three-figure innings – five of them against first-class sides – and enjoyed the additional distinction of making a hundred on his first appearance at Lord's in an important engagement when he scored 118, not out, against the MCC.

From the personal point of view he was probably disappointed at doing little of note in the one Test match which the team engaged in against England at Lord's but, captaining the side in the absence of the Maharajah of Porbandar and K. S. Ghanshyamsinhji of Limbdi, he showed himself admirably suited for the duties of leadership in what were, after all, rather difficult circumstances.

Over and above his batting, he could claim to be a distinctly useful change bowler, rather on the slow side of medium, his best performance being when he took five wickets for 21 runs against Leicestershire.

He was also a very fine fielder, and it was owing to a severe blow he received in the Test match, when trying to catch Ames, that he could not do himself justice when his turn came to go in against England.

Off the cricket field he had a somewhat retiring deposition and was very modest as to his own abilities, but, able to speak English quite well, he always proved an interesting man to whom to talk about the game. He is ADC to the Maharajah Holkar of Indore.

WISDEN 1934

The death of India's greatest cricketer in 1933 created many column inches within Wisden.

RANJITSINHJI by Sir Stanley Jackson

The news of the death in India in April last of His Highness the Jam Saheb of Nawanagar, better known to the cricket public throughout the world as K. S. Ranjitsinhji, was received with profound regret by his innumerable friends in this country. It seems but natural that an appreciation of His Highness and his remarkable career upon the cricket field should appear in *Wisden* in the volumes of which his achievements are chronicled and provide a lasting testimony to his skill.

There must be many who knew Ranji better than I did during the later period of his cricket career in this country, but for some years after we first met in Cambridge in 1892 I had the pleasure of his close friendship, and many indications of a confidence and goodwill which in later years I realised was but a natural return of a high caste Indian gentleman for what he regarded as some special act of friendship or service...

The first time I can remember seeing him play cricket was early in the summer term at Cambridge in 1892. I had heard of an Indian playing occasionally for Trinity in 1891, but only as one who with coaching and practice and less resort to unorthodox methods might become a useful cricketer. One day in 1892 on my way up to Fenner's I noticed a match in progress on Parker's Piece, and seeing a rather unusually large crowd of spectators, I stopped to watch. As luck would have it Ranji was at the wicket. After a short exhibition of brilliant and certainly unorthodox strokes I thought Ranji was stumped, but much to the satisfaction of the crowd the umpire decided in his favour. I left the scene not particularly impressed.

I spent the winter months of 1892–93 playing cricket with Lord Hawke's team in India and I have no doubt now that my experience during that tour awakened in me a sympathetic interest for Indians which perhaps in 1892 I did not possess to the same degree. At Fenner's in the early part of the summer term of 1893 I saw Ranji at the nets, being bowled to by two fast bowlers whom I recognised as Lockwood and Richardson of Surrey, who with other county professionals came in those days to Cambridge to get fit for the county season. When I had finished my practice Ranji was still at it, but with two fresh bowlers. I mentioned to C. M. Wells that I thought Ranji seemed to be overdoing the practice; and when Wells made this suggestion, Ranji replied, 'I find I am all right for half an hour but cannot last. I must now master endurance.'

In later days I had many opportunities of remembering this remark when consistent centuries appeared to demonstrate that he had succeeded in his objective and justified his efforts at practice. Ranjitsinhji had a passion for cricket and was determined to excel. He had that confidence in himself that springs from natural ability. That he possessed capacity for application and perseverance was further shown by his skill as a shot and as a fisherman, and later in the more serious walks of life, by his success as a ruler and administrator in his State...

I had the pleasure of giving Ranjitsinhji his Blue in 1893. He was a brilliant slip and played several good innings in the University Matches at Cambridge. The University Match tried him highly. He received an ovation on going in to bat, which, meant as an encouragement, proved, I know, an embarrassment. He made only a few runs. He quickly became a great favourite with the public, a position he gained not only by his skill as a cricketer but in no small degree by a personality made additionally attractive by a modest demeanour and invariable courtesy which is a natural attribute of a Rajput. The disappointment at his failure, which was rare, was almost as great as the pleasure enjoyed from his success, even amongst the most enthusiastic supporters of his opponents. I am reminded of an occasion during a Test match at Manchester when, staying with friends, I sat next to a lady at dinner who bemoaned her fate at having come a long way only to be disappointed by Ranji's failure. I, personally, felt duly subdued as I had myself made 128 that day!

A figure so prominent in the cricket life of this country for so many years must necessarily have had an influence on the game one way or another. Ranji certainly played the game as all would wish to see it played. Perhaps he was fortunate to have played at a time when many have declared cricket in this country was at its best. My friend Gilbert Jessop referred to him as 'The most brilliant figure during cricket's most brilliant period' and 'It was during the nineties that cricket reached its pinnacle as a national game and Ranji was one of those who helped to put it there.' Ranjitsinhji had no desire to be placed on a pinnacle... His example was an inspiration to his own people in India, and his main desire to feel that the part he had played in the game was for its good.

'When I have finished,' he once said, 'I hope I may be remembered not only for the success it has been my fortune to enjoy as a player, but rather as one who tried his best to popularise the game for the game's sake.'

When an unfortunate stroke of fate deprived him of that priceless possession to which he owed so much – the sight of one of his eyes – he showed a fortitude in adversity which none could help but admire; but if this meant the end of his cricket it did not prevent him from seeing his way along the difficult path of statesmanship when called upon to undertake the high responsibility of Chancellor of the Chamber of Princes at a time of crisis in India's future – a position he filled with success.

I think it will be generally agreed that the game of cricket gained by Ranji's association with it, as also can his innumerable friends feel that they gained much by their association with so good a sportsman.

OBITUARY, by Sydney Southerton

Almost the greatest tribute to the memory of H. H. the Jam Saheb of Nawanagar, whose sudden death at Delhi, on April 2, came as such a shock to the world of cricket, is the fact that everywhere he was referred to as 'Ranji'. It is scarcely necessary to add that this contraction of his name was used with true affection early in his career and remained to the end.

Born at Sarodar, Kathiawar, India on September 10, 1872, Kumar Shri Ranjitsinhji came of ancient Rajput stock. He received his earliest lessons in cricket while at school at Rajkumar College, Rajkote, and when in 1888 he paid a visit to England he was... a batsman of some skill but very unorthodox in his methods. Actually he played no cricket of any note until he went into residence at

Trinity College, Cambridge, where he secured a place in the college eleven. Probably because he was an Indian he attracted a certain amount of attention but nobody who watched him playing for Cambridgeshire in 1892–93, and for Cambridge University when he was given his Blue by F. S. Jackson in 1893, had the least idea that they were looking at a man who, in a few years, was to dazzle the world and bring about such an alteration in the methods of batting as definitely to mark a turning point in the history of the game. It is not too much to say that by his extraordinary skill Ranjitsinhji revolutionised cricket, the effects of his wonderful play on the leg-side being seen day after day down to the present time.

If a little crude and most certainly unreliable at the outset, Ranjitsinhji was blessed with a most versatile brain and the capacity for application which in course of time made him one of the most brilliant batsmen ever seen. Quite individual and distinctive in style, he possessed exceptional keenness of eye, besides such power and flexibility of wrist, that on a fast wicket he could do almost anything in the way of scoring. Admitting the use of the word in connection with cricket, genius could with the greatest truth be applied to him. Thanks to his special gifts he could – and did – take the good length ball off the middle stump and glance it to leg with a measure of certainty no one else has ever equalled or even approached. In this way he was no safe model for any player of average skill, for the attempt to bring off many of his strokes must have been fatal to most people...

Deciding to stay in England after leaving Cambridge, Ranjitsinhji duly qualified for Sussex, and in 1895 commenced a memorable association with that county which continued unbroken up to 1904. No happier augury for his future success could have occurred than when on the occasion of his first appearance for Sussex, against the MCC at Lord's, he scored 77 not out and 150. That summer he obtained 1,775 runs and averaged nearly 50. A year later this performance was completely eclipsed. His average went up to nearly 58 and he registered no fewer than 2,780 runs. This was the highest aggregate obtained by anyone up to that date and, what was of greatest importance, bigger than that of W. G. Grace – 2,739 in 1871 – which had stood as a record for a quarter of a century. The seasons of 1901 and 1904 also brought Ranjitsinhji aggregates of over 2,000 runs, while in 1899 and 1900 he exceeded 3,000, his totals respectively for these years being 3,159 and 3,065. In 1900 he had the remarkable average of 87. Altogether in the course of his career he scored 24,567 runs with an average of 45, and played 72 three-figure innings – ten during the summer of 1896. On 14 occasions he reached 200, obtaining all these scores for Sussex and five of them in 1900... It must be mentioned too that in 1896 he accomplished the feat of making three consecutive hundreds, getting 100 and 125 not out against Yorkshire immediately following 165 against Lancashire. In the match with Yorkshire he went in on the second evening, but had not scored at the drawing of stumps, so that he really made two separate hundreds on the same day...

He was, however, always insistent that the best innings he played on a hard wicket was his 234 not out at Hastings in 1902 when, in the match between Sussex and Surrey, 1,427 runs were scored and only 21 wickets went down. Richardson and Lockwood were among the Surrey bowlers, but Ranjitsinhji batted so superbly that he made both of them look just ordinary. His driving was wonderful. Some years afterwards he said to me, apropos of this innings and without any trace of boasting in his remarks, 'I think I could have stayed there forever, for the ball looked as big as a balloon the whole time I was in.' By a sad coincidence, Hastings was the ground on which in 1920 he played his last match in England – Sussex v Northamptonshire. He had then grown very stout and suffered from the grave disability of having lost one of his eyes, through an accident when out shooting. I saw both these matches and well remember the feeling of sorrow which came over me when I realised the inevitable change which the passage of years had wrought in his wonderful powers of execution. It is of interest to know, however, that his one idea of coming back and playing cricket after the War was prompted by his desire to write another book on cricket, with special emphasis on the art of batting with only one eye. As he said at the time, he could deal with good length balls almost as well as formerly, but the long-hop or half-volley caused him real trouble in properly focusing his sight.

Ranjitsinhji was captain of Sussex for five years – 1899 to 1903. Returning to India after the summer of 1904 he did not play again until 1908 when he turned out and obtained over 1,100 runs. There came a similar interval after that, and in 1912, returning once more to first-class cricket, he made more than 1,100 runs.

Taking part in 14 Test matches – five in Australia – he scored in the course of those games 989 runs with an average of nearly 45. When, in the winter of 1897–98, he formed one of A. E. Stoddart's second team to Australia, he played an innings of 175 at Sydney, but as an England cricketer his great triumph was that at Manchester in 1896 when he scored 154 not out in superb style, being so completely master of the Australian bowling that, could he have got anybody to stay with him, he might have saved England from defeat...

So has passed a great character in the history of the game. We may never see his like again, for he burst on the cricket horizon at the start of what has been described as its most brilliant era, when there existed scope for introducing new ideas and methods.

I count myself unusually fortunate to have been a witness of many of his great performances, and even more privileged to have enjoyed his friendship. To me Ranjitsinhji was the embodiment of all that a cricketer should be – generous in defeat, modest in success and genuinely enthusiastic regarding the achievements of either colleagues or opponents.

SUSSEX

A remarkable paean of praise to the ailing Duleep was disguised as a report of the Sussex season.

Captain: K. S. Duleepsinhji (retired)

Sussex began under something of a cloud, for before the campaign opened it was known that they would not enjoy the assistance or again be under the leadership of K. S. Duleepsinhji. Unhappily the visit he paid to Switzerland, in the hope of bringing about an improvement in his health, did not have the desired effect and he was told that it would be better for him to give up all ideas of cricket for the summer in order to have a better chance of complete recovery later on. As it happened the pulmonary disease from which he was suffering, took, if anything, a firmer grip of his system. Duleepsinhji had to content himself with reading and listening about the manner in which his side were acquitting themselves and, towards the end of the season, he knew definitely that he had played his last ball in county cricket. In a letter which breathed a spirit of hope, but in which it was clear he felt his career was ended, he wrote definitely resigning the captaincy of the Sussex eleven. Thus, after an all too brief sojourn among us there passed from the game he had adorned with such conspicuous grace and success, one of the most beautiful batsmen of recent years. English cricket in general and that of Sussex in particular will be all the poorer for his enforced absence. A young man of singular charm of character; extremely modest of his own wonderful ability; and with a love for the game which transcended his joy in all other pastimes, Duleepsinhji will always be remembered as one of the outstanding personalities during his period in first-class cricket.

THE MCC TEAM IN AUSTRALIA AND NEW ZEALAND, 1932–33,
by S. J. Southerton

On the other side of the world, the Nawab of Pataudi was involved in the Bodyline tour, though he did not play a central role in events.

Pataudi also made four hundreds, starting the tour with one each in the first two matches at Perth. Then at Sydney, just like his famous countrymen Ranjitsinhji and Duleepsinhji, he signalised his first appearance in a Test match by playing a three-figure innings. Both Sutcliffe and Pataudi began in wonderful style, the former making four hundreds in his first six innings, and the latter four hundreds in his first nine attempts. Pataudi took part in the second Test match, but after that was left out of representative engagements.

Australia v England
First Test, played at Sydney, December 2, 3, 5, 6, 7, 1932

Hammond, if not quite so dashing as a little time previously at Melbourne, was eminently good, but Pataudi – like two other famous Indians, Ranjitsinhji and Duleepsinhji, reaching three figures in his first Test match – was, for the most part, plodding and rather wearisome to watch. He did not show the Sydney public anything like the great array of strokes of which he is known to be capable of executing and seemed on the whole disinclined to take the slightest risk with balls which apparently were quite safe to hit.

WISDEN – 1935

MCC IN INDIA 1933–34, by Hubert Preston

When the MCC team captained by A. E. R. Gilligan visited India in the winter of 1926–27, two matches against All-India produced close struggles which earned recognition in a Test match at Lord's in 1932. Although beaten by 158 runs, India then shaped so well that the need for a far stronger side for a subsequent visit was apparent. So, D. R. Jardine, the victorious captain in Australia the winter before, was chosen to go out with a really powerful team in the autumn of 1933.

Decisive wins came in two of the Tests and England held a big advantage in the drawn game at Calcutta until the loss of two wickets spoiled the final position, but, unlike the previous side which went through a heavy programme without a reverse, Jardine's team suffered defeat from Vizianagram by 14 runs.

This break in the regular run of defeats or drawn matches must give encouragement to the further development of the game in India. A marked advance was noticeable already throughout the tour in the great improvement in the condition of the grounds, the accommodation provided and the increased attendances. All these important points meant real progress, but cricket itself had not risen to the same degree as the authorities had shown in their preparations for the visit. The public interest taken in every engagement helped to make the trip very enjoyable.

Of the Indian team, the captain, Nayudu, was no doubt the best all-round cricketer in the country. Amar Nath, who played a great innings in the first Test, the Yuvraj of Patiala and Merchant stood out prominently as batsmen. Nissar, the fast bowler, looked scarcely so good as when over here, but Amar Singh fully upheld his reputation for length and spin, notably when bowling round the wicket. Mushtaq Ali, a slow left-hand bowler and good right-hand batsman, should make a name.

Apart from individual superiority man for man, England naturally benefited from the skill of Jardine as a captain. Nayudu did not show sound judgement either in using his bowlers or in placing his field. The one victory gained and the good uphill struggle in the second match with England should influence the players to exercise more control and study more closely the essentials necessary to become first-class...

While criticising the England side, consideration must be given to the exhaustion due to continuous travelling and playing in the extreme heat of India. Some of the side gave signs of being tired out... In batting, three amateurs stood out over all the professionals. Jardine, Walters and Valentine usually were at the top of their form. On the whole, however, the Englishmen scarcely adapted themselves to the matting wickets as well as anticipated. In England batsmen have to play on such a variety of pitches changing from day to day that it was surprising that some of the team failed to come up to expectations under conditions new to them. But the heat, travelling and constant social functions, always very pleasant, could be held responsible for anyone failing to do himself full justice.

England v India
First Test, played at Bombay, December 15, 16, 17, 18, 1933

Victory for England by nine wickets was the result of the first Test soon after lunch on the fourth day. Nichols and Valentine stood out conspicuously in a satisfactory performance. The Essex fast bowler worked with unflagging zeal in the great heat and did specially good service when India had pulled the game round to some extent... Nissar bowled much the best for India; keeping up a good pace he sent Jardine's off stump flying with a specially fast ball. He and the other bowlers were not sure of the fieldsmen, but there was nothing better in the match than the catch made by Jamshedi, the slow bowler, in dismissing Townsend, a very hard return being held beautifully.

When India batted a second time, facing as arrears their first innings total, two smart catches from snicks off Clark suggested a collapse, but Amar Nath and his captain raised the total from 17 to 59 by extremely good cricket. A bruised hand troubled Nayudu, who was slow compared to the rapid scoring of his partner. Amar Nath reached 102 before stumps were drawn and seemed set again in the morning when Nichols brought off his wonderful catch. At the wickets altogether three hours and a half Nath hit 21 fours in his 118 – a particularly fine effort for a first appearance against England. He and Nayudu put on 186 – the largest partnership in the match – but the remaining seven wickets went down for 55 runs, Nichols being mainly responsible for England having such a light task to accomplish. It is noteworthy that in the two innings of India, while six men were leg before, Verity was the one bowler to hit the stumps; and, of his two successes earned in this way, one came on the first the other on the last day.

India 219 and 268 (Amar Nath 118, C. K. Nayudu 67; Nichols 5-55).
England 438 (B. H. Valentine 136, C. F. Walters 78, D. R. Jardine 60;
Nissar 5-90) **and 40-1 wicket**. England won by nine wickets.

WORCESTERSHIRE

Pataudi took part in only six County Championship matches, but it is hoped that this splendid batsman will turn out regularly during this coming summer. When Pataudi did play last year he showed brilliant form as his average of over 91 proves. His not out innings of 214 against Glamorgan was a magnificent effort.

WISDEN — 1936

CRICKET IN INDIA

The Bombay Quadrangular Tournament took place after an interval of five years.

Mohammedans v Parsees: November 24, 25, 26, 1935. Mohammedans 334 (Nazir Ali 197; H. J. Vajifdar 4-64). Parsees 101 (Baqa Jilani Khan 4-80) and 232 (H. J. Vajifdar 52, S. H. M. Colah 43; M. Nissar 4-69). Mohammedans won by an innings and one run.

Hindus v Europeans: November 27, 28, 1935. Hindus 299 (L. P. Jai 94; R. J. O. Meyer 4-64). Europeans 121 (F. B. T. Warne 49; Amar Singh 6-42, S. R. Godambe 4-33) and 146 (R. J. O. Meyer 51; Godambe 5-31, Amar Singh 4-50). Hindus won by an innings and 32 runs.

Mohammedans v Hindus: December 1, 2, 3, 4, 1935. Mohammedans 209 (M. Hussein 86; Amar Singh 5-78) and 198 (Wazir Ali 44; S. R. Godambe 4-56, Amar Singh 4-70). Hindus 180 (C. K. Nayudu 97; M. Nissar 6-69) and 127 (Nayudu 53; Nissar 4-56, Mushtaq Ali 3-15). Mohammedans won by 100 runs.

No mention is made of the Ranji Trophy, a regional rather than community-based tournament first competed for in 1934–35, nor of its first winners: Bombay.

WISDEN — 1937

For the first time, Wisden *reported on matches between Indian sides and a team that was not from England – an Australian side which toured at the same time as their Test side was touring South Africa.*

AUSTRALIANS IN INDIA, 1935–36

Played 23: Won 11, Lost 3, Drawn 9

With their representative side in South Africa, a team of Australians, many of them veterans, went to India and had matters all their own way for the greater part of the tour. The tiring effects of extreme heat and constant travelling eventually told their tale. Three of the last seven matches were lost, but 11 victories and nine drawn games in the full programme of 23 fixtures showed that India could not produce sides capable of extending under normal conditions what was practically Australia's second eleven.

Of four representative games, the Australians won the first by nine wickets and the second by eight wickets, but the third brought their first defeat, by 68 runs, and another close struggle in the fourth ended in India winning by 33 runs. The other reverse was a disaster at Secunderabad where the Australians lost by an innings and 115 runs. This was by far the most emphatic victory ever gained by an Indian eleven over a visiting team, and in making a record score of 413, Moin-ud-Dowlah lost only five wickets before declaring.

The trip came about through the efforts of the Maharajah of Patiala. The Australian side, not recognised officially, consisted of a blend of former Test players, many of whom had finished with first-class cricket several years before, and promising players of the younger generation like the Tasmanian, R. O. Morrisby.

INDIA IN ENGLAND, 1936, by W. H. Brookes

It is to be hoped the tour undertaken by a team of cricketers from India in England during 1936 will have a beneficial effect upon Indian cricket, but there is no getting away from the fact that the results achieved did not come within measurable distance of what had been expected. Playing 28 first-class matches, India won no more than four of them. They beat Minor Counties in an innings, and Ireland by ten wickets and overcame both Lancashire and Hampshire, but in the fixture at Liverpool, Lancashire had nothing like full strength in the field and the success at Bournemouth was gained by a margin of only two runs.

The difficulties inseparable from the selection of a representative India side can be fully appreciated only by those in close touch with the game in that country. Some very good players were sent but they did not blend and the lack of teamwork offset the value of individual performances. Merchant, Mushtaq Ali and Ramaswami proved themselves no mean exponents of batting and Nissar, although not reproducing such devastating form with the ball as when in England four years previously, placed several good bowling feats to his credit. Some of the players, however, were handicapped through inexperience of matches of three days' duration. Accustomed to innings lasting three hours apiece in which batsmen need to score quickly, they found difficulty in adapting their style to the altered circumstances. The middle of the batting all too often lacked stability.

Most unfortunately, dissension developed among members of the party and, although much of the gossip was exaggerated, many of those who watched the Indians last season formed the impression that there was a want of harmony on the field. If a tour of India cricketers is to be successful, differences of creed will have to be forgotten. Another blow to the prospects of the team came a week before the first of the Test matches when it was announced that Amarnath had been sent back to India as a disciplinary measure.

This drastic action – unparalleled in the history of modern cricket – deprived the team of their most successful all-round player, for Amarnath had scored more runs than anyone else (613 in 20 innings) and had dismissed 32 batsmen at a cost of under 21 runs per wicket. His feat in the match with Essex at Brentwood of registering two separate hundreds and his clever bowling against Middlesex at Lord's had proved emphatically his worth to the side. A clear and convincing explanation of the reason for this stern measure was withheld at the time, and after the players returned to India a special committee enquired into the affair.

Altogether, 22 players were called upon during the tour. The members of the official team were:

Maharaj Kumar of Vizianagram (Captain)
Major C. K. Nayudu
S. Wazir Ali
Mahomed Nissar
P. E. Palia
L. Amarnath
S. Banerjee
Amir Elahi
M. J. Gopalan
D. D. Hindlekar
M. Baqa Jilani
L. P. Jai
S. Mahomed Hussain
K. R. Meherhomji
V. M. Merchant
Mushtaq Ali
C. Ramaswami

C. S. Nayudu joined the team in June; Amar Singh, M. Jahangir Khan and Dilawar Hussain in accordance with an arrangement made before the tour was begun, assisted in several matches, and S. M. Hadi played in two games.

Merchant was far and away the outstanding batsman and, despite his absence from several matches, he scored 1,745 runs for an average of 51.32 and hit three hundreds. No one else on the side was quicker to find his form and when from June onwards the Maharaj requested him to go in first he played some admirable innings. He and Mushtaq Ali, in scoring 203 together in the second innings of the Manchester Test match, set up a record first-wicket partnership against England in England. The same two batsmen previously had made 215 for the second wicket against Minor Counties. Another notable performance by Merchant was that in the match with Lancashire at Liverpool where he carried his bat for scores of 135 and 77.

The leadership of the Indian team was no sinecure, and the Maharaj Sir Vijaya Vizianagram – he received a knighthood during his visit here – carried far more cares and worries than are usually the lot of the captain of a touring team. He did not accomplish anything out of the common in batting but could not alone be held responsible for the limited success of the side. Cricket is essentially a team game, and in a band of players divided amongst themselves, the will to pull together was not often apparent…

On the whole, India's bowling possessed nothing like the steadiness and venom shown by the 1932 side… Now and again there were glimpses of brilliance but in comparison with the live and accurate work of the players who came to England four years previously the fielding was no more than moderate.

England v India
First Test, played at Lord's, June 27, 29, 30, 1936

During the early cricket, India held their own and, in fact, gained an innings lead of 13 runs. Amar Singh and Nissar both bowled admirably in England's first innings, but on Tuesday they had a heartbreaking task on a dead slow wicket and England in the end won easily… Well as Allen bowled, his work was outclassed by that of Amar Singh who, when England went in on an improved wicket, maintained a superb length and swung the ball either way. With a very short run, Amar Singh was able to bowl for a long spell without losing his steadiness. In his first nine overs, he took four wickets for 13 runs and half the England side were out for 41… At the end of an exciting day's cricket, England were 15 runs behind with three wickets to fall, but next day when, following more rain, play was held up until quarter-past two, the innings was finished off in 19 deliveries for two additional runs…

As artificial means were used to dry the actual wicket – a procedure adopted for the first time in a Test match in England – it was problematical how the wicket would play when India batted again. At first, the ball kicked up and rose at different heights, and although the conditions improved, an early collapse by India in which four wickets fell for 28 runs could not be retrieved.

India 147 (G. O. Allen 5-35) **and 93** (G. O. Allen 5-43). **England 134** (M. Leyland 60; L. Amar Singh 6-35) **and 108-1 wicket** (H. Gimblett 67 not out). England won by nine wickets.

England v India
Second Test, played at Manchester, July 25, 27, 28, 1936

During the Second Test, the Indian opening batsmen, Vijay Merchant and Syed Mushtaq Ali, helped set a record for most runs scored in a day's play in a Test match – 588 – a record that still stands today. Their share of this massive total was an unbroken partnership of 190.

In striking contrast to what occurred in the Lord's match, the second of the Test engagements produced several fine individual batting performances on either side. Hammond on his return to the England team was at the top of his form in hitting a faultless 167 and when India batted a second time Merchant and Mushtaq Ali, scoring 203 together, set up a record first-wicket partnership against England in England. England's bowling was made to look moderate and although having to face arrears of 368 India waged such a splendid uphill fight that when bad light intervened at quarter to four on Tuesday they were leading by 22 runs and had half their wickets in hand. Whether England could have forced a win had further play proved possible can only be conjectured. The easy-paced pitch left the fast bowlers powerless and although Robins worried the batsmen India had the satisfaction of putting together their highest total against England…

Bearing in mind their first-innings performance, India appeared to be facing a hopeless position but Merchant and Mushtaq Ali quickly cleared away thoughts of a collapse. Revelling in an unusual number of full-pitches bowled to them these two quick-footed batsmen, by fine strokeplay all round the wicket, put 190 runs up before stumps were drawn. Merchant often jumped in to drive Robins and also cut well; his partner, who hit 15 off an over from Allen, hooked short balls by supple strokes and completed his hundred in two and a quarter hours. Only six wickets fell on Monday and 588 runs were scored.

Play on Tuesday began after a light shower. Robins and Verity were quickly brought on and when 13 runs had been added Mushtaq Ali was cleverly caught off a hard return. His efforts and those of Merchant in this stand brought exactly as many runs as India scored in the first innings, and the pair were together more than two and a half hours during which Mushtaq Ali sent the ball 17 times to the boundary… With the innings defeat averted, India batted more soberly and it was generally agreed they had an even chance of saving the game when the weather intervened, bad light compelling an abandonment.

India 203 and 390-5 wickets (V. M. Merchant 114, S. Mushtaq Ali 112, C. Ramaswami 60); **England 571** (W. R. Hammond 167, J. Hardstaff 94, T. S. Worthington 87, R. W. V. Robins 76, H. Verity 66 not out). Match drawn.

CAMBRIDGE UNIVERSITY

Another Indian player had a distinguished season in England in 1936, playing for Cambridge University. A developing all-rounder, he played a number of good innings and took 6-11 in 16.4 overs as the University dismissed Warwickshire for 43.

Jahangir Khan, in a very busy season, much of his time being given to helping the Indian touring team, developed into a forcing batsman of lasting quality when he scored 133 off the full strength of the Nottinghamshire bowling and he was mainly responsible for the sensational dismissal of Warwickshire.

CRICKETERS OF THE YEAR 1937

V. M. MERCHANT

The second Test tour to England by India gave the man Wisden described as 'India's original batting hero' the chance to show that he was as good as his scores at home indicated.

Vijay Madhavji Merchant, the outstanding batsman of the India team in England last season, was born in Bombay on October 12, 1911. He first took part in the game at the age of eight at Bharda High School, Bombay, where he captained the Junior team and when only 15 put together scores of 124 and 100 (both not out) in a match for the Seniors.

Going to Sydenham College, Bombay, Merchant captained the team, and in 1929 was chosen for the Hindus in the Quadrangular Tournament. This recognition gained, he improved by leaps and bounds. In 1931, when the college won the Shield for the first time in its history, Merchant scored 504 runs, average 84, and took 29 wickets for 12.13 runs apiece – both records in Bombay inter-collegiate cricket.

In the same year, playing in the Moinuddowla Gold Cup Tournament, he scored 157 for the Freebooters XI against Aligarh University, and such form against some of the best bowlers in the land earned him an invitation the following year to participate in the national trials, but for private reasons he could not accept.

Fortunately Merchant was not lost to India cricket. During the 1933 tour of D. R. Jardine's team, Merchant, playing for Bombay Presidency against MCC, scored 19 not out and 67 not out, and thereby hangs a tale.

Prior to that game Merchant, as he himself admits, felt a slight apprehension in facing fast bowling. Since, he has feared no bowler, and this is how the transition occurred. In the second innings, Merchant received a blow on the chin from a ball

V. M. Merchant.

delivered by Nichols, the Essex fast bowler, and was led injured from the field. An English doctor in attendance patched him up (Merchant today bears a scar in witness of the happening), refused to let him use a looking-glass, and sent him out to resume his innings. He stayed three hours and took out his bat.

This performance brought Merchant back into the limelight and, chosen for India, he played in the three Test matches that year although he achieved nothing out of the common with 178 runs in six innings. In the Silver Jubilee Tournament games held in 1935 at Delhi as trials for the 1936 tour, he scored in four innings, 3, 125 not out, 81 and 100 not out, and although, owing to a strained shoulder, he could not play against the Australian team in any of the representative matches, he was selected on his Tournament form for the tour in England.

It should be interpolated here that Merchant was never an opening batsman in India, and was asked to go in first in this country only when Palia lost form and Hindlekar was injured. Merchant began in England with 366 runs in seven innings and then fell out of the game for three weeks owing to a damaged finger; it was on his return that he was requested to open the innings.

Landmarks along his road of progress here were, in his own opinion, his first hundred in England – the 151 he made against Somerset – and his scores of 135 not out and 77 against Lancashire at Liverpool. In the Test matches, he did yeoman work in scoring 33 and 114 at Manchester, where the game was saved, and 52 and 48 at The Oval, and in all three-day matches registered 1,745 runs, average 51.32.

Although barely more than 5ft 7in in height, Merchant does not allow his comparatively small physique to handicap him in stroke production. What he lacks in reach he makes up by his perfect footwork and quick eye. He is not averse to going out to drive fast bowlers, he employs the hook as a safe scoring stroke, and delights onlookers by the neat skill of his glances and general placing to leg.

His defence tells of long study of the game. Yet, except for a little coaching by the games master at his school, he is self-taught in the arts of cricket. Merchant, however, offers his thanks to L. P. Jai for much learned through force of example. For two years he played under that stylish cricketer for Bombay, and to Jai, Merchant considers he owes more for his cricket success than to any other individual.

Merchant bowled a good deal at school and college, but of late years has not exploited his medium-pace off-spin bowling to any extent. A smart picker-up, he has a slight preference for the outfield. None of his relatives have met with success as cricketers, but he is coaching two younger brothers who are playing for their school.

WISDEN – 1938

At the end of the decade, two noble stalwarts of India's development as an international power died.

OBITUARY

Cooch Behar, Prince Victor of, died on October 30, aged 53. Educated at Eton, he captained the State team of Cooch Behar in 1910–11. He was well known at Lord's and for many years acted as intermediary for the cricket authorities in India, especially regarding touring sides. He was keenly interested in Indian Gymkhana and arranged for several men to go out as coaches.

WISDEN – 1939

OBITUARY

Patiala, The Maharajah of, President of the Cricket Club of India, died on March 23, at the age of 46. At the opening of the Brabourne Stadium, Bombay, when Lord Tennyson's team played there in December 1937, the Maharajah expressed the hope that 'the stadium will become to India what Lord's ground is to England'. That was typical of his keen interest in cricket when poor health compelled him to give up active participation in the game at which he was proficient as a free-scoring batsman and keen field. His successor, the Yuvaraja of Patiala, playing for India, was top scorer with 24 and 60 in the third representative match against D. R. Jardine's team at Madras in 1934, and also did well against Lord Tennyson's side.

LORD TENNYSON'S TEAM IN INDIA

Lord Tennyson's side toured in the winter of 1937–38, playing five 'unofficial Tests'. It was very much a tour led by nobles on both sides: when Tennyson's team played the Jam Sahib of Jamnagar's XI at Jamnagar, among the Jam Sahib's team were Prince Ranvirsinhji, Prince Yadavendrasinhji, Prince Indraviyajasinhji and Prince Jayendrasinhji. The Jam Sahib's XI won by 34 runs, thanks mainly to the all-round skills of the rather less noble Vinoo Mankad and Amar Singh. The first 'Test' was particularly notable in that it included the first instance of natural disaster stopped play to be reported in Wisden.

Played 24: Won 8, Lost 5, Drawn 11

The team which, under the sponsorship and captaincy of Lord Tennyson, toured India during the winter of 1937–38 did not meet with the success anticipated.

Although A. P. F. Chapman, W. R. Hammond and T. W. Goddard declined invitations to join the party and Yorkshire did not permit M. Leyland to make the trip, there seemed justification for Lord Tennyson's description of the side as 'probably the strongest ever to visit India'. The players, however, laboured under the disadvantage of strange conditions, both of weather and wickets, and a pronounced sicklist, and while they won three of the five 'unofficial Tests' they lost five of the 24 fixtures. Misfortunes undoubtedly told heavily against the team. Captain Jameson and Parks at no time enjoyed good health; Smith, Pope, Hardstaff and Langridge all suffered from minor ailments on occasion; Lord Tennyson was attacked by dysentery; and knee trouble kept Gover out of all but two of the last nine matches. In the circumstances, the record could not be regarded as unsatisfactory, particularly in view of the good form shown by Indian elevens...

Under the able captaincy of V. M. Merchant, India were a difficult side to beat, even though Merchant, failing as a batsman after his triumphs in England in 1936, scored only 98 runs in nine 'Test' innings. One young player in V. Mankad came to light. Protégé of A. F. Wensley, the former Sussex professional now a coach in India, Mankad proved himself a splendid batsman, replete with a variety of well-executed, powerful strokes, sound defence and the right temperament for the big occasion. This native of Jamnagar left a lasting impression on the touring team, against whom, in 11 innings, he scored 558 runs (including 113, not out, in the fourth 'Test') at an average of 62. In addition to his batting prowess, Mankad bowled left-hand spinners with considerable skill, and fielded beautifully, particularly at short leg. Amar Singh, with his combination of speed and immaculate length, was easily the best bowler who assisted India. In the five 'Tests', he took no fewer than 36 wickets.

Lord Tennyson's Team v India
First 'Unofficial' Test, played at Lahore, November 13, 14, 15, 16, 1937

Lord Tennyson's Team won by nine wickets.

A brief but severe earthquake shock held up the game for two minutes on the second day.

BOMBAY PENTANGULAR TOURNAMENT, 1937
(WON BY MUSLIMS)

With the inclusion of a Rest XI, the usual Quadrangular Tournament became a Pentangular competition, but before they had played a match, the Hindus withdrew. Muslims beat the Parsis, the Rest and Europeans.

WISDEN — 1940

NOTES ON THE 1939 SEASON, by R. C. Robertson-Glasgow

The MCC tour of India, which was to have taken place this present winter, was naturally cancelled. A moderately strong, if by no means representative, team had accepted invitations. Some of our best cricketers had decided on rest, in view of the visit to Australia due in the winter of 1940–41, and now most unlikely of achievement.

OBITUARY

Rubie, Lieut-Col. Claude Blake, CBE, ED, died on November 3 after an operation, aged 51. He was the appointed manager of the cricket team that would have toured India during the winter had not the war intervened. A well-known member of MCC he used to keep wicket occasionally for Sussex.

WISDEN — 1941

One of the first great Indian bowlers died in 1940, and was given a full obituary, a sign of the reputation that Indian cricket was beginning to gain in the 1930s. With the onset of war, and despite cancelled MCC tours, there was no reason why Wisden *should not give more space to first-class 'Cricket in the Empire', but India still attracted little attention. It was not until the 1941 edition that the Ranji Trophy, now fully established as India's leading competition, received its first mention.*

CRICKET IN INDIA 1939–40

The Cricket Championship of India for the Ranji Trophy was won by Maharashtra, who beat United Provinces by ten wickets in the final at Poona. The outstanding feature of the tournament was the all-round cricket of V. S. Hazare of Maharashtra, who scored 619 runs (average 154.75) and took 20 wickets for 22.90 runs each. Against Baroda, Hazare scored 316 not out, a record individual innings for a three-day match in India.

In their four championship matches Maharashtra scored 2,686 runs, averaging 55.95 runs per wicket.

OBITUARY

Amar Singh, one of the best cricketers produced by India, died at Rajkot on May 20. A very good right-hand fast-medium bowler with easy delivery, he swung the ball; and pace from the pitch made him difficult to time. Seldom failing as a taker of wickets, he seemed to reserve his most effective work for the big occasion. Tall, of athletic build, Amar Singh, besides being such a capable bowler, batted freely and fielded brilliantly. Born in December 1910, he passed away when in his prime.

Coming to England in 1932, he stood out as a prominent member of the All-India team, dismissing 111 batsmen at a cost of 20.78 each and scoring 641 runs with an average of nearly 23. In the one match played against England he created a good impression at Lord's. Four batsmen fell to him and in an uphill struggle he played a very good innings of 51. After the tour he became a Lancashire League player for the Colne club, who released him for a few matches in 1936 when India rose to the status of three Tests. In these engagements with England Amar Singh took ten wickets and averaged 31 with the bat. So well did he bowl at Lord's that he dismissed four of the first five England batsmen for 13 runs and altogether sent back six batsmen for 35 in 25 overs and a ball, so enabling India to lead by 13 on the first innings. England won comfortably by nine wickets, but nothing in the match was more noteworthy than the bowling of the Indian between two batting collapses by his own side. At Old Trafford he hit up 48 and was not out, while at The Oval he gave a brilliant display with the bat, making 44 out of 51 in half an hour.

These exhibitions of free hitting were in keeping with his most noteworthy performance in 1932, when, going in last but one at Liverpool, he played a grand innings of 131 not out against Lancashire; his chanceless hitting was remarkable. His batting average for the 1936 tour was 33.30 in 11 innings; second in the bowling list, he took 26 wickets at 23.50 each.

Against England touring teams Amar Singh met with special success, notably when Lord Tennyson led a side in the winter of 1938. In five representative fixtures, described as unofficial Tests, he took 36 wickets at a cost of 16 runs apiece, and was largely responsible for India gaining two victories. When Tennyson's team won the rubber match by 156 runs Amar Singh took nine wickets in 12 overs – all he sent down in the two innings.

CRICKET IN INDIA, 1940–41

The Bombay Pentagular Tournament was won by the Muslims, who beat the Rest in the final by seven wickets. Hindus did not take part in the tournament.

WISDEN — 1944

There was no mention of Indian cricket in the 1942 edition, and very little the following year. But in 1944 the new editor, Hubert Preston, included for the first time something approaching a comment on domestic Indian cricket.

CRICKET IN INDIA

On December 3, 4 and 5 (1943), at the Brabourne Stadium, remarkable cricket took place in the final match of the first Pentangular Tournament contested since 1941. V. M. Merchant scored 250 not out for the Hindus, who declared with five wickets down for 581. The Rest were dismissed for 133, and in the follow-on lost five men for 62, but V. S. Hazare made 309, he and his brother, Vikram, who contributed only 21, adding 300 in five hours and a half. Despite this extraordinary display The Rest were beaten by an innings and 61 runs.

Hindus 581. The Rest 133 and 387 (V.S. Hazare 309)

V. S. Hazare previously held the Indian record with 316 not out at Poona in the season 1939–40, but V. M. Merchant beat this with 359 not out for Bombay v Maharashtra in the Indian Cricket Championship on January 2, 1944.

No further details about Merchant's record innings were ever published in Wisden.

WISDEN – 1945

Towards the end of the war, several English county cricketers were serving in the armed forces in India, and found time to play a little cricket. However, Wisden *reported their efforts rather more fully than those of their Indian team-mates.*

English county cricketers with the Forces in India assisted Europeans in the Pentangular Tournament at Bombay in November 1944, but Muslims won the competition, just beating Hindus, victors in the two previous tournaments, by one wicket in the four-day final. It was the most successful of Bombay's annual cricket festivals and crowds up to 35,000 visited the Brabourne Stadium.

Europeans failed to qualify for the semi-final, losing to Parsis on the first innings, 343 to 479, in a match confined to three days. Hardstaff (Nottinghamshire), their captain, and Denis Compton (Middlesex) batted brilliantly, Hardstaff showed his finest driving form while making 150 in the first innings and 76 not out in the second. Compton scored 79 not out in the second innings and helped Hardstaff in an unfinished partnership of 146. R. T. Simpson, the young Nottinghamshire batsman, scored 69 in the first innings and assisted Hardstaff to add 142. R. S. Modi became the first Parsi to record a double century in any representative tournament. He took almost seven hours over 215, which helped his side materially in gaining their first innings lead.

The Hindus reached the final, thanks mainly to a score of 221 not out by V. J. Merchant, Parsis being beaten on the first innings. Merchant hit 21 fours in an excellent all-round display lasting six hours. V. Mankad spent five and a half hours over 128 runs; he and Merchant put on 270 for the third wicket.

Muslims beat The Rest on the first innings in the other semi-final. Most successful batsmen for the winners were G. Mahomed (106) and M. Ghazali (108 not out). M. Sathasivam scored 101 for The Rest.

In the final, which ended on November 29, Hindus, 18 behind on the first innings (Hindus 203, Muslims 221) made 315 in their second innings, G. Kishenchand contributing 118 not out and Merchant 60. After a splendid struggle, Muslims managed to obtain the necessary 298 runs, the winning hit being made with their last pair together. K. C. Ibrahim, batting all the last day for a patient 137 not out, took chief part in the notable victory.

Hardstaff, Compton and Simpson played many fine innings in other matches, and P. Cranmer (Warwickshire) and P. F. Judge (Glamorgan) shone as bowlers.

WISDEN – 1946

As the war ended, the editor called for cricket, and its civilizing influence, to resume around the world as quickly and as completely as possible. So strong was the message that this edition devoted six pages to an 'official' tour of India by the Australian Services Team.

NOTES BY THE EDITOR, by Hubert Preston

Directly after the end of the season Dr H. V. Evatt, Australian Minister for External Affairs, appealed to the MCC to send a side to Australia as soon as possible, with the natural outcome of the acceptance of a definite invitation from the Australian Cricket Board of Control for England to visit Australia in the 1946–47 season. On the same occasion Dr Evatt stressed that the tour of the Australian Services team which sailed in October last to India was official. So, with the Dominions, West Indies and New Zealand putting teams in the field, the whole British Commonwealth of Nations became identified actively with cricket almost before the joyous shouts for peace, raised on the collapse of Japan, ceased to echo. And now a very powerful side from India, under the leadership of the Nawab of Pataudi, further accentuates the happy relations which cricket brings to all competing countries.

AUSTRALIAN SERVICES TOUR IN INDIA

On their way home from England in October 1945, the Australian Services team broke their journey and fulfilled a series of ten games in India, including three representative matches. They were regarded as the first official side from the Commonwealth to visit India.

Tired after their programme of 50 matches in the British Isles, and without their opening bowlers, R. G. Williams and A. G. Cheetham, the Australians failed to extend their opponents as they had done in England....

Two of the representative matches were drawn, but the third, and final, at Madras, brought easy victory for India. Though the majority of the zone matches were drawn, they were keenly contested. Batting for East Zone at Calcutta, D. Compton, of Middlesex, was out for nothing in the first innings, but hit 101 in the second.

The games provided the Indian cricket authorities with a good opportunity to watch possible players for the tour to England. R. S. Modi, V. M. Merchant and M. R. Rege took the eye with especially fine innings.

WISDEN – 1947

In 1946, in the year before independence and partition, India became the first overseas team to undertake a Test tour of England after the war.

INDIA IN ENGLAND 1946, by R. J. Hayter

In one important particular India's 16 cricketers who visited England in 1946 accomplished more towards raising the status and dignity of their country's sport than was achieved by either of the two previous touring sides. While the politicians at home argued the rights of independence, the cricketers abroad showed to the world that they could put aside differences of race and creed and join together on and off the field as a single unit, working as one for the same cause. These young men came as their country's ambassadors. By their cricket they won the hearts of the English public; by their modesty and bearing they earned the respect and admiration of everyone with whom they came into close contact. In anything like reasonable weather crowds everywhere flocked to India's matches. A profit of £4,500 in such a dreary summer told eloquently of their popularity.

By winning 11 and losing only four of their 29 first-class matches, the Indians did better than their 1932 and 1936 predecessors. Had they enjoyed the warmth of sunshine and hardness of wickets so much more suited to them and their style of play than the rain, storms, biting cold and sodden turf all too often met in 1946, they would undoubtedly have been even more successful. Yet, in spite of the handicaps under which they laboured, the team themselves were not satisfied with their performances, which fell below the hopes of their countrymen, who anticipated that England would be given a much harder fight in the Test matches. True, both at Lord's and Manchester, there were periods when India held the advantage, but England fought their way to a ten-wickets victory in the First Test and were baulked only by the barest of margins in the Second. Rain won the Third, at The Oval.

In order to view the tour in correct perspective it must be emphasised that, while English cricket lay nearly dormant for six years of war, the game in India went on practically unaffected, so that the Indians prepared confidently, hoping to prove themselves worthy of a place in the highest sphere of international cricket. Additional factors thought to be in their favour were the inclusion of six men, Merchant, Mushtaq Ali, Amarnath, Hindlekar, Banerjee and C. S. Nayudu, thoroughly experienced in English conditions from their 1936 visit, the Nawab of Pataudi's acceptance of the captaincy, and the knowledge that the English season would necessarily be one of rehabilitation.

On anything approaching a batsman's wicket the Indians usually made big scores... For all their huge totals, the Indians sometimes jeopardised their chances of victory by unnecessarily slow batting. Pataudi's declaration at the start of the season that when India were batting the scoreboard would move fast was not always carried into practice. One important reason for this lack of aggression was the repeated failures of the two most daring stroke-players, Amarnath and Mushtaq Ali, whose big innings, though all too rare, remained some of the most pleasant memories of a pleasant tour.

No praise could be too high for Merchant, who, on any reckoning, must be accounted one of the world's greatest batsmen. The first Indian to score 2,000 runs on a tour, Merchant gave of his best in every situation, showing a degree of concentration and determination, especially on a big occasion such as a Test match, more developed and controlled than any batting of some of his team-mates. He hit seven hundreds, two double centuries, shared in 15 out of 26 three-figure stands made for India, and exceeded 50 in 20 out of his 41 innings. His cutting, both square and late, touched the heights of brilliance; he hooked, drove and played the ball off his legs with masterly certainty, and, with all his triumphs, remained a charming, unassuming man and a studious captain whenever Pataudi was absent. His 128 at The Oval in the Third Test was the highest ever played for his country against England.

In emerging from almost complete retirement to lead his country, the Nawab of Pataudi took a big risk of spoiling his own reputation in England as a successful classical batsman. Unfortunately he did not enjoy the best of health and was liable to strains which caused him to retire from the field on a number of occasions and to miss altogether too many games. Though Pataudi scored four hundreds, was third in the batting averages, and at times gave evidence of his former superlative skill, he was but a shadow of the Pataudi England knew so well...

Few men have accomplished finer deeds on their first cricket tour to England than did Vinoo Mankad, India's left-arm slow bowler and right-hand batsman, who set the seal on consistently good work by becoming the first Indian ever to perform the double event of 1,000 runs and 100 wickets in a season. No member of any touring team had accomplished this feat since L. N. Constantine did so for

West Indies in 1928, and R. Howorth, the Worcestershire all-rounder, was the only other man who gained this distinction in 1946.

India's big drawback in bowling was the lack of an opening pair of real penetration, comparable with the Nissar-Amar Singh combination of 1932. Extenuation for Banerjee's moderate performances could be found in that a man who thrived on hard work received too few opportunities to bowl himself into his full power. When given a fast wicket, as at Liverpool, Banerjee showed himself able to unsettle the early batsmen, but he could not gain a place in any of the Test teams. With Sohoni also unable to cause much trouble to English batsmen, the main burden of attack was thrown upon the all-rounders, Mankad, Amarnath and Hazare...

... During the season Amarnath and Mankad signed contracts to play in League cricket in England in 1947. Hafeez remained behind to study philosophy at Oxford University.

Surrey v India
Played at The Oval, May 11, 13, 14, 1946

A record-breaking last wicket stand between Sarwate and Banerjee featured India's first victory of the tour. Although Merchant and Gul Mahomed put on 111 for the third wicket, nine men were out for 205 when the last pair came together. They were not separated for three hours ten minutes, their partnership of 249 being the highest ever recorded for the last wicket in England. Never before in history had nos. 10 and 11 in the batting order each scored a century in the same innings. Both Sarwate and Banerjee gave masterly displays and neither at any time appeared in difficulties. Fishlock drove well for Surrey, who collapsed badly before the Indian spin bowlers. Nayudu, dismissing Fishlock, Bennett and A. V. Bedser, performed the hat-trick.

India 454 (C. T. Sarwate 124 not out, S. Banerjee 121, Gul Mahomed 89, V. M. Merchant 53; A. V. Bedser 5-135) and **20 for one wicket. Surrey 135** (L. B. Fishlock 62) and **338** (R. J. Gregory 100, Fishlock 83; Sarwate 5-54). India won by nine wickets.

The three Test matches did not go India's way: they were unlucky to meet Alec Bedser in his debut series, who took 11 wickets in each of his first two Tests.

England v India, by Hubert Preston
Third Test, at The Oval, August 17, 19, 20, 1946

Merchant maintained his mastery without ever becoming menacing as a hard hitter, and then lost his wicket unluckily. He started for a short run, was sent back by Mankad but moved too slowly and Compton, running behind the bowler from

Last Wicket Record At Oval. C.T. Sarwate and S. Banerjee, who created records by scoring 249 for the last wicket against Surrey at Kennington Oval. The stand was the highest for the last wicket in England, and never before had Nos. 10 and 11 batsmen each scored a century in the same innings.

CRICKETERS OF THE YEAR 1947

M. H. MANKAD

The man who held together the first post-war (and last colonial) Indian team to visit England, in 1946, was Vinoo Mankad, by any measure one of India's greatest cricketers of all time.

Mulvantrai Mankad, known throughout the world by his cricket nickname of Vinoo, left-arm, slow bowler and right-hand batsman, so distinguished himself on his first tour in England as a member of the 1946 India team that, both in performance and ability, he became recognised as the leading all-rounder of the season. Fittingly he crowned his great debut before the English public by completing the coveted 'double' of 1,000 runs and 100 wickets, a feat accomplished by only one other player, R. Howorth of Worcestershire, whose record was slightly inferior to that of Mankad. Not since L. N. Constantine achieved the feat in 1928 had a member of a team visiting England accomplished this all-round performance until Mankad made cricket history as the first Indian ever to do so.

As chief agent in India's attack Mankad was called upon in first-class matches to bowl 1,160 overs, 380 in excess of any of his colleagues, and as many as three times as many as either Banerjee, Sohoni, Sarwate or Nayudu. In so doing he took 129 wickets, more than twice as many as the next most successful Indian bowlers, Hazare and Amarnath (56 each). As a batsman, accustomed at home to going in first, he was given no settled place but used rather as a utility man. In spite of so much bowling responsibility and the irregular batting position Mankad showed himself a very fine player. Seven times he shared in century partnerships, on four occasions with Merchant, the other three with Hazare. Mankad took part in the biggest stands of the tour for the first, fourth, sixth and eighth wickets, putting on 293 with Merchant against Sussex, 332 with Hazare against Yorkshire, 227 unfinished with Hazare against Middlesex and 110 with Merchant against Lancashire, at Old Trafford. Moreover, Mankad opened with Merchant in the Lord's Test and for a good time in the second innings looked capable of demoralising England's bowling.

These stood out as some of his batting triumphs, whereas in bowling he consistently presented a problem to English batsmen. Although called upon to bowl so often on all types of wickets, Mankad rarely departed from a perfect length and, even if not carrying all before him on a wet wicket he was rarely mastered. Indeed but for the shortcomings of some of his fieldsmen, his number of wickets might have been increased by as many as 40 to 50.

Mankad, born on April 12, 1917, at Jamnagar in the Nawanagar state, began to play cricket regularly when a pupil at Nawanagar High School. There he received

tuition from Albert Wensley, the Sussex professional, and to Wensley he readily attributes much of his bowling success. Wensley taught him the art of flighting, variation of pace and spin, and advised him to discard off-breaks because of the possibility of losing his natural grip and action for the more deadly leg-break. Mankad's batting came under the guidance of K. S. Duleepsinhji and when still at school Mankad accomplished an all-round performance which put him on the path to fame. In the final for the High School Shield he took 13 wickets against Alfred High School, Rajkot, was top scorer for Nawanagar with 35 in the first innings and, after his school lost seven wickets for 80 when needing 153 to win, Mankad turned the scales with a freely hit 92 not out.

He first appeared in big cricket for Western States in the Ranji Trophy in 1935. Next year, the Nawanagar Cricket Association, in the first season of its formation, won the Ranji Trophy and Mankad played a leading part in the success. Even then he was little known outside his state until Lord Tennyson's team toured India in 1937–8. In the unofficial Tests he headed both bowling (14.53) and batting (62.66) averages, and Lord Tennyson was stated to have given his opinion that Mankad would step into the World's Best XI. After leaving Nawanagar, Mankad played for the weaker Gujrat team and his opportunities for big cricket became more scarce until in 1945 he toured Ceylon with the representative Indian side. One performance by Mankad, when he took eight All-Ceylon wickets, did much to re-establish his reputation and in the same year he bowled so well against the Australian Services XI that A. L. Hassett, the Australian captain, freely tipped him as a certainty to do well on the English trip.

So necessary was Mankad to the Indian team in England that he missed only two matches, and those on account of an injury which slightly affected his bowling for the remainder of the season. When fielding at cover-point against Surrey at The Oval in May he jarred an ankle and his left elbow; subsequently he found that he could not deliver the faster ball, which went with his arm, either so quickly or so often as before. Nevertheless, this same delivery was responsible for a large proportion of his wickets. Many English batsmen confirmed that though they were prepared for it beforehand they could not always detect its coming when at the wicket. Mankad, of slightly round-arm action, takes only a few steps before delivery near the extreme edge of the crease. He imparts an unusual amount of spin to his stock ball, the leg-break to right-hand batsmen. His batting varies from the stolid to the adventurous according to the situation and his place in the order. This example of team spirit has characterised his constant approach to the game.

mid-on, kicked the ball on to the stumps – an incident reminiscent of that by Joe Hulme, another Arsenal and England forward, who in the same way dismissed Iddon of Lancashire in 1938 when Middlesex visited Old Trafford. This was a sad finish to a remarkable display of skilled concentration lasting five hours and a quarter. Merchant hit 12 fours, excelling in late cuts and pulls, while placing on record the highest innings [128] for India in a Test match against England.

India 331 (V. M. Merchant 128, S. Mushtaq Ali 59); **England 95 for three wickets**. Match drawn.

THE RANJI TROPHY 1945–46

Holkar won the trophy for the first time in its 12 years' existence, triumphing over Baroda in the six-day final at Indore. In the semi-final against Mysore six Holkar batsmen hit individual hundreds, the innings total of 912 for eight wickets declared breing a record in India, and Mysore conceded the match. The other semi-final ended in a tie, and Baroda beat Southern Punjab by the spin of a coin.

Holkar v Mysore
Semi-final, played at Indore, March 2, 3, 4, 5, 1946

Holkar 912 for eight wickets declared (B. B. Nimbalkar 172, M. M. Jagdale 164, K. V. Bhandarkar 142, C. T. Sarwate 101, C. K. Nayudu 101, R. Pratapsingh 100). **Mysore 190** (G. M. Rajasekhar 83 not out, C. T. Sarwate 9-91) and **509 for six wickets declared** (B. K. Garudachar 164, M. M. Jagdale 4-70). Mysore conceded the match, Holkar winning by an innings and 213 runs.

OBITUARY

Beet, George, achieved his ambition of umpiring in a Test match before he died on December 13, at his home in Derby. Appointed to the umpires' list in 1929, he stood regularly, and at length was chosen for the England and India Test at Manchester in July 1946. On the way home by train from that game, Beet was taken seriously ill and rushed to Derby Infirmary for an operation. From this illness he never recovered.

WISDEN – 1948

OBITUARY

Sewell, Mr Edward Humphrey Dalrymple... died on September 21, aged nearly 75. Born in India, where his father was an Army officer, he was educated at Bedford Grammar School... In a curiously varied life he returned to India as a civil servant, and his very powerful hitting enabled him to make many big scores at an exceptional rate of scoring. The first batsman in India to make three consecutive hundreds, he also twice exceeded 200. Sometimes he enjoyed the advantage of having Ranjitsinhji for captain.

WISDEN — 1949

India's first ever Test tour to Australia, in 1947–48, was not a success on the pitch. The Australians won the series by four games to nil, with one game lost to the weather.

INDIA IN AUSTRALIA, by Leslie Smith

India cannot have happy memories of their tour in Australia during 1947–48. Of the 14 first-class matches played, only two brought victories compared with seven defeats. In the Test matches they were outclassed: four were lost; in three Australia batted only once; and such was the superiority of the Australians that except in one instance the result looked a foregone conclusion before the end of the first day.

Needing all possible good fortune, India actually experienced the reverse, for bad luck dogged them throughout the Test series. In four of the five games Bradman won the toss and twice weather conditions made the pitch treacherous when India batted. On the only occasion when Amarnath called correctly India led by 81 on the first innings, but they were unable to force home the advantage because of rain, which reduced cricket to less than ten hours in six days and the match was left drawn…

The inability of Merchant and Modi, two of the most reliable batsmen on all types of pitches, to make the trip undoubtedly proved an immense handicap. The team was unbalanced, with practically everything depending on the captain, Amarnath, Mankad and Hazare. Phadkar, particularly in the Tests, Adhikari, Kishenchand, Sarwate, Rangachari and Sen, the wicketkeeper, were all useful members of the side, but there were too many failures, several of the party doing practically nothing with either bat or ball.

India were not at their best in the field, several catches being dropped, but the party impressed everyone by their keenness and they were immensely popular throughout the country.

Australia v India
Fourth Test, played at Adelaide, January 23, 24, 26, 27, 28, 1948

Although they gained another overwhelming success, and in so doing won the rubber, the match was a personal triumph for Hazare, who followed Bradman's example in the Third Test and hit a hundred in each innings. Against such a powerful attack as that possessed by the Australians, this was a truly remarkable performance. To balance this, however, Bradman was once again in irresistible form, hitting a double hundred.

Australia 674 (D. G. Bradman 201, A. L. Hassett 198, S. G. Barnes 112,
K. R. Miller 67). **India 381** (D. G. Phadkar 123, V. S. Hazare 116) and **277**
(V. S. Hazare 145, H. R. Adhikari 51; R. R. Lindwall 7-38).
Australia won by an innings and 16 runs.

WISDEN – 1950

Throughout the 1940s, big scores were being made in Indian domestic cricket, and 1948–49 provided the apogee with one team set a world record 959 to win a match in the Ranji Trophy and the sad tale of the ultimate nearly man, B. B. Nimbalkar.

CRICKET IN INDIA 1948–49

Despite the visit of the West Indies, the Ranji Trophy, conducted for the first time on an open draw basis and not on the zonal system, drew considerable interest. After a break of three seasons, Bombay regained the Trophy. Their main strength was in their batting, K. C. Ibrahim, D. G. Phadkar and M. K. Mantri being particularly prominent.

The tournament was marked by the setting up of new world records. B. B. Nimbalkar (443 not out) and K. V. Bhandarkar (205) added 455 for the Maharashtra second wicket against Kathiawar at Poona, so beating the 451 scored by D. G. Bradman and W. H. Ponsford in 1934. Nimbalkar's innings, which lasted eight hours 14 minutes and included 49 fours, was the highest individual score in India cricket. He was only nine short of Bradman's world record when Kathiawar conceded the match.

The Bombay v Maharashtra semi-final aggregate of 2,376 runs for 38 wickets surpassed the 2,078 for 40 wickets by Bombay and Holkar in 1944–45. In the same match nine three-figure innings were played, and U. M. Merchant and D. G. Phadkar (Bombay) and M. R. Rege (Maharashtra) scored a century in each innings and Maharashtra were set a world record 959 to win.

Kathiawar v Maharashtra
Played at Poona, December 16, 17, 18, 1948

Kathiawar 238 (Thakur Saheb of Rajkot 77, D. G. Choudhuri 4-46).
Maharashtra 826 for four wickets (B. B. Nimbalkar 443 not out,
K. V. Bhandarkar 205, S. D. Deodhar 93).
Maharashtra won on first innings, Kathiawar conceding the match.

Bombay v Maharashtra
Played at Poona March 18, 19, 20, 21, 22, 23, 24, 1949

Bombay 651 (M. K. Mantri 200, U. M. Merchant 143, D. G. Phadkar 131, P. R. Umrigar 57, Y. N. Gokhale 4-35) and **714 for eight wickets declared** (D. G. Phadkar 160, U. M. Merchant 156, K. M. Rangnekar 94, M. N. Raiji 75, K. C. Ibrahim 59). **Maharashtra 407** (M. C. Datar 143, M. R. Rege 133, K. K. Tarapore 6-119) and **604** (S. D. Deodhar 146, M. R. Rege 100, S. G. Palsule 97, M. C. Datar 86, Sham Joshi 57). Bombay won by 354 runs.

WEST INDIES IN INDIA 1948–49, BY R. W. THICK

At international level, in the winter of 1948–49, India continued challenging new Test opponents, as West Indies embarked on their first ever tour of the subcontinent. The tour broke new ground in terms of transport arrangements as well.

West Indies broke fresh ground in 1948–49 with a visit to India, where their batting strength astonished their hosts, and victory in the fourth match of the series enabled them to win the Test rubber. The other four encounters, like eight more of the tour, failed to produce a definite result, and West Indies, who won six first-class matches, suffered only one defeat.

Apart from the fixtures which ended in victory for West Indies, the Tests occupied five days, and doubtlessly four were drawn because both sides lacked fast bowlers up to international standard. Unfortunately for West Indies, Hines Johnson could not make the trip. Few batsmen relish the ball which buzzes in the air on account of its tremendous speed, and until bowlers are found who can combine increased velocity with accuracy of length and direction it is to be feared that many representative matches will end in stalemate. Another weakness which manifested itself was the inability of leg-break bowlers to cause much trouble...

Although Worrell, a fine batsman, did not make the trip for West Indies, the continued absence of Merchant for health reasons, which kept him at home during the tour in Australia, dealt India a bigger blow. Experiments to find a reliable opening pair were largely disappointing, and another obstacle was the failure of Amarnath to find his best Test form. Hazare, Adhikari, Mushtaq Ali and Phadkar were all seen to advantage, but rarely did India's batting equal that of their opponents in technique or attractiveness. Mankad won the admiration of friend and foe alike by clever left-arm slow bowling, the view being expressed that he had no peer in the world...

Enthusiasm for cricket in India proved unbounded and record attendances almost everywhere assured financial success for the tour. West Indies travelled by ship to England and then went by air to and from India. After exhaustive train journeys to several places, the Indian Cricket Board of Control arranged the same form of long-distance air travel for other engagements. This provided a pointer for those who organise visits to countries where players may become fatigued by ordinary transport in extremely hot weather.

India v West Indies
Fifth Test, played at Bombay, February 4, 5, 6, 7, 8, 1949

India almost won the final Test, but Goddard's tactics in slowing the game down prevented the hosts from gaining what would have been their first ever Test victory.

Goddard, West Indies captain, won the toss for the fifth time in the Tests, but his side made a poor start on the turf pitch. Phadkar's deliveries often ran away late and he soon dismissed Rae, who fell to a great catch by Mushtaq Ali at short leg. The same bowler beat Walcott with a magnificent delivery which went through at considerable speed, and two wickets were down for 27. In spite of muscle trouble, however, Stollmeyer batted confidently, and Weekes helped him add 110 for the third wicket. Yet West Indies' total of 235 for five wickets at the close showed that they were never really at their best…

On the second day Phadkar and Mankad quickly finished the innings, the last five wickets falling for the addition of 51. At the end India's position was also far from bright, half the side being out for 132. Gomez and Atkinson, both medium-pace, and the more speedy Trim generally held the upper hand, and India found themselves 93 behind. The last two days produced interesting and exciting cricket. Rae earned chief honours with the bat in West Indies' second innings, when Phadkar, Mankad and Banerjee were most successful bowlers.

Set 361 to win with 395 minutes left, India decided to go for the runs, and their position looked promising when Hazare, who hit a fine century, and Modi put on 137 for the fourth stand. The final over came with India requiring 11 for success, and as Sen appeared unlikely to bat, Phadkar and Ghulam Ahmed were virtually their last pair. Phadkar added five more, but an enthusiastic if disappointed crowd saw victory elude India's grasp by six runs. For West Indies, Jones, while taking five wickets for 85 in 41 overs, accomplished the best bowling of his career.

West Indies 286 (J. B. Stollmeyer 85, E. D. Weekes 56) and **267** (A. F. Rae 97). **India 193** and **355 for eight wickets** (V. S. Hazare 122, R. S. Modi 86; P. E. Jones 5-85). Match drawn.

OBITUARY

Hindlekar, D. D., one of the best wicketkeepers ever produced by India, died at Bombay on March 30, aged 40. He was one of the small band of cricketers who opened an innings and went in last in separate Test matches. Hindlekar toured England in 1936 and 1946 and altogether played in four Test matches. At

Manchester in the Second Test in 1946 he and Sohoni, the last pair, stayed together for the last 13 minutes of the match and warded off defeat. During the 1936 tour he opened the innings in the First Test at Lord's, but subsequently chipped a bone in a finger and also was troubled by blurred vision. Ten years later a strained back kept him out of several matches.

His choice for the 1946 visit to England was unexpected, for he was then 37, but such was his form in the Bombay Pentangular final of 1945–46 that he could not be overlooked. Never spectacular but always sound, both behind the stumps and when batting, Hindlekar was a cheerful personality and an extremely popular member of the touring parties.

WISDEN – 1951

THE COMMONWEALTH TEAM IN INDIA

In the disappointment over the MCC decision not to send a team in 1949–50, India found great consolation from the fine cricket of the all-professional Commonwealth side, composed largely of players prominent in league cricket in Lancashire, which stepped into the breach…

Since the primary requirement of a league professional is that he should be an all-rounder, it was hardly surprising that the side proved entertaining, versatile and such a great attraction in all parts of India, Pakistan and Ceylon that a second tour was arranged for the following winter…

Financially, the tour was a distinct success, and it did much to develop the great and ever-increasing interest in cricket in India.

Two more Commonwealth tours followed, in 1950–51 and 1953–54. Both were highly successful.

OBITUARY

Wazir Ali, Major Syed, the former Indian Test match cricketer, died in Karachi on June 17, aged 46, after an operation for appendicitis. Elder brother of S. Nazir Ali, another Test player, Wazir Ali appeared in seven Test matches – all against England. He toured England in 1932 and 1936 and played against England in India in 1933. A fine batsman with a keen eye and a wide range of powerful strokes, Wazir Ali hit six hundreds during the 1932 tour and scored 1,725 in all matches. On his second visit to England he was handicapped by a finger injury. He missed a month's cricket, but although unable to do himself justice he hit the highest score for the Indians during the tour – 155 not out against an England XI at Folkestone. He led the Indian team which won matches against visiting Australian sides in India in 1935 and 1936.

WISDEN — 1952

In preparation for the Indian tourists' arrival for their tour, the 1952 edition published an article by Vijay Merchant. This was the first article ever published on Indian cricket, apart from tour and match reports. It was a long piece, and it revealed the divisions that lay within Indian cricket as much by what Merchant did not write as by what he did.

TWENTY YEARS OF INDIAN TEST CRICKET, by Vijay M. Merchant

The Imperial Cricket Conference gave India Test match status for their first official tour of England in 1932. That was a red-letter day in the history of Indian cricket and the stepping-stone to the exchange of official visits between India and most of the other cricketing countries. Of the previous visits to England, that of the semi-official side of 1911 was the most notable. Although that team contained some of the finest Indian cricketers, it experienced difficulty in overcoming even the lower-placed counties.

Batting and bowling talent was present, but fielding let India down and the side did not possess the temperament to recover from a difficult situation. In addition, the Maharajah of Patiala, the captain, did not enjoy good health. After playing in the first few matches, he went on a tour of the Continent and took with him Col. K. M. Mistry, his ADC. Col. Mistry was the best batsman on the Indian side, and his absence from the remaining fixtures created a gap which was never filled. He had made a big impression on English critics by his 78 against the MCC at Lord's and the public looked forward to more innings from him…

Wonderful Hitting

The next meeting of Indian and English cricketers came in 1926, when a team under Arthur Gilligan visited India. Including as it did such outstanding personalities as Maurice Tate, Andy Sandham, Jack Mercer, George Geary and Bob Wyatt, the MCC side was most successful and provided considerable education to Indian cricketers both old and young. One match on that tour is still talked about by those who saw it. Playing for the MCC against the Hindus at Bombay, Guy Earle, of Somerset, scored 130 in which he hit eight sixes and 11 fours. People in Bombay had never seen such hitting and never expected to see the like of it again. In the Hindus' innings, however, C. K. Nayudu outshone this performance. He made 153 in 100 minutes by even fiercer hitting. Nayudu's innings contained 11 sixes and 13 fours and, in point of merit, was the best I have seen by an Indian cricketer in any land. Although Nayudu never again touched that form, his display will ever be green in the memory of those fortunate enough to be present…

The MCC [sent] a strong side to India in 1933–34. They paid Indian cricket a high compliment by appointing Douglas Jardine as captain and sending cricketers like Walters, Bakewell, Nichols, Clark and Hedley Verity... Above all, Jardine's captaincy impressed India more than any single feature or individual performance. His shrewd tactics and ability to get the best out of his men were an object lesson not only to Indian cricketers but to Indian captains as well. He never gave away anything or asked for any concession, and India came to understand how relentlessly he must have pursued his method of attack in Australia in 1932–33. England has possessed few captains with the tenacity and singleness of purpose reflected in Douglas Jardine.

In Jardine's tour, India found one player of particular merit, L. Amarnath. In addition, many of the weaknesses which have been the curse of Indian cricket for some years were exposed. The tour showed clearly that India lacked solidity in batting and could not consolidate a good position after a fine start. It also showed that India did not possess the tenacity to turn the tables when odds were against them. Above all it exposed our fielding weakness. Time and again Indian cricket has suffered because of fielding lapses, and even now after nearly 20 years those lapses persist...

An Unhappy Appointment

In 1936 India sent her second official team to England. The tour began with a severe handicap in the captaincy of the Maharaj Kumar of Vizianagram. Originally the Nawab of Pataudi was appointed captain but, because of bad health, he withdrew. Subsequently, Vizianagram was appointed captain. Vizzy had done a great deal for Indian cricket and when in 1931 he invited Hobbs and Sutcliffe to India to play for his team in a series of matches in India and Ceylon, he gave Indian cricketers and public an opportunity to see two of the world's greatest batsmen in action.

The captaincy of India was quite a different matter. On his form he would not have found a place in any good side, but the authorities in India did not seem to realise that captaincy of a country's team on an official tour meant more than individual status or the ability to make good speeches. So far as cricket was concerned, he was a dismal failure. He also made the sad mistake of insisting on playing in as many matches as possible. Neither in the field nor in batting was he an acquisition and, more often than not, the team virtually played with ten men.

The unfortunate Amarnath incident also marred that trip. Similar incidents have occurred in most touring sides, but the drastic action of sending Amarnath home not only was a blot on Indian cricket, but considerably weakened the team in all the Test matches... The action against Amarnath seemed to be out of place at the time...

India went to England again in 1946. For the first time we were captained on tour by a man who deserved a place in the team on his merits as a cricketer. The Nawab of Pataudi had achieved notable things in England, and India welcomed his abilities both as captain and batsman. We were fairly and squarely beaten in the First Test match at Lord's and just managed to save ourselves from defeat at Manchester. The Oval Test was a washout. India, however, did well against most of the counties and financially the visit proved successful…

India undertook a new venture in 1947–48 when a team was sent to Australia, but with three of the best players staying at home, we could not hold the strong Australians who, under the captaincy of Don Bradman, proved as invincible as they were against W. R. Hammond's MCC team the previous year. Amarnath led India; he batted extremely well in the first-class matches, only to fail in the Tests. The pick of our batsmen were Hazare, Phadkar and Mankad, whose great efforts were spoiled through lack of support…

While visiting teams average between 50 and 55 runs an hour in representative matches, India have not been able to average more than 35 to 40. Unless, therefore, their fielding – particularly catching – improves considerably and the rate of scoring is speeded up, it will be very difficult for India to go far in international cricket.

Vijay Hazare… has done more for Indian cricket in the last five years than any other player and, from the point of batting technique and the number of runs scored, should rank amongst the first six in the world at present. Temperamentally he is extremely sound and devoid of nerves. If he can quicken his rate of scoring, few men would be superior to him in contemporary cricket.

Effect of Partition
The partition of India has deprived Indian cricket of some outstanding cricketers. Abdul Hafeez Kardar, Fazal Mahommed [sic], Khan Mahommed and Imtiaz Ahmed would have helped considerably to strengthen the Indian team. Today Khan Mahommed is the fastest bowler in this subcontinent and India has no one among the medium-paced bowlers who can be put in the same category as Fazal Mahommed; Kardar is sufficiently well known in England; Nazar Mahommed is a most attractive and dashing opening batsman – India's biggest need today; and Imtiaz Ahmed is an outstanding opening batsman who demonstrated his abilities last year against the Second Commonwealth Team by scoring 300 runs in the last match. That is the highest score made by any Indian or Pakistani cricketer against a visiting team.

Above all, the partition has deprived India of future fast bowlers. In the past, India often relied for fast bowling on the Northern India people who, because of their height and sturdy physique, are better equipped for this kind of bowling than the cricketers of Central India or the South. Now this source of supply has ceased and the gap has not yet been filled. Some time may elapse before India possesses a fast bowler of the calibre of Mahomed Nissar who hailed from the Punjab…

I am writing several months before the team will be chosen and I hope that Vijay Hazare, who should be an admirable captain, will be given a large proportion of young cricketers. In India too much premium has always been placed on experience and too little faith in youth. Over a period of years this policy has been disastrous. In the Indian team today are men who not only played in 1936 but as far back as 1933–34. Many promising cricketers have had their careers cut short through not receiving opportunities at the right time. Too many have retired soon after returning from a tour. Until and unless the authorities take courage in both hands and give more opportunities to young men, India's inherent weakness will continue and no improvement will be possible.

CRICKET IN INDIA, 1950–51

In Indian domestic cricket, Holkar continued to pile up the runs on their way to another Ranji Trophy success, although Ghulam Ahmed would not have been cheering them on.

Twenty teams participated in the Ranji Trophy championship during the 1950–51 season, East Punjab being new entrants. Holkar regained the trophy which they had won twice before... A feature of the Championship was the emergence of Gujerat as a strong contender. They appeared for the first time in the final, and were defeated by Holkar. Until last season Gujerat were the 'wooden spoonists' of the competition. On their way to the final they beat Baroda (holders), Bombay and the Services XI...

S. Mushtaq Ali (Holkar) distinguished himself by hitting a century in each of the four matches he played. Ghulam Ahmed achieved a world record bowling performance in one innings against Holkar. His figures were 92.3-21-245-4, and so he sent down three more balls than did A. L. Valentine for West Indies against England at Nottingham in 1950.

Jasu Patel, batting No. 9, scored 152 for Gujerat against Holkar in the final. He and Nakhuda added 136 runs for the tenth wicket, the last partnership of the match, but this could not save Gujerat from defeat.

Ranji Trophy Final – Holkar v Gujerat

Holkar 429 and 443. Gujerat 327 and 356. Holkar won by 189 runs.

WISDEN – 1953

In the winter of 1951–52 and the summer of 1952 England played India home and away. India gained their first ever Test victory during the winter, but in England came up against Fred Trueman at his quickest.

MCC TOUR OF INDIA, PAKISTAN AND CEYLON, 1951–52,
by Leslie Smith

Taking everything into consideration, the MCC team which toured India, Pakistan and Ceylon in the winter of 1951–52, did as well as could have been expected.

They began the tour under a big handicap, knowing they were being termed England's second string, and hard as they tried to prove that false, they never really succeeded...

In the Test matches with India, England shared the honours, each side gaining one victory, with the remaining three drawn. The tour lacked colour and, except perhaps in one or two instances, failed to show English cricket at its best. At the same time it must be emphasised that cricket in India is very much different from that in England. Pitches there are practically all of the slow, lifeless type, unhelpful to either batsmen or bowlers. These, plus the trying heat and humidity, made it sheer hard work with little reward forthcoming. The bowlers, particularly, had a most difficult tour. On not more than four occasions did the faster men find pitches which gave the slightest encouragement, and for them it generally meant an over or two at full pace while the shine remained on the ball, then a drop to three-quarter speed to conserve energy...

India, for the most part, looked a better-balanced side, with strength in batting making them extremely difficult to dismiss cheaply. Roy, a definite discovery, scored more runs than any other Indian batsman in a Test series against England, Hazare made centuries in the first two Tests, and good support came from Gopinath, Umrigar, Phadkar and Adhikari, with others occasionally rising to the occasion. India possessed by far the best bowler on either side in their slow left-hander Mankad, whose achievement of taking 34 wickets in the series on pitches seldom suitable to him was a great performance. Shinde bowled superbly at Delhi and Ghulam Ahmed showed good form in the last two Tests, but without Mankad India's attack would have been weak. England were slightly superior in the field, especially in ground work, but taken all round India were the sounder combination.

INDIA'S FIRST TEST VICTORY AGAINST ENGLAND

Fifth Test, at Madras, February 6, 8, 9, 10, 1952

India made history by recording their first Test victory, and they did it in emphatic style. Undoubtedly they were the superior all-round side and they went all out for success from the first ball. Their hero was Mankad, who bowled superbly in each innings, taking 12 wickets in the match for 108. His performance of 8-55 in the first innings has seldom been bettered in Test cricket when it is considered that the pitch gave him little assistance.

Mankad's bowling inspired the whole side, the fielding being far better than in previous matches and the batting possessed a more adventurous spirit, necessary for the occasion. England disappointed badly. There was no real reason for the batting collapse in the first innings which virtually decided the match. Hopes that they could stage one of their renowned recoveries were dashed when the pitch turned difficult after the third day.

Yet again India made five changes from their previous side. Manjrekar, Nayudu, Shinde, Joshi and Adhikari stood down for Mushtaq Ali, Amarnath, Gopinath, Divecha and Sen. As originally chosen the side included Adhikari and omitted Umrigar, but a wrist injury due to a fall gave Umrigar another opportunity which he seized splendidly. Carr led England for the first time, Howard standing down with pleurisy, this being the one change from the Kanpur side.

Carr won the toss, giving England a 3–2 advantage in the series, but they were soon in difficulties, Lowson being bowled by a splendid breakback with three scored. Spooner and Graveney looked like bringing about a recovery, but the advent of Mankad at 65 changed the course of the match. Two or three times Mankad almost lured Graveney out of his ground before the batsman could resist no longer and moved forward to a ball well on the off and was stumped.

Spooner and Robertson added 60 for the next stand, but again just when England looked to be getting themselves out of trouble a wicket fell, Spooner, who stayed two hours 50 minutes, being caught at cover off Hazare's second ball. For a change, Watkins failed and Poole was never comfortable. With half the side out for 197 only two recognised batsmen, Robertson and Carr, remained. They made a good effort with a partnership of 47 before Robertson was brilliantly caught and bowled after a stay of four and a half hours. Mankad followed this by taking the last four wickets which fell for 22, three of them stumped when lured forward by the flight.

During the afternoon the death of King George VI was announced and arrangements were changed, the second day being made the rest day. Subsequently India batted consistently, with Roy again in fine form. Fourth out at 191, he scored his second century of the series and hit 15 fours in 111, made in three hours 50 minutes. India really took control after the fall of the fifth wicket, Phadkar and Umrigar adding 104 and Umrigar and Gopinath 93 in 80 minutes. Umrigar took out his bat for 130 after four hours 35 minutes, a splendid effort following a run of disappointing scores in the Tests.

England, 191 behind, survived the last quarter of an hour on the third day, but with the pitch wearing they were soon struggling next day. Robertson again batted well and made top score for the second time, Watkins showed he was still full of fight, but they were almost alone in their resistance and the match ended before tea on the fourth day. The scenes at the finish were surprisingly subdued, but the Indian officials and players were delighted at the first victory by their country at the 25th attempt to win a Test match.

ENGLAND

	1st Innings		2nd Innings
F. A. Lowson b Phadkar	1	– c Mankad b Phadkar	7
R. T. Spooner c Phadkar b Hazare	66	– lbw b Divecha	6
T. W. Graveney st Sen b Mankad	39	– c Divecha b Ghulam Ahmed	25
J. D. Robertson c and b Mankad	77	– lbw b Ghulam Ahmed	56
A. J. Watkins c Gopinath b Mankad	9	– c and b Mankad	48
C. J. Poole b Mankad	15	– c Divecha b Ghulam Ahmed	3
D. B. Carr st Sen b Mankad	40	– c Mankad b Ghulam Ahmed	5
M. J. Hilton st Sen b Mankad	0	– st Sen b Mankad	15
J. B. Statham st Sen b Mankad	6	– c Gopinath b Mankad	9
F. Ridgway lbw b Mankad	0	– b Mankad	0
R. Tattersall not out	2	– not out	0
Extras (b 4, l-b 4, n-b 3)	11	Extras (b 7, l-b 2)	9

1-3 2-71 3-131 4-174 5-197 6-244 7-252   266   1-12 2-15 3-68 4-117 5-135 6-159 7-159   183
8-261 9-261 10-266   8-178 9-178 10-183

First innings – Nissar 26–3–93–5; Phadkar 16–2–49–1; Divecha 12–2–27–0; Amarnath 27–6–56–0;
Ghulam Ahmed 18–5–53–0; Mankad 38.5–15–55–8; Hazare 10–5–15–1
Second innings – Nissar 18–5–42–1; Phadkar 9–2–17–1; Divecha 7–1–21–1; Amarnath 3–0–6–0 ;
Ghulam Ahmed 26–5–77–4; Mankad 30.4–9–53–4

INDIA

	1st Innings
Mushtaq Ali st Spooner b Carr	22
P. Roy c Watkins b Tattersall	111
V. S. Hazare b Hilton	20
V. Mankad c Watkins b Carr	22
L. Amarnath c Spooner b Statham	31
D. G. Phadkar b Hilton	61
P. Umrigar not out	130
C. D. Gopinath b Tattersall	35
R. V. Divecha c Spooner b Ridgway	12
P. Sen b Watkins	2
Ghulam Ahmed not out	1
Extras (b 8, l-b 2)	10

1-53 2-97 3-157 4-191   (9 wickets declared) 457
5-216 6-320 7-413 8-430 9-448

First innings – Statham 19–3–54–1; Ridgway 17–2–47–1; Tattersall 40–9–100–2; Hilton 39–13–94–2;
Carr 19–2–84–2; Watkins 14–1–50–1; Robertson 5–1–18–0

UMPIRES: B. J. Mohoni and M. G. Vijayasarathy
India won by an innings and eight runs.

INDIA IN ENGLAND, 1952, by Leslie Smith

India returned home at the end of the 1952 tour of England well satisfied with a profit of over £11,000, but far from happy about their performances on the field. Frankly, they were a big disappointment and few countries have finished with such a poor record. Admittedly they lost only five matches, but they won no more than four of their first-class games and offered little opposition in the Tests. No fewer than 20 of the 29 games were drawn – a fact that showed the biggest failing of the team.

From the moment the Indians arrived there seemed to be an attitude of defensive caution in their play, and the longer the tour progressed and the failures continued the more pronounced it became. Defeat was the horrid ogre in their path, and to ward it off they retired into a cave, pulled a massive rock over the entrance and attempted to defy all efforts to dislodge them. Against the battering rams of Trueman and Bedser when opposed to the full strength of England, this proved useless, as would probably have been any tactics they might have adopted. But the same methods could hardly be excused when they were opposed to county sides. India were weak as a representative team, but certainly not as bad as they made themselves appear. A more vigorous policy would probably have brought greater success and even more financial reward.

Having beaten England at Madras and gained the first Test victory in their history a short while before they sailed, the Indians were expected to do a good deal better than their predecessors on tour. It soon became obvious that this was not to be, and in the four Tests they were outclassed. They lost the first three and the weather saved them in the last.

People in India failed to understand why their side did so badly, not realising that there is a wide difference in the game of cricket as played in the two countries. It was this difference which the team could not overcome. In India pitches, with one or two exceptions, are completely lifeless, giving no encouragement to bowlers of any type. Batsmen get a false sense of security, and as long as they discard risks and concentrate on punishing only the bad balls they are in little danger. Hence the massive totals and slow rate of run-getting often found in matches in India. The most serious result is that fast bowling has become a lost art, for, as Statham and Ridgway found there, during the MCC tour, it is merely a waste of time pounding away in the heat with such little reward. For all their energy, the ball came off so sluggishly that batsmen had plenty of time to step back and watch it right on to the bat.

This was a terrific handicap to India in England and explained to a large extent the disintegration before Trueman. Few of their batsmen had ever faced such speed and they did not know whether to play forward or back. The ball which flew round their head was a new thing to them – and they had no answer to it. Without a real fast bowler on their own side, there could be no question of retaliation.

Quick spin, too, baffled them, for again they rarely meet it. A side which goes on tour inexperienced in facing fast bowling and the quickly turning ball has little hope of succeeding. The remedy lies in the hands of the Indian authorities, who, if they expect their country to become a world power in cricket, must make every endeavour to introduce more pace into their pitches.

England v India
First Test, at Leeds June 5, 6, 7, 9, 1952, by Leslie Smith

History was made in the match which, if not reaching the high standard expected from Test cricketers, was crammed with exciting incidents, remarkable collapses and gallant recoveries. But, above all, were the events which occurred at the commencement of India's second innings. They went in facing a first innings deficit of 41, and within a few minutes the match seemed almost over. India lost their first four wickets without a run scored and the crowd were stunned into silence as the drama unfolded before them. No Test side had ever before made such a bad start to an innings...

In the course of the first 14 balls Trueman claimed three wickets and Bedser one. Only the dismissal of Gaekwad by Bedser was the result of the ball doing the unexpected. Trueman upset Roy, Manjrekar and Mantri by his fiery pace and hostility... Trueman, in his first Test, emerged as England's most successful bowler with seven wickets for 166 runs, but lively as he was, weak batting on the part of the Indians helped him.

England won by seven wickets.

Only six years after leading India in England, the only man to have played cricket for both India and England died, at a very young age.

OBITUARY

Nawab Iftikhar Ali of Pataudi, who died after a heart attack while playing polo at New Delhi on January 5, at the age of 41, will always be associated with Ranjitsinhji and Duleepsinhji as three great Indian batsmen who became leading figures in English cricket. Pataudi, known as 'Pat' throughout the world, achieved the rare distinction of representing England and India in Test Cricket.

Born at Pataudi in the Punjab on March 16, 1910, he went to Chiefs' College, Lahore, and received cricket coaching from M. G. Salter, the Oxford Blue. Going to England in 1926, he obtained further guidance from Frank Woolley, the Kent and England left-hander. In October 1927 Pataudi went to Oxford, but had to wait until 1929 before gaining his Blue. That season he accomplished little with the bat until the University Match, when his innings of 106 and 84 went a long way towards saving the game.

The Worst Start In Test Cricket. This was the scene at Headingley on the third afternoon of the First Test when India began their second innings by losing four men without a run on the board. There was no parallel to this collapse in the history of Test cricket. With the first two balls of his second over F. S. Trueman dismissed M. K. Mantri and V. L. Manjrekar and here V. S. Hazare, who went in sixth, has just averted a possible hat-trick.

The following year he disappointed against Cambridge, but on his third appearance in 1931 he reached the height of his powers. In form from the start of the season, he scored 1,307 runs in 16 innings and finished top of the Oxford batting with the splendid average of 93. In successive innings he made 183 not out against The Army at Folkestone, 165 and 100 against Surrey at The Oval and 138 and 68 against H. D. G. Leveson Gower's XI at Eastbourne. Even this he overshadowed with a remarkable 238 not out against Cambridge at Lord's, the highest individual score ever made in the University Match...

His health was never strong and he was not always fit when touring Australia with D. R. Jardine's team in 1932–33. Nevertheless, he added another great triumph to his name by scoring a century in his First Test match and helping England to victory by ten wickets at Sydney. He played in the next Test but did little, and was left out for the remaining three games.

Pataudi did not allow his disappointment to upset him, and on returning to England he was again in fine form for Worcestershire, his adopted county. In 1934 he was once more chosen for England against Australia, but scored only 12 and 10 at Nottingham in the First Test, and ill health handicapped him afterwards. Although making occasional appearances for Worcestershire, he virtually dropped out of the game, but surprised everyone by returning to England as captain of the Indian touring team in 1946. He showed glimpses of his class, notably when becoming one of four batsmen to score a hundred in the same innings against Sussex at Hove, and finished third in the averages, but he was again handicapped by ill health and he failed in the three Test matches.

After that tour Pataudi again dropped out of cricket, but he made one more attempt to return. In November 1951 MCC approved an application for Pataudi to be regarded as still qualified to play for Worcestershire, and it was expected that he would appear occasionally for the county, despite his age of 41. He died a few weeks later.

A quick-footed batsman with a splendid eye, Pataudi possessed a wide variety of strokes, but did not have the fluency of his Indian predecessors, Ranjitsinhji and Duleepsinhji. He was also a fine hockey and billiards player and an accomplished speaker, although some considered his wit to be sharp and cynical. After the partition of India and Pakistan, Pataudi, a Muslim, found himself without a State to rule, but preserved his ruling status and was employed in the Indian Foreign Office in New Delhi. He left three daughters besides an 11-year-old son, who has shown promise of developing into a good cricketer.

CHAPTER 4
ON LEVEL TERMS: 1953–1983

From 1952, when India recorded her first Test victory, against England, until 1983, when India won the World Cup against the odds, Indian cricket was growing both domestically and internationally. Following partition in 1947, Pakistan began to play international cricket in 1952, visiting India for five Tests in October that year. Further afield, as the English counties embraced the idea of overseas stars within their ranks from the 1960s onwards, many Indian players became as familiar as the local heroes to the English – and Wisden *reading – public. The Indian Test side varied in quality during this period, as did every other Test side, but some great players emerged onto the world stage. India was taken seriously as an opponent in all forms of the game, and no more did any country risk sending a substandard side to India, which began to be known as a cricketing fortress where victory for the visitors was well nigh impossible.*

WISDEN – 1953

PAKISTAN IN INDIA, 1952

Pakistan's performance on their entry into official Test cricket was not without encouragement for the future. They gained only one victory in 12 first-class fixtures, but individual achievements suggested that they possessed the youthful talent on which to build for subsequent engagements.

The superiority in spin bowling gave India mastery… That was mainly because India could call upon Mankad. The Pakistan batsmen were never comfortable against his cleverly varied left-arm slows.

Mankad missed one Test and yet claimed 23 of the 75 wickets taken. During the third match – his 23rd appearance for India – he completed the double of 1,000 runs and 100 wickets and became the fifth player to accomplish the feat in Test cricket. He followed M. A. Noble and G. Giffen (Australia) and W. Rhodes and M. W. Tate (England).

As on the tour of England in 1952, Ghulam Ahmed's off-breaks proved a valuable foil to Mankad's deliveries, but, oddly, his most notable feat occurred with the bat. At New Delhi he and Adhikari added 109 in the best last-wicket stand in any Test for India.

India included no fewer than 26 players in the five Tests and, with Hazare not available for the final game in Calcutta, they introduced D. H. Shodhan, a young left-handed batsman from Gujerat. He was a big success, hitting a century when it was most needed. L. Amarnath, Shodhan's captain on that occasion, is the only other player to have scored 100 on his first Test appearance for India, although Ranjitsinhji, Duleepsinhji and the Nawab of Pataudi did so when representing England.

Wisden *is wrong: Duleepsinhji did not hit a century on debut, although he did hit a century on debut against Australia.*

INDIA'S FIRST TEST VICTORY AGAINST PAKISTAN

This was Pakistan's first ever Test match, but Wisden *only afforded it a few lines of description.*

First Test, at Delhi, 16, 17, 18 October 1952

The cleverly varied left-arm slow bowling of Mankad on a pitch responsive to spin proved too great an obstacle for Pakistan. Mankad's most deadly spell came after Nazar Mohammed and Hanif Mohammed made 64 for the opening stand. In 16 overs he took six wickets, and his final figures of eight wickets for 52 in the first innings and 13 wickets for 131 in the match were both new records for Indian Test cricket. Ghulam Ahmed gave good support with off-spinners, but it was as a batsman in a record last-wicket stand of 109 in 80 minutes with Adhikari that he won the admiration of the crowd. Ghulam hit two sixes and five fours. Kardar and Imtiaz Ahmed were Pakistan's only convincing batsmen against spin.

India 372 (Adhikari 81*, Hazare 76, Ghulam Ahmed 50; Amir Elahi 4-134). **Pakistan 150** (Hanif Mohammad 51; Mankad 8-52) and **152** (Mankad 5-79, Ghulam Ahmed 4-35). India won by an innings and 70 runs.

WISDEN – 1954

INDIA IN WEST INDIES 1952–53

In 1953, an Indian side visited West Indies for the first time. The Indian fielding, long seen as one of their weak points, had improved greatly.

Visiting West Indies for the first time early in 1953, India undertook their fourth Test series inside 18 months and, although their cricket showed signs of staleness, they did better than many people expected. From the winter of 1951–52, when MCC visited them, to the end of the West Indies tour in April 1953, India met England in nine Tests, Pakistan in four Tests and West Indies in five Tests. Of these, India won three, lost six and drew nine. They failed to gain a victory over West Indies, but lost only one match, the other four being drawn. That was the only game of the tour in which the Indians were defeated. Their solitary first-class success came against Jamaica.

By far the most impressive feature of India's cricket was their ground fielding, which reached great heights. The catching was not always in the same class, but there was little doubt that their brilliant outcricket had much to do with maintaining interest on the tour. Also the fact that West Indies found it difficult to establish a mastery helped, and the crowds were larger than anticipated. Twice the gates had to be closed in the First Test at Port of Spain, and the ground record was broken for one day when 22,000 watched the cricket. As a satisfactory profit was forthcoming, the decision of India to undertake the tour, which at one time looked like being cancelled, was justified.

From a playing point of view the big successes were Gupte, a little leg-break and googly bowler, and Umrigar, the hard-hitting batsman. Gupte, who was unlucky to be omitted from the tour of England, flighted and spun the ball so cleverly that few of the West Indies' batsmen faced him confidently. During the tour Gupte took 50 first-class wickets, only seven less than the number obtained by the rest of the bowlers put together. Umrigar, with plenty of power behind all his strokes, averaged over 62 both in Tests and in all matches.

WISDEN – 1956

OBITUARIES

Baloo, Mr Palwankar, who died in India on July 4, aged 78, played for the Hindus from 1907 to 1920, doing much good work as a slow left-arm bowler. His death occurred on the day which for so long had been printed in *Wisden* Births and Deaths as the date of his birth, which actually was March 19. His best analysis for the Hindus was eight wickets for 43 runs in the second innings of the Parsees in the 1919 Quadrangular Tournament.

He toured England with the 1911 All-India team, heading the bowling averages with 114 wickets, average 18.86, in all matches. During that tour his chief feats were eight wickets for 103 v Cambridge University; seven for 83 v Lancashire and eight for 15 in the two innings of Ulster at Belfast.

Shinde, Sadashiv G., who died in Bombay on June 22, aged 31, played in seven Test matches for India between 1946 and 1952. A slow leg-break and googly bowler, he toured England in 1946 and 1952 without much success. His best performance in a Test match was in the first England innings at New Delhi in 1951–52, when he took six wickets for 91 runs.

INDIA IN PAKISTAN 1954–55

India first visited Pakistan to play Test cricket in the early months of 1955. Wisden was very disapproving of the cricket played.

The first official Test series to be played in Pakistan did little credit to cricket generally. Pakistan and India faced each other like two boxers tentatively sparring for an opening, but being afraid to strike the first blow in case some unexpected counter might be forthcoming. With neither side prepared to take the initiative the series ended in stalemate, all five Tests being drawn for the first time in history. Fear of defeat remained uppermost in the minds of the two teams and it does appear that until the two countries realise that the loss of a Test match is not the shattering tragedy they seem to imagine, games between them are likely to remain dull and practically devoid of interest.

Perhaps the years will bring greater understanding on the cricket field, but it is to be hoped that in the meantime the public will not lose interest in the game. Certainly on this tour the crowds were large and enthusiastic, but the many who must have been watching international cricket for the first time saw little to make them want to go again. Both sides adopted the same defensive batting tactics and negative bowling to deep-set fields. As a result the average rate of scoring in the Tests was barely 30 runs an hour.

WISDEN – 1957

NEW ZEALAND IN INDIA 1955–56

Just a year later, New Zealand, then the weakest Test side, toured India for the first time, but lost the series by two Tests to nil, with three drawn. By now, India had met every other Test-playing nation, apart from South Africa, who they would not meet until the 1990s.

INDIA'S FIRST TEST VICTORY
AGAINST NEW ZEALAND

The tour report stated that, 'The New Zealanders... achieved results much below the level which had been hoped for, but circumstances were against them. The frequency of the Tests... gave almost no opportunity for players out of form to find their touch, especially as many matches were played on matting pitches...'

Second Test, at Bombay, December 2, 3, 4, 6, 7, 1955

On a pitch of easy pace, India made an uncertain start, losing three wickets for 63 runs before Mankad and Kripal Singh mastered the steady but not dangerous attack. They added 167 for the fourth wicket. Mankad continued to bat splendidly after the partnership was broken, and he equalled the then Indian individual Test record score of 223, set up by Umrigar in the previous match. Batting for nearly eight hours, Mankad hit 22 fours. Despite a sound innings by the left-hander, Sutcliffe, New Zealand were unable to avoid the follow-on in face of accurate bowling, well handled by Umrigar, and keen fielding. Gupte, who turned his leg-breaks appreciably despite the easy nature of the pitch, proved difficult, and he again troubled New Zealand in their second innings. Sutcliffe defended dourly, but apart from MacGibbon and Moir, none of the other batsmen offered prolonged resistance.

India 421 (Mankad 223, Kripal Singh 63; Cave 3-77). **New Zealand 258** (Sutcliffe 73; Gupte 3-83) and **136** (Gupte 5-45, Mankad 3-57). India won by an innings and 27 runs, with four hours to spare.

In India, V. Mankad, P. R. Umrigar and V. L. Manjrekar batted splendidly and fully demonstrated the limitations of the New Zealand attack. Kripal Singh and N. J. Contractor batted with great promise for the future, but the main feature of the Test series was the superb performance of Gupte, the leg-break bowler, who took 34 wickets, average 19.67.

India v New Zealand
Fifth Test, at Madras, January 6, 7, 8, 10, 11, 1956

India wound up the high-scoring series by breaking more records and gaining an overwhelming victory. Mankad and Roy, the Indian opening batsmen, mastered the New Zealand bowlers on an easy-paced pitch, and they were not parted until after lunch on the second day. They made 413, a record for Test cricket, surpassing

359 made by Hutton and Washbrook for England against South Africa at Johannesburg in 1948–49. Mankad scored 231, and passed the Indian individual Test record of 223 which he and Umrigar each made earlier in the series. India's 537-3 set up a new record total for that country, beating 498-4 declared in the First Test. The first-wicket partnership was also the best by an Indian pair in first-class cricket, exceeding 293 by V. M. Merchant and Mankad for the Indians against Sussex at Hove in 1946.

India won by an innings and 109 runs.

Australia also toured India on their way back from England at the end of 1956, but three spin-dominated Test matches produced little excitement, except for Australian fans as their team won by two matches to nil.

WISDEN – 1958

'Cricket In India 1956–57' occupied three pages of copy, as this edition gave outline scores for all 21 Ranji Trophy matches. There was over a page of commentary, too.

P. Chatterjee, of Bengal, who took 15 wickets in the match against Madhya Pradesh the previous season and so became India's first bowler to achieve the feat, gained further distinction when he took all ten wickets in Assam's first innings, his figures being 19-11-20-10.

BENGAL SILVER JUBILEE

A party of 12 players managed by Mr C. G. Howard, the Lancashire secretary, flew to India on Boxing Day 1956 for two four-day festival matches as part of the Silver Jubilee celebrations of the Bengal Cricket Association. They lost their match against the West Bengal Chief Minister's XI but beat the [Cricket Club of] India President's XI.

WISDEN – 1959

The Indians came again to England in 1959, and Wisden *welcomed them with an article entitled 'India Be Bold!' by Vijay Merchant. After several years of turgid and only slightly successful Test encounters against all comers in the previous decade, it was sensible advice, but in the event they proved to be neither bold nor successful. Merchant, never one to mince his words and with his status as one of India's greatest batsmen to protect him, made it clear what he thought of India's cricket, her cricketers and, especially, her selectors and administrators.*

INDIA, BE BOLD! by Vijay Merchant

Indian Cricket is at the crossroads. After 27 years in the international sphere we seem to have got nowhere and have only five victories to our credit in Test matches. Of these, one was registered against a second-rate England eleven in 1951–52; two against Pakistan on their initial tour of India in 1952 and two against a weak New Zealand team in 1955–56. Normally, victories in Test matches reflect the standard of the game in a particular country. There is not the slightest doubt that in the case of Indian cricket this reflection is absolutely true. Our standard has gone down considerably since we were given Test recognition in 1932...

Let us, therefore, examine the causes which have contributed to the comparatively low standard of our cricket. More than at any other time, the government has given its full patronage to the game both in cash and in kind and thus at least one of the obstacles for the improvement of the game has been removed. Even so, we have made little progress.

Indian cricketers of today are not inclined to put in the same effort that marked the determination of our players of a previous generation... The outlook on the game has completely changed. There is a greater tendency than ever before to play more scientific and defensive cricket. We play now not so much to win matches as not to lose them. During the last five years our rate of scoring has gone down so considerably that except against weaker sides we have not been able to register victories...

Our selectors rely mostly on the number of runs made by individual batsman rather than the manner in which the runs have been scored. Time and again an excellent innings of 35 or 40 has been ignored and a slow-moving sketchy innings of 70 or 80 has earned a place for the batsman in the Test team. Again, a single failure in a representative match has brought about the downfall of a batsman, thereby making him and others extremely slow and cautious...

Indian cricket needs organising. We have our National Championship for the Ranji Trophy but the performances put up are not given due recognition. Whenever a visiting team arrives in this country we make a new start with cricket camps, trial matches, performances against the visitors in the preliminary fixtures, etc., but form in our premier tournament is hardly ever taken into consideration. Thus, except for the semi-finals and the finals there is no interest in this tournament on the part of the selectors or organisers.

India has no fast bowlers and for many years no effort has been made to find one. Our selectors are waiting for someone ready made... There must be a five-year plan to pick very young well-built cricketers who have a flair for fast bowling and are prepared for hard work. As a necessary step we shall have to change the nature of our pitches and make them fast enough to give real encouragement to fast bowling...

We try to maintain certain policies and principles instead of being practical. In 1952 we lost the services of Vinoo Mankad because our selectors were not prepared to give him an assurance that he would be one of the party for England that year. Mankad is a professional who plays regularly in English League cricket. His club – Haslingden – wanted to know by the end of October 1951 whether his services would be required for India or if he would be available for the club in 1952. They had to make their own arrangements for that year and were keen to get another good professional in case Mankad was not available. Mankad explained the whole position to the Indian board but the selectors were not prepared to give him the necessary assurance that he would be one of the 17!

Finally, party politics and personal prejudices have affected our organisation and consequently our cricket. I do not know how much cricket there is in our politics but there is a lot of politics in our cricket. Sport in India has become sufficiently important now for people with high ambitions to intervene by getting the necessary votes to gain a majority on the board. Appointments of captain, manager, selection committee, coaches, etc., have become much more important than cricketers themselves and the welfare of the game. The annual general meeting of the Board of Control for Cricket in India has become of greater significance than the semi-finals or finals of the Ranji Trophy tournament.

Let our batsmen remember throughout the tour that the bat was made for them to hit the ball, not the other way round. A courageous team is bound to add laurels to Indian cricket and would come back with happier memories than those of our last visit in 1952. Let us not follow the bad examples of some recent Test crawls by England, South Africa and Australia. I say, INDIA, BE BOLD!

WISDEN – 1960

INDIA IN ENGLAND 1959

Bold or not, India lost the series in England by five games to nil, the first (but unfortunately not the last) time India had been so humiliated. The old problems of the captaincy, the opening bowlers and the lack of keenness in the field were highlighted again.

There can be no denying that the Indian tour of 1959 was a disappointment for the team as well as for the British public. Twelve months ago *Wisden* recorded that in recent years no touring team has gone through such a lean time as did the New Zealanders. Now we have India with a more dismal story, for they suffered 11 defeats – five more than the New Zealanders – and their seven wins in 35 matches were exactly the same.

While the New Zealanders arrived during the worst summer on record and had to contend with persistent rain, there was no excuse for India as they enjoyed one of the finest summers in living memory and, moreover, man for man they were a more talented bunch, but they never harnessed their resources. Instead, they performed as a set of individuals.

Seven years had elapsed since the previous side under V. S. Hazare visited England, but far from building up a combination in the meantime for this vital tour India relied mainly on immature youngsters. They left the impression that since they have ceased to employ English coaches their standard of cricket has receded considerably. They were no match for England, who for the first time won all five Tests in the same series.

One of India's biggest problems, that of captaincy, has been with them for many years. Their whole approach to the game gave the impression of needing revision, for their cricket appeared to be tainted with the same faults that in this modern age have spoiled the game as a spectacle in nearly all parts of the Commonwealth, including England. These blemishes were the negative attitude to batting and bowling and the disinclination to take the slightest risk, so that cricket becomes boring and drives the paying public to seek their entertainment elsewhere.

The main defects were the lack of top-class opening batsmen who would have set the innings on a sure foundation, the need of genuine fast bowlers of the Nissar-Amar Singh brand, and until late in the tour a tendency to slothful fielding.

D. K. Gaekwad was not the first visiting captain to tour England and play well below his best form. The Baroda player never suggested that he had the verve and personality to carry this exacting task, and he appeared a sick man midway through the tour. He did well to miss only one Test match… A more active approach to all he did, especially his field placing, would have been welcome.

Manjrekar, India's most attractive and prolific run-getter for years, was in the hands of the doctors and masseurs before he appeared in the nets and it was always a struggle to keep him fit. Arriving terribly overweight, Manjrekar was constantly struggling in the field and all too often the sub fielder was called to his rescue…

In mid-July it was decided to invite Baig, the Oxford Freshman, to replace the crippled Manjrekar and this proved a wise move. After his brilliant form in the Parks, the young Hyderabad player hit two centuries in his first two games for his countrymen, 102 v Middlesex and 112 in the second innings of the Old Trafford Test, and in all he made three centuries in his 12 games for the touring team. Baig's approach to the game was pleasant to observe and his influence could do much to restore India's cricket. For one so small, he was extremely powerful all round the wicket and his ability to hook fast bowling stamped him as a great player in the making. Equally sprightly in the field, Baig's inclusion strengthened the outcricket and his throwing was fast and accurate. Baig's maiden Test century and the manner of his dismissal by Dexter's brilliant pick-up and throw will be talked about at Old Trafford for a long time.

Coming to the bowlers, first and foremost were the opening pair, Desai and Surendranath, though neither was above medium-fast. Desai had rare ability and it was a pity that he had to be brought to England almost straight out of junior cricket. He possessed that very rare attribute of being able to bowl outswingers to right-handed batsmen and he had endless courage. He found himself terribly overworked in the Tests; the Leeds crowd must have wondered from where he obtained his stamina as he toiled with little respite. 'Tiny' was a very popular player on all the grounds and he returned to India a vastly improved cricketer. Surendranath, the Army bowler... spent hours bowling down the leg side to batsmen who offered no strokes to such tactics and there was much dull cricket to watch...

Borde, despite a broken finger injury in the first Test which put him out of action for five matches, almost completed the double and was the tourists' outstanding cricketer. Attractive to watch in any position on the field, his happy approach to every phase in the game made him popular everywhere... Kripal Singh, chosen as a promising all-rounder, was a profound disappointment. He scored 309 out of his 879 runs after the last Test match. He was unable to do any substantial bowling owing to his spinning finger soon becoming sore and he spent much time in the doctor's hands, despite the beautiful English summer. He never looked happy nor interested in the important phase of fielding...

Despite their lack of success, the Indians were always a happy party off the field and the way they disported themselves wherever they went made them extremely popular under their efficient and genial manager, His Highness the Maharajah of Baroda. India's total share of gate receipts was £30,000 which gave them a profit of £5,000.

Shortly after the tourists arrived back in India, news came through of the death of one of their greatest cricketers.

OBITUARY

Duleepsinhji, Kumar Shri, who died from a heart attack in Bombay on December 5, aged 54, was among the best batsmen ever to represent England and certainly one of the most popular. Ill health limited his first-class career to eight seasons, but in that time he scored 15,537 runs, including 49 centuries, at an average of 50.11. A remarkably good slip fieldsman, he brought off 243 catches. 'Duleep' or 'Mr Smith', as he was affectionately known in cricket circles, was in the Cheltenham XI from 1921 to 1923, and when captain in the last year headed the batting figures with an average of 52.36, his highest innings being 162. He also met with considerable success as a leg-break bowler and in 1922 was top of the averages with 50 wickets at 13.66 runs each, but he rarely bowled after leaving school... He got his Blue as a Freshman, scoring 75 in the University Match, and also played against Oxford in 1926 and 1928. Illness kept him out of the side for most of the 1927 season.

His career with Sussex, whom he captained in 1932, began in 1926 and he headed the county averages in every season until 1932, when doctors advised him not to take further part in cricket. In 1930 he hit 333 in five and a half hours against Northamptonshire at Hove, which still stands as the highest individual innings played for Sussex and beat the biggest put together by his famous uncle, K. S. Ranjitsinhji – 285 not out against Somerset at Taunton in 1901; three times he reached three figures in each innings of a match… and in 1931 he registered 12 centuries, four of them in successive innings.

He made 12 appearances for England and in his first against Australia at Lord's in 1930 he obtained 173. Of this display a story is told that, when Prince Duleepsinhji was at last caught in the long field from a rash stroke, his uncle remarked, 'He always was a careless lad.'

Tributes included:

Sir John Hobbs: 'He was an extremely popular personality and did not have an enemy on the field. He was a brilliant player.'

R. Aird: 'He was not only a very great cricketer, but he also possessed a charming and gentle nature which endeared him to all his many friends.'

H. Sutcliffe: 'There was no better man to play with. He was never out for personal glorification, his great concern being for the success of the team. He was a real joy to watch and was, above all, a first-class man.'

WISDEN – 1961

As India were recording their first ever Test victory against Australia, Wisden was still printing obituaries of Indian princes, whether or not they had a great deal to do with cricket.

OBITUARIES

Bhopal, The Nawab of, Air Vice-Marshal H. H. Sir Hamidullah Khan Sikander Saulat, who died on February 4, aged 65, captained the cricket XI at the Mahomedan Anglo-Oriental College at Aligarh and also won a cap for hockey. He became one of the most celebrated polo players in India and was also a keen lawn-tennis player, yachtsman and fisherman.

Mistri, Colonel K. M., who died on July 22, aged 84, was a splendid left-handed batsman and useful bowler. Most of his first-class cricket in India was for the Parsees, for whom he first appeared in 1893 in the annual Presidency matches, but he was a member of the India team who visited England in 1911. He had been Chairman of the Indian Selection Committee.

AUSTRALIA IN PAKISTAN AND INDIA, 1959–60

After regaining the Ashes from England the previous winter, the Australians completed a short but highly successful tour of the subcontinent of Pakistan and India in 1959–60. In three crowded months they played eight Tests and three other first-class games, losing only one, the second Test against India at Kanpur where they went down by 119 runs against the off-spin of Patel.

There was no question of this being an A tour. The Board of Control picked their 15 best players, seven of them with previous Test experience in India – R. Benaud, the captain, A. Davidson, R. N. Harvey, P. Burge, R. R. Lindwall, K. Mackay and C. C. McDonald.

INDIA'S FIRST TEST VICTORY AGAINST AUSTRALIA

Second Test, at Kanpur, 19, 20, 21, 23, 24 December 1959

The chief architect of India's first Test victory over Australia since the two countries first met in 1947 was Patel, the Ahmedabad off-spin bowler, who took 14 wickets for 142 runs. In the Australian first innings Patel exploited newly-laid turf and achieved an analysis of 9-69 – India's finest Test bowling performance. Then on the last day, amid scenes of great excitement, he routed Australia a second time and took five more wickets for 55 runs.

For Australia Davidson, the fast bowler, took 12 wickets for 124 and twice regained the initiative for his side. India collapsed alarmingly on the first day. Benaud began the slide after lunch, and Davidson pressed home the advantage when India slumped from 38 for no wicket to 152 all out.

At first the India bowlers failed to gain any assistance from the pitch when Australia replied and 71 runs were scored before Patel dismissed Stevens. Then a remarkable transformation took place. Patel took eight wickets for 24 runs and the Australian lead was restricted to 67.

Contractor (74) and his colleagues showed improved form during the India second innings and Australia were left requiring 225 for victory.

McDonald, Harvey and Kline, who scored 73 between them, batted confidently enough, but the other seven – Rorke was absent ill – mustered only 20 against Patel and Umrigar and India won comfortably.

India 152 (Davidson 5-31, Benaud 4-63) and **291** (Contractor 74, Kenny 51; Davidson 7-93). **Australia 210** (McDonald 53, Harvey 51; Patel 9-69) and **105** (Patel 5-55, Umrigar 4-27).
India won by 119 runs.

CRICKET IN INDIA, 1959–60

Wisden's *Indian correspondent, S. K. Gurunathan, was given more space as Indian cricket came out of the international shadows. Five and a half pages were devoted to the Ranji Trophy. It was, however, an uneventful season, with Bombay winning for the 11th time in the 26 years of the competition.*

[Baroda's] match with Saurashtra had to be abandoned after a day's play as most of the members of the Saurashtra team were near-relations of K. S. Duleepsinhji, who died while this match was in progress.

Bombay's batting strength was again in evidence as much through seasoned players like Umrigar, Apte and Ramchand, who each played a three-figure innings once or more, as it was through rising youngsters such as Amroliwalla. Haridikar and Adhikari, the last named giving the impression of being a Test prospect in the near future.

WISDEN – 1962

Subcontinental cricket reached its nadir at about this time – dull and not particularly skilful – the series between the visiting Pakistan team and India coming in for particular criticism. However, later in 1961, the England team's tour, despite being their first ever Test series defeat by India, was incredibly successful as the financial power of the Indian market was being noticed for the first time. But, perhaps the most important event, as far as Indian cricket was concerned, in the 1961 season took place on a road near Brighton.

PAKISTAN IN INDIA, 1960–61

Compared with the exciting series between Australia and the West Indies, the Pakistan tour of India was, in marked contrast an extremely dour affair. All five Tests were drawn and, in fact every one of the 15 first-class games ended in a stalemate.

This was the second time that the two countries had played completely drawn series but the first time that every match played by a touring side was ended in a draw. In addition, the five draw encounters meant that the countries have now partaken in 12 successive undecided Tests.

…The chief aim of the contestants appeared to be to uphold national prestige by avoiding defeat rather than to take the risk of trying to enforce a decision. Cricket was a secondary interest. In the Tests Pakistan average 35 runs per 100 balls; India 39 runs per 100 balls.

Scoring was so slow that on only 11 of the 25 days allotted to the Tests did the aggregate of runs reach 200, and on nearly half of these occasions the quicker tempo came on the last day when a decision was out of the question.

NOTES BY THE EDITOR 1962, by Norman Preston

During the highly concentrated tour of India, Pakistan and Ceylon, the England team took part in eight Test matches and won only one. That was sufficient to give them the series against Pakistan, the other two games being drawn, but against India two games were lost and three drawn. So for the first time in history India won the rubber against England. The tour may not have shown English cricket at its best but it drew remarkable crowds, just on two million people watching the 24 matches, with approximately 1,200,000 at the Tests alone. MCC might well have to consider how they can make the most of such enthusiasm, especially as the next full-scale tour to those countries is not due until 1971–72.

OXFORD UNIVERSITY IN 1961, by G. Kitchen

Overshadowing all else in the events of Oxford University cricket in 1961 was the unfortunate car accident at Hove which deprived the team of their highly talented captain, the Nawab of Pataudi, for all subsequent engagements including the match against Cambridge. His captaincy had been an inspiration to a side already well equipped in talent and experience and his fielding, as always, set a fine example.

Above all, the Nawab, by his dazzling, if unorthodox, batting made the season memorable for all who saw him in action. Up to the time of his injury he had made 1,216 at an average of 55.27 and he appeared certain to surpass his famous father who thirty years earlier scored 1,307 runs in a season for the Dark Blues.

WISDEN – 1963

In the 1963 edition, Wisden's 100th year, it published an article that looked back over the entire history of international cricket. For India, the author picked out a few of its greatest players.

STARS OF THE TESTS, by E. M. Wellings

Of similar eminence in Indian Test cricket was V. M. Merchant, though he cannot be claimed as his country's greatest batsman. Before India played Test cricket Ranjitsinhji, Duleepsinhji and Pataudi represented England, and each scored a century in his first Test against Australia.

Ranji would be recognised as the leader of the trio, though if he was appreciably better than Duleep, whose career was interrupted and then cut short by ill health, he must have been quite amazing...

Some bowlers of great stature have not been linked with any particular partner, sometimes because there have not been suitable partners. In addition to any previously mentioned they include... India's Amar Singh, a fast-medium bowler to be mentioned in the same breath as Tate and Bedser.

CRICKET IN INDIA, 1961–62, by S. K. Gurunathan

For the first time, a zonal tournament was organised and in the fitness of things, a trophy named after that great cricketer Duleepsinhji, was instituted. It was a step in the right direction and the Board of Control deserves congratulations. The tournament, though a knockout one, afforded another opportunity for top cricketers to try their skill in the highest company.

MCC TEAM IN INDIA, PAKISTAN AND CEYLON, 1961–62, by Leslie Smith

Between October 8, 1961 and February 20, 1962, the MCC cricketers took part in one of the most strenuous tours undertaken by any side. They played 24 matches in India, Pakistan and Ceylon, including eight five-day Tests, three in Pakistan and five in India.

The original tour plans had to be changed because India subsequently arranged a trip to West Indies in the February. This meant a strange programme, with three games, including one Test, being played in Pakistan, followed by the complete Indian part of the tour and then a return to Pakistan to finish the programme.

... England were not represented by their full-scale side. Players like Cowdrey, Statham and Trueman would almost certainly have made a big difference and, perhaps, tipped the balance in England's favour, for there was never much between the Test teams.

This business of leading players declining certain tours needs consideration by the authorities. India rightly point out that they have never seen a full-strength MCC side and resent the fact that the star players make a habit of turning down the trip.

Admittedly English players find the tour harder and less comfortable than any other, but this scarcely justifies players, once they are established, picking and choosing which tour they want to make. It is no secret that in general the men who go to India, Pakistan and Ceylon regard themselves as a second eleven, often play like it and are caustic about the stars who stay at home.

India and Pakistan, for their parts, deserve the best, for the enthusiasm there has grown remarkably in a few years... The leading personalities for India were

Manjrekar, in batting, Borde and Durani for their all-round skill, and Contractor for his imaginative captaincy...

The umpiring was reasonable, although criticism came here and there. India took the unusual course of appointing ten different umpires to officiate in the five Tests so that almost inevitably standards differed. It was agreed by both captains that a smaller panel would be more suitable.

The English players never did accustom themselves to the different type of food, the all-too-many functions and the unusual living conditions, but in the main they were a cheerful set of players.

A couple of months after the series win against England, India embarked on a tour to rival the one to England in 1959 in terms of its lack of success.

INDIA IN WEST INDIES, 1961–62, by Dicky Rutnagur

After their triumph against England in 1961–62, India had reason to embark on their tour of the West Indies with hope and great heart, if not with glowing optimism, but they returned home vanquished in all five Tests and the colony game against Barbados...

India, even had they given of their best, might not have won a Test against a side of such immense all-round strength, but they should not have lost four of the five Tests so easily, and should have drawn the Third Test comfortably...

Circumstances, to an extent, militated against the touring side touching peak form in the West Indies. The heavy domestic season, which had started in August instead of in November, had taxed their energy, determination and concentration beyond measure, and it was folly on the board's part to hustle them into a tour in so short a time after the end of the home season.

The Indians took the field under a hot Trinidad sun within 12 hours of arrival from wintry London and New York. A crop of pulled muscles and stomach disorders was inevitable, and throughout the tour the players' nostrils were filled with the odours of drugs and liniments.

A nasty accident to Contractor, the captain and opening batsman, halfway through the tour, had the team in a state of shock, anxiety and extreme unhappiness. What most of the outside world heard about the incident was that Contractor was struck through ducking to a ball delivered by Charles Griffith, which never rose beyond the height of the stumps.

Contractor did not duck into the ball. He got behind it to play at it – he probably wanted to fend it away towards short-leg – but could not judge the height to which it would fly, bent back from the waist in a desperate, split-second attempt to avoid it and was hit just above the right ear...

The saving grace of the Indians' performance on this tour was their ground fielding, which was as good as that of any contemporary Test side. Surti was outstanding. If the catching had touched even half these heights, the Indians would have saved themselves a lot of humiliation.

Barbados v India
At Bridgetown, March 16, 17, 19, 1962

This was a sordid and unhappy section of the tour. Overshadowing all else was the injury to Contractor, who was hit over the right ear by a ball from the fast bowler, Griffith, at the start of the first innings. This bowler was later no-balled for 'throwing' in the match but while this occurred, Contractor was fighting for his life. He had been rushed to hospital with a fractured skull and immediately underwent an emergency brain operation, which undoubtedly saved his life. A specialist brain surgeon was flown from Trinidad and another operation followed. A blood clot had formed from the fracture and pressed on the brain. Three of his team, Borde, Nadkarni and Umrigar, gave blood for Contractor, as did the West Indies captain, Worrell. Manjrekar, too, was injured in the first innings. He was hit on the nose and retired hurt but courageously batted a second time and scored 100 not out.

Barbados won by an innings and 95 runs.

OBITUARY

De Mello, Mr Anthony Stanislaus, who died at New Delhi on May 24, aged 61, was at his request buried wearing the colours of the MCC, of which he was very proud to be a member. Though he did not get a Blue while at Cambridge, he did much to develop cricket in India, bearing a major part in the formation of the Board of Control, of which he had been president, and the Cricket Club of India.

WISDEN – 1964

OBITUARY

Nissar, Mahomed, who died at Lahore on March 11, aged 52, played as a fast bowler in six Test matches for India against England. Tall and well built, he was specially dangerous with the new ball, possessing the ability to make it swing and break back. He twice visited England. In 1932, under the captaincy of the Maharajah of Porbandar, he headed the India bowling averages for first-class matches with 71 wickets, average 18.09, and in the only Test match that year dismissed five batsmen for 93 and one for 42...

As a member of the Maharaj Kumar of Vizianagram's team in 1936, he topped the Test averages with 12 wickets at a cost of 28.58 runs each and, with 66 wickets for 25.13 apiece, proved the most successful Indian bowler in all first-class games.

He took part in two Tests against D. R. Jardine's side in India in 1933, taking five wickets for 90 runs in the first innings of the opening match of the series.

WISDEN – 1965

In 1963–64, England toured India again. The tour was remembered more for the illnesses than for the cricket: the five Tests were all left drawn.

MCC TEAM IN INDIA, 1964, by E. M. Wellings

An eight-week tour of India containing five Test matches was an interesting MCC experiment in January and February 1964. It is the general wish today to shorten overseas tours. A five-Test series could, obviously, be crammed into a shorter period, but whether such congestion of important fixtures is desirable is very much open to question...

A short tour has special problems. It requires the chosen Test players to be almost continually in action, while the reserves are liable to find too little cricket to maintain their interest. Yet the risk of injury and illness is no less at the start of a short than a long tour. Hence adequate reserves are essential, and in order to exercise them seven minor games to five Tests should be the minimum ratio. An additional hazard in India is the risk of stomach trouble, which, in fact, struck severely at this MCC team. Having learned from experience, MCC arranged for their team – and the attending writers – to take tinned food from England for use in the more remote cricketing centres, where European cooking is not understood. There was some slight criticism of this action from touchy folk in India, but that should not prevent MCC acting similarly on future tours. The tinned food was in some places very necessary.

All five Test matches were left drawn... That unsatisfactory state of affairs was not surprising to those familiar with Indian playing conditions. And the fact that most matches were doomed to be drawn almost from the outset did not seem to disturb spectators. More than 1,000,000 watched the ten games, and day after day the Test grounds, whose capacity varied between 30,000 and 45,000, were packed. Financially the tour was a rousing success, though the nature of the play inflicted sore wounds on the game of cricket.

When pitches are made so slow and true that a competent craftsman could bat successfully with a broom handle, incentive is missing. Throughout the series India played as though reconciled to the conditions. In no match did they make a serious attempt to win, even when England were a makeshift collection of players in the Bombay Test. Yet they were led by the Nawab of Pataudi, who was certainly not without aggression and enterprise when he played in English first-class cricket.

India v England
Second Test, at Bombay, January 21, 22, 23, 25, 26, 1964

England were deprived of all except two of their specialist batsmen. Following Barrington's injury, an attack of stomach trouble removed Edrich, Sharpe and Mortimore before the match and Stewart at teatime on the first day. The ten-man side then consisted of two specialist batsmen, two wicketkeepers, of whom Parks reverted to his first role as specialist batsman, four quick bowlers and two spinners. Yet India played so apprehensively on the defensive that they never seriously challenged this makeshift team.

This was a spineless Indian performance, but a superb one by England, whose spirit on this testing occasion was magnificent. They put the sort of fire into their outcricket that distinguishes the best Celtic rugger pack, and they fought splendidly with the bat.

Match drawn.

AUSTRALIA IN INDIA AND PAKISTAN, 1964

After a short rest following their tour of England, the Australians visited India and Pakistan on the way home. Only Test matches were played. In the three-match series in India, each side won one game with the third drawn…

Simpson, the Australian captain, enjoyed a specially successful time and showed no sign of the staleness which affected some of his team. Lawry supported him well, their first-wicket partnerships in India being 66, 91, 35, 59, 97 and 115…

In India, McKenzie added 13 more wickets to his rapidly growing tally in Tests. Nadkarni, the slow left-hander, did even better for India, his 17 wickets costing 13.70 runs each. The Nawab of Pataudi, the captain, was easily the most successful batsman and his century at Madras was a fine effort.

India v Australia
Second Test, at Bombay, October 10, 11, 13, 14, 15, 1964

India won by two wickets and drew level in the series after a close fight. The issue might well have been different had O'Neill been fit. He went down with stomach pains just after the start and could not bat in either innings.

WISDEN – 1966

OBITUARY

Vizianagram, The Rajkumar of, Sir Gajapatairaj Vijaya Amanda, who died in Benares, Northern India, on December 2, aged 59, captained the Indian team in England in 1936. He showed his strength of character before the first Test match by sending home as a disciplinary measure India's most successful all-rounder, L. Amarnath, who had scored more runs than anyone and hit two centuries in the game against Essex at Brentwood. In three matches against England, 'Vizzy', as he was known in the cricket world, scored only 33 runs, his highest innings being 19 not out at Lord's. On the whole tour, however, his aggregate reached 600, including 60 from the University bowling at Oxford, average 16.21. Three times he was elected President of the Board of Control for Cricket in India. He was a member of the Indian Legislative Assembly.

WISDEN – 1967

As the Indians prepared to visit England again, Dicky Rutnagur surveyed Indian cricket for the benefit of Wisden *readers. This edition also included a list compiled by the eccentric but brilliant Rowland Bowen that threw up some surprising facts about Indian cricket.*

INDIAN CRICKET – ITS PROBLEMS AND ITS PLAYERS,
by Dicky Rutnagur

Of all the forms of their culture the British brought to India, none thrust its roots as deep as cricket. Though India has dominated international hockey for almost four decades, cricket is far more a part of the national scene than the only team game at which we have been world champions.

Growing audiences at Test matches do not alone indicate the extent of cricket's popularity in the country. More significant is the appreciable rise each year in the number of clubs and tournaments at all levels – a sure sign that the game is constantly recruiting more players.

The only pity is that cricket in India, for social and economic reasons, will always be an urban game and its growth, therefore, is in peril of being retarded by the shortage of grounds in the overcrowded towns and cities. This handicap must be overcome if the enthusiasm for the game is to be reflected truly in playing standards at the highest level.

Finance, fortunately, has been no problem in recent years. A succession of tours has made for the accumulation of large reserves and the enthusiasm whipped up by Test cricket has spread to Ranji Trophy matches which, in many places, are more largely attended than at any time since the war.

Of course, the money taken at these games is not sufficient to support the whole structure of the game, but at least there is plenty left over from Test matches receipts to develop cricket at school and university level.

The continuance of this happy state of affairs depends largely on the 1967 Indian team. They tour both England and Australia within the year and if they take back sizeable returns, the government of India will in future be more free in sanctioning foreign exchange for inward tours and minor tours abroad, like the proposed Colts' visit to England two years ago, which never came off because sterling was not made available.

Their approach, even more than results, will bring the Indians the goodwill they need. Their undoing on the last two visits was their outlook, and I have always felt that better cricket could have been extracted from both the 1952 and 1959 sides by captains more imaginative than Hazare and Gaekwad...

India's Test fortunes have been mixed during the eight years since they were last in England. In this span, they have played six series at home and one abroad, and of the 32 Tests involved, five were won and eight lost, while 19 were drawn. India won two of the seven series, and lost two.

This is by no means a glittering record, but certainly more striking than what was achieved in earlier years. The ratio between defeats and wins is small, but considering that no part was played by the weather, the large proportion of unfinished matches is depressing. I saw every one of these 19 draws, and by my estimate, at least half of them did no credit to the approach of the players...

Not many months ago, some of us sat round to pick an Indian team of all-time greats. Anybody who has indulged in this popular pastime knows how much argument it can produce, but on this occasion, the matter was settled quickly, tempers were not roused and few claims were greatly disputed. The team decided was: V. M. Merchant, S. Wazir Ali, L. Amarnath, V. S. Hazare, V. L. Manjrekar, C. K. Nayudu, Vinoo Mankad, L. Amarsingh, N. S. Tamhane, M. Nissar, S. P. Gupte.

These great cricketers gave India a magnificent start in the international sphere and before passing to later events, one should mention that the 1932 side were superb in the field, an attribute applied to few Indian sides afterwards...

SOME DATES IN INDIAN CRICKET HISTORY,
Compiled by Rowland Bowen

1721	Cricket played by mariners of the East India Company's ships at Cambay.
1792	The Calcutta Cricket Club already in existence (perhaps the second oldest cricket club in the world) as a match was played against Barrackpore and Dum Dum.
1797	Cricket being played in Bombay.
1804	First recorded century in India: 102 by Robert Vansittart for Old Etonians v Rest of Calcutta.
1840	Indians known to be taking part in cricket matches...
1854	First known publication on cricket in India – *Calcutta Cricket Club Matches 1844–54* – this is also the first known book of scores outside the British Isles.
1864	First known match between Madras and Calcutta...

1889   First known instructional book on cricket in Marathi – published in Baroda.

1890   Parsi Cricket Club formed in Shanghai: probably the first Indian cricket club to be established outside India.

1891   H. H. Maharao Umedsinghji of Kotah became first Indian to take all ten wickets in an innings (at Mayo College)…

1933-44 D. R. Havewalla scored 515, the record for all grades of Indian cricket. His team was thereby enabled to make 721 (the highest score hitherto by an Indian team) in reply to its opponents 446, and to win by an innings.

OBITUARIES

Ghulam Mohamed, who died in Karachi on July 21, aged 68, toured England with the Maharajah of Porbandar's All-India team in 1932. He proved a big disappointment, taking only three wickets in first-class matches at a cost of 95.33 runs each, but on the matting pitches of his own country he achieved much success with left-arm deliveries of medium pace. He played for the Mohammadans in the Sind Pentangular and Bombay Quadrangular tournaments.

Gurunathan, S. K., who died on May 6, aged 58, was Sports Editor of *The Hindu* and a well-known figure in sporting journalism in India. He wrote with authority on almost all games, but cricket was his speciality. He covered over 50 Test matches in which India took part, including the tour of England in 1952. He contributed to *Wisden* and to *The Times*, and was the author of many books, including *Story of The Tests* and *Indian Cricket*, an annual publication on the lines of *Wisden*.

WISDEN – 1968

INDIA IN ENGLAND, 1967, by Norman Preston

Never has a touring team endured such misfortune as befell the Nawab of Pataudi's combination who came for the first half of a dual Test season.

Owing to the atrocious weather which prevailed in May they spent most of their time in various pavilions watching the rain and when they were able to play the wet pitches and miserable conditions provided little opportunity for them to produce their true form. Injuries, too, hit the side severely. Of the two main opening bowlers, Guha was fit for only one Test and Mohol never faced England, while the third new-ball bowler, the left-handed Surti, was also absent from the third Test when Kunderan, a wicketkeeper, and Subramanya began the attack in England's first innings and Pataudi in the second…

The Indian Board of Control entertained high hopes of the young but inexperienced team they decided to send abroad… Only Pataudi and Borde had previously played first-class cricket in England, but while the captain led his men admirably and played many fine innings, including 64 and 148 in the Headingley Test, Borde failed completely in the three Test matches, scoring only 60 runs in his six innings as against 724 runs in his other 18 first-class innings...

As the Nawab of Pataudi frequently pointed out, there has been no incentive for anyone to bowl fast in India over the past 20 years and until the lifeless pitches are changed the desired improvement in the standard of fast bowling will not materialise...

While Pataudi stood out by himself among the batsmen, the number one wicketkeeper, Engineer, often gave the side a fine start with his enterprising strokeplay... More also should be heard of Wadekar, a stylish and consistent left-hander who, despite never reaching three figures, scored 835 runs, average 37.95...

The need for genuine spin bowling in their own country was emphasised by the fine work of Chandrasekhar, who excelled with pacey right-handed googlies, Prasanna, off-spin and Bedi, the Sikh, a natural left-arm slow bowler, who did turn the ball and provided a colourful picture with his blue and sometimes maroon turban.

Poor catching often let down the side despite the shrewd field setting of the Nawab, who, by reason of his association with Oxford University and Sussex, generally knew any frailties of the opposition. When the sun shone and things were going well for them the standard of fielding rose to considerable heights and one hopes that when India come next time to England the weather will be much kinder to them, especially in May.

England v India
First Test, at Headingley, Leeds, June 8, 9, 10, 12, 13, 1967, by Norman Preston

India, hit by the weather in May with little chance of accustoming themselves to English conditions, entered the match without a victory to their credit and their reputations so sullied that only small crowds attended, the best being on Saturday when 12,000 were present... Yet, despite all their misfortunes the gallant Indians struggled bravely, Pataudi batted magnificently for 64 and 148 and Engineer, in both innings, Wadekar and Hanumant showed excellent form. Indeed, India, 386 behind on the first innings, accomplished the rare feat of passing 500 in the follow-on...

On Friday, England treated the depleted Indian attack mercilessly and in three and a half hours put on 269 before Close declared. Boycott finished with 246 not out, the highest individual innings for any Test between England and India, as well as his own highest in first-class cricket. He hit one six and 29 fours and did not make a false stroke, but his lack of enterprise met with much disapproval and the selectors dropped him for the next Test.

England won by six wickets with two and three-quarter hours to spare.

CRICKETERS OF THE YEAR 1968

THE NAWAB OF PATAUDI (JNR), by D. J. Rutnagur

Only four fathers and sons have both been chosen as Cricketers of the Year, and curiously enough, two of these cases occurred in 1968. The younger Nawab was joined in the 1968 list by Jim Parks, whose father James (J. H.) Parks, had been one of the Five in 1938. For the record, the only other fathers and sons in this list to date are Micky and Alec Stewart (1958 and 1993) and Peter and Shaun Pollock (1966 and 2003).

It is debatable whether it is an asset or otherwise to be born the son of a famous man, especially if one has aspirations in the same sphere in which the father made his mark. Comparisons are inevitable, and comparisons can be so unnerving and oppressive to the one being compared.

Mansur Ali, The Nawab of Pataudi, who captained India in England last summer, inherited more than a princely title when he was born at Bhopal on January 5, 1941. Also handed down to him was a talent for cricket which made his father an outstanding batsman during one of cricket's most prosperous eras.

The younger Nawab has followed gloriously in his father's footsteps, and that in spite of the severe handicap of losing the use of his right eye as the result of a motor car accident, in 1961. Pataudi came to greatness without the guiding influence of his father, although anyone who knows him has no doubt that he has always been inspired by his memory. He was only 11 – in fact it was on his birthday – that the former Nawab died of heart failure while playing polo in New Delhi.

Young Pataudi could not have seen his father play cricket many times, and if he did, he was too young then to form impressions of his style and technique. And as critics have said, the similarity between their styles is faint indeed…

Not many months after his father died, in 1952, Pataudi came to England. The passenger list of the ship on which he travelled included many illustrious cricket names. There was Vinoo Mankad, making his annual trip to play in the Lancashire League; then there were the three Ws and Ramadhin, returning from Australia at the end of the West Indies tour. Pataudi played deck games with them and their constant company further stoked his cricketing ambitions.

Hardly could Frank Worrell have imagined then that in ten years, almost to the month, his young shipmate would be walking out with him to toss for innings in a Test match. This happened in Barbados, when Pataudi took over the Indian captaincy from Contractor, who lay in hospital, gravely ill. Pataudi then had played in only three Test matches and, at 21, became the youngest captain ever in international cricket…

Pataudi's Test record in 24 matches is 1,643 runs, including a double century and two centuries against England, one against Australia (on his first appearance against them) and two hundreds against New Zealand. He has played 43 innings at an average of 40.17. These figures are respectable enough, but could hardly be considered to fulfil the expectations held out by his brilliance in his four years at Winchester and in his first year at Oxford...

He went up to Oxford, in 1960, and like his father before him, scored a century against Cambridge in his first University Match. Later that year, he made his debut in Indian cricket, playing in a couple of Ranji Trophy matches for Delhi; but having come straight out of the English winter, he could do himself little justice.

Oxford honoured him with their captaincy in 1961, the first Indian to lead either University, but before the University Match came along he was involved in that dreadful accident. The season, till then, had seen him at the height of his powers. By the end of June, he had collected 1,216 runs (average 55.27) and was not far from equalling his father's high aggregate in the Oxford season of 1931.

Contrary to predictions that he would never play cricket again, Pataudi was back in flannels during the Indian season immediately following, and was called up by the Test selectors for the third Test against England...

When the Australians played a short series in India... Pataudi emulated his father by scoring a century on his first appearance against them. It was a masterly innings and the manner in which he dominated Veivers and Martin was memorable. His captaincy also was more purposeful and enterprising and, in the next Test, he led India to a brilliant and dramatic win, contributing 86 and 53 to this unforgettable victory...

Then, at Headingley in the first Test, last summer, he played his epic innings of 148 which lifted India out of the dark pit of despair. India lost in spite of his courageous effort, but in defeat they took away as much honour as the winners...

As a Test captain, he could have reached greater stature had his tenure not coincided with a period of very lean bowling resources. This weakness and the low standard of fielding seem to frustrate him, which perhaps explains his periodic urge to call it a day.

However, it is vital to the revival of Indian cricket that he should continue, for there is no doubt that both while batting and fielding he strikes a tremendous personal example.

OBITUARIES

Hussain, Dr Dilawar, who died at Lahore on August 26, aged 60, was a batsman-wicketkeeper who played in three Tests, all against England, between 1933 and 1936. As an undergraduate at Cambridge in 1936, he assisted the team led by the Maharaj Kumar of Vizianagram when the other two wicketkeepers, D. D. Hindlekar and K. R. Meherhomji, were unfit, and in 17 first-class innings scored 620 runs, average 44.28. A defensive player, he had an ungainly crouching style but possessed unwearying patience coupled with admirable determination. In the Second Test against D. R. Jardine's team at Calcutta in 1933 he opened the innings and made 59 and 57, being the first wicketkeeper to score fifty in each innings of a Test.

Nayudu, Colonel Cottari Kanyaiya, who died at Indore on November 14, aged 72, captained India in their first Test match with England. That was at Lord's in 1932 when, despite a painful hand injury received when fielding, Nayudu made top score, 40, in the first innings... As a small boy he played for the Hislop Collegiate High School, Nagpur, whom he captained, and while still at school appeared for Modi, of which club he also became captain. In 1926–27 at Bombay, he gained prominence by hitting 153 (including 11 sixes and 13 fours) out of 187 in just over 100 minutes for Hindus against A. E. R. Gilligan's MCC team. Though never on the winning side in a Test match, he helped Vizianagram to inflict by 14 runs the only defeat of the tour upon D. R. Jardine's powerful MCC side in 1933–34, taking four wickets for 21 runs in the second innings. Tall and well proportioned, Nayudu was specially strong in driving, bowled accurately at slow-medium pace and was a fine fielder. He also shone at hockey and Association football.

WISDEN – 1969

Under the Nawab of Pataudi, and with the help of a powerful spin attack, India rediscovered the art of aggressive batting, away from home, at least.

INDIA IN AUSTRALASIA, 1967–68, by T. L. Goodman

The Indian team led by the Nawab of Pataudi failed to win a first-class match and were beaten by Australia in all four Tests. They arrived with obvious shortcomings for Australian conditions, primarily the complete absence of fast bowling. The insipid nature of the opening attack, some instability in the batting and a good deal of untidy fielding in the first half of the tour combined to suggest a substandard Test series. But Pataudi's gallant batting under physical difficulties inspired an uplift; moreover, the teamwork, and especially the fielding, improved so that India made a splendid fight of the third Test, in Brisbane, where for a time they seemed to have a good chance of victory. Again in the fourth Test, in Sydney, they threw out a challenge, but failed to sustain it.

Much of their batting was aggressive and flavoured by neat stroke-making; thus the team provided some entertaining days and there were some outstanding personal successes. The tour was of considerable value to the visitors; it also assisted the Australian selectors in picking a team for England.

The tourists had some wretched periods in their first few weeks. At that stage they suffered severely from the absence of Pataudi, who pulled a hamstring muscle when fielding in the opening first-class match, against Western Australia. He missed the first Test in Adelaide, and how serious was the effect of his absence was shown by his resourceful and courageous batting in the subsequent Tests: he had successive Test scores of 75, 85, 7, 48 and 51...

The Nawab of Pataudi's pugnacious batting was the most memorable of the tour – it had a touch of genius. India's captain had long since had to rearrange his technique because of the almost total loss of vision from his damaged right eye, and in Melbourne and thereafter he was handicapped by his leg strain. He could not move down the pitch and had to play mostly off the back foot. Yet he still hit the loose ball hard; sometimes he lifted the bowlers, including the speed men, McKenzie and Renneberg, to the outfield. He played the hook shot daringly. Australian crowds, happy to see Pataudi having an occasional slice of luck, fully appreciated the class and character of his batting. He usually batted when his team were in difficulties, and with the peak of his cap pulled down to shade that blurred right eye, he often looked an heroic figure.

Surti was such a capable player, one who applied himself wholeheartedly to the job in hand, that the Queensland Cricket Association were happy to engage him as a coach and to play in the inter-state competition in the following few seasons. This left-hander proved a versatile bowler, beginning at medium pace (sometimes he shared the new ball) and changing to leg-spin, usually with good control. Surti and Prasanna each took 34 wickets in first-class matches and Surti scored most runs, 557. Surti was one of the best fieldsmen.

The lightweight Prasanna, after being let down by fieldsman in early games, took six wickets in an innings of the Melbourne Test and repeated that feat in Brisbane... His off-spin bowling contained the basic principles of length, direction, spin and flight. He frequently deceived batsmen in the air. He spun the ball more decisively than an Australian bowler, indeed, on some days he spun it when no home player could spin at all. Prasanna was rated among the most impressive off-spinners to tour Australia since the war – in the class of Tayfield, Laker, Titmus and Gibbs. In the Brisbane Test, Bedi, the left-handed leg-spinner who had bowled tidily against New South Wales, proved a good foil for Prasanna.... Engineer always looked an exciting, if venturesome, opener; he scored a fine century against Western Australia and he played other good innings, but too often he fell to a rash stroke.

From 1968, the English county game was opened up to overseas players. Wisden's editor was lukewarm in his appreciation of Farokh Engineer, who nevertheless went on to become a true Lancashire favourite.

NOTES BY THE EDITOR, 1969, by Norman Preston

The innovation permitting each county to engage one overseas cricketer on immediate registration every three years without residential qualification, was, as I predicted, a great success. For too long county cricket had been stifled by dour, safety-first methods. The overseas players by their enterprise and natural approach brought a breath of life into the three-day match... F. M. Engineer, from India, was somewhat disappointing with the bat, but pleased Lancashire immensely with his wicket-keeping.

WISDEN – 1970

CRICKET IN INDIA 1968–69, by P. N. Sundaresan

Bombay emphasised that they are still the top team in the country by winning the Ranji Trophy for the 11th year in succession and for the 20th time since the start of the championship in 1934...

At the end of the Ranji Trophy final, R. B. Desai, the India and Bombay pace bowler, announced his retirement from first-class cricket. Popularly known as 'Tiny' because of his small build, Desai appeared in the limelight when the West Indies team toured the country in 1958–59; he served his state and country well with his great-hearted medium-fast bowling. Desai bowled his heart out on the dead pitches in India and even when he was just over 25 he lost his regular place in the India side. A more judicious use of his talent both in the Ranji Trophy and other matches could have preserved him as a penetrating bowler for a longer period. His early disappearance from the Test scene was also an argument for the preparation of fast pitches in the country, which is still groping to find a replacement for Desai who, it has to be borne in mind, was never as fast as even D. G. Phadkar.

WISDEN – 1971

NEW ZEALAND IN INDIA AND PAKISTAN, 1969, by R. T. Brittenden

In India, New Zealand were beaten in the first Test at Bombay, but won the second at Nagpur comfortably and were on the point of a crushing victory at Hyderabad when a violent half-hour storm drenched the ground and made further play impossible...

New Zealand were better equipped with fast bowlers than India and Pakistan, their fielding was distinctly better, and although their batting was only a little less fallible, it showed more resource in very difficult conditions. In India there were sharply turning pitches... India averaged about 31.2 runs an hour, Pakistan 34.3, New Zealand 35.7 and 37.8; and even those modest rates would have been unattainable had batsmen not taken their lives in their hands on many occasions...

Although the cricket was not of very high quality, the attendances were much larger than in 1965. There were about 432,000 spectators at five games in India.

AUSTRALIANS IN CEYLON AND INDIA, 1969-70,
by P. N. Sundaresan

The two-month Australian tour of Ceylon and India, from October to December in 1969, provided keen cricket and stirred tremendous public interest... The daily attendance for the Tests ranged from 35,000 to 50,000, only the limitation on accommodation keeping out many more... India's victory in the Third Test at Delhi also added fire to the enthusiasm of the fans. The tour was marred by disturbances – a riot at Bombay, an invasion of the crowd on to the field at Calcutta and stone-throwing at Bangalore – so much so that one heaved a sigh of relief when the programme was concluded...

Australia won the Test series by three matches to one, with victories in the First, Fourth and Fifth Tests. They were beaten in the third match at Delhi... The three-one triumph in the series, however, was not as clear or comfortable as the margin suggested. India had a great opportunity to win the final Test at Madras when their spin attack took a firm grip on the game, but vital fielding lapses in both innings enabled Australia to come out on top. If India had won they would have squared the rubber, which would have been a truer indication of the form of the series.

The Tests resolved into a tremendous battle between the Australian batsmen and the Indian spinners, the left-arm Bedi, and the two off-spinners Prasanna and Venkataraghavan. Bedi and Prasanna, especially, struck as penetrative a combination as Lock and Laker, the Englishmen, or Valentine and Ramadhin, the West Indians. The trio shared 726.3 of the total 929.1 overs delivered in the Tests and claimed 59 of the 70 wickets that fell to bowlers...

The Indian batting lacked depth and failed to match the bowling skill. The drawback was that the established batsmen, Wadekar, Pataudi and Engineer – Borde, Sardesai and Surti were dropped after their failure in the first Test – were not certain of making big scores and thus failed to bind the innings together with the support of the young batsmen, who had their baptism in Test cricket. There was only one century for India, by G. R. Viswanath, in the second innings of the second Test at Kanpur in which he made his debut. He scored 137 runs. Just 20 years old, Viswanath impressed everybody with his dash and skill. He might be the pivot around which the Indian batting could be built for the future...

India's performance in the series was a big improvement on that against New Zealand, who came earlier in the year. The Indian selectors, except for recalling Borde and Sardesai for the first Test, stuck to their policy, set afoot in the earlier series, of choosing a young side, despite the strong criticism that this aroused.

OBITUARIES

Sen, Probir, who died in Calcutta on January 27, aged 43, kept wicket for India in 14 Test matches between 1947 and 1952, taking part in two tours abroad – in Australia in 1947–48 and England in 1952. He made his first-class debut when 17 in 1943 for Bengal, whom he later captained, and also played for Calcutta University. Before retiring in 1958, he helped in the dismissal of 125 men and as a right-handed batsman hit 2,461 runs in first-class cricket, average 23.66. His highest innings was 168 against Bihar at Jamshedpur in 1950–51, he and J. Mitter putting on 231 for the ninth Bengal wicket. He had also represented East Bengal at Association football and hockey.

Godambe, Shankarrao Ramachandra, who died on December 6 (1969), aged 70, was a member of the India team who toured England in 1932 under the captaincy of the Maharajah of Porbandar, scoring in all matches 200 runs, average 10.52, and taking with swing bowling 28 wickets for 25.46 runs apiece. He represented Bombay in the Ranji Trophy competition and the Hindus in the Quadrangular Tournament, in the 1925 final of which he hit 61 and 51 not out. For the Hindus against A. E. R. Gilligan's 1925–26 MCC team at Bombay, he (58) partnered C. K. Nayudu while the last-named hit 153, including 11 sixes and 13 fours, in 100 minutes.

Jai, L. P., who died on January 29 (1968), aged 66, was in his day among the leading Indian batsmen. He scored 1,278 runs, average 31.95, for Hindus in the Quadrangular (later Pentangular) Tournament, with 156 against the Muslims in 1924 the highest of his three centuries; and he captained the side when they won the Pentangular Tournament in 1941. He hit 774 runs, average 43.00, in Ranji Trophy matches for Bombay, whom he led to victory in the competition in 1934–35. His one Test match appearance for India was against A. E. R. Gilligan's England team in 1933, and he toured England with little success in 1936. He had been vice-president of the Bombay Cricket Association and a Test selector.

WISDEN – 1972

In 1970 and 1971, India's Test team came of age, winning in the West Indies and in England within 12 months – their series win in England the first in almost 40 years of Test cricket.

INDIA IN THE WEST INDIES, 1971, by D. J. Rutnagur

The 1970–71 tour of the West Indies was, till then, India's most successful cricket venture abroad. West Indies, the only country they had not so far beaten, were mastered in the Second Test. This win decided the series in India's favour. Only once before had they won a rubber away from home, 3–1 against New Zealand, in 1968...

The Indians' overall record of two wins, one defeat and nine draws could well have read six wins, one defeat and five draws had Wadekar, their new captain, adopted a more positive approach. His bowlers always looked match-winners, but the batsmen were not encouraged to give them the opportunity to go for the kill. Little consideration was given to the entertainment of the crowds which, at all centres, were big enough for the tour to yield an appreciable profit.

While victory in the series opened a new chapter in the history of Indian cricket, West Indies suffered the disappointment of losing their fourth successive rubber and their second at home...

Gavaskar's arrival on the Test scene, at 21, was near phenomenal. Despite missing the First Test through a finger injury, which he aggravated by nail biting, Gavaskar amassed 774 runs at an average of 154.80. He had to sit out all three first-class games in Jamaica and yet he finished with 1,169 runs (av. 97.41). Only Hendren and Sandham have scored more runs in a West Indian season.

Gavaskar's achievements equalled, surpassed or approached several important records. No Indian batsman had hitherto made 700 runs or more in a single series. Only K. D. Walters before him had scored a century and a double-century in the same Test. Gavaskar fell only five runs short of E. D. Weekes' aggregate of 779, the highest in a series between the West Indies and India. Gavaskar also established a new record for the highest aggregate in a maiden Test series (703 by G. A. Headley in 1929–30 was the previous highest). Only one other batsman can pride himself on a higher average for a series than Gavaskar – Sir Donald Bradman (201.50 v South Africa, in 1931–32 and 178.75 v India, in 1947–48)...

Although Chandrasekhar, later the scourge of England, was left at home, the Indian bowlers excelled themselves, the three main spinners, Prasanna, Bedi and Venkataraghavan, between them taking 48 of the 68 Test wickets that fell to the bowlers. All of them were remarkably accurate and even if the pitches tended to aid them, there is no doubt that their mastery in flighting the ball gave them a great advantage.

Prasanna, one of the world's leading off-spinners, missed two Tests through finger injuries, but the rapid advance of Venkataraghavan during the tour enabled India to make light of Prasanna's absence. Venkataraghavan captured 22 Test wickets and 41 on the whole tour. Using his height, he got a surprising amount of bounce from even the slower pitches. Only S. P. Gupte, who took 50 wickets in 1952–53, has taken more wickets on an Indian tour of the West Indies...

India's first-string wicketkeeper, Krishnamurthy, improved as the tour progressed, but earlier did not quite look ready for Test cricket. Both as wicketkeeper and as batsman, Engineer was sorely missed. He was left out because of the Indian board's policy not to consider cricketers who had not made themselves available for the preceding domestic season.

Their long-awaited win over the West Indies will prove a source of inspiration and confidence to the Indians in future engagements. Although rudely shocked by the result, West Indies are not likely to be dispirited, because enthusiasm for the game has never been higher in any of the West Indies territories. Its development is receiving much dedication from administrators and ex-cricketers, and there is ample promise of West Indies cricket coming back to the forefront in the near future.

INDIA'S FIRST TEST VICTORY AGAINST WEST INDIES

Second Test, at Port-of-Spain, March 6, 7, 9, 10, 1971

The arrival of Gavaskar on the Test match scene was the difference between the two sides.

It was India's first win in 25 Tests between the two countries. Undoubtedly, luck held with India all the way, but this cannot detract from the high quality of the batting of Gavaskar and Sardesai and outstanding bowling by their four spinners. Spin bowlers dominated the match. For the West Indies, Noreiga, the 35-year-old off-spinner, captured nine wickets for 95 runs in India's first innings.

Despite the fact that the pitch was tailor-made for spinners, winning the toss was very much a mixed blessing for, on the first day, the ball rose awkwardly almost as often as it kept low. In fact, the first ball of the match was a shooter. It bowled Fredericks off his toe and, at one stage, West Indies were 62-4. Sobers, trying desperately to plunder runs before the innings petered out, was bowled at 108, trying to sweep. Charlie Davis, playing his first Test at home, scored 71 not out and enabled West Indies to reach a respectable score. Only the two fast bowlers, Holder and Shillingford, afforded any assistance while Davis defied the Indian spinners.

When India batted, the first stroke of luck they enjoyed was the dropping of Gavaskar, then only 12, by Sobers, at slip, off Holder. He and Mankad put on 68 runs for the first wicket. Gavaskar then continued to play the role of anchorman while Sardesai asserted himself. The pair added 96 runs for the third wicket. Sardesai scored another century, batting just as commandingly as in the first Test. Gavaskar and Wadekar were out to successive balls, but Sardesai found another stubborn partner in Solkar. Their stand of 114 for the fifth wicket enabled India to lead by 138 runs. Solkar, in the early stages of this partnership, was lucky to be twice dropped off Sobers, then bowling an extremely deadly spell of wrist spinners.

India's big lead notwithstanding, the initiative lay with the West Indies at the end of the third day. They had gone 12 runs ahead with only one second-innings wicket lost. An unfortunate accident, before the start of the fourth day's play, again turned the wheel of fortune. Davis, one of the overnight not-outs, was struck over the eye while practising in the nets, and he had to go to hospital to have the wound stitched. By the time he returned, Fredericks (through a suicidal run out), Sobers, Lloyd and Camacho were all out for the addition of only 19 runs to the overnight total. Undaunted, Davis again batted for the remainder of the innings, scoring 74.

India had about eight hours to get the 124 runs they needed to win, but they took no chances and with Gavaskar in full cry, completed their task on the fourth day.

West Indies 214 (Davis 71*; Prasanna 4-54, Bedi 3-46) and **261** (Fredericks 80, Davis 74: Venkataraghavan 5-95). **India 352** (Sardesai 112, Gavaskar 65, Solkar 55; Noreiga 9-95) and **125 for three wickets** (Gavaskar 67*; Barrett 3-43). India won by seven wickets, with a day to spare.

INDIA IN ENGLAND, 1971, by D. J. Rutnagur

In Bombay, the birthplace of Indian cricket, unprecedented scenes were witnessed on the night of August 24, the day India beat England in the Third Test match at The Oval. There was dancing in the streets. Revellers stopped and boarded buses to convey the news to commuters. In the homes, children garlanded wireless sets over which the cheery voice of Brian Johnston had proclaimed the glad tidings of India's first Test victory in England, a victory which also gave them the rubber.

As in the West Indies, the spin attack was the cornerstone of India's success in the Test series and their overall record of seven wins and only one loss – a distinguished performance on a short tour. Of course, the inclusion of Chandrasekhar gave it a sharper edge and its effectiveness was enhanced no less by the vast improvement in fielding standards. For this, credit goes mainly to the manager, Lieut. Col. H. R. Adhikari who, to borrow from football parlance, was a 'tracksuit' manager.

Chandrasekhar, Bedi, Venkataraghavan and Prasanna comprised one of the most versatile spin combinations that any country has ever sent on tour. Of the 244 wickets that fell to bowlers on the whole tour, these four captured 197 and in the Tests, Chandrasekhar, Bedi and Venkataraghavan accounted for 37 as against 11 by the two seamers, Abid Ali and Solkar. Masters of their craft, the spinners bowled well even under unfavourable conditions and at Lord's and The Oval, where the pitches assisted them, they were quite menacing.

Although most of England's batsmen had faced him in 1967, Chandrasekhar posed even more problems than on his first visit. Venkataraghavan returned for his second tour a much improved bowler, possessing greater variations in pace and flight, and seemingly able to extract more bounce than he did earlier in his career. With 63 victims, he was the highest wicket-taker on the tour.

Bedi bowled tirelessly, and in the challenging manner of the classical left-arm spinner. He must rank amongst the finest bowlers of his type to have toured this country. Prasanna, whom many (Garry Sobers included) consider the world's best off-spinner today, failed to gain a Test place. India could not afford the luxury of two bowlers of a type and Venkataraghavan's superior batting and fielding ability gained him preference...

None of the batsmen performed feats which could be called outstanding. But Gavaskar and Wadekar both made a thousand runs and Viswanath, though he scored three centuries before the First Test, just failed to emulate them. There were many times when we saw glimpses of Gavaskar's undisputed class. Had he resisted the temptation to drive early in his innings, he might have made many more runs...

Engineer's availability for the Test matches made the difference between defeat and victory. At The Oval, he batted most sensibly during a difficult period in the first innings and his experience of playing in a tense situation – which most of his team-mates lacked – came in just as handy in the final stage of the battle for victory. Although it was a long time since he had kept to the Indian spinners – and taking Chandrasekhar needs a lot of practice – Engineer's performance behind the stumps was of the highest class...

In the field, as already mentioned, Wadekar's team were far superior to any previous Indian side in England. Solkar shone in all positions. Close to the wicket, he, Wadekar and Venkataraghavan took their catches expertly. It was also a measure of the Indians' fitness that they kept remarkably free of injuries and illnesses.

England v India
Third Test, at The Oval, August 19, 20, 21, 23, 24, 1971, by Geoffrey Wheeler

---

India made cricket history by winning a Test match on English soil for the first time. In doing so, they brought to an end England's record run of 26 official Tests without defeat. The Indian match-winner was the wrist-spinner Chandrasekhar who took 6-38 as England were dismissed in their second innings for 101 runs, their lowest score against India and their third lowest total since the war. For once the all-rounders and bowlers could not redeem the failures of the established batsmen.

The Indians were left 173 to make in the fourth innings and by consistent batting on a slow, turning pitch gained a victory which gave them the series. It was an unexpected win, for until Chandrasekhar's inspired spell on the fourth day England seemed to have the match well in hand...

India finished the fourth day with 76-2. Gavaskar was lbw to Snow without scoring, but Mankad played his longest innings of the series and then Wadekar and Sardesai denied England a breakthrough. Next morning, Wadekar was run out attempting a quick single to d'Oliveira before a run had been added. The tension was high and the Indians, avoiding all risks, took three hours to make the last 97 runs… Sardesai and Viswanath batted in dedicated fashion and when they were out Engineer struck some telling blows. Abid Ali cut the winning boundary to bring the jubilant Indian supporters racing on to the field to acclaim their heroes, who had shown that their success in the West Indies was well merited and in no way a fluke. So India won in England for the first time in 39 years.

England 355 (A. P. E. Knott 90, J. A. Jameson 82, R. A. Hutton 81) and **101** (B. S. Chandrasekhar 6-38). **India 284** (F. M. Engineer 59, D. N. Sardesai 54; R. Illingworth 5-70) and **174 for six wickets**. India won by four wickets.

CRICKETERS OF THE YEAR 1972

B. S. CHANDRASEKHAR, by D. J. Rutnagur

By no means the first in the line of Indian spinners, Chandrasekhar was the first to be chosen as a Cricketer of the Year purely for his bowling. A withered bowling arm meant that he was always a figure of some controversy, like Muralitharan three decades later.

India's first Test victory on English soil came in the wake of a most dramatic turn in fortunes, England being toppled from the commanding position of a 71-run lead in the first innings. Batting again, they were put to flight in a matter of only two and a half hours. The havoc was wrought by Bhagwat Subramaniam Chandrasekhar who, in a spell of 18.1 overs, captured six wickets for only 38 runs.

Chandrasekhar's match-winning effort at The Oval was the climax of a highly successful tour performance. He took 50 wickets in all first-class matches, 13 of them in the Tests. Although such figures were no novelty to Chandrasekhar, his success on this trip will have for him a special significance, for he had spent the four previous years in the backwoods. Even six months earlier, no place could be found for him in the side that toured the West Indies. His selection for England was influenced, one believes, by the view that English batsmen are vulnerable against wrist-spin…

There is a fairytale flavour to the story of Chandrasekhar's career. Born on May 18, 1946 in Bangalore (also the birthplace of Colin Cowdrey), Chandrasekhar suffered an attack of poliomyelitis when he was only five years old. Recovery and convalescence meant his spending three months in hospital, but once he came home his parents encouraged him to live the normal life of a five-year-old. He has never forgotten how much he owes to all around him for the courage and confidence they gave him at that vital stage of his childhood…

Chandrasekhar must be unique in that he has turned his deformity, a withered arm, into an instrument of success. The belief is that the thinness of his arm gives it the flexibility of whipcord, enabling him to produce the extra bite in his top-spinner. Indeed, Chandrasekhar is not a wrist-spinner in the classical mould. He is, in fact, medium-paced. Top-spinners and googlies are his stock-in-trade, although it is not that he never delivers a leg-break. In fact, several Indian batsmen have said that he now turns his leg-break more sharply than ever before.

He is able to generate enough pace to have once bowled a bumper in a Test match. The paradox of that incident was that the target of the bumper was Charlie Griffith. The blow got home, although not as painfully as it would have done if the roles had been reversed. This, incidentally, happened in the last innings of the 1966–67 series, at Madras.

Chandrasekhar did not arrive in big cricket through the customary channels of the Inter-State schools' championship and the Inter-University competition. When only just past his 17th birthday, he went straight from club and schools cricket to the Mysore side. Three months later, he was a Test player.

With 25 wickets in four Ranji Trophy games, Chandrasekhar was picked for the Board President's XI (a team of Test candidates) to face the 1964 MCC team in their opening fixture. Although he took only one wicket, that of Sharpe, he made an impression, not least through inducing an unaccepted slip chance from Ken Barrington. Chandrasekhar inevitably made his debut in the second Test of that rubber. He took five wickets in that match, but his effectiveness waned as the series progressed. There were various reasons for this. But an important one was that Cowdrey joined in the fray from the third Test onwards and brought his masterly technique to bear the job of coping with the awkward newcomer. Chandrasekhar to this day maintains that only three batsmen have played him with complete assurance – Cowdrey, Sobers and Barrington.

The Australians played a three Test series in India later that year and got so badly entangled in Chandrasekhar's web of mystery that they were beaten in the first Test, at Bombay, where Chandrasekhar was able to extract added bounce from a pitch now relaid on a foundation of bricks…

Chandrasekhar's first venture abroad, the England tour of 1967, brought further glory – 57 wickets, including 16 in the Tests. They were reward for bowling around 700 overs. His statistics must be judged also in the light of the most deplorable fielding seen in modern first-class cricket…

In England last summer, Wadekar got the best out of him by using him as sparingly as possible. Test matches entailed just as much bowling as on the previous trip, but his quota for the whole tour was 200 fewer overs. Of course with Prasanna, Venkataraghavan and Bedi having developed so much in the intervening years, Wadekar had more scope to nurse Chandrasekhar than did Pataudi. Division of labour, no less than a phenomenal improvement in India's close catching, made for the glorious comeback of this gentle, cheerful sportsman.

WISDEN — 1973

CRICKET IN INDIA 1971–72, by P. N. Sundaresan

The rise in stature of Indian cricket in the international cricket scene, following the twin triumphs in the West Indies and England in the 1970–71 season, was reflected in the home season of 1971–72. This concluded in April with Bombay winning the Ranji Trophy championship for the 14th year in succession with traditional aplomb. There was tremendous enthusiasm at the playing level, while the attendance at important matches, especially in Bombay, reached new proportions. The most significant aspect of such upsurge was the excellent performances of youngsters in the Ranji Trophy, Duleep Trophy, National Defence Fund and other matches.

It is interesting to note that of the young players subsequently listed – R. D. Parkar, Parthasarathy Sharma, V. S. Vijayakumar, A. A. Ismail, S. Chakravarthy, P. M. Salgoankar, P. K. Shivalkar, R. K. Tandon, N. Mehta, S. K. Hazare and Madan Lal, only the last named went on to enjoy any sort of prolonged international success.

WISDEN — 1974

MCC IN INDIA 1972–73, by Clive Taylor

Unlike most suspense stories the surprise in the MCC tour of India, Pakistan and Sri Lanka came at the beginning when the First Test match against India at Delhi just before Christmas was won by the impressive margin of six wickets. It was a match which nobody expected England to win, least of all the England players whose only preparation after a lay-off of three months had been three matches, only one of which at Hyderabad against the President's XI, which could have passed for a Test side, was of real quality.

Before the First Test, Tony Lewis and his players would have been prepared to get out of it without defeat, relying on further practice to prepare them for other encounters in the series. The Indians, who never seemed to be referred to as anything except the world champions by their millions of followers, were a very confident side.

It says much for the effort made by this England party that India were never as confident again. Yet in the end the overall results of the tour were disappointing. In eight Test matches England won only that first one, lost the series 2–1 to India and featured in a depressing series of three drawn Tests in Pakistan, which would probably still have ended that way had they gone on playing for the rest of their lives, so slow were the pitches.

It was a disheartening record for a team who came so close to defeating India, who on their own wickets are one of the game's major powers. Just one reasonable innings by any of the specialist batsmen in each of the Tests at Calcutta and Madras would have seen England leading the series 3–0…

For England's players the main part of this tour was taken up with efforts to find a way to counter Bedi and Chandrasekhar, the two most destructive spinners in the world. In the course of it Chandrasekhar took 35 wickets, Bedi 25 and Solkar leapt about in the leg-trap like a hungry trout. That was a bowling series.

WISDEN – 1975

INDIA IN ENGLAND, 1974, by Dicky Rutnagur

For India, the 0–3 defeat by England in the 1974 series marked the end of an era of unprecedented success in Test cricket. In the three years preceding, India had won all the three series they contested – two of them abroad. Of their previous 13 Test matches, four were won and only one lost.

They had beaten England twice during this span – in England, in 1971 (1–0) and again at home (2–1), in the winter of 1972–73. In the context of this record, India's total eclipse was surprising.

The weather was outrageously unkind to the tourists while they prepared for the Test series. It was at its coldest and wettest during the opening Test, at Old Trafford. But the weather was by no means the decisive factor. The team had its shortcomings, some of which have applied to every Indian team to have toured England since the war…

The Indians… showed no conviction, not even in the county matches. Basically, their batting was not much weaker than in 1971. It was shown up more by the size of England's totals and more purposeful bowling than they encountered either in 1971 or, in the home series, 1972–73.

In fact, Gavaskar, who was such a big disappointment on both those occasions, came forth with effective performances in his first three innings of the series, starting with a very sound century. Simultaneously, Viswanath also gave evidence of his class and ability. Engineer, after failing in the First Test, lent weight to the batting with innings of substance and dash in each of the remaining encounters…

As captain, Wadekar had obviously used up all his luck in building up his hitherto unbeaten record. To add to all his problems, the coin just would not fall the way he called. The only time it did, at Edgbaston, he might have been better off losing the toss. There came a stage when all judgement about bowling changes and field placings seemed to have deserted him.

Ironically, this was the first Indian team to go through an English tour without losing to a county, but this record was no compensation for massive defeats in all three Test matches.

England v India
Second Test, at Lord's, June 20, 21, 22, 24, 1974, by Norman Preston

This was an extraordinarily one-sided contest, yet for three days India, handicapped because Chandrasekhar injured a thumb on the first day, put up gallant resistance, but compelled to follow on late on Saturday evening 327 runs behind, they capitulated in 77 minutes on Monday morning for 42, their lowest Test total and the lowest ever in a Test at Lord's.

The match was notable for several other milestones. England's total of 629 was their highest at Lord's and their highest against India as well as their best since making 654-5 against South Africa at Durban, 1938–39. They had also only once surpassed the margin of victory, an innings and 579 runs against Australia at The Oval, 1938. It was also England's first win at Lord's for five years... Bedi, who bowled continuously and exceedingly well on Friday until relieved just before tea, joined I. A. R. Peebles (The Oval, 1930) and L. O'B. Fleetwood-Smith (The Oval, 1938) as the only bowlers to concede 200 runs in a Test innings in England.

... Time permitted only two overs on Saturday night when India batted a second time, and on Monday morning in a heavy atmosphere Arnold revelled in swinging the ball either way. He made the breakthrough and Old completed the debacle, Hendrick, who might have done just as well, being merely a spectator. The full attendance was 65,373; receipts £50,445.

England 629 (D. L. Amiss 188, M. H. Denness 118, A. W. Greig 106; B. S. Bedi 6-226). **India 302** (F. M. Engineer 86, G. R. Viswanath 52) and **42** (C. M. Old 5-21). England won by an innings and 285 runs.

England v India
Prudential Trophy, First Match, at Headingley, July 14, 1974

For the first time, England and India played two one-day internationals (of 55 overs per side) after the Test series. England won them both, with India's lack of experience in the short version of the game being very obvious. Lessons were quickly learnt.

Although India exceeded all expectations by scoring 265, English expertise in the one-day game was finally decisive and victory came with 23 balls to spare. England were behind the required run-rate in the early stages but a skilled innings by Edrich, whose 90 occupied only 26 overs, ended Indian hopes of causing a surprise. Wadekar's field settings in defence of his side's handsome total were difficult to understand and the England batsmen picked up ones and twos at will. Edrich was particularly adept and when he was fifth out at 212 the only threat to England was the weather. The last two overs were played in really heavy rain and the crowd sheltered under umbrellas while Greig, Knott and Old knocked off the remaining runs.

England won by four wickets.

CRICKET IN INDIA 1973–74, by P. N. Sundaresan

Karnataka, which is Mysore's new name, following a political decision to change the name of the state, ended the 15-year-old reign of Bombay as the national cricket champions. The holders lost in the semi-final to Karnataka – the match was drawn but the decision went in favour of the latter on first innings lead – and they went on to defeat Rajasthan in the final and to annex the Ranji Trophy for the first time…

A. L. Wadekar, Bombay and West Zone's captain, would like to forget the season. He began by losing the Irani Cup match to the Rest of India, led by Prasanna; captaining West Zone, Wadekar lost to North Zone, and he ended the season by losing Bombay's hold on the Ranji Trophy.

OBITUARY

Patiala, The Maharajah of, latterly Lieut-Gen. Yadavindra Singh, died on June 17 in The Hague where he had been Indian Ambassador to Holland since November 1971. He was 61. In his only Test match, against England at Madras in February 1934, he made India's top score, 60, but his side were beaten by D. R. Jardine's team by 202 runs. A tall, graceful batsman, he played for the Hindus in the Quadrangular Tournament and captained Southern Punjab in the Ranji Trophy, scoring 132 against Rajputana in 1938–39. He was chosen for the 1936 tour of England but state business caused him to decline. The Yuvraj played in many representative matches against touring sides from overseas and in minor cricket he hit about 50 hundreds, including 284 against a Bombay XI at Patiala in 1938. His father was a noted patron of cricket, besides being a first-class player and was donor of the Ranji Trophy.

WISDEN – 1976

The first World Cup was held in 1975: India failed to make it to the semi-finals, but were keen to host the next event.

THE PRUDENTIAL CUP: WEST INDIES – WORLD CHAMPIONS

The first World Cup, officially called the Prudential Cup, proved an outstanding success. Blessed by perfect weather, ideal conditions prevailed. Altogether 15 single-innings matches, each confined to 60 overs, were played in England between June 7 and June 21. There were a few one-sided contests among some tremendous and keenly fought struggles. The highlight came in the final at Lord's where Australia and West Indies were in combat from 11am until 8.45pm when the Duke of Edinburgh presented the cup to Clive Lloyd, the West Indies captain.

When the ICC met in London towards the end of June member countries were invited to submit ideas for the next World Cup. India had already said that they were keen to act as hosts, but several members thought it was hard to beat England as the venue. The main view for this reasoning was the longer period of daylight in England in June when 60 overs for each side can be completed the same day.

England v India
Prudential World Cup, at Lord's, June 7, 1975

England won by 202 runs before a crowd of nearly 20,000. Receipts £19,000.

With Amiss in his best form and admirably supported by Fletcher, England ran up the highest score in this country for a 60-over match, although later in the summer it was beaten by Hampshire in the Gillette Cup. Both sides relied almost entirely on seam bowlers, which meant that India left out Bedi, a decision that caused much surprise. Timing the ball perfectly, Amiss raced to 98 out of England's 150-1 before lunch and altogether he made his 137 out of 245 by the 51st over and struck 18 fours. A feature of the cricket was the great outfielding of Ghavri, but the runs flowed so freely that finally Old (two sixes and four fours) helped himself to 51 off 28 balls in 35 minutes.

India, in turn, gave such a disappointing exhibition that even their own large contingent of supporters showed their disapproval. The culprit was Gavaskar, who sat on the splice throughout the 60 overs for 36 not out. Neither G. S. Ramchand, India's manager nor the captain, Venkataraghavan, agreed with the way Gavaskar performed. It was said that the pitch was slow and he took the opportunity to have some practice.

India v East Africa
Prudential World Cup, at Headingley, June 11, 1975

India won by ten wickets as East Africa's batsmen were quite obviously in a class of cricket 'above them'. Their batsmen were without the technique necessary to score runs off accurate Test class bowling and the bowlers, performing on a surface which had nothing to offer, had little to give other than all-out effort... East Africa were all out in the 56th over and apart from some steady bowling by Frasat with the new ball the India openers, Gavaskar and Engineer, had no difficulty in overhauling the East Africa score of 120... Other than Yorkshire members, officials and guests, only 720 people paid for admission.

WEST INDIES IN INDIA AND PAKISTAN AND SRI LANKA, 1974–75,
by Dicky Rutnagur

The fourth tour undertaken by the West Indies of the Indian subcontinent was remarkable... For the first time, every Test match of a series in India produced a definite result and the Fifth Test started against the dramatic background of India having levelled the rubber after being overwhelmed in the first two Tests. Despite India's gallant rally, West Indies deserved to win the final Test and the series, as there was never any question of their all-round superiority...

The Indian cause in the Test matches suffered from a combination of power-politics amongst the administration, Gavaskar's unavailability for three Tests through injury, and conservatism on the part of the selectors.

Wadekar having failed on the England tour and gone into retirement, Bedi and Engineer were the two leading candidates for the captaincy. Bedi was not considered for the post and even left out from the First Test on flimsy disciplinary grounds while Engineer was disqualified by the fact that he was based overseas. So Pataudi, despite no performance of any merit in domestic cricket, was reinstated as captain.

No doubt, Pataudi led the side well, but he was injured while fielding in the First Test and even when he returned for the Third, could not find his form. A tremendous burden thus fell on Viswanath, who at last acquired the habit of making consistently big scores in keeping with his talent and class.

OBITUARY

Ali, Syed Nazir, who represented India in their first Test match in England, died in Lahore in February at the age of 68. First attracting attention by some good bowling against the MCC in India in 1926–27, he then spent several years in England, making one appearance for Sussex in 1927 and playing regularly in club cricket round London. In 1930 he represented the Club Cricket Conference against the Australians at Lord's and had the distinction of getting Bradman's wicket. When he was chosen as a member of the Indian side in England in 1932, he had thus the advantage of considerably greater experience of English conditions than most of the other players. By then he had become more of a batsman than a bowler and was third in the batting averages with 1,020 runs at an average of 31.87, his highest score being 109 against Essex. He was also third in the bowling, but took only 23 wickets. A match against the MCC in India in 1934 concluded his Test career. He was an attacking batsman and a particularly fine driver, and a fast-medium right-hand bowler who could move the ball both ways. In later years he was a prominent administrator in Pakistani cricket. His elder brother, Wazir, also played for India.

WISDEN – 1977

After a pleasant tour of New Zealand during the winter of 1975–76, the trip to the West Indies the following year provided a nasty shock.

INDIA IN THE WEST INDIES, 1976, by Dicky Rutnagur

As at the end of the tour, the Indian team trudged along the tarmac towards their home-bound aeroplane at Kingston's Norman Manley Airport, they resembled Napoleon's troops on the retreat from Moscow. They were battle-weary and a lot of them were enveloped in plasters and bandages. The bandages were the campaign ribbons of a controversial and somewhat violent final Test which the West Indies won to prevail 2–1 in a four-Test series.

Following an overwhelming win for the West Indies in the opening contest in Barbados, the second in Trinidad was drawn, with India very much on top. At the same venue, India won the third in a blaze of glory, their triumph being achieved by scoring over 400 runs in the final innings – a feat that had only one precedent in the history of Test cricket.

Both sides went into the series suffering from a common disadvantage. Only a month earlier, the West Indies had finished a long and exciting tour of Australia during which they had lost the Test series by a humiliating margin. India undertook the West Indies tour directly after a visit to New Zealand. Undoubtedly, this tour had been less demanding on skill and stamina than the West Indies' campaign in Australia. But it did handicap the Indians in that they had an arduous journey of 62 hours from New Zealand and then went into the first match in the West Indies in little over a day, having had no opportunity to accustom themselves to totally different conditions…

It must be said that even during the early days of struggle, Bedi's tactics were constructive and positive. Indeed the Indians proved very resilient…

Inevitably, Gavaskar and Viswanath were the pillars of the Indian batting. Gavaskar, who sustained a bad facial injury in New Zealand, missed the first two matches but found his touch straight away, looking every bit the brilliant player he is. But he could not get himself to concentrate and build a long innings till the Second Test.

Viswanath, having discovered his form in New Zealand, batted effortlessly from the start in the West Indies, although he seemed to have an unfortunate knack of attracting balls that kept unplayably low. Men of short stature both, Gavaskar and Viswanath were happiest batting in Trinidad. Gavaskar, as in 1971, made centuries in both the Test matches there while Viswanath played the match-winning innings in the Third Test… After repeated early collapses, the Indians experimented with Gaekwad as an opening batsman and Mohinder Amarnath as No. 3. Gaekwad's height, his dogged determination and sound judgement of direction fitted him for his new role.

In the bloody Kingston Test, he batted a day and a half in the teeth of hostile fast bowling and seemed to have established himself as an opening batsman for a long time to come. But eventually he ducked into a ball that did not rise to the expected height and took a blow which put him in hospital and might well have killed his taste for the assignment.

West Indies v India
Third Test, at Port of Spain, April 7, 8, 10, 11, 12, 1976

India scored over 400 to win this Test, a feat accomplished only once before – by Australia against England, at Headingley, in 1948. Their victory was the climax of a very brave second-innings recovery.

Gavaskar and Viswanath both batted at their best to meet the big challenge in the second innings and Mohinder Amarnath was outstanding while playing the role of anchor. But India's achievement reflected poorly on the three West Indies spin bowlers who could make so little headway on a worn, turning pitch. In contrast, all three of India's spinners bowled magnificently in both innings.

West Indies built up a seemingly impregnable position over the first two days… On the last day, India's target was 269 in six hours. After completing his century, Gavaskar lost his touch and eventually succumbed in trying to move back into top gear. Mohinder Amarnath, who had helped Gavaskar to put on 108, did not have the skill to dominate and in the second hour, the score rate slumped to 22. Amarnath had become particularly bogged down after surviving a return chance to Imtiaz Ali, at 37. Time was still on India's side at lunch when 206 were required in four hours.

In 45 minutes after the resumption, they added 26 and then Lloyd took the new ball, 29 overs after it was due. Julien bowled very loosely with it and with Viswanath getting after him, India now began to make rapid advance. In eight overs with the new ball, 37 runs were scored.

Viswanath was now inspired. Using his feet, he bent the spin attack to his will and his century came out of 147 runs, with 13 fours. The pair, who put on 159 in all, took India to within 67 of their objective and then Viswanath, backing up too far, was run out. The statutory overs began five minutes later.

India were not thrown out of their stride by Viswanath's dismissal. Patel took command of the spin attack, which collapsed under the pressure and India got home at a gallop, with seven overs to spare.

West Indies 359 (I. V. A. Richards 177, C. H. Lloyd 68; B. S. Chandrasekhar 6-120) and **271 for six wickets declared** (A. I. Kallicharran 103 not out). **India 228** (M. A. Holding 6-65) and **406 for four wickets** (G. R. Viswanath 112, S. M. Gavaskar 102, M. Amarnath 85). India won by six wickets.

West Indies v India
Fourth Test, at Kingston, April 21, 22, 24, 25, 1976

This was a stormy Test, with accusations from the Indians of persistent intimidatory bowling after three of their batsmen were put out of action in their first innings. However, the Test will not be remembered only for the controversy. The cricket for the first three days was highly combative, promising a much keener finish.

The virgin pitch had an immense bearing on the tactics of West Indies as also the result. The bounce at each end was vastly different and even at one particular end was variable because of an undulation on a fast bowler's length, the ball rising from it to alarming heights. It was the unpredictability of bounce that contributed to the unsafe manner in which the Indian batsmen took evasive action and, consequently, suffered nasty injuries.

This is not to say that there was no short-pitched bowling. There was a surfeit of it – overdone, in fact, to the extent where the umpires should have intervened. A lot of the short-pitched bowling was delivered by Holding from round the wicket to minimise the batsman's scope of drawing away from his stumps...

The first day, shortened by bad light, belonged to India… India's problems set in the following morning when, at 199, the new ball was taken. In three overs with it, Holding reduced India to 216-3, having Mohinder Amarnath and Viswanath caught at backward short-leg. Viswanath was caught off the glove, the impact leaving a finger both fractured and dislocated. The fall of the fourth wicket at 280 would suggest that West Indies' offensive had been checked. But, in fact, two batsmen, Patel and Gaekwad, had meanwhile retired with injuries that put them out of the match. Patel, facing Holder, took his eye off the ball and edged it on to his mouth. Gaekwad was struck just above the left ear, having ducked into a ball that was not too short, but the bounce of which bore no relation to its length. In this instance, the irregularity in the pitch seemed responsible.

India's first innings total of 306 was overtaken by the West Indies reply of 391 and when Holding had Gavaskar caught at short-leg in the third over of the second innings, India's spirit was broken. They slid to 97-5 in less than three hours and at that point, the innings closed as five batsmen in all absented themselves because of injury. In addition to Viswanath, Patel and Gaekwad, who were hurt during the Indians' first innings, Bedi and Chandrasekhar had damaged fingers while attempting return catches during the West Indies' innings. At first it was thought that Bedi had declared again – with India only 12 runs in front – and it was only after West Indies had won that a statement was issued by Bedi that the Indian innings should be recorded as completed.

INDIA	1st Innings		2nd Innings	
S. M. Gavaskar b Holding	66	– b Julien b Holding	2
A. D. Gaekwad retired hurt	81	– absent hurt	
M. Amarnath c Julien b Holding	39	– st Murray b Jumadeen	60
G. R. Viswanath c Julien b Holding	8	– absent hurt	
*D. V. Vengsarkar b Holding	39	– lbw b Jumadeen	21
D. B. Patel retired hurt	14	– absent hurt	
S. Madan Lal lbw b Daniel	5	– b Holding	8
S. Venkataraghavan lbw b Daniel	9	– b Holding	0
†S. M. H. Kirmani not out	0	– not out	0
B. S. Bedi*	absent hurt	absent hurt	
B. S. Chandrasekhar	absent hurt	absent hurt	
Extras (b 6, lb 6, w 12, nb 21)	45	Extras (nb 6)	6

1-136 2-105 3-216 3-237*   (6 wickets, declared) 396   1-5 2-68 3-97 4-97 5-97   (all out) 97
3-273* 4-280 5-306 6-306

First innings – Holding 28–7–82–4; Daniel 20.2–7–52–2; Julien 23–10–53–0; Holder 27–4–58–0;
Jumadeen 3–1–8–0; Fredericks 3–1–8–0
Second innings – Holding 7.2–0–35–3; Daniel 3–0–12–0; Julien 3–0–13–0; Holder 6–2–12–0;
Jumadeen 7–3–19–2

WEST INDIES	1st Innings		2nd Innings	
R. C. Fredericks run out	82	– not out	6
L. G. Rowe st Kirmani b Bedi	47	– not out	6
I. V. A. Richards b Chandrasekhar	64		
A. I. Kallicharran b Chandrasekhar	12		
*C. H. Lloyd c & b Chandrasekhar	0		
†D. L. Murray c sub b Chandrasekhar	71		
B. D. Julien b Chandrasekhar	5		
M. A. Holding c sub b Bedi	55		
V. A. Holder not out	36		
R. R. Jumadeen c Gavaskar b Venkataraghavan	3		
W. W. Daniel c Amarnath b Venkataraghavan	11		
Extras (b 1, lb 2, nb 2)	5	Extras (nb 1)	1

1-105 2-186 3-197 4-206 5-209 6-217   391   (0 wickets) 13
7-324 8-345 9-352 10-391

First innings – Madan Lal 7–1–25–0 ;Amarnath 8–1–28–0; Chandrasekhar 42–7–153–5; Bedi 32–10–68–
2; Venkataraghavan 51.3–12–112–2; Vengsarkar 0.5–0–7–0
Second innings – Madan Lal 0–1–0–5–0

West Indies won by 10 wickets.

WISDEN – 1978

MCC IN INDIA 1976–77, by Dicky Rutnagur

After severe and depressing losses to Australia and West Indies in successive home summers, the tide turned for English cricket during the 1976–77 tour of India and Sri Lanka. For the first time in five ventures since the Second World War, England beat India on their own soil.

The margin of England's victory in the series was decisive: 3–1. And the extent of England's superiority in achieving these three wins was no less convincing – an innings and 25 runs, ten wickets and 200 runs. MCC were undefeated in the eight other first-class matches on the tour although only one of them was won.

A historic aspect of the English triumph in the Test series was that no other touring side in India had ever before clinched the rubber over the first three Tests. As India came back to win the fourth and strongly contest a highly exciting final Test (the only one to be drawn) there was no evidence of slackening effort on the part of the tourists.

In analysing the series, it must be pointed out that India looked as weak as they have ever done in their 42 years in international cricket. What slight potential they had as a team they did not realise until after the series was decided…

The Indian batting seemed desperately short of Test-class material and the shortage was emphasised because Viswanath, who had a very successful series against New Zealand just before, suffered almost total loss of form. The other leading batsman, Gavaskar, played three notable innings, including the only Indian century of the series, but there were other occasions when he showed a marked reluctance to shoulder responsibility…

The Indian spinners as a combination suffered from the failure of the batsmen to give them totals big enough to bowl at, at least in the first three Tests. Fielding support also was inadequate – certainly not up to Test standards. No batsman of any quality was seen in the matches outside the Tests and, on this evidence, the revival of India as a Test force did not appear to be close at hand.

India v England
Third Test, at Madras, January 14, 15, 16, 18, 19, 1977

The unfortunate 'Vaseline' incident took place just before the innings subsided. Lever, who took 5-59 in the innings (two of them on the previous day) was reported by umpire Reuben to be carrying on his person a strip of surgical gauze impregnated with Vaseline. He considered it to be a breach of Law 46.

The MCC authorities did not deny the presence of the offending strip of gauze, but offered an explanation for its use. Their version of how it came to be discovered by the umpire did, however, conflict with that of Mr Reuben. The umpire said that it came adrift while Lever was delivering the ball. MCC, on the other hand, claimed that Lever found it a hindrance and discarded it himself.

The MCC explanation for the bowler having possession of the gauze strip was this: 'During the morning session, both Lever and Willis had suffered from smarting eyes because of sweat running into them from the forehead. So, on the advice of the team's physiotherapist, Mr Bernard Thomas, they went out wearing these gauze strips which were intended to divert the trickle of perspiration away from their eyes.'

Ken Barrington, the MCC manager, said that while there had been a technical breach of the law governing fair and unfair play, the offence was totally unintentional. At a press conference the following day, the rest day, the captain and manager emphasised in further defence of Lever that the gauze strips were not worn until after lunch and that by then England had made such large inroads into the Indian innings, that such unfair methods were quite unnecessary.

Fuel had been added to the fire by Bedi, the Indian captain, stating after the incident that even at Delhi, during the first Test, he had suspicions that a polishing agent of some kind had been used.

More was to be heard of the 'Vaseline' incident at the end of the fourth day, on which England played themselves into a winning position... After close of play, two statements were issued on the affair. The secretary of the Indian board, Mr Ghulam Ahmed, said that the tour committee of the board had considered the umpire's report and other available evidence and could not come to a definite conclusion whether the intentions of the bowler were deliberate or not. He added that the board had conveyed all its findings to the TCCB in London.

While this statement left the impression that the Indian board was not satisfied one way or the other, Mr Barrington said that the Indian board and captain Bedi had accepted our explanation that this was not a direct infringement of the laws of the game. In a day or two, a statement came from Lord's that the TCCB was satisfied with the explanation received from Messrs Barrington and Greig.

England won by 200 runs.

WISDEN – 1979

To a great extent, the Packer revolution passed India by, at least in its direct impact. No Indian players were in the original group who signed up, so when India toured Australia in 1977–78, they were able to take a full strength side. They were still not quite good enough for Australia's second eleven.

INDIA IN AUSTRALIA, 1977–78, by D. J. Rutnagur

India's third tour of Australia was not seen to suffer from competition by the newly established World Series Cricket. The Australian public soon gave its vote to the traditional game and, overall, the Test matches drew bigger attendances than on the Indians' previous visit, in 1967–68. Only in Perth, the newest of Australia's Test venues, were the crowds of disappointing size.

Both Australia and India responded magnificently to the challenge of WSC and to the enthusiasm of those who watched and followed the Test matches. The tourists kindled the flame of public interest by winning every state game leading up to the First Test.

In what turned out to be a fascinating series, Australia won the first two Tests, but both in desperately close finishes. In each of them, also, fortunes ebbed and flowed intriguingly from day to day, sometimes from session to session. Moreover, both sides batted attractively and bowled positively. Hence, the series was made. Then India won the Third and Fourth Tests, both more decisively than Australia had won the two preceding encounters. The two-all situation set up the series for a glorious finish, and the finale was indeed dramatic and exciting. Australia won the six-day final Test on the last day after India, in an heroic second-innings recovery, had made a record losing score of 445 ...

The Indians... performed well above the form they showed in their last series, against England the previous winter. In some respects, they were unlucky to lose. However, for a side containing a very small proportion of players who had previous experience of Australian conditions, they were fortunate that, after a dry spring, the pitches lacked their customary pace.

One had anticipated before the start of the tour that India would be almost solely dependent on Gavaskar and Viswanath for their runs. And, indeed, they were the highest scorers in Test matches, with aggregates of 450 and 473 respectively, and with averages of above 50. Gavaskar hit three centuries in nine innings, but only once made a two-digit score in the first innings of a Test match. Viswanath, who surprisingly did not make a single hundred, came into his own after India were two down in the series...

Of the Indian bowlers, the three seamers, Madan Lal, Mohinder Amarnath, and Ghavri, all bowled well at times, but India suffered from not having a single bowler of anything approaching genuine pace. Hence all depended on the spinners. Day in and day out, Bedi was the outstanding member of the quartet. He took 54 first-class wickets on the tour and 31 in the Tests. Chandrasekhar was slow in touching his peak, and by the time he did Australia had gone two up in the series. However, he won the Third Test, at Melbourne, taking 12 wickets in the match, and he was also prominent in India's victory in the Fourth, at Sydney.

Australia v India
Fifth Test, at Adelaide, January 28, 29, 30, February 1, 2, 3, 1978

With India putting on a record losing total in the second innings of 445, the deciding Test ended on a highly exciting note – a finale becoming an evenly fought series. The one unfortunate feature of this memorable contest was the strong feeling that crept in, albeit briefly, when, on the third day, the Indians showed displeasure over at least three umpiring decisions. The volatile Bedi expressed his criticism of the umpiring in the strongest terms...

Australia continued to build on the fine start and finished with a total of 505, the highest of the series by either side. When India batted, Thomson bowled as fast and as accurately as he has ever done. Though his participation in the match was limited, it had immense bearing on the result. He removed Gavaskar and Mohinder Amarnath, the main pillars of the Indian batting, while India lost three wickets for 23 runs. There was a worthwhile partnership of 136 between Viswanath and Vengsarkar, but thereafter India never looked like matching Australia's massive total.

With six days allotted to this match, Simpson did not enforce the follow-on when India were bowled out halfway through the third day. The Indian spinners recaptured their form in the second innings, but half-centuries by Darling and Simpson saw Australia to a total of 256, which left India 493 runs to win – or more than 14 hours to bat out for a draw. Their only comfort was that Thomson was still unfit to bowl...

Viswanath and Amarnath batted right through the morning of the fifth day, adding 131 before Viswanath fell to the second new ball, at 210. Amarnath carried on to make 86, and with Vengsarkar batting with composure, India continued their struggle in an encouraging manner... India were 348-6 at Vengsarkar's dismissal. The seventh-wicket pair, Kirmani and Ghavri, got sufficiently entrenched for the Australians to start worrying. However, the third new ball gave them the decisive breakthrough. Still, India fought to the bitter end.

Australia won by 47 runs.

OBITUARIES

Mankad, Mulvantrai, affectionately known to cricketers throughout his life by his schoolboy nickname of 'Vinoo', died in Bombay on August 21, aged 61. He was the greatest all-rounder that India has yet produced. In Tests he scored 2,109 runs with an average of 31.47 and took 162 wickets at 32.31. He made five centuries and twice took eight wickets in an innings. Against New Zealand at Madras in 1955–56 he scored 231, still a record for India in a Test, and with P. Roy put on 413 for the first wicket, a record for any Test. His average for that series was 105. When India at Madras in 1952 gained their first victory over England, his bowling was almost wholly responsible. On a wicket which gave him little assistance he took 8-55 and 4-53.

His most famous feat was v England at Lord's in 1952 when going in first he scored 72 and 184. In the second innings he went straight to the wicket after bowling 31 overs that day. In the whole match he bowled 97 overs and took 5-231. England won by eight wickets, but Mankad's performance must surely rank as the greatest ever done in a Test by a member of the losing side. Indeed in assessing his record one must remember that of the 44 Tests between 1946 and 1959 in which he played India won five only.

His first-class career started in 1935, but it was against Lord Tennyson's team in India in 1937–38 that he came into real prominence. With a batting average in the unofficial Tests of 62.66 and a bowling average of 14.53, he headed both averages, and Tennyson is reported to have said that he would already get a place in a World XI. In 1946 for India in England he made 1,120 runs and took 129 wickets. He remains the only Indian ever to have accomplished this feat and no member of any touring side has achieved it since.

In 1947 he went into league cricket and, though he remained available in India during the winter, when they came to England in 1952, he was released for the Tests only. Indeed the Lord's Test was his first first-class match that season. He captained India in Pakistan in 1954–55. In his first-class career, which ended in 1962, he scored 11,480 runs with an average of 34.78 and took 774 wickets at 24.60.

As a batsman, he had great powers of concentration and a strong defence. His record stand with Roy lasted over eight hours and they were not separated till after lunch on the second day. At the same time, if a ball wanted hitting, he hit it. Many will remember how at Lord's in 1952 the match had barely been in progress half-an-hour when he hit Jenkins high over the screen at the Nursery End. He had a fine cover-drive and hit well to leg. Like many players of great natural ability he did not in attack worry overmuch about the straightness of his bat. In fact he was essentially a practical batsman who was prepared to go in cheerfully whenever his captain wanted and adapt his tactics to the state of the match.

As a bowler, he was a slow left-hander of the old-fashioned orthodox type, varying his natural leg-break with a faster one which came with his arm and got him lots of wickets. His figures in 1946 are the more creditable when one realises that for most of the tour he was suffering from an injury which made this ball tiring and difficult to bowl. As a boy he had experimented with the chinaman but was fortunately persuaded by that shrewd coach, Bert Wensley, to abandon it. For some years he was undoubtedly the best bowler of his type in the world.

Ghorpade, Jaysingh, who died in Baroda on March 29 aged 47, was for some years regarded as one of the best all-rounders in India, a beautiful strokeplayer, who was always looking for runs, a useful leg-spinner and a magnificent field in the covers. But it must be said that, for a player of this reputation, his performances in the highest class were disappointing. A member of the sides in the West Indies in 1952–53 and in England in 1959, he played in eight Tests between 1953 and 1959, and in these his batting average was only 15 and his highest score 41 against England at Lord's, when he helped Contractor to add 83 for the fourth wicket. Moreover, India being rich at that time in leg-spin, he was seldom given a bowl and never took a wicket in a Test... However, such was his reputation as a fieldsman that he was almost always twelfth man in any match in which he was not playing. He always played in spectacles. At the time of his death he was chairman of the Indian Selection Committee.

WISDEN – 1980

INDIA IN PAKISTAN, 1978, by Dicky Rutnagur

Pakistan and India, who had confronted each other twice on battlefields since they last played a Test match, resumed cricket contact after almost 18 years when India undertook an eight-week tour of Pakistan which included three Test matches. Pakistan, distinctly the stronger side, won the Second and Third Tests. The First was drawn.

The warmth and enthusiasm with which the Indians were received, plus the cordial relations between the players, made it plain enough that the renewal of cricketing rivalry between the two neighbouring countries was long overdue. Indeed, cricket authorities on both sides of the border are eager to make up for the lost years...

It would be hypocritical to say that the tour and the Test series were totally free of incidents and controversy. But there was no more tension and friction than is usual these days in Test matches between any two countries.

However, the tour would have been happier without the notorious Sahiwal incident, on the occasion of the last of three one-day internationals. As the Indians, with plenty of wickets in hand, approached their target, Sarfraz Nawaz indulged in an excess of bumpers which were obviously out of the batsmen's reach. There was no intervention from the umpires and Bedi, the Indian captain, conceded the match in protest. His action raised controversies both in Pakistan and at home...

The Indian batting did not live up to the reputation and standards established in Australia a year earlier. Morale gradually declined in the face of a surfeit of short-pitched bowling. Head and shoulders above everyone else was Gavaskar, with scores of 89, 8 not out, 5, 97, 111, and 137... Not once in the entire series did India bowl out Pakistan. The striking rate of their bowlers was one wicket every 66 runs. The might of Pakistan's batting emphasised the fact that India's celebrated spinners were over the hill. The Indian attack looked absolutely forlorn... And in addition, Kirmani had a disastrous tour, both with gloves and bat.

India's one consolation was the emergence of 19-year-old Kapil Dev as an all-rounder of considerable worth. A clean and hefty striker of the ball, he made some useful runs in the lower order, and also showed promise of developing into an excellent fast-medium bowler.

Pakistan v India

One-day International, at Sahiwal, November 3, 1978 (40 overs)

Pakistan 205-7 (Asif Iqbal 62, Majid J. Khan 37). **India 183-2** (A.D. Gaekwad 78 not out, S. Amarnath 62). India conceded the match in protest against an excess of bumpers sent down by Sarfraz Nawaz.

INDIA IN ENGLAND, 1979, by Norman Preston

On their ninth tour of England, the first official one was in 1932, the Indian cricketers did not do themselves justice... England recorded their highest total of 633-5 when they beat India by an innings and 83 runs in the First Test at Edgbaston, but in the three remaining Tests India held their own, thanks mainly to the splendid batting of Gavaskar, Viswanath, Vengsarkar and, to a lesser degree, of Chauhan.

In recent years, India were indebted to the skill of their spin bowlers, Chandrasekhar, Prasanna and Bedi. This time they left off-spinner Prasanna at home, and Chandrasekhar and Bedi accomplished little in the Tests. A strained Achilles tendon troubled Chandrasekhar and he appeared only in the First Test. On Venkataraghavan fell the responsibility of captain, but he had a disappointing tour. His off-spin caused such few problems that his six Test wickets cost 57.50 runs apiece.

Consequently, a tremendous amount of work fell on the two opening bowlers: Kapil Dev, a 20-year-old all-rounder and the youngest member of the party, and Ghavri, a left-hander with both bat and ball. Kapil Dev stood out by himself as the main attacker, but his 16 Test wickets cost 30.93 runs each.

England v India

Fourth Test, at The Oval, August 30, 31, September 1, 3, 4, 1979, by Terry Cooper

The match was drawn after the most gripping closing overs in a home Test since the draw at Lord's against West Indies in 1963, a match it closely resembled, as all four results were possible with three balls left. Gavaskar's inspiring and technically flawless 221 earned him the Man of the Match award and brought that rarity in recent Tests in England – a final day charged with interest. Botham played the major part in preventing an Indian victory and confirmed his status as man of the series. As the teams fought each other to a standstill, there were many Englishmen in the crowd who would not have displayed their customary dejection at a Test defeat.

Gavaskar's innings was the highest by an Indian against England, overtaking the unbeaten 203 by the younger Nawab of Pataudi at Delhi in 1963–64, and his stand of 213 with Chauhan surpassed the previous-best opening partnership for his country against England – 203 by Mushtaq Ali and Vijay Merchant at

Manchester in 1936. India's 429-8 – they were set 438 in 500 minutes – was the fourth-highest score in the fourth innings of a Test. To reach their target they would have needed to set a new mark for a side batting fourth and winning, but this generation of Indian batsmen have some notable performances in that department and the job did not frighten them...

Botham achieved the three runs he needed to reach the landmark of 1,000 runs and 100 wickets in his 21st Test, beating the 23 Tests required by Vinoo Mankad for this double...

Botham, as bowler and fielder, sent India sliding into trouble, taking two wickets and holding two catches, and India had subsided to 137-5 when bad light halted the game 40 minutes early. Botham's second catch was remarkable. Bairstow could only parry the ball when Vengsarkar edged Willis. The ball struck Brearley on the boot, flew upwards, and as Bairstow came across to retrieve it, Botham grabbed it one-handed at second slip...

At 76 for no wicket on the fifth morning, India wanted roughly a run a minute. Their rate was never brisk – 48 in the first hour, 45 in the second, and 44 in the third... England were despairing of wickets when, after five and a quarter hours, Chauhan edged Willis. The despair soon returned as Vengsarkar joined Gavaskar in an accelerating stand which produced 153 at better than a run a minute. Gavaskar masterminded the show, doing all the thinking and playing most of the shots. Tea came at 304-1 and, after a mere six overs between the interval and five o'clock – England ruthlessly slowed down the game – the last 20 overs began at 328-1 with 110 wanted, and India favourites...

Yashpal Sharma and Gavaskar rattled the score along to 389, when Botham returned with eight overs left. It was a gamble by Brearley, for Botham had looked innocuous during the day. But he struck with the key wicket, Gavaskar drilling a catch to mid-on shortly after England had taken a drinks break – a rare move, tactically based, with the end so near. Gavaskar's memorable innings lasted eight hours nine minutes, and he hit 21 fours, most of them coming from firm clips past mid-wicket and his unexpectedly powerful cover-drive. However, his cool control of the developing crisis was missed by India as much as his runs... Botham's final four overs brought him an absolutely crucial three for 17. A target of 15 from the last over was too much, and the climax came with fielders encircling the bat.

England 305 (G. A. Gooch 79, P. Willey 52) and **334 for eight wickets declared** (G. Boycott 125, D. L. Bairstow 59). **India 202** (G. R. Viswanath 62) and **429 for eight wickets** (S. M. Gavaskar 221, C. P. S. Chauhan 80, D. B. Vengsarkar 52). Match drawn.

CRICKETERS OF THE YEAR 1980

S. M. GAVASKAR, by D. J. Rutnagur

Until Sachin Tendulkar came along to break virtually all the Indian batting records, the bulk of them were held by their greatest opening batsman, Sunil Gavaskar.

Sunil Manohar Gavaskar was born in Bombay on July 10, 1949, with the scent of bat oil in his nostrils, for his father was still a very active club cricketer and his uncle from his mother's side, M. K. Mantri, was Bombay's and India's wicketkeeper. In the circumstances, it was no surprise that a toy cricket bat was among his earliest possessions, and that the infant Gavaskar's afternoon naps were followed by practice against the bowling of a doting mother and the houseboy.

The most prolific Indian batsman ever in Test cricket says that he learnt to read numbers from scoreboards. While children of his age went to bed listening to tales of *Little Red Riding Hood* and *Goldilocks*, Gavaskar had his little ears trained to the radio and the voices of John Arlott and Rex Alston describing the Test matches of 1952, in which uncle Madhav was engaged. For him, the big bad wolf was F. S. Trueman.

When Gavaskar went visiting his uncle, he would ask him to unlock his wardrobe and display his various caps, sweaters and blazers, the colours of Bombay University, Bombay and India. The child that stared at them with awe was to win all those colours himself before he was 20 and to wear them with great distinction.

Last summer's memorable Oval Test, in which Gavaskar scored his epic 221, was his 50th. At that point, with a home season of 13 Test matches to follow, he had played more Test matches than any Indian except Bishan Bedi, Polly Umrigar and Gundappa Viswanath.

Gavaskar has made and broken records at all levels of the game. Flip through the statistical section of *Wisden*'s Indian counterpart and his name figures on almost every page. During the recent 1979-80 series against Australia, he became the first Indian to complete 5,000 runs in Test cricket. At the end of it, with 22 hundreds, he stood third (jointly with Walter Hammond and Colin Cowdrey) in the international list of Test century-makers. The only two in front were Sir Donald Bradman (29) and Sir Garfield Sobers (26). The diminutive Indian has also established himself as the most successful opening batsman in Test history, having made three more centuries than any other (Sir Leonard Hutton).

Gavaskar's three-figure Test scores include three double-centuries, the first of which was made in only his fourth Test and came on the heels of a century in the first innings of that same game – the Fifth Test of India's 1971 series in the West Indies. India went into this Test match, at Trinidad's Queen's Park Oval, leading 1–0, having won the second Test on the same ground a few weeks earlier.

But for Gavaskar's 124 in a total of 360, India would probably have lost that six-day final Test, for West Indies scored 526 in reply. Danger still lurked when Gavaskar scored 220 in the second innings, but eventually India came near to winning it. The remarkable feature of Gavaskar's marathon batting in that match was that both innings were played under the handicap of an agonising toothache which deprived him of adequate sleep. He refused painkillers lest they made him drowsy or slackened his reflexes.

Although he missed the First Test – in fact, he did not play at all on the Jamaica leg of the tour because of an infected fingernail – Gavaskar aggregated 774 runs in that, his first series. After scoring 65 and 67 not out in his maiden Test (the one in which India beat West Indies for the first time) Gavaskar had already notched up two centuries, in the Third and Fourth Tests, before performing his tremendous feat in the Fifth...

Immediately after his phenomenal debut in the West Indies, Gavaskar had a good tour of England, although his Test scores were not quite compatible with his triumphs in the Caribbean... After his double-century in Trinidad, there was a gap of seven Test matches and the five representative games in Australia before Gavaskar compiled his next Test hundred, against England at Old Trafford in 1974, which he himself regards as his best innings. He has not looked back since, and on two more occasions he has scored separate hundreds in a Test match.

As is obvious from Gavaskar's Test record, he is capable of intense concentration and discipline. But he summons these virtues only when India are in trouble or when he senses the chance of a win. He is not one for making big scores just for the sake of records. When he sets his sights high, he builds his innings with meticulous craftsmanship, limiting himself to the stroke he plays best – drives through the covers, past the bowler, and between mid-on and mid-wicket. But when he lets his hair down, his range of shots and the power behind them are quite astonishing. He can lay claims to a six at the Melbourne Cricket Ground. As an exhibition of brilliant batsmanship in a Test match, his 205 against West Indies at Bombay two winters ago was outstanding.

An executive with a textile firm, Gavaskar, educated at St Xavier's School and St Xavier's College, is married and has a son, named after his boyhood hero and one-time West Indian adversary, Rohan Kanhai. Gavaskar's sister Kavita (means poetry) is married to the other Indian batting genius, Gundappa Viswanath. It is mind-boggling to contemplate the talent of their offspring – when he arrives.

WISDEN – 1981

THE AUSTRALIANS IN INDIA, 1979–80, by Dicky Rutnagur

The Australians' third full tour of India was of historic interest on two counts. It was Australia's final campaign before the compromise between the Australian Cricket Board of Control and World Series Cricket took effect, and it was important from their opponents' viewpoint because India won a series (2–0) against Australia for the first time. The two countries had previously contested seven rubbers over 31 years, during which India had won only five Tests to Australia's 19, with six drawn...

The result of the Test series was not unexpected, for the Australians were relatively inexperienced, ten of the party of 15 never having toured before. Moreover, they were all new to conditions on the Indian subcontinent. They did have some early advantage in that India had just returned from a long and strenuous tour of England and had had no time at all to acclimatise before going into the first Test. Furthermore, India themselves were in the throes of rebuilding their side...

The series marked the end of an era in Indian cricket as, for the first time in 11 years, India took the field without any of their three great contemporary spinners, Chandrasekhar, Bedi and Prasanna. Venkataraghavan also lost his place after the first two Tests... But the main wicket-taker, with 28 victims, was pace bowler Kapil Dev, who showed how much he had benefited from the tour of England...

To suit Australia's convenience, the tour was scheduled for an unusually early time in the season, when the monsoons had not quite receded. The first two Test matches, played in September, were both drastically affected by the weather and it was fortunate that the others were free of interference. The Indian board would be unfair to the paying public if, in future, they arranged tours starting any earlier than mid-November.

THE PAKISTANIS IN INDIA, 1979–80, by Dicky Rutnagur

Much the same Pakistan side that had totally outplayed India at home a year earlier and won the series 2–0, went down by the same margin in a tense, controversial rubber of six Tests. The result could have been 3–0 for India, after a brave second innings recovery, were close to winning the Second Test. However, Pakistan dominated the dead final Test, which was drawn.

The marked turn of fortunes in a year was wrought by several factors, of which India's advantage of playing at home was the least significant. The most prominent reason for India's ascendancy was the development as an opening bowler of Kapil Dev who, with 32 wickets, was the leading wicket-taker of the series for either side. And with an abundant infusion of new players, India were stronger than 12 months earlier, much of the added strength coming from greater mobility in the field and superior catching...

The Pakistanis, whose only win on tour was against a weak East Zone side, would not come to terms with their shortcomings. Instead, they looked elsewhere for the cause of their failures. They alleged bias on the part of the umpires and in Bombay, during the Third Test, they accused the ground authorities of doctoring the pitch after the match had started. After a stormy Fourth Test, in which Sikander Bakht kicked down the stumps after having an appeal disallowed, Asif Iqbal talked of calling off the rest of the tour. Although such an action would have had severe repercussions, both at political level and in the cricket world, the Indian players would not, they said, have been too sorry. The atmosphere on the field had been soured and standards of conduct had dropped to deplorable levels...

For all that the Pakistanis' comments on the umpiring were in bad taste, there was no doubt that it was deficient in standards. It has been remarked on adversely by the Australians as well. The Indian board must take steps to improve it and one way would be to induce former first-class players to take up umpiring. As elsewhere, umpiring in India is no longer a financially unattractive occupation.

THE GOLDEN JUBILEE TEST, by Dicky Rutnagur

India v England
at Bombay, February 15, 17, 18, 19, 1980

With the rival sides fatigued, both mentally and physically, at the end of an arduous season, the Test match to celebrate the Golden Jubilee of the Board of Control for Cricket in India produced poor cricket. But it was redeemed by an extraordinary all-round performance by Botham, whose versatility was in full bloom. There was hardly a session on which he did not bring his influence to bear, performing the unprecedented feat of scoring a century and capturing 13 wickets in a Test. Taylor, the England wicketkeeper, also established a new world Test record by taking ten catches in the match.

To England, after the Test series in Australia, this success, even if inspired by one man, brought welcome relief. But for India, the defeat ended an unbeaten run of 15 Test matches, four of which they had won.

With the pitch uncharacteristically grassy, England were at no disadvantage from losing the toss; even less so as an overcast sky was a further aid to swing and cut on the opening morning. The Indians, jaded after playing 16 Tests in the past seven months, could not summon the application and discipline needed to combat these conditions and were bowled out in less than a day for 242, Botham taking 6-58 and Taylor taking seven catches. India would have fared even worse but for gallant resistance from the lower order of their batting.

Batting as indifferently as they did in Australia, England at 58-5 looked most unlikely to match India's score, let alone build on the advantage created by their bowlers. But they were only 13 runs behind when they lost their next wicket two hours 20 minutes later. Botham, batting for 206 minutes and hitting 17 fours, scored 114 in an innings which was responsible and yet not lacking in enterprise. His stand of 171 with Taylor was England's best-ever sixth-wicket partnership against India. Taylor remained entrenched until the third day was more than an hour old and altogether scored 43 in a stay of four and a half hours. Yet their stand could have been cut short at only 85 when umpire Hanumantha Rao upheld an appeal against Taylor for a catch behind the wicket, off Kapil Dev. Taylor hesitated and protested at the decision. Viswanath, the Indian captain, who was fielding at first slip, was as certain as the batsman that there had been no contact and persuaded the umpire to rescind his verdict...

India 242 (I. T. Botham 6-58) and **149** (I. T. Botham 7-48). **England 296**
(I. T. Botham 114; K. D. Ghavri 5-52) and **98 for no wicket**.
England won by ten wickets with a day to spare.

OBITUARIES

Banerjee, Shute Nath, who died in Calcutta on October 14, 1980, aged 67, became the first Bengali to play Test cricket when he won his only cap against West Indies in Bombay in 1948. A right-arm fast-medium bowler, he took 1-73 in West Indies' first innings and 4-54 in their second. He is perhaps best remembered for having, in 1946, on the second of his two tours to England, helped C. T. Sarwate add 249 in three hours ten minutes for the Indians' last wicket against Surrey at The Oval. This is still an Indian record and the second-highest last-wicket partnership ever made. Batting at No. 11, he joined Sarwate at 205-9 and hit 121. Sarwate finished with 124 not out... He captained Bihar from 1942 until 1958.

Naoomal Jeoomal, who died in Bombay on July 18, 1980, aged 76, served the game of cricket for many years, first in India and, after partition, in Pakistan. As a member of the Indian side to England in 1932 he opened their innings at Lord's in their first-ever Test match, scoring 33 and 25, and played twice more against England, in India in 1933–34. His highest score in England was 164 not out against Middlesex in 1932 and in India 203 not out against Nawanagar in 1938. In the 1950s he became Pakistan's national coach. He lived to enjoy the Jubilee Test match between India and England in Bombay in February 1980.

WISDEN – 1982

THE INDIANS IN AUSTRALIA AND NEW ZEALAND, 1980-81,
by Dicky Rutnagur

To win the Third Test, at Melbourne, after being 182 runs behind on the first innings, was a notable achievement by Sunil Gavaskar's Indian side. But apart from that victory, which drew the series, they had a very moderate tour – in New Zealand as well as in Australia. New Zealand outgunned them in both one-day internationals, and for the first time in seven meetings, India lost a Test rubber (0–1) to New Zealand.

In Australia, India lost the opening Test, at Sydney, in three days, being overwhelmed by a vintage innings of 204 by Greg Chappell and the fast bowling of Lillee and Pascoe. Even though Patil played a memorable innings of 174, they were on the brink of defeat in the Second Test at Adelaide, and although India must be given credit for rising above the handicap of three injured bowlers to win the final Test at Melbourne, the surprisingly poor quality of the Australian batting in the second innings has to be taken into account...

Gavaskar's one Test innings of substance, the 70 at Melbourne, ended in a dreadful scene. Given out lbw to Lillee, Gavaskar indicated that he had edged the ball on to his pad, and was so enraged that he wanted to forfeit the match, ordering his partner, Chauhan, to walk off with him. The bewildered Chauhan followed him towards the dressing room, but the Indian manager, Wing-Commander Durrani, intervened before Chauhan actually left the playing arena. Such a bizarre incident not only brought controversy over the umpiring to a head but also revealed the stress which Gavaskar felt from his personal lack of performance as well as that of his team...

On the happier side was the fairytale Test debut of Ravi Shastri, a 19-year-old left-arm spinner from Bombay, who was pulled out of a Ranji Trophy match in Kanpur and despatched to reinforce the touring party. He arrived in Wellington on the night of the First Test, in which he took six wickets for 63 runs. Tall and gangling, Shastri, more alike in style to Durani than Bedi in that he pushed the ball through, took nine more wickets in the two following Tests. His calm, sensible batting lower in the order raised promise of his developing into a useful all-rounder, and his fielding too was an asset.

An article in this edition covered much ground that earlier editions had reported on fully, but the author made some interesting points.

A HALF-CENTURY OF TEST CRICKET – INDIA: 1932–1982,
by Michael Melford

The influence of different types of pitch on Anglo-India series needs to be discussed. In the wetter type of English summer, Indian touring teams have been at a hopeless disadvantage. They did strike one of the best English summers this century in 1959 – but with one of their weakest sides. On other tours they have often been undone by fast bowlers and the lifting ball; even by spin because the English turning pitch differs from its Indian counterpart and anyhow is no help to batsmen or bowlers who are short of confidence. Thus it is that, after 50 years and nine tours, The Oval Test of 1971 is the only one of 29 Tests in England which India have won.

By contrast, they began to produce pitches at home which showed off their spin bowling, quick-footed batting and agile close fielding to full advantage. In a way it was a reaction to the plumb and lifeless pitches on which two sides could play for a week without either winning or losing. In another sense it was a defensive measure to meet the chronic shortage of Indian fast bowlers, a matter largely of physique and climate which became the more acute when the northern provinces were detached to form Pakistan...

Although India were swamped 5–0 in England in 1959, a series in India remained an entirely different operation. At this time India may have lacked strokeplaying batsmen, fast bowlers and positive captaincy, but these were ailments which could be covered up or mended at home, as they soon were when the young Nawab of Pataudi took over. When, in 1961–62, Ted Dexter led the strongest MCC side to visit India so far, England lost the last two Tests, and the series 2–0.

By now huge crowds were watching cricket in India. Within a few years they were to become bigger still, as concrete (and non-inflammable) stadia were built to meet demand. Also to meet demand, MCC sent another team, under M. J. K. Smith, only two years later in 1963–64 for a short tour into which five marvellously dull drawn Test matches were crammed. To the crowds the lack of action seemed to be no great disappointment. A Test match was still a rare and wonderful occasion, an opportunity for cheerful vandalism, a good-humoured event despite the lifeless mud pitches, the almost unvaried spin bowling, the leisurely tempo and the shortage of strokes...

My own recollection of that tour is of hour after hour of the forward defensive stroke, of cricket as placid and predictable as the smoke going straight up from the chimneys beside the Ganges. Nevertheless, it had its macabre humour, as when England were so short of players with stable stomachs that two of the fit ones,

Bolus and Barrington, set themselves to stay at the wicket at all costs and gave the left-arm spinner, Nadkarni, the distinction of bowling 131 successive balls without conceding a run. I seem to remember that one of the less serious injuries was sustained by an England bowler who, having beaten the bat for the first time in hours, threw his arms in the air in excitement and strained his back.

OBITUARIES

Amir Elahi, who died on December 28, 1980, aged 72, could lay claim to two unusual distinctions: he was one of only 12 cricketers to have played for two different countries and one of the 20 oldest cricketers to have played in a Test match. He appeared once for India, against Australia at Sydney in 1947, and five times for Pakistan, all in India in 1952–53. In his last Test match, at Calcutta, he was 44.

Having begun life as a medium-paced bowler, he turned to leg-breaks and googlies, and it was in this latter role that he was best known. On his first tour, to England in 1936, he met with limited success (17 wickets at 42.94). In Australia, too, in 1947–48, he found wickets hard to come by (eight at 65.87), as, indeed, he did when, after partition, he went with Pakistan to India (thirteen at 38.76). In the Ranji Trophy, however, he was a prolific wicket-taker (193 wickets, 24.72), mostly for Baroda, whom he helped to win the competition in 1946–47, shortly before becoming a Pakistan citizen. His finest hour with the bat (he was most at home at No. 11) was when he shared a last-wicket partnership of 104 (a Test rarity) with Zulfiqar Ahmed for Pakistan against India at Madras. Amir Elahi's share was a surprising 47. To meet him and talk about his cricketing days was always a pleasure.

Palia, Phiroz Edulji, who died in Bangalore on September 9, 1981, aged 71, played twice for India, each time at Lord's, in 1932 and 1936. Having pulled a hamstring in the field in the 1932 match, he batted at No. 11 in the second innings in a vain attempt to save the match for India. Palia was a left-hand batsman, wristy and attractive, and a useful bowler of the orthodox slow left-arm type. More was expected of him in England, certainly as a batsman, than he achieved. Despite batting high in the order, in 37 first-class innings his top score was 63 against Oxford University in 1936. His highest first-class score, 216, was in the Ranji Trophy for United Provinces against Maharashtra in 1939–40. After his retirement he kept in touch with the game as a Test selector and radio commentator.

WISDEN – 1983

ENGLAND IN INDIA AND SRI LANKA, 1981–82,
by John Thicknesse

The first sentiment to be expressed about England's tour of India is relief that Mrs Gandhi, India's Prime Minister, allowed it to take place. Because of the presence among Fletcher's 16 players of Boycott and Cook, who had both been in South Africa in the recent past, the tour was in doubt until days before the party left London's Heathrow airport. The Cricket boards of both countries feared that cancellation might lead to a black–white split in cricket, and in the fortnight following an announcement by the Indian government that Boycott and Cook were unacceptable, there was ceaseless activity in London, Delhi and Bombay to ward off that disaster. Boycott's absence in Hong Kong on holiday added to the difficulties, but after a week of suspense he joined Cook in declaring his repugnance to apartheid, and Mrs Gandhi was placated...

For the huge crowds who came to watch in India, the disappointment of the series was that, after losing the First Test on a poor pitch in Bombay, England lacked the penetration to harry a confident Indian side who, with batting down to No. 10, were content to hold on to their lead. Of the last five Tests, the only one that looked like reaching a result was that in Calcutta, where England's declaration left them six hours to bowl India out on a pitch on which the ball was keeping low and turning. But with 70 minutes lost to smog on the final morning, and Gavaskar once again immovable, that game also petered out.

INDIA IN ENGLAND 1982, by John Woodcock

It hardly seemed satisfactory that a tour by England to India should be followed almost immediately with one by India to England. But that is as it was, and it gave England the chance to avenge their defeat, suffered on the subcontinent, a few months earlier. Of the three Test matches, England won the first and drew the last two. Although poorly attended, the series contained some good and interesting cricket, to which Sunil Gavaskar's Indian side, the tenth to visit England in an official capacity, made a generous contribution.

Of the 16 players, three, Ghulam Parkar, Suru Nayak and Randhir Singh, arrived uncapped. Ashok Malhotra and Pranab Roy had each played in only two Test matches. The others were widely experienced. Besides Gavaskar himself, the world's most prolific opening batsman, they included a glorious all-round cricketer in Kapil Dev, whose jousts with Botham were among the features of the summer, two seasoned batsmen of high quality in Dilip Vengsarkar and Gundappa Viswanath (Gavaskar's brother-in-law), a top-class wicketkeeper in Syed Kirmani, and a successfully teasing orthodox left-arm spinner in Dilip Doshi. That they managed to win only one of their 12 first-class matches was because of their bowling, which was very short of depth. Madan Lal, at medium pace, occasionally moved the ball about effectively, and Ravi Shastri, only 19, showed promise as a tall spinner (orthodox left-arm).

CRICKETERS OF THE YEAR 1983

KAPIL DEV, by Scyld Berry

In an era of great all-rounders (Ian Botham, Imran Khan, Richard Hadlee were his rivals), Kapil Dev was by no means out of place. But having been to both Chandigarh and Welwyn Garden City, I struggle to find any similarity between the two, a fact that says nothing but good about Chandigarh.

India's tour of England [in 1982] made a quiet start to the summer. But the Test series was lent excitement by the rivalry between Ian Botham and an Indian who, by his exuberant performances, challenged the title unofficially held by Botham of being the finest contemporary all-rounder. During the series against England, Kapil Dev again proved himself a fine fast-medium bowler, but it was his batting which secured for him the player of the series award. His scores were 41, 89, 65 and 97; and every time he went in, after the first of those innings, he seemed to be on course for the fastest Test century ever made in terms of deliveries received.

Only in recent decades have Test centuries been regularly recorded in terms of deliveries as well as minutes, and it was considered that the one by Roy Fredericks off 71 balls at Perth in 1975–76 was the fastest until research discovered that Jack Gregory's at Johannesburg in 1921–22 came from four balls fewer. Kapil Dev, in his second innings of the Lord's Test, hit 89 off 55 balls. Although he fell short of the record then, it would be surprising if he does not break it on some occasion in his career, so quick is his eye, so clean his hitting, so laughing and cavalier his manner.

This amateurish, or at least old-fashioned, approach is readily comprehensible if seen against his background. Kapil Dev Nikhanj was born in Chandigarh, a model Welwyn Garden-type city in the northern foothills of India, which serves as the capital of Punjab and of Haryana, being on the border of the two states. Kapil Dev, a Punjabi, plays for Haryana. His official date of birth is given as January 6, 1959, although in that part of India the year of birth is not always registered at the time and can be altered to suit convenience. As it stands, however, Kapil Dev goes into history as the youngest man to have made 1,000 Test runs and taken 100 Test wickets.

His parents came from what is now Pakistan. They emigrated at Partition from near Rawalpindi – if they had not, Kapil Dev might have been opening the bowling for Pakistan with Imran Khan. After a while of wandering, Kapil Dev's father settled in Chandigarh to become a building and timber contractor in the new city. The family business remains prosperous: in other words Kapil Dev does not play cricket for a living but for pleasure...

By his own admission, India's position in their first innings at Lord's was the most awkward he faced: hounded by Bob Willis and Botham, India were 45 for five wickets. Kapil Dev had to be circumspect, but clearly the chafing shackles were going to be thrown off at the next opportunity. That came on the fourth evening,

after Dilip Vengsarkar had worn down England's bowling but India were still in arrears in the follow-on. Kapil Dev then hit 89 out of the 117 runs which India added in 15 overs. Test cricket can have seldom seen such exuberance. His runs might have come off even fewer than 55 balls if Dilip Doshi had not been the last man in and Kapil Dev forced to neglect some runs in order to keep the strike. When he finished off his evening's work by taking England's first three wickets in four overs, he had enjoyed as glorious a session of play as any immortal of the game.

In the Second Test at Old Trafford, Kapil Dev reached his 50 off 33 balls, well on course again for breaking the record. India, once again, were under pressure to avert the follow-on: but after Kapil had emerged at 173 for six wickets, the remaining 53 runs required were scored in even time. Towards the end of his innings of 65 he slowed down, which does not suit him or his special talent. For Kapil Dev as a batsman has the almost unique ability to launch himself straight into fourth gear, with over-drive his variation.

His cleanness of hitting and precision of timing were repeated at The Oval. Again India faced the follow-on: when Kapil Dev entered their last five wickets still had to make 147. He promptly hit, between interruptions, 97 off 92 balls in 102 minutes. When Botham offered the bait of a slower ball, the uncomplicated Kapil put it straight into the distant Vauxhall Stand. During what was otherwise a promising first term of captaincy by Willis, Kapil Dev's partnership of 130 in 27 overs with Syed Kirmani threw England into some disorder.

Before returning to Northamptonshire after the series, Kapil Dev enjoyed a mid-season working holiday in the United States, which may again exemplify his attitude to the game. When back with his county the carefree hitting continued with two whirlwind hundreds in the Championship, one on an under-prepared pitch at Eastbourne. His 50 would arrive in even time, his century – if it came – in about two hours. Dennis Brookes said he had seen no one at Northampton with such a gift for hitting and timing since Colin Milburn.

Less to Northamptonshire's delight, the amateur attitude – playing for the pleasure of it – has manifested itself in Kapil Dev's bowling as well. Understandably, as India's one quick bowler, he has been worked to the full during an intensive Test programme. It was the opportunity to take the new ball in 25 Test matches in the space of only one year and 110 days which helped him to his world record of performing the Test double in the shortest-ever time. (Botham reached his 1,000 Test runs and 100 wickets in longer time but four fewer Tests.) The last thing he needs in India's off-season is the grind of daily bowling.

As he remains the only strike bowler on India's horizon, Kapil Dev may soon decide to devote his energies to India's cause to the exclusion of the county game. But even if he is lost to the English scene, he will not be forgotten after his all-round displays of rubbery exuberance, which were enough to evoke the memory of Learie Constantine.

CHAPTER 5

THE ONE-DAY GAME TAKES CENTRE STAGE: 1983–2000

Until the 1983 World Cup, India had been perpetual also-rans in the one-day game. Sunil Gavaskar's notorious 36 in 60 overs in the 1975 World Cup was what people remembered of India's limited-overs efforts, rather than the – rather occasional – victories against other teams in one-day internationals. But the 1983 World Cup changed all that. As the editor of Wisden *wrote in his notes, 'They brought warmth and excitement in the place of dampness and depression.' India had not even reached the semi-finals before 1983, and now they won the title. This sparked a massive interest in the limited-overs format in India, and began what seems today like a terminal decline in interest in Test cricket on the subcontinent.*

WISDEN – 1984

India had a very busy and largely unproductive winter in 1982–83, being what most people considered was a poor preparation for the World Cup.

THE INDIANS IN PAKISTAN, 1982–83, by Qamar Ahmed

In a one-sided series Pakistan beat India by three Tests to none, their victories at Karachi, Hyderabad and Faisalabad all being achieved by large margins. They also won the series of one-day internationals. Imran Khan's team plundered the mild Indian attack almost to their hearts' content, breaking record after record as the season progressed. The consistency and scoring feats of Zaheer Abbas, Mudassar Nazar, Javed Miandad, and to a slightly lesser extent Mohsin Khan, destroyed the Indian bowlers...

India's poor showing was due mainly to patchy batting and weak fielding. Many catches were dropped at crucial moments. In addition, except for Kapil Dev, none of their bowlers posed any real threat to the home batsmen. Madan Lal had to return to India because of a badly bruised heel. India relied principally on their three left-arm spinners, of whom Dilip Doshi, the most experienced of them, did not show his best form after the first Test. Ravi Shastri, another of them, had injury problems, and the turbaned Maninder Singh did not enjoy the best of luck.

An umpiring controversy in the middle of the six-Test series, when the manager of the Indian team, the Maharajah of Baroda, was critical of local standards, blew over with the release of a statement by Sunil Gavaskar, the Indian captain, expressing his confidence in the umpires of Pakistan. Although, yet again, politically motivated rioting marred the last Test in Karachi, the series was played, on the whole, in a cordial atmosphere.

Pakistan v India
Sixth Test, at Karachi, January 30, 31, February 1, 3, 4, 1983

Crowd demonstrations, thought to have been prompted by students protesting against arrests made at a university campus brawl, and high scores made this a typical Karachi Test. The fourth day's play had to be abandoned after lunch, because of the rioting. In completing his sixth Test century Mudassar passed 2,000 runs for Pakistan, and Wasim Bari became only the fourth wicketkeeper to claim 200 Test victims. For India Amarnath made his fifth Test hundred and his third of the series, reached in 238 minutes in the last hour of the last day. He and Kirmani also reached 2,000 Test runs. Shastri's maiden century for India, which he scored as a stop-gap opener, was an outstanding achievement.

India 393 for eight wickets declared (R. J. Shastri 128, D. B. Vengsarkar 89) and **224 for two wickets** (M. Amarnath 103 not out, S. M. Gavaskar 67). **Pakistan 420 for six wickets declared** (Mudassar Nazar 152, Mohsin Khan 91). Match drawn.

INDIA IN WEST INDIES, 1982–83, by Tony Cozier

For a combination of reasons, India's fifth Test series in the West Indies fell disappointingly short of the hard-fought drama of the previous two, in 1971 and 1976. Rain, which affected every Test in varying degrees, made the third meaningless. West Indies won two of the other four and had the better of the two drawn matches. At no stage of any match were India in a position to win, although the West Indian bowling often lacked the penetration which has become its hallmark.

India arrived direct from a trying series in Pakistan, in which they had been badly beaten. The consequence of their defeat was the replacement of their long-standing captain, Sunil Gavaskar, by the dynamic all-rounder, Kapil Dev, besides a number of other critical team changes, notably the exclusion of Gundappa Viswanath, after 89 Tests, and the left-arm spinner Dilip Doshi.

The new formula made little difference...

THE SRI LANKANS IN INDIA, 1982–83, by P. N. Sundaresan

Sri Lanka have never won a Test in India. Their first tour there set the trend.

Sri Lanka lost all three one-day internationals during their first official tour of India, in September 1982. However, they drew the one Test match, in Madras, and won a one-day, limited-overs match against Delhi, the Ranji Trophy champions...

It was Krishnamachari Srikkanth who upset Sri Lanka's plans in the one-day internationals, his personal scoring-rate of 1.3 runs a ball (244 runs off 195 balls) having a telling effect.

THE PRUDENTIAL WORLD CUP, 1983

The third World Cup, the last to be sponsored by the Prudential Assurance Company, began with two fine surprises, when India beat West Indies and Zimbabwe beat Australia in the opening round of matches, and ended with the greatest surprise of all, when India beat West Indies again, this time in the final at Lord's. None of the eight sides had to make do without a victory...

Of the 27 matches played, only three were not begun and finished in a day. Many were played in warm sunshine, and throughout the competition, from June 9 to 25, interest ran high. After losing their opening match, West Indies carried all before them until failing, for the first time, to win the final. Australia had a disappointing fortnight, and with Imran Khan unfit to bowl for them, Pakistan were a shadow of the side which had trounced India and Australia in the previous winter...

India's unexpected success (they were quoted at 66 to 1 before the competition began) came under a young and relatively new captain (Kapil Dev) and owed much to the presence in their side of three all-rounders (Kapil Dev, Roger Binny and Mohinder Amarnath) who, at critical moments, found enough in the conditions to help form an effective attack. Who would ever have thought before a ball was bowled that the leading wicket-takers in the competition would be the Sri Lankan De Mel and Binny, with his gentle medium-pace?

Each side received 60 overs. No bowler was allowed more than 12 overs per innings and, to prevent negative bowling, the umpires applied a stricter interpretation than in first-class cricket in regard to wides and bumpers.

The total amount of the Prudential Assurance Company's sponsorship was £500,000, and the gate receipts came to £1,195,712. The aggregate attendance was 232,081, compared with 160,000 in 1975 and 132,000 in 1979. The surplus, distributed to full and associate members of the International Cricket Conference, was in excess of £1,000,000, this being over and above the prior payments of £53,900 to each of the seven full members and one of £30,200 to Zimbabwe.

In addition to the trophy and silver-gilt medals for each player, India received £20,000 for their victory. As runners-up West Indies won £8,000. The losing semi-finalists, England and Pakistan, each won £4,000. There were also awards of £1,000 to the group winners, plus Man of the Match awards (£200 for the group matches, £400 for the semi-finals and £600 for the final).

India v Zimbabwe
at Tunbridge Wells, June 18, 1983

A remarkable match contained one of the most spectacular innings played in this form of cricket. India, who had chosen to bat on a pitch from which the ball moved a lot, were 9-4 – soon to be 17-5 – when their captain, Kapil Dev, came in. No one could foresee then that a week later India would be winning the whole tournament; indeed, qualification for the semi-final was in grave doubt. With Binny and Madan Lal, Kapil Dev took the score to 140-8 and by then was in full flow. Kirmani provided sensible support in an unbroken ninth-wicket stand of 126 in 16 overs while Kapil Dev, with six sixes and 16 fours in all, reached 175, beating the previous highest for the tournament, Glenn Turner's 170 for New Zealand against East Africa at Edgbaston in 1975. The match was still not firmly in India's hands, for Curran, who with Rawson had been responsible for India's early disasters, played a dashing innings of 73, and it was not until he was ninth out at 230 in the 56th over that India were safe.

Man of the Match: Kapil Dev. India won by 31 runs.

World Cup Final: India v West Indies
at Lord's, June 25, 1983, by Wilfred Wooller

India defeated on merit the firm favourites, winning a low-scoring match by 43 runs. It was an absorbing game of increasing drama and finally of much emotion. The result, as surprising as, on the day, it was convincing, had much to do with the mental pressures of containment in limited-overs cricket.

Amarnath was named Man of the Match by Mike Brearley for a stabilising innings of 26 against hostile fast bowling after the early loss of Gavaskar, followed by his taking three late West Indian wickets, Dujon's being especially important. Dujon and Marshall had lifted West Indies, needing 184 to win, from 76-6 to 119-6, a recovery based on the calm application of sound batting principles and one which was threatening to achieve after all the result which everyone had expected.

Lord's, groomed like a high-born lady, bathed in sunshine and packed to capacity, was at its best when Lloyd won the toss and invited India to bat: a distinct advantage, it seemed, for his battery of fast bowlers. The Lord's wicket often

INDIA

S. M Gavaskar c Dujon b Roberts	2
K. Srikkanth lbw b Marshall	38
M. Amarnath b Holding	26
Yashpal Sharma c sub b Gomes	11
S. M. Patil c Gomes b Garner	27
*N. Kapil Dev c Holding b Gomes	15
K. B. J. Azad c Garner b Roberts	0
R. M. H. Binny c Garner b Roberts	2
S. Madan Lal b Marshall	17
†S. M. H. Kirmani b Holding	14
B. S. Sandhu not out	11
Extras (b 5, l-b 5, w 9, n-b 1)	20

1-2 2-59 3-90 4-92 5-110   **183**
6-111 7-130 8-153 9-161 10-183

Roberts 10–3–32–3; Garner 12–4–24–1; Marshall 11–1–24–2; Holding 9.4–2–26–2; Gomes 11–1–49–2; Richards 1–0–8–0

WEST INDIES

C. G. Greenidge b Sandhu	1
D. L. Hayes c Binny b Madan Lal	13
I. V. A. Richards c Kapil Dev b Madan Lal	33
*C. H. Lloyd c Kapil Dev b Binny	8
H. A. Gomes c Gavaskar b Madan Lal	5
S. F. A. F. Bacchus c Kirmani b Sandhu	8
†P. L. J. Dujon b Amarnath	25
M. D. Marshall c Gavaskar b Amarnath	18
A. M. E. Roberts lbw Kapil Dev	4
J. Garner not out	5
M. A. Holding lbw Amarnath	6
Extras (l-b 4, w 10)	14

1-5 2-50 3-57 4-66 5-66 6-76   **140**
7-119 8-124 9-126 10-140

Kapil Dev 11–4–21–1; Sandhu 9–1–32–2; Madan Lal 12–2–31–3; Binny 10–1–23–1; Amarnath 7–0–12–3; Azad 3–0–7–0

India won by 43 runs.

inclines to extravagant morning life. Now it never lost this capacity to allow movement off the seam, sufficient to be of much significance later in the day for the medium-paced attack of Madan Lal and Sandhu, who removed the cream of the West Indian batting, and for the seemingly inoffensive Binny, who accounted for the dangerous Lloyd.

There was an explosive start to the match, Garner hurling the ball down, chest-high on the line of the off-stump. Roberts, fast but flatter, had Gavaskar caught at the wicket in his third over. To score off such an attack was a problem, but Srikkanth showed how: he hooked Roberts for 4, pulled him for 6 and square drove him to the Tavern boundary like a pistol shot. Yashpal, released from the constraints of speed, drove the slow spin of Gomes high and wide to the off, but straight to cover point. At lunch India were 100-4. Afterwards Kapil Dev perished at deep long-on and Patil lost concentration. Madan Lal, Kirmani and Sandhu added 31 late runs, but India's total of 183 seemed many too few.

West Indies started badly. Greenidge padded up to the deceptive Sandhu and was bowled. Richards, however, swept the total swiftly and effortlessly to 50. Then, when 33, he mistimed a hook and Kapil Dev took a fine catch over his shoulder, running back towards the mid-wicket boundary. Madan Lal followed with two more quick wickets, those of Haynes and Gomes. All three fell for six runs in 19 balls. Lloyd drove Binny to mid-off and immediately after tea Bacchus was caught at the wicket. It remained for Amarnath to break the partnership between Dujon and Marshall which, just in time, he did. India were an entertaining and well-drilled team, learning and improving as they progressed towards the final.

The attendance was 24,609, including members.

NOTES BY THE EDITOR, by John Woodcock

The World Cup was a great success and India's victory a splendid surprise. They brought warmth and excitement in the place of dampness and depression. In the early years of limited-overs cricket no one, themselves included, took India seriously. Their strength lay much more in waging battles of attrition.

Now, on pitches which had had no time to quicken up after all the rain, their lack of fast bowling was not the hindrance it might have been. Three of their batsmen could also bowl, which was vital for the way it shortened their tail. When, after beating West Indies in the final at Lord's, they flew home, it was to be fêted through the length and breadth of India. Not six months later they were being pilloried for having capitulated to the same West Indian side. Indian crowds, like the game itself, can be unmercifully fickle.

CRICKETERS OF THE YEAR 1984

M. AMARNATH, by Scyld Berry

A surprisingly downbeat evaluation of Lala Amarnath's son ends by wondering whether he has feet of clay – hardly the qualification for a Cricketer of the Year.

On May 3, 1983, Mohinder Amarnath reached his 1,000 Test runs for the year. No one has achieved that target by so early a date, and while it has to be admitted that he was enabled to do this feat by playing a plethora of Test cricket, it should be acknowledged that he could hardly have triumphed in more adverse circumstances than on Indian tours of Pakistan and the West Indies. Moreover, during the 1982–83 season Amarnath hit more runs – 2,355 at an average of 81 – than anyone else has ever done in a first-class season outside England. Still on the crest of a wave, he followed up by winning Man of the Match awards in the World Cup semi-final against England and in the final against West Indies, when India achieved one of the game's most unexpected victories.

Yet Amarnath, and India, merely had walk-on parts during the first two World Cup tournaments. And in England he had an even lower profile than elsewhere, since he had played only two Test matches there, both in 1979 and without distinction. So the half-year or so of personal success that the Indian enjoyed, as triumphant as any cricketer can have known, came as a surprise to most followers of the game in England.

Mohinder Amarnath Bhardwaj, or Jimmy as he prefers to be known, was born in Patiala on September 24, 1950. His father, Lala Amarnath, who scored India's first Test century, was employed in the retinue of the sports-loving Maharajah of Patiala to encourage the development of cricket within his north Indian state.

From the start Lala was an influence upon his three sons, all of whom played first-class cricket (the oldest of them, Surinder, going on to represent India as a left-handed batsman). The father, renowned as something of a martinet, taught Mohinder to love cricket to the exclusion of all other games. Another paternal instruction was that any short ball was there to be hooked.

Although Mohinder made his Test debut as a medium-pace in-swing bowler (like his father) against Australia in 1969, batting soon became his chief concern and the hook his forte. The stroke helped him to his first major success in Australia in 1977–78 during the World Series controversy, and again when India toured Pakistan and the Caribbean last winter. But the hook has been the reason behind not only his ups but his downs.

Early in 1979, in a Test match against Australia in Bombay, Amarnath emerged in a solar topee (again in imitation of his father), tried to hook Rodney Hogg and fell on his wicket. Later that year, during India's tour of England, he was hit on the head half a dozen times and kept refusing to wear a helmet. The culmination came

when he failed to pick up a ball from Richard Hadlee out of a dark background at Trent Bridge: he missed the ball and it fractured his skull. It was several months before Amarnath could play again; and then he found that the injury had damaged his eyesight. So as a temporary measure he wore spectacles, and as a permanent one he adopted an open-chested, crouched stance after the style of Jim Parks or the late Ken Barrington. But his courage had in no way been impaired…

Amarnath… felt a renewed determination to prove himself at international level. He duly did so during India's visit to Pakistan in 1982–83. While Imran Khan harassed his colleagues, taking 40 wickets in the six-match series for fewer than 14 runs each, Amarnath scored three centuries and three fifties in his ten innings.

In the West Indies immediately afterwards he carried on against Roberts, Marshall, Holding and Garner from where he had left off against Imran and Sarfraz. He was selected as the player of the series on either side after hitting 598 runs in his nine innings. The hook shot stood him in good stead while his team-mates tried vainly to contend with the imitation of Bodyline which Malcolm Marshall delivered from round the wicket…

This purple patch continued into the World Cup, where Amarnath scored 237 runs in eight innings (twice run out), and was an effective reserve seamer even though his run-up had dwindled to an amble. Since the competition followed a month after India's series in the Caribbean, he was by then well attuned to West Indian pace. Indeed this familiarity with the West Indies bowling is one reason that Amarnath gives for India's winning of the cup. The presence of good fielders and strokemakers, not all that common in Indian sides of the past, was another factor, along with the slow pitches that prevailed.

His bowling at Old Trafford, where the pitch had no grass and was very uneven was as important as his 46 (run out) when India chased a modest England total. In the final he stood firm while the West Indian bowling was at its most hostile and Srikkanth went for his ebullient shots at the other end. Together they shared the highest partnership of the match. Finally his amiable, almost apologetic medium pace finished off three of the last four wickets for 12 runs.

However, and sadly, the man whom Imran Khan amongst others called the best player of fast bowling in contemporary cricket was brought down to earth during the latter half of the year. In the home series against Pakistan and in the first two Tests against West Indies, he was unable to reach double figures. Whether the reason was delayed shellshock or related to that inexplicable phenomenon known as form, the Indian god was found to have feet of clay.

OBITUARY

Manjrekar, Vijay Laxman, who died in Madras, where he had gone for a sportsmen's gathering, on October 18, 1983, aged 52, was a conspicuously good player of fast bowling in an era when India had few of them. Having played in the first of his 55 Tests in 1951–52, against England at Calcutta, he soon showed his quality by making 133 in his first Test in England (at Headingley) in June, 1952, when only 20. Coming in at 42 for three on the first morning, with Trueman and Bedser on the warpath (and Laker to follow), he and his captain, Hazare, rescued India's innings with a fourth-wicket partnership of 222, which still stands as a record between the two countries.

. If, as the years passed, problems of weight slowed him down, he had sufficiently nimble footwork and enough natural ability always to be a dangerous opponent and often a joy to watch. Like many of the best Indian batsmen, he was small and a fine cutter and hooker...

He made seven Test centuries, the highest his 189 against England at Delhi in 1961–62 and the last of them in his final Test innings, against New Zealand at Madras in February 1965... An occasional off-spinner, a serviceable wicketkeeper and in his early days a fine cover fielder, he played at different times for no fewer than six sides in the Ranji Trophy – Bombay, Bengal, Andhra, Uttar Pradesh, Rajasthan and Maharashtra. In Test matches he scored 3,208 runs (average 39.12), took one wicket, held 19 catches and made two stumpings.

WISDEN – 1985

CRICKET IN INDIA 1983–84, by P. N. Sundaresan

The 1983–84 season marked the 50th year of the Ranji Trophy championship, the country's premier competition. India's triumph in the 1983 Prudential Cup would have served as an ideal background to the 'golden jubilee' of the championship, but tours by Pakistan and West Indies consumed a major portion of the playing days and rather pushed it into the background. Besides this, India's performances against the touring teams, particularly West Indies, resulted in sufficient loss of prestige for the Indian Cricket Board to set up a panel of experts, which included cricketers of the stature of P. R. Umrigar and M. A. K. Pataudi, to evaluate the causes of this. In their findings the panel stressed that such domestic fixtures as the Ranji Trophy championship should be disturbed as little as possible when foreign teams visited the country. The chairman of the committee, the Maharajah of Baroda, a former board president, referred to this as 'a dangerous trend'.

Bombay regained the Ranji Trophy after a lapse of two seasons, defeating Delhi in the final on first innings... With Dilip Vengsarkar making a brilliant 123 and skipper Sunil Gavaskar, in his new role as a middle-order batsman, guiding the innings in masterly fashion, Bombay amassed 625. Gavaskar's unbeaten 206 (532 minutes, with 25 fours) was the climax to a season in which he overhauled two Test records – Sir Donald Bradman's 29 centuries and Geoffrey Boycott's aggregate of 8,114 runs.

The effect of the World Cup win, as well as local political and economic decisions, meant that one-day internationals were beginning to become the preferred diet of Indian cricket fans.

THE PAKISTANIS IN INDIA, 1983–84, by Dicky Rutnagur

This tour, including three Test matches and two one-day internationals, initiated what was intended as an annual exchange of short visits between the two neighbouring countries. However, the maiden venture received a disappointingly lukewarm response.

Dogged by bad weather, the three Tests were all drawn. India won both one-day internationals, which, unlike the Tests, were well patronised. Another limited-overs match, played for the Prime Minister's Fund under floodlights at an athletics stadium in New Delhi, built for the previous year's Asian Games, was a sell-out and nearly 100,000 spectators still occupied the vast terraces when the match, interrupted by an electrical fault, finished well after midnight.

Only the last Test, played at Nagpur, drew a full house every day. The First Test, at Bangalore, a city with rich cricketing traditions, started before a crowd of only 15,000, which, by Indian standards, was very few. There was little more support for the Second Test although Jullundur was staging a Test match for the first time. There were various, unconnected reasons for low attendances, the one common factor being the adverse weather. This was not an unforeseen problem, September and early October being a time of year when the monsoons are still active. In Bangalore, the sale of tickets was depressed by the state government withdrawing the exemption of entertainment tax on sporting events. At Jullundur, many would-be spectators were kept away by the political turmoil and violence that was prevalent in the region at the time. A heavy police presence and irksome security measures did not create the ideal atmosphere for a Test match.

THE WEST INDIANS IN INDIA, 1983–84, by Dicky Rutnagur

West Indies went through an arduous itinerary with little challenge to their authority. They won the six-Test series 3–0, which was as big a margin as any previous West Indian side had achieved in India, and made a clean sweep of the five one-day internationals, thus avenging their two shock defeats by India only a few months earlier in the Prudential World Cup in England...

By the end of the series, India had played 29 consecutive Tests without a victory, their longest barren stretch ever. Although West Indies were clearly the superior side, India's efforts suffered from poor planning and rigid selecting. Another principal reason for the disparity between the two sides was the total eclipse of Mohinder Amarnath, who had been India's batting mainstay during the previous winter. In five Tests in 1983–84, three against West Indies, he scored 12 runs. However, Sunil Gavaskar was back in his accustomed place as the leading India run-getter although his performances varied sharply. A third of the way through the series he told the selectors that he no longer relished going in first and it was when batting at No. 4 that he made 236 not out in the final Test, his 30th three-figure innings in Test cricket, which took him past Sir Donald Bradman's record...

If India's batting was undependable, their bowling was hopelessly inadequate, even in helpful conditions. Only Kapil Dev, who took a record 29 wickets for India against West Indies, matched up to the standards of Test cricket... Attendances at the Test matches were good, though only the fifth in Calcutta drew capacity crowds each day. Improved television coverage was thought to have affected the gates, but it proved less of a counter-attraction when it came to the one-day internationals. India's World Cup success could, it seemed, have altered the tastes of the cricket-watching public.

OBITUARIES

Banerjee, Jitan N., who died on January 18, 1984, aged 78, was the first Indian cricketer to captain a Bengal team, though it was under T. C. Longfield that he played for them when they won the Ranji Trophy in 1938–39. He was a right-arm medium-paced bowler with good control.

Rangnekar, Khandu Moneshwar, who died in Bombay on October 11, 1984, aged 67, was an attractive left-handed batsman who scored 2,548 runs for Maharashtra, Bombay and Holkar in the Ranji Trophy with an average of only just under 50. The largest of his first-class hundreds were 217 for Holkar against Hyderabad in 1950 and 202 for Bombay against Maharashtra in 1940. Chosen for India's tour of Australia in 1947–48, he played in three Test matches but had a disappointing tour. He had hit 102 and 17 not out on his first-class debut, for Maharashtra against Western India, at Poona in 1939–40, and in all first-class matches, from 1939 until 1964, he made 4,602 runs, average 41.45, including 15 centuries, and took 21 wickets at medium pace. A vice-president of the Indian Board of Control, he also became President of the Bombay Cricket Association.

WISDEN – 1986

The editor, John Woodcock, asked Sir Donald Bradman to write an article for Wisden. The great man responded with a piece in which his analysis of the one-day game was absolutely spot on.

WHITHER CRICKET NOW?
by Sir Donald Bradman

Undeniably the limited-over game caters for a plethora of fast and medium-pace bowlers who tend to bowl just short of a length. In general it discourages, in fact it almost tolls the knell of, the slow leg-spinner. But here again one must acclaim the marvellous leg-spin bowling of the young Indian, Sivaramakrishnan, who proved against the best batting in the world in Sydney and Melbourne early in 1985 that he could bowl his ten-overs stint, get wickets and still be economical. I don't doubt that O'Reilly, Grimmett, Benaud, Verity and others would have done the same. So perhaps, after all, the game is highlighting the fact that top-quality spinners can and will survive any challenge.

THE AUSTRALIANS IN INDIA, 1984–85, by Mike Coward

It took some time for the full relevance of Australia's brief goodwill tour of India, to play a series of one-day internationals, to become apparent. In the end, what started as a public relations exercise to help the Indian authorities celebrate the Golden Jubilee of the Ranji Trophy had a considerable impact on Australian cricket. Indeed, the shock waves are still being felt.

From a cricketing standpoint, it was a most successful undertaking. Australia won the five-match series 3–0 – the matches at Trivandrum and Jamshedpur were abandoned after rain – which was a considerable achievement after India's success in the World Cup the previous year. However, with the benefit of hindsight, Australia's first success in such a series on the subcontinent can be seen to have been the least significant happening.

While he had personal success, Kim Hughes lost support within his team and within a few weeks had resigned the Australian captaincy. The Indian excursion culminated with a gala dinner in Bombay, a priceless moment in the history of Indian cricket, and on their way home several of the Australian players had their first significant contact with representatives of the South African Cricket Union. Clandestine discussions with organisers of rebel teams took place in Singapore, leading in April 1985 to another major crisis for Australia's cricketing authorities.

The visit to India will also be remembered for the farce of Jamshedpur, where a one-day international could not be started as scheduled because the players' gear had been misplaced by officials. This was an incident which caused great embarrassment to the Board of Control for Cricket in India, who have been charged with the responsibility of organising, jointly with Pakistan, the 1987 World Cup.

India, who had reinstated Sunil Gavaskar as captain following Kapil Dev's sequence of failures after their 1983 World Cup triumph, did not seem as intensely committed to the one-day series as the Australians and were comprehensively beaten. Kepler Wessels was named man of the series. The Australians, who proved very popular, won prize money of 25,000 rupees (£2,000), most of which they donated to a home for crippled children in Ahmedabad.

ENGLAND IN INDIA (AND SRI LANKA), 1984–85
by John Thicknesse

England got more than they bargained for on their tour of India, and it was much to their credit that they became the first team from any country to win a series there coming from behind. Within a few hours of their arrival in New Delhi, in the early morning of Wednesday, October 31, they were awoken with the news of the assassination of Mrs Gandhi, the Indian Prime Minister. The memory of this was still fresh when, on the eve of the first Test, less than four weeks later, the British Deputy High Commissioner, Mr Percy Norris, a cricket-lover who had entertained the touring party at a reception in his home the previous evening, was shot dead as he was being driven to his Bombay office. Both outrages took place within a mile or two of where the team were staying.

In political and world terms, Mrs Gandhi's assassination of course had the greater impact, and for 72 hours India's capital city, while safe for those content to obey High Commission advice to stay close to their hotel, was an uneasy place to be. Happily, thanks to a generous gesture from the Sri Lankan Cricket Board, and the sympathetic co-operation of that country's president, who had flown to New Delhi for the funeral and invited the team to share his plane on the return journey, they found sanctuary in Colombo. There, for the next nine days, they found opportunities for play and practice which would have been impossible in India during the period of official mourning.

Mr Norris's murder affected them more personally, and with a Test due to start next day they felt under threat themselves. Had the decision been left to the team, or more particularly to a majority of the representatives of the British press, there is little doubt they would have taken the first available flight home. But as in Delhi, Tony Brown, the England manager, retained his sense of perspective, took advice from all relevant bodies, including the Foreign Office, and after consultation with the Test and County Cricket Board at Lord's, decided the best course was to stay and play…

Nevertheless, to safeguard the team, the itinerary was revised to postpone until near the end their appearance in the north of India, where because of the large Sikh population there was continuing unrest. Armed guards and escorts also became such a feature of the tour that before long they were hardly noticed. The fixture against North Zone, which was due to have been played at Jammu, was switched to the Wankhede Stadium, Bombay, between the First and Second Tests. With Kapil Dev resting from the North Zone team, it was predictable that spectators for that game would be numbered in hundreds; but the smallness of the crowds was generally a disappointing feature of the tour. Only for the one-day internationals, and an abortive Test in Calcutta, were Ground Full signs in use…

When the Kanpur Test was drawn, England had won a winter series for the first time for six years, and also, by 4–1, the one-day internationals. Creditably as they performed, however, they owed a lot to India's shortcomings. Sunil Gavaskar's lack of form – 140 runs compared to 500 against Fletcher's team – was probably the biggest factor in the turnabout: having got his 30th Test hundred behind him, against West Indies 12 months before, and so passed Sir Donald Bradman's record, he seemed short of motivation. Following a quarrel about division of prize money, there were signs, too, of disharmony within his team, of which a foolhardy stroke by Kapil Dev, helping England win the Delhi Test, and his subsequent dropping were symptomatic. The minimum 80-overs-a-day playing condition cut out the petty timewasting that had marred Fletcher's tour, while the emergence of a top-class umpire in V. K. Ramaswamy in the last two Tests was a relief to all concerned.

India v England
First Test, at Bombay, November 28, 29, December 1, 2, 3, 1984

A combination of bad batting in England's first innings and erratic umpiring by Swaroop Kishen in their second helped India end a sequence of 31 Tests without a win in a fast-moving and entertaining match. Their previous victory had also been at the Wankhede Stadium and at England's expense, just over three years earlier when Fletcher's team lost by 128 runs and protested about the umpiring.

India won by eight wickets.

BENSON AND HEDGES WORLD CHAMPIONSHIP OF CRICKET, 1984–85, by John Woodcock

Who remembers India's victory in this 'World Championship'?

To mark the 150th anniversary of the founding of the state of Victoria, the Victorian Cricket Association promoted what they called a World Championship of Cricket. The seven Test-playing countries entered representative sides, England and India arriving straight from their meeting in India, New Zealand and Pakistan from theirs in New Zealand, and Sri Lanka and West Indies already being in

Australia. At a cost of over £3 million, lights were installed on the Melbourne Cricket Ground: to see them switched on for the first time, during the opening match between England and Australia, there was a crowd of 82,494. Of the 13 matches, nine were in Melbourne and four in Sydney.

The tournament was won by India, who played excellent cricket throughout, winning all their five matches comfortably.

OBITUARIES

Malik, Sardar Hardit Singh, CIF, OBE, died at Delhi in October 1985, aged 90. Educated in England from the age of eight, he headed the batting averages at Eastbourne College and, going up to Balliol, attracted attention in the Freshmen's match in 1913 and in the Seniors' match in 1914 but did not have a game for the University. However, playing five matches for Sussex in August 1914, he scored 71 against Leicestershire and 49 against Middlesex and showed himself fully up to first-class form. He was in fact playing for Sussex in the Canterbury Week when war was declared on August 4, and at the time of his death he was the last survivor of the Week before 1919. After gallant service in the Royal Flying Corps during the war, in which he was shot down and wounded, he returned to Oxford for a year in 1920, played a second time in the Varsity golf match and had a trial in the cricket side without success. For Sussex, however, in the Horsham Week he played a brilliant innings of 106 against Leicestershire. He and Albert Reif put on 175 for the seventh wicket at a tremendous pace.

He played no county cricket after 1921, but his turbaned figure was for many years a familiar sight on English golf courses when the demands of a distinguished career in the Indian diplomatic service, where he was his country's first High Commissioner to Canada and later their Ambassador in Paris, allowed. A man of great charm, he was widely loved.

Merchant, Udaykant Madhavji, who died in Bombay on February 7, 1985, following a stroke, aged 68, was the younger brother of Vijay Merchant, by whom he was somewhat overshadowed. He was, however, a considerable batsman in his own right, as is shown by a career batting average in first-class cricket of 55.78.

Phadkar, Dattatreya Gajanan (Dattu), who died in Madras, following heart surgery, on March 17, 1985, aged 59, was a right-arm medium-paced bowler and a forcing batsman, and, as such, one of India's best all-rounders in the years after the Second World War. He played in 31 Tests between 1947 and 1959... After making 115 against England at Calcutta in 1951–52, a match in which he also took four wickets, he had the misfortune to make his one tour of England in 1952, a wet summer when Bedser was at his best and Trueman was an emerging force. Phadkar's best score in that series was 64 in India's second innings at Headingley, after their first four wickets had gone down for no run...

In the Ranji Trophy he played for Maharashtra, Bombay, Railways and Bengal, captaining Bombay for whom he had an especially successful season in 1948–49 with a batting average of 114… He scored 1,229 runs in Tests (average 32.34) and took 62 wickets (average 36.85). He served at different times as an Indian Test selector and was made an Honorary Life Member of MCC in 1969. Two months before he died he came to the press box at Eden Gardens, Calcutta, to inform the editor of *Wisden* that he had been born not on December 12, 1925, as in the *Almanack*, but two days earlier.

WISDEN – 1987

By the mid-1980s, the proliferation of one-day tournaments was getting out of hand. Apart from three ODIs against Sri Lanka on their tour there, India took part in the Benson and Hedges World Series Cup in Australia and against Australia and New Zealand (Australia beat India by two games to nil in the best-of-three final), the Sharjah Challenge Cup in Sharjah, against Pakistan and West Indies (West Indies won), The Austral-Asia Cup at Sharjah and featuring India, Australia, Pakistan and New Zealand (Pakistan beat India by one wicket off the final ball of the final). They did not, for some reason, take part in the Asia Cup in Sri Lanka.

THE INDIANS IN SRI LANKA, 1985–86, by R. Mohan

Lacking any kind of match practice for months after the 1984–85 home season had ended, and with a team hastily assembled in August, the Indians were under-prepared for their visit to Sri Lanka. They were also at a further disadvantage in conditions which the Sri Lankan seam attack was accustomed to exploiting. The home team had trained assiduously for months, and for this reason alone the fledgling Test nation deserved the historic and emotive maiden win it scored in the three-match series.

India's bowling was even more limited than usual, but what let the team down was the batting. This never attained the levels it had in the two limited-overs successes earlier in the year – first in Melbourne and then in Sharjah. The political background against which this series was organised, with the Indian government viewing it as a diplomatic initiative, was never likely to inspire confidence in cricketers touring the island in troubled times.

With only two three-day matches and a one-day international before the First Test, the Indians were hardly in a position to find their form before the three Tests were played off the reel. Indeed, with a bit of luck the Sri Lankans might well have won the First Test, rain robbing them of a session of play on the final day. However, the chance that had slipped away was encashed in the Second Test in which the Sri Lankans outbowled and outbatted the Indians. In the final hour, Rumesh Ratnayake dived to take a return catch from a defiant Kapil Dev to end the Indian innings and signal a fine triumph. Sri Lanka had seized the chance which India had given them by losing four first-innings wickets cheaply on the fourth morning, the home batsmen sparkling as they set up a target which the Indians could not be expected to attain. Only some unconvincing umpiring, about which the Indians unfortunately stated their misgivings in very clear terms, detracted from the merits of a splendid victory...

With Sunil Gavaskar opting to bat in the middle order, India were never given a solid start in the series. Krish Srikkanth made runs consistently for the first time in a revived Test career, but of the senior middle-order batsmen, Dilip Vengsarkar waged a near-lone battle for India...

The young Indian leg-spinner, Laxman Sivaramakrishnan, injured a finger on his bowling hand early on tour and never played the expected role of strike spinner.

INDIA'S FIRST TEST VICTORY AGAINST SRI LANKA

When Sri Lanka toured India in 1986–87, it was spin again that dominated as India recorded their first victory against the comparative newcomers in the sixth Test between the two countries.

Second Test, at Nagpur, December 27, 28, 30, 31, 1986

India recorded their first victory in Tests against Sri Lanka. The Sri Lankans, having chosen to bat first, were disconcerted to see the ball turning so soon on a pitch and were all out before tea on the first day. Ranatunga's brave, stroke-filled 59 from 77 deliveries provided their only relief as Yadav, with well-flighted off-spin, and Maninder Singh, slow left-arm, with good support from the close-in fieldsmen, exploited some nervous handling of spin bowling. Yadav's figures were his best in Tests.

India's consolidation of their position was held up by bad light on the first day and rain and a damp outfield on the second, when the Sri Lankans were quirky about resuming in such conditions. Amarnath, returning after injury in place of the injured Azharuddin, and Vengsarkar drove home India's advantage after the former had shared a century stand with Lamba, who opened instead of Gavaskar. Amarnath batted for six minutes under six hours and became, at 61, the fourth to score 4,000 runs for India. His hundred was his 11th in Tests, Vengsarkar's was his 13th. Gavaskar, recovered from the fever that had indisposed him, made possible a declaration at lunch on the fourth day with a versatile 74 off 79 balls, revealing his adaptability in a situation requiring quick runs. From one over from

Ranatunga he took 18 runs, including two successive sixes. For three hours in the afternoon, Maninder mesmerised the opposition to return career-best figures of 7-51 and finish with ten wickets in a Test for the first time. Only the left-handed Ratnayeke, batting for two hours 50 minutes, and Mendis, striking out boldly, provided any resistance.

Sri Lanka 204 (Ranatunga 59; Yadav 5-76, Maninder Singh 3-56) and **141** (Ratnayeke 54; Maninder Singh 7-51). **India 451 for six wickets declared** (Vengsarkar 153, Amarnath 131, Gavaskar 74, Lamba 53). India won by an innings and 106 runs.

THE INDIANS IN AUSTRALIA, 1985–86, by Dicky Rutnagur

The fifth Indian team to visit Australia for a Test series surpassed its predecessors only in that it finished the tour (excluding the World Series Cup matches) unbeaten. But its merit is more exactly reflected by the fact that, for the first time in three tours, India failed to win a Test match – and that at a time when Australia were reckoned to be at their weakest ever.

It was to the disadvantage of the Indians that the tour was very short, and this handicap was the more severely felt because rain interfered with every first-class match save the first, against South Australia, which the tourists won… That scope for practice was so limited was an encumbrance which the Indians brought on themselves by asking for an abbreviated itinerary, preferring to play earlier in a one-day competition in Sharjah. Just prior to this series, India had lost a rubber to Sri Lanka while Australia were beaten by New Zealand. In some eyes, therefore, the series was seen as a contest for international cricket's wooden spoon. And often the quality of both teams' play merited such a tag, Australia particularly plumbing low depths.

India's main batsmen scored abundantly. Sunil Gavaskar was the most prolific, registering two centuries and averaging 117.33 in the Tests. However, except for Krish Srikkanth and, once, Mohammad Azharuddin, the others did not fit their rate of scoring to the side's needs. In the last Test the first three batsmen all hits hundreds, but so slow were Gavaskar and Mohinder Amarnath over their record second-wicket stand that Kapil Dev had to promote himself to make up lost time.

Kapil Dev took eight wickets in the first innings of the opening Test. But otherwise the Indians' bowling strength was centered on their two finger spinners, Ravi Shastri and Shivlal Yadav, and one of the reasons for India's inability to convert their superiority into wins was the loss of form of their young leg-spinner, Laxman Sivaramakrishnan. Inadequate as it was, India's young bowling was made to appear even less effective by substandard fielding.

THE INDIANS IN ENGLAND, 1986, by Graeme Wright

As the Indians began their tour in cold, rainy weather in the West Country, two questions came to mind. Why were they filling the first half of a twin-tour summer when, having toured first in 1982, they could have followed New Zealand in 1986? And could their bowlers, on the evidence presented, bowl England out twice to win a Test match?

The answer to the first question was that it was the choice of India's Board of Control. With two tours of India scheduled for 1986–87, they wanted their international players fresh at the start of the season rather than returning from a tour of England. While sensible, this none the less condemned Kapil Dev's team to the colder, more unsettled half of the English season. And the wisdom of it was called into question when India went into the first one-day international, having lost a third of their playing time to the weather...

India won the first one-day international; they won the Texaco Trophy; and they beat England in the first Test, so winning their second Test in England and their first at headquarters. In doing so they answered, convincingly, the second question, and they did so again at Headingley, embarrassingly, dismissing England for 102 and 128...

In Dilip Vengsarkar, India had the batsman of the series. At Lord's and at Headingley, his hundreds were the platform from which India pushed for victory. In both innings of both Tests he top-scored for India, was rarely forced to play a false stroke, and made every movement elegant...

A winning team is usually a happy one, but it was greatly to India's advantage, and to the credit of the players concerned, that during the Indians' tour of Australia, Kapil Dev and Gavaskar had formed a bond of friendship, the outcome of which was to be India's most successful tour of England.

England v India
Second Test, at Headingley, June 19, 20, 21, 23, 1986, by Derek Hodgson

Hammonds Sauce Works Band, playing in front of the Football Stand, was the indisputable success for England during a match which India won by a resounding margin in under three and a half days. This victory, their first in England outside London, gave them a decisive 2–0 lead in the three-match series. Summing up England's performance, their chairman of selectors said, 'We were outplayed in every department'.

... The respective wicketkeepers, French, in his first Test and More in his second, made an excellent impression... The same, regretfully, cannot be said of those spectators who tried to recreate the human wave effect by synchronised waving of the arms when Azharuddin was batting on Friday afternoon. Their mindless imitation of the football crowds at the World Cup in Mexico did not help the batsman's concentration and left Headingley's reputation as a ground for cricket lovers as much in tatters as the reputation of the England team.

India won by 279 runs.

CRICKETERS OF THE YEAR 1987

D. B. VENGSARKAR, by Dicky Rutnagur

Dilip Vengsarkar, by no means the greatest nor most well remembered of the Indian batsmen on the late 20th century, holds the unique record among touring batsmen of scoring a century on each of his three Tests at Lord's. Ricky Ponting and Michael Atherton, among many other distinguished players, have never scored a Test hundred at Lord's, while even Don Bradman only managed two in four visits, but Vengsarkar scored three.

The view has always been held overseas that the true test of batsmanship is making runs in England, where conditions can alter with the passing overhead of a cloud and where pitches can vary so much in character. Even in contemporary times of covered pitches, the touring batsman still takes added glory from success in England.

One who has triumphed on every tour of England is Dilip Balvant Vengsarkar, born in Bombay on April 6, 1956, who holds the unique record of scoring a century on every one of his three Test appearances at Lord's. And this tall, elegant batsman reached his zenith in the summer of 1986 when his two hundreds, one at Lord's and another at Headingley, on one of the poorest Test pitches seen in England for some years, went so far towards India's achieving their 2–0 win in the three-match series. He finished it with an average of 90, by some margin the highest of any Indian batsman in England. Any suspicions that these hundreds were scored against a weak England team can be discounted. In each instance, Vengsarkar, having come in at the fall of the second wicket, was still short of his century when joined by the No. 11 batsman. They were innings of the highest quality.

India's selectors have seldom been regarded as over-adventurous, but they could scarcely resist picking Vengsarkar in his first season of first-class cricket after seeing him make 110 in less than even time on a turning pitch against Prasanna, Bedi and Minna, a leg-spinner who was then regarded as a Test prospect. This classic innings was played in the annual fixture between the Ranji Trophy champions and the Rest of India, and when Vengsarkar went in, Bombay, the champions, were 100-3 and needing to score 211 to obtain a lead on first innings.

At that time, in 1975, the middle order of the Indian batting was fairly settled and the only vacant place was as Sunil Gavaskar's opening partner. Playing very straight as he did, Vengsarkar seemed to fit the role, but blooded against Sri Lanka, he was not an immediate success. He was out for 0 and 17 and was dropped for the remaining representative games. However, he held the selectors' attention by making a dour century against the touring team for the Indian Universities, and before he was quite 20, he earned himself a place in the tour party to New Zealand and the West Indies in the spring of 1976.

Vengsarkar does not hail from a cricketing family, but his interest in the game was kindled when he was little more than a toddler as his home overlooked a large

patch of green which is one of the main nurseries of Bombay cricket. Part of it was the home ground of Dadar Union, a club of high repute and tradition. Young Vengsarkar watched from his bedroom window, and when he was a little older he joined other boys in the neighbourhood in impromptu mid-week games. Nor was it just that he lived and grew up in the right environment. He was sent to the right school, King George, which produced many cricketers who played for Bombay and not a few who went on to play for India, including such greats of Indian cricket as Manjrekar and Gupte. By 11, he was in King George's junior team as well as in the First XI, playing in the highly competitive Harris Shield competition (named after Lord Harris)…

No sooner was he out of school than Vengsarkar was recruited by Dadar Union. Playing for the club alongside Gavaskar provided a close study in the building of a major innings, and this experience was quickly applied to his cricket at university, where he studied, and later graduated in, commerce. In 1974, Vengsarkar amassed 240 in the semi-finals of the collegiate competition and 170 against Delhi in the final of the Inter-University tournament. It was his passport into Bombay's Ranji Trophy squad, although he spent his first season in the reserves before getting his call in 1975, when Eknath Solkar was injured. He lost no time in establishing himself, and after only one season of first-class cricket climbed to the next level – a Test cap.

On the first leg of his maiden tour, in New Zealand, Vengsarkar played in all three Tests, opening the innings with Gavaskar each time, but without scoring over 30. There were no major scores either in the two Tests he played in the West Indies, but in the second of them he gave a clear hint of his promise and class. That was the contentious final Test match at Kingston, which was played on a newly laid pitch of very uneven bounce. The West Indies pace bowlers, Holding, Daniel, Holder and Julien, were not averse to pitching short and three Indian batsmen took no further part in the match after being injured in the first innings. Indeed, Bedi declared as a protest against West Indies' intimidatory bowling. However, Vengsarkar, using his height to cope with the steep bounce, came out of the struggle with distinction, considering his lack of experience against pace bowling, scoring 39 and then 21 in the second innings, when five Indian batsmen were absent injured. Notwithstanding this display of skill, he was not a fixture in the Test side until the tour of Australia in 1977–78, but from then until the series against England last summer he had missed only three Tests. By the time he returned to India for the series against Australia, he had 85 appearances to his name and an aggregate, including 11 centuries, of 4,985: only Gavaskar and Viswanath have scored more runs for India.

Although he frequently passed 50, Vengsarkar had to wait until his 17th Test match before achieving his maiden hundred: an occasion when he shared a record second-wicket stand of 344 with Gavaskar against West Indies, in Calcutta, in 1978–79. He has made runs everywhere, but all his overseas Test hundreds have been scored in England, where his reach and his technique of playing the ball late stand him in such good stead, as he demonstrated so amply last summer.

OBITUARY

Lall Singh, who died in Kuala Lumpur on November 19, 1985, aged 76, appeared for India against England in the inaugural Test match between the two countries. Of Indian origin, he was born in Malaya, as it was then, and was the only Malayan to play for India. A century for the Federated Malay States led to his travelling to Calcutta, sponsored by a Kuala Lumpur businessman, for trials for the side to visit England in 1932, and scores of 99 and 48 won him inclusion. In the only Test match of the tour, his scores were 15 and 29, and in the second innings he put on 74 in 40 minutes with Amar Singh for the eighth wicket. In England's first innings he had run out Woolley from mid-on, and it was for his brilliant fielding, as much as his entertaining batting, that he left an impression. 'It would be idle to pretend,' said *Wisden*, 'that he had a particularly strong defence.' In all matches on the tour he made 520 runs, with a highest score of 52.

WISDEN – 1988

The Australians, Pakistanis and Sri Lankans all toured India in 1986–87, while the Indians also took part in the Champions Trophy in Sharjah and the Sharjah Cup, in neither of which they impressed.

THE AUSTRALIANS IN INDIA, 1986–87, by R. Mohan

The 11th Test series between Australia and India earned its place in posterity when the first of the three matches, at the Chidambaram Stadium, Chepauk in Madras concluded excitingly in the second tie in Test cricket. It had taken almost 84 years and 498 Tests to produce the first tie, between Australia and West Indies at Brisbane in December 1960; the second came only 26 years later, but there have been so many Test matches of late that this was the 554th Test since that first historic finish at the Gabba...

Kapil Dev went without a wicket in a series for the first time, and this certainly dented India's ambition of sustaining the winning vein struck several months earlier in England. Border, on the other hand, had cause to feel satisfied with the way the tour panned out for his young and inexperienced side... Neither captain, however, should have drawn any satisfaction from a series which saw relations on the field deteriorate from day to day. There were far too many incidents of gamesmanship, with the Indians reacting to the pattern of behaviour set by the visitors.

India v Australia
First Test, at Madras, September 18, 19, 20, 21, 22, 1986

On a hot and humid Monday, one of the most memorable Test match finishes was witnessed by some 30,000 spectators at Chepauk. For the second time in 1,052 Tests, the result was a tie, and coincidentally Australia had been involved each time. Yet there had been little hint of such a climax on the first four days; indeed, as India were being outplayed on the first three days, the thoughts of some Australians were possibly inclined to an innings victory. Only an inspired century against the odds by the Indian captain, Kapil Dev, precluded the possibility of India having to follow on after Australia had amassed their highest total in India – 574 in 742 minutes...

On the second day, Jones cemented the solid start, first reaching his maiden Test hundred and then extending it to Australia's first double-hundred in a Test in India. Batting in all for 8 hours 23 minutes, facing 330 balls and hitting two sixes and 27 fours, Jones had to battle against the difficult weather conditions and overcome bouts of nausea and leg cramps...

With 18 needed off the last 30 balls, the match seemed to be India's, but when Chetan Sharma, caught on the boundary, and More were dismissed in one over by Bright, a third possible result – an Australian victory – was sighted for the first time that day. Yadav, who had struck Matthews for six to take India within seven runs of victory, was next out, bowled off his pads by Bright, leaving India 344-9 with eight balls remaining. Maninder Singh defended the last two balls from Bright, which gave Shastri the strike for the last over, from Matthews. He blocked the first ball and, scenting victory off the second, hit a shade too eagerly: the ball went in front of deep square leg off a thick inside edge and a misfield enabled two runs to be taken safely. The next ball he placed calmly towards mid-wicket for the single which eliminated the possibility of an Australian win. Maninder defended the fourth ball, with some difficulty, and at 5.18pm was leg-before to Matthews's penultimate delivery.

Australia 574 for seven wickets declared (D. M. Jones 210, D. C. Boon 122, A. R. Border 106) and **170 for five wickets declared. India 397** (Kapil Dev 119, R. J. Shastri 62, K. Srikkanth 53, M. Azharuddin 50; G. R. J. Matthews 5-103) and **347** (S. M. Gavaskar 90, M. Amarnath 51; R. J. Bright 5-94, G. R. J. Matthews 5-146). Match tied.

THE SRI LANKANS IN INDIA, 1986–87, by R. Mohan

India's long-awaited success in a home series was made possible by the Sri Lankans' reluctance to come to terms with spin bowling on a sporting pitch in the Second Test and on a doubtful one in the Third. With their 2–0 victory in the

Tests, India thus avenged their unexpected defeat in Sri Lanka the previous season...

It was a tour devoid of controversy. So affected was the visiting team by the loss of the Test series that the one-day series was handed over on a platter, despite the fact that Sri Lanka had won the first match convincingly. It may have been some consolation for Sri Lanka, however, that the emerging players made a greater impact overall than the experienced ones, for from the point of view of the country's cricket, this gave confidence for its future.

THE PAKISTANIS IN INDIA, 1986–87, by R. Mohan

A run of 11 successive draws between India and Pakistan was dramatically arrested by the quality, or rather lack of quality, of a Test match pitch designed to produce a result. In contrast to the languorous pace at which the first four Tests had been played, the final Test in Bangalore, a centre notorious in the previous decade for flat wickets, was enthralling throughout. After pitches which had blunted the edge of Pakistan's pace attack and provided nothing for spin bowlers against Indian batsmen so accustomed to such bowling, it seemed at times that the batsmen were now treading through a minefield. It was a test of nerve which India, despite having dominated many phases of the first four Tests and having bundled out Pakistan for next to nothing in the first innings, failed...

Sunil Gavaskar's feat of completing 10,000 runs, Imran's felicity with the bat, which belied the position at which he generally batted, the progress of Ramiz Raja as an opening batsman, the dashes of brilliance shown by Srikkanth, Vengsarkar and Azharuddin – easily the outstanding fielder in the two teams – and the wily performance of the spinners, Tauseef Ahmed, Iqbal Qasim and Maninder Singh: such were the high points of what would otherwise have been a not so memorable series.

India v Pakistan
Fifth Test, at Bangalore, March 13, 14, 15, 17, 1987

Pakistan won this match to record their first series win in India, their seventh Test win against India, and only their third victory in any series outside Pakistan. The behaviour of the pitch, so encouraging to spin bowling, provided a match of riveting theatre, although both captains had anticipated seaming conditions...

Batting first after winning the toss, Pakistan responded to panic induced by the turning ball with extravagant strokeplay that was not so much bold as foolish. Maninder, despite mixing the bad with the good, returned career-best figures of 7-27, including a spell of four wickets in 13 balls. Pakistan tumbled to their lowest score against India. The home side, in turn, were made to struggle...

On the fourth day, on a pitch which allowed even an off-spinner to bowl bouncers, Gavaskar gave a masterly exhibition of technique and judgement. Only when he was out, having batted five hours 23 minutes and faced 266 balls for his 96, caught at slip off a ball that kicked off a good length, could Pakistan assume victory.

Pakistan 116 (Maninder Singh 7-27) and **249. India 145**
(D. B. Vengsarkar 50; Iqbal Qasim 5-48, Tauseef Ahmed 5-54)
and 204 (S. M. Gavaskar 96). Pakistan won by 16 runs.

OBITUARIES

Joshi, Padmanabh Govind (Nana), died in Pune on January 8, 1987, aged 60. A sound wicketkeeper and useful, versatile right-hand batsman, he appeared in 12 Tests for India over nine seasons. He had already announced his possibilities as a batsman with a dour, unbeaten 100 for a combined team against 'Jock' Livingstone's Commonwealth side at Nagpur in 1949–50 when he was called up by India in 1951–52 for the First Test against Nigel Howard's England side. He took two catches and made two stumpings in the first innings but was not required to bat, yet India dispensed with his services until the Fourth Test, then dropped him again for the Fifth, so establishing a pattern which prevailed until 1960–61, when he played in his final Test, against Pakistan at Bombay. He scored 52 not out and with R. B. Desai added 149 for the ninth wicket which was still a record for India against all countries at the time of his death.

Kripal Singh, Amritsar Govindsingh, died in Madras on July 22, 1987, aged 53. Coming into the side for India's first Test match against New Zealand, at Hyderabad in 1955–56, he hit an unbeaten 100 on debut and with Umrigar (223) added 171 for the fourth wicket. When India began uncertainly at Bombay in the next Test, he scored 63 and added 167 for the same wicket with Mankad, who emulated Umrigar's score of 223. With 36 in his only other innings, Kripal Singh finished the series with an average of 99.50. He did little in two Tests against Australia in 1956–57, but a half-century against West Indies at Madras in his one match of their 1958–59 series helped secure him a place in the 1959 team to England. There, however, he was a disappointment.

... Recalled in 1961–62 for the series against England after taking a career-best 6-14 and 6-35 for Madras against Hyderabad, he appeared in the First Test alongside his brother, Milkha Singh. Their father, Ram Singh, had represented India in two unoffical tests against Ryder's Australian team in 1935–36 and against Lord Tennyson's 1937–38 team, and two other brothers, Satwender and Harjinder, also played first-class cricket. He... later became a Test selector, and would have become the chairman of selectors in August 1987.

Merchant, Vijaysingh Madhavji, died in his native Bombay on October 27, 1987, aged 76. An opening batsman of orthodox technique and seemingly endless patience, on his two tours of England with Indian teams he was the leading batsman with 1,745 runs average 51.32, in 1936 and 2,385, average 74.53, in 1946. In India, his runs were legion; his average in the Ranji Trophy championship was 98.75 from 3,639 runs. But often these runs were accumulated on surfaces almost too perfect, especially at the Brabourne Stadium in Bombay, and so it was his batting in English conditions that provided the measure of his greatness... Not a tall man, only 5ft 7in, but strong, like Gavaskar in another generation he built his technique on classical footwork. And always there was his concentration and determination...

In his ten Test matches, he scored 859 runs with an average of 47.72, and in his 146 first-class matches he totalled 13,248 runs for a career average of 71.22, which is second only to Sir Donald Bradman's of 95.14. He hit 44 hundreds, including ten double-hundreds and one triple.

WISDEN – 1989

RELIANCE WORLD CUP, 1987–88, by Scyld Berry

Despite being played on home soil and in neighbouring Pakistan, India's defence of their World Cup title did not go quite according to plan.

The fourth World Cup was more widely watched, more closely fought, and more colourful than any of its three predecessors held in England. Any doubts about it were dispelled by the opening matches when Pakistan, the favourites, were run close by Sri Lanka; when India, the holders, were beaten by Australia by one run; when England succeeded in scoring 35 off their last three overs to beat West Indies; and when the gallant amateurs of Zimbabwe lost by only three runs to New Zealand.

If the rest of the Reliance Cup, as it was officially known and seldom called, could not quite live up to such a start, the experiment of an oriental World Cup was still acknowledged to have been a great success. The semi-finals in Lahore and Bombay held the subcontinent by the ears and eyes, even if they did not produce the results desired by the tens of millions who were following the matches on radio and television. The arrangements for the final, at Eden Gardens in Calcutta, were praised to the full by the winning Australian captain, and rightly.

Any drawbacks resulted from the geographical enormity of the two host countries and the determination of the Indo-Pakistan Joint Management Committee to spread the games around as many as 21 venues. It was the equivalent of staging a tournament in Europe, barring only the Soviet Union, without quite the same facility of transport and telecommunications. Fewer centres would have meant less travelling, a shorter and more compact competition – it took six weeks against less than a month for the 1983 World Cup – and increased enjoyment all round. For successive matches, the Sri Lankans were shunted from Peshawar, in the North-West Frontier Province of Pakistan, to Kanpur in central India, back to Faisalabad, then across the border again to Pune: two-day journeys every time, with hours spent in transit lounges at airports waiting for flights.

Nevertheless, in circumstances which were perhaps more arduous than they need have been, the organisers did excellently. In return, the weather was kind to them. To all intents, only one match was affected by rain, when Australia and New Zealand were reduced to 30 overs each in Indore. (Happily, the rule that a match could not be carried over to its second day was never exposed in its absurdity.) Otherwise the matches were of 50 overs per side, and on good pitches totals similar to those in previous 60-over World Cups were raised. Viv Richards, and West Indies as a team, set up new records against Sri Lanka for World Cup innings…

Batsmen were not troubled by dew when batting first, as some had feared, but by the strain of batting second. Out of 27 matches, 19 were won by the side batting first. The received wisdom had been to bowl first in one-day internationals and to determine the target. Now every side wanted to bat first, then watch the opposition – fatigued by three and a half hours' fielding in the heat – make mistakes and panic as the run-rate climbed to seven and eight an over. The side batting first played the ball according to its merits; the side batting second seemed to play it according to the run-rate required.

In this context, Australia were fortunate to bat first in five of their six qualifying games, and to be able to do so again in their semi-final and final, on pitches which lost what bounce they had. This luck aside, they were still the team most deserving of victory: they appeared to put the most into the tournament – the sweat was dripping from the peaks of the batsmen's caps when they warmed up in Madras – and they gained their first success of note since 1984. England, the runners-up, arrived with a specialist in tropical diseases and a microwave oven but with only three batsmen capable of scoring at a run a ball. They won whenever their bowlers were able to make up for the deficiencies in their batting.

Co-hosts India and Pakistan, as holders and favourites, had been expected to meet in the final but never met at all, not even in a hastily conceived third-place play-off match which fell through owing to the exorbitant demands of some players. Indeed, it was perhaps as well that their paths never crossed, for there were reports of communal conflict in India after the semi-final results… In a sense, India handicapped themselves by playing in the weaker qualifying group, much as England had in 1979. In both cases the hosts qualified without having the weak links in their bowling exposed. India's batting was collectively the most brilliant in the tournament but not always the most effective. The demands of their crowds for spectacular hitting, and enticing awards from a sponsor for every four and six they hit, cannot have been beneficial influences; likewise a never-settled dispute which the senior Indian players had with their board over insignia.

SUNIL GAVASKAR – THE LITTLE MASTER, by Tony Lewis

Wisden marked the retirement of Sunil Gavaskar with a tribute article by Tony Lewis, former England captain and future MCC president, whose only tour as England captain had been to India at the start of Gavaskar's career. This was the first time such a tribute had been paid to an Indian player.

It is tempting to write an appreciation of Sunil Gavaskar in extravagant language so that it matches the pinnacle to which he took his batsmanship. Reflect on the career of a man who played in more Test matches, scored more runs and hit more hundreds in Test cricket than any other and you think in heroic terms. Imagine his beginnings in Bombay and the romance flows. It is 1951, he is two years old, up on the balcony of his parents' flat in the Chikalwadi district, defending a door with a toy bat as a tennis ball, gently propelled by Meena, his mother, bounces towards him. Link that to the fairytale last appearance at Lord's, where he had never scored a century. In MCC's 200th-birthday match he constructed an innings of 188, all patience and style, which demonstrated to many who had not seen him in his pomp that here was art fined down, skills chiselled to something simple yet beautiful and lasting.

However, ornate language does not suit Sunil Gavaskar, even though Sir Donald Bradman rightly described him as an ornament to cricket. Gavaskar is a man who does not live in luxury though he could afford to. His middle-class English accent is cultured and he is articulate, but he is frugal with his words, often preferring silence. His eyes can twinkle and he has a relish of fun; he delivers the one-line joke like a knockout punch and is mischievous in mimicry. Yet Sunil Gavaskar's eyes can also turn to fire, his face burn with anger, and deep in the small frame you can hear the fighting spirit of the old Marathas thunder.

It is impossible to think of Sunil without his wife, Marshniel, known to the cricket world and her friends as Pammi. Think of solid partnerships – Hutton and Washbrook, McGlew and Waite, Greenidge and Haynes, Mohsin and Mudassar, Marsh and Boon, Contractor and Roy, and you would have to say Gavaskar and Pammi. This is not because Sunil's opening partners have changed so often, but because with Pammi, whom he married in 1974, he merges; he gossips and relaxes. Also he has someone to share his drive. Once the object was a massive collection of runs; now business ambition, which has always floated just under the surface, gives them the purpose they need in everyday life.

I first saw Sunil Gavaskar bat when I led MCC in India in 1972–73. We had been warned to expect something special by his incredible performances in his first Test series in the West Indies in 1971–72. He scored 774 runs in eight innings at an average of 154.80, including 124 and 220 in the Fifth Test at Port-of-Spain. He had not been as successful in England later in 1971 but now, about to play his first Test in India, he had the subcontinent longing to greet a little master.

Gavaskar reminded me of Geoff Boycott – detached, insular, totally within himself and not given to banter with players, umpires or even his partner. He looked neat, 5ft 4in tall, and strong in the legs and forearms. His kit was clean, his appearance smart. Another Boycottism, I thought; preparation perfect for the pursuit of runs. And more Boycott in the sideways stance, the small first movement of the back foot, the sharp downward angling of the bat in the forward defensive stroke. He scored slowly, but it was important for him and for India that he took as much practice as possible against the English bowlers before the Test series begun. His concentration was absolute.

Of course, Bombay already knew about Sunil Gavaskar's single-mindedness. His father, Manohar Gavaskar, had been a fine batsman and wicketkeeper in club cricket, and his maternal uncle, Madhav Mantri, had played four times for India. The former fired his enthusiasm, the second shaped his thinking. By the age of 20 he had put away all childish strokeplay and made 327 for Bombay University in a trophy match. In our particular Test series runs eluded him, but that just meant that he had a more realistic base from which to develop. Soon I was watching him from the commentary boxes around the world and my pleasure in seeing him bat has not wavered over 15 years.

Quite unforgettable was his 101 out of 246 against England at Old Trafford in 1974. Cold north-west winds drove in squalls, bringing only the seventh day of rain in Manchester since mid-February. The pitch was firm and bouncy, Willis, Old and Hendrick were hostile, whacking in short balls. Underwood and Greig were the slower bowlers and they gave nothing away. Gavaskar first demonstrated how brave he was. He kept his eye on the ball and swayed either side of the high bounce, but when the ball was pitched up he was immediately forward to drive it straight. This is where Gavaskar was a better player than Boycott. Overall Boycott lost his strokes, or maybe through parsimony he cut them out; Gavaskar reduced risk too, but never lost the spring off the back foot which sent him firmly into the drive.

Sunil Gavaskar has never been a dedicated net-player, and he never appears to thrive on too heavy a programme of cricket. It is interesting to note that he scored 39 per cent of his first-class runs in Test cricket, whereas Boycott's percentage was 17. He has an independent mind and sees a much wider world than cricket available to him. For example, when he joined Somerset in 1980 he was unhappy. At close of play the Somerset cricketers would be off to the beer tent where they would chat about cricket. Sunil prefered to retreat from cricket to different conversations and take a quiet glass of wine with his dinner.

Gavaskar was India's Test captain 47 times. He won his first three series from 1979–80 but later was accused of being too defensive. His final tally was nine wins, eight losses and 30 draws. Thoughtful and authoritative, he was easily the best cricket brain of the Indian side for most of his career. Consequently it was hard for him to accept the captaincy of the younger Kapil Dev, and to the embarrassment of Indian players these two outstanding personalities clashed. There have been many tales of their enmity, but I must write honestly that I have never witnessed it. If anything, the Kapil–Sunil impasse was fuelled as much by the media as by what went on behind dressing-room doors.

Indian cricket has now lost a great player. He became a better one-day cricketer as he came to enjoy the game more in his later days. He has proved everything and he delighted in leading India to victory in what was called the World Championship of Cricket in Australia in 1984–85. His perverse moments were now behind him: as when he walked off the field and took Chetan Chauhan with him as a demonstration against Australian umpiring; as when he called the Indian selectors 'court jesters'; as when he refused ever to play again in Calcutta after he had delayed a declaration against David Gower's team and almost caused a riot.

Only the good thoughts remain and they are precious. Sunil Gavaskar will be remembered for his rolling walk to the crease, his forearm padded against the fast bowlers. His deflections to fine leg will remain clearly etched, as will his firm pushes in a wide arc on the leg-side, his drives, of course, and his lethal cut to square third man. But I will recall most the best player of spin bowling I have ever seen, always balanced, forever with time whether playing right out to the pitch of the ball or back to watch and wait.

Sunil and I shared a car in Sharjah recently and he talked urgently about his ambitions in sports publishing, video and television. He had that same resolute look in his eye; the second game has started. You would not wish to be Mr Gavaskar's opponent in any field.

THE WEST INDIANS IN INDIA, 1987–88, by Dicky Rutnagur

Dicky Rutnagur, as ever, did not mince his words.

The interests of cricket were not best served by either the timing of this tour or the cavalier fashion in which the Board of Control for Cricket in India, influenced by financial considerations and driven by internal politics, chopped and changed the itinerary even after the tour had started. The World Cup tournament, which was so vigorously promoted and which had only just ended, left the country with no appetite for any form of international cricket except the overs-limit variety. The Test matches, regrettably, were received as enthusiastically as sandwiches filled with the leftovers of the Christmas turkey. The thrilling First Test, at Delhi, was played before very thin crowds and on no day of the series was any ground completely full.

In such an atmosphere, the first-class games outside the Tests also suffered from lack of support. Member associations of the Indian board were reluctant to host these fixtures, yet all clamoured to stage one-day internationals. To meet this demand, the board went to the extent of cancelling, at the 11th hour, the Second Test match at Nagpur and substituting it with two one-day internationals in addition to the five originally scheduled. Nagpur had initially been allotted this Test match when Kanpur was unable to stage it. Mr Jackie Hendriks, the West Indians' manager, was unhappy at the shortening of the Test series, which he considered to be the main business on the agenda, and he accepted the rearrangement most reluctantly. He was told by board officials that Nagpur had backed out of staging the Test match, but officials of the local association denied the allegation. Instead of the Test match, Nagpur was given a one-day international and the other went to Calcutta, whence the pressure for the revision of the programme originated…

West Indies won the Charminar Challenge one-day series 6–1, as well as the match at Ahmedabad, and most of their victories were gained decisively. Yet, crowds flocked to them. The low attendances at the Test matches, however, left the host associations incurring heavy losses.

The 1–1 result of the four-match Test series was not a true index of the strength of the teams. While West Indies were not the side they once were, they were distinctly superior. A more appropriate result would have been 2–1 in their favour, although even then it would not have been a just one. The Indian victory in the final Test was gained on a Madras pitch that made a mockery of Test cricket.

India v West Indies
Fourth Test, at Madras, January 11, 12, 14, 15, 1988

India won with a day to spare, the most decisive of their six victories against West Indies. Its main author was a new cap in Hirwani, a bespectacled, 19-year-old leg-spinner, who had the assistance of an under-prepared pitch which afforded turn from the opening day. In the circumstances, the scales were tipped heavily in India's favour when Shastri, captaining for the first time in a Test match, won the toss. Hirwani captured eight wickets in each innings to equal the Australian R. A. L. Massie's feat of taking sixteen wickets on his debut, against England at Lord's in 1972. If Hirwani was able to give the ball air, as he did and challenge the batsmen to counter-attack, it was because of India's first-innings total of 382, which was owed principally to a dashing 109 by Kapil Dev, scored off only 119 balls and including 17 fours…

The pitch, if a nightmare for the batsmen, made equally high demands on the wicketkeepers, and More deserved much credit for stumping six batsmen in the match, five of them in the second innings. Both figures were a record for stumpings in a Test.

India 382 (Kapil Dev 109, Arun Lal 69) and **217 for eight wickets declared** (W. V. Raman 83). **West Indies 184** (I. V. A. Richards 68; N. D. Hirwani 8-61) and **160** (A. L. Logie 67; N. D. Hirwani 8-75). India won by 255 runs.

OBITUARIES

Gaekwad, Lieut-Col. Fatesingrao, who died in Bombay on September 1, 1988, at the age of 58, was as the Maharajah of Baroda a popular manager of the Indian touring team to England in 1959. Later he managed the Indian teams to Pakistan in 1978–79 and 1982–83, by which time the Indian royal families had lost their titles by government edict. A right-hand batsman of some style, and there was considerable style in all Jackie Baroda did, he first appeared as a 16-year-old for Baroda in the Ranji Trophy in 1946–47 and continued in the side until 1957-58, for four years as captain... He was president of the Board of Control for Cricket in India from 1963–64 to 1965–66 and an honorary life member of MCC. A man of wit, humour and great personal wealth, he was a Member of Parliament in India from 1962 to 1967 and did much for the World Wildlife Fund. Radio listeners in Britain and beyond came to know him as a member of the BBC commentary team.

Jahangir Khan, Dr Mohammad, who died in Lahore on July 23, 1988, aged 78, played four Test matches for India in the 1930s and, after partition, made an important contribution as a player, administrator and selector to the development of cricket in Pakistan. His son, Majid, captained Pakistan, as did his nephews, Javed Burki and Imran Khan. All three emulated him in gaining Blues; Majid like his father at Cambridge, his cousins at Oxford. An elder son, Asad, won his Blue at Oxford...

It was in 1936 also that there occurred the sparrow incident with which his name has become associated. Playing for Cambridge against MCC at Lord's, he was bowling to T. N. Pearce, who had just played a defensive push when it was noticed that the bails had been dislodged. It was then that a dead sparrow was found beside the stumps. The unfortunate bird was stuffed and subsequently displayed in the Memorial Gallery at Lord's; but while legend has it that the sparrow was struck by the ball in flight, it is thought no one actually saw this happen.

Wankhede, Seshrao Krishnarao, who died in Bombay on January 30, 1988, aged 73, was president of the Board of Control for Cricket in India from 1980–81 to 1982–83. But it was as president of the Bombay Cricket Association from 1963–64 that he played his most far-reaching role in Indian cricket affairs. For more than 30 years the Association had been dissatisfied with a situation which saw them beholden to the Cricket Club of India for the distribution of profits from Test and first-class cricket at the Brabourne Stadium, which the CCI owned, and for the allocation of seats for Test matches there. When in 1971, with England due to tour India in 1972–73, the CCI would not agree to provide more seats for the Association's member clubs, the BCA at Wankhede's instigation decided to build its own stadium and so vacate its tenancy of the Brabourne Stadium, leaving this famous, splendid ground with little more than its history. Since 1973–74 virtually all international and first-class cricket in Bombay has been played at the stadium which bears Wankhede's name.

WISDEN – 1990

1989 was a quiet year for the Indian Test side, which was not strong, and a mediocre year in the one-day game. India won the Asia Cup, held in Bangladesh, but underperformed in the Sharjah Cup.

THE NEW ZEALANDERS IN INDIA, 1988–89, by R. Mohan

Although Richard Hadlee had sworn never to set foot again on the Indian subcontinent, the prospect of making the world Test bowling record exclusively his proved irresistible. To the delight of the country's many cricket-lovers, he came to India after an absence of 12 years, and it was soon evident that he was a performer of an entirely different class this time. On his previous visit he was a young man looking to earn a reputation; now he was the champion on a mission. And after 18 minutes of the start of the Test series, Hadlee had his 374th Test wicket when Arun Lal edged into the slips. His feat was warmly applauded and he went on to dominate the series with a technically faultless display of the use of the cricket ball. His 18 wickets were the basis on which the visitors contested and provided an interesting series which was not decided until the Third and last Test.

THE INDIANS IN THE WEST INDIES, 1988–89, by Dicky Rutnagur

Even without playing to their full potential, West Indies were vastly superior to India in both the Test matches and the one-day internationals. They won the Test series of four matches 3–0 and made a clean sweep of the overs-limit rubber of five. From the Indian viewpoint, the tour was one of the most disastrous they have undertaken. Even outside the Tests, they were sometimes embarrassed and failed to win any match at any level…

For the first time since his retirement, India truly felt the absence of Sunil Gavaskar. They were immensely unlucky with the weather on the early part of the tour, and they also suffered harshly from injuries… Already, prior to the start of the series, India had lost the services of Krishnam Srikkanth, valuable for his experience as well as for his ability to carry the attack to the bowling. His tour ended in the last one-day international when his forearm was fractured by a ball from Bishop. Srikkanth had shown signs of good form from the first match of the tour. From the Second Test onwards, there was a continuing deterioration of a long-standing groin injury carried by Mohammad Azharuddin. That the problem became so acute as to reach crisis proportions was as much the fault of the player himself as of the Indian board for allowing the injury to remain untreated for over a year. The other experienced batsman in the side, Vengsarkar, was completely undermined by Bishop and, unquestionably, was weighed down by the demands of captaining an inadequate side.

Although Navjot Singh Sidhu recorded the highest score by an Indian on tour, 286 against Jamaica, and followed it up with a brave century in the final Test, the outstanding Indian batsman of the tour was Sanjay Manjrekar, who scored a maiden Test century in the Bridgetown Test... He headed the aggregates and the averages for the series, but more than that he caught the eye with his judgement of direction and his technique of playing fast bowling. Sidhu's success was achieved more by keenness of eye than mastery of technique, the most obvious imperfection being an initial backward movement of the right foot...

The outstanding Indian bowler was Kapil Dev. His tally of 18 wickets in the series, at a very respectable average of 21.38, did less than full justice to the skills he showed in conditions not best suited to his pace... The most disappointing aspect of the series was India's inability to take advantage of a turning pitch in the Third Test, at Port-of-Spain. Their failure and their rout underlined the decline of the art of spin bowling in a country where it abounded only a few years earlier... The leg-spinner, Narendra Hirwani, failed by a long way to live up to the reputation gained from taking 16 West Indian wickets in his maiden Test and 20 in the only other three he had played since. As expensive as he was lacking in penetration, Hirwani... suffered from lack of guidance from his captain and from his setting of fields, for which ridiculous can be the only fitting description...

As captain, Vengsarkar could not inspire his team either by personal performance or by force of personality. Yet at the end he publicly denounced his side as lacking courage and sense of purpose. In truth, the team's performance reflected a marked lack of class in its components.

OBITUARY

Sharma, Narendra (Changa), who died on May 20, 1989, aged 35, made his Ranji Trophy debut for Jammu and Kashmir in 1977–78 as an off-spinner and in eight seasons of championship cricket took 39 wickets at 42.38 apiece. He had curiously deformed thumbs, which caused him problems in gripping the bat, but with his unique bowling grip he was able to spin the ball considerably.

WISDEN — 1991

India toured New Zealand and Pakistan during the winter of 1989–90. In New Zealand, where India lost the Test series 1–0, Wisden noted the progress of a young star in the making. Sixteen-year-old Sachin Tendulkar batted with the poise of a player twice his age. At Napier, 80 not out overnight, he seemed destined to become the youngest batsman to score a Test century, but he added only 8 more runs the next morning. In Pakistan, all the Tests were drawn – no surprise there. The surprise was the acceptance of umpiring decisions.

THE INDIANS IN PAKISTAN, 1989–90

Two cricketers made a quiet and yet very effective contribution to the tenth series between India and Pakistan. They were not players. John Hampshire and John Holder, both from England, were the third country umpires invited to officiate in the four Test matches, and their presence changed the nature of cricket contests between these two Asian neighbours. The frisson was missing. Events on the field were far less contentious, with both teams accepting the umpires, and their rulings, in good faith. The occasional mistakes, some glaring, did not lead to flare-ups, with the result that the atmosphere was refreshingly free of suspicion. Teams had been touring Pakistan for years without any firm belief that they could, or even would be allowed to, win a Test. In this series, the relations between the two sides were cordial and the cricket, if not spectacular, was highly competitive.

The neutral umpires stood only in the Tests, not in the one-day series, and conjecture was that their presence had much to do with the 0–0 result. That line of thinking, however, paid little regard to the splendid manner in which Sanjay Manjrekar held together the Indian batting. Pakistan had the better of the exchanges in the first two Tests but were unable to translate their advantage into victory.

THE INDIANS IN ENGLAND, 1990, by R. Mohan

The supremacy of cricket as England's summer sport was in question... A certain amateur spirit was needed if cricket was to recapture its glory, and the Indian tourists, led by Mohammad Azharuddin, had that spirit. The fear of losing has often been responsible for dull Test cricket, but India, accustomed to winning abroad once in a blue moon, had none of that fear. Moreover, with conditions so dry that hosepipe bans were being imposed in Britain, the Indian batsmen found themselves in their element. They scored heavily from their earliest games, making 15 first-class hundreds, six of them in Tests, and their double victory in the Texaco Trophy one-day internationals suggested how attractively they could perform. The Tests would revolve around their success in using these batting skills to support the notoriously weak bowling.

The fate of the series lay in the toss at Lord's. With so many batsmen among the runs, most captains would have grabbed first strike the moment the coin came down in their favour. This is where captaincy may have let India down. Graham Gooch, soon to make this summer his *annus mirabilis*, may not have believed his ears or his luck when England were asked to bat. For while the mild cloud cover at the time of the toss was contrary to the forecast, any moisture in the pitch could only have been imagined. Not without reason did the sagacious Mike Brearley write that the decision was pusillanimous. Moreover, the divisions in Indian cricket were soon emphasised as the team's cricket manager, Bishan Bedi, was reported to have disassociated himself from the decision to put England in, though he made a belated attempt to assuage the players' feelings by denying the words attributed to him…

Until the last Test, India's batsmen were always left to battle against the odds, chasing one massive England total after another, but their talented line-up, and especially the brilliant Azharuddin, did much to re-establish the virtues of positive batting. The Indian captain's breathtakingly audacious hundred at Lord's signified the difference between the English straight bat, wielded with control rather than subtlety, and oriental wristiness, which lends itself to innovation…

India were let down by their lack of cold-blooded professionalism… It was after the senior batsmen had displayed the same lack of commitment on the final day at Old Trafford that Sachin Tendulkar completed his conquest of English hearts, saving his side from defeat and scoring the sixth century of the match en route. There should be many more Test hundreds for Tendulkar; what made his first so special were the circumstances in which he made it, as a 17-year-old coming to the rescue of his country. Yet those who had seen him stand up to a barrage of bouncers from the Pakistani fast bowlers at Sialkot the previous winter would have had no doubts about his genius, or his capacity to set an example to colleagues old enough to be father figures. He had already… dazzled the crowd at Lord's with an unbelievably athletic catch of the sort that only players of his age can attempt…

The happy ending for England brought down the curtain on a popular show. The Indians had been model tourists, ever willing to please the spectators and never once questioning the umpiring, the crowded itinerary (twice they went straight from a Test into six days of first-class cricket), the long coach rides in a criss-cross programme, or even some hotels with less than adequate service. Relations between the teams were excellent. Neither two poor umpiring decisions in successive overs at Old Trafford, when India were poised to match England's total, nor the couple of warnings for attempting to interfere with the ball were allowed to dampen the good cheer.

The Indians left England happier for their visit, convinced that the future would be brighter and that a nucleus of players had been found to serve them for some time to come.

England v India

First Test, at Lord's, July 26, 27, 28, 30, 31, 1990, by John Thicknesse

By using Shastri to open the batting, India made room to play the 17-year-old Bombay student, Tendulkar, who in England's second innings brought off as wonderful an outfield catch as Lord's has seen, holding Lamb's straight drive one-handed at knee height after hurtling more than 30 yards from wide long-off to a point behind the bowler...

India were 430-9, needing 24 to save the follow-on. Kapil Dev watched Hirwani survive the last ball of Fraser's over, played the first two of Hemmings's defensively, then ripped into the next four and drove each one for six. Three of them were enormous, clattering the scaffolding, one was simply big; all were magnificent. With the very next delivery, Fraser had Hirwani lbw. India had scored 78 in 15.1 overs, and the devil-may-care Kapil had become the first man to hit four sixes running in a Test. It was an unexpected way to save a follow-on.

England 653 for four wickets declared (G. A. Gooch 333, A. J. Lamb 139,
R. A. Smith 100 not out) and **272 for four wickets declared** (G. A. Gooch 123,
M. A. Atherton 72). **India 454** (M. Azharuddin 121, R. J. Shastri 100,
Kapil Dev 77 not out, D. B. Vengsarkar 52; A. R. C. Fraser 5-104) and **224**.
England won by 247 runs.

CRICKETERS OF THE YEAR 1991

M. AZHARUDDIN, by R. Mohan

The gloriously stylish but ultimately fallen hero of Indian cricket at the very end of the 1900s was Mohammad Azharuddin. All those old phrases like 'wristy strokes' and 'oriental artistry' that had been first used for Ranji but largely discarded after Duleep's retirement, came out again for Azhar. A Muslim educated at a Christian school, captaining the national side made up largely of Hindus and Sikhs, perhaps he never quite fitted in, but to watch him bat in his prime was sheer joy.

Last summer, a new definition was given to oriental artistry as Mohammad Azharuddin, India's captain, time and again placed the ball through square leg and mid-wicket with a wristy turn of the bat at the instant of impact. Line seemed to mean little, length everything, as he feasted on England's bowling with hundreds at Lord's and Old Trafford to follow successively on one against New Zealand in Auckland. They set the crackers bursting in the cosmopolitan neighbourhood of Vithalwadi, in celebration not just of Azharuddin's success, but also of the return of the touch which five years earlier had launched his international career so spectacularly. Three hundreds against England in his first three Tests. That was early in 1985, and the 21-year-old was hailed as a prophet among the Indian pantheon of batting demi-gods. He was also beginning the struggle to cope with the expectations of a nation and his awe of his own reputation.

Mohammad Azharuddin was born on February 8, 1963 in Hyderabad, capital city of the Deccan plateau state of Andhra Pradesh... In 1981–82, at the age of 18, he made his first-class debut in the Ranji Trophy. Such exposure was rather easily attained in a Hyderabad side which was going through a transition, but the experience shaped his batting even as it toughened him mentally.

National recognition came on the heels of a double-hundred for South Zone in January 1984, in the Duleep Trophy, with a place on the Under-25 tour of Zimbabwe... His breakthrough came later in the season after David Gower's England team, beaten in the First Test, had come back to square the series in Delhi. In contentious circumstances Kapil Dev was dropped from the side and Azharuddin was brought in to replace Sandeep Patil for the Calcutta Test. The rest is history...

While there were centuries to be made on the plumb pitches at home, there were none abroad until his first visit to Pakistan in 1989–90. By then, following an unhappy tour of the West Indies, where fast and short-pitched bowling had provided a searching test of his technique, his place in the side was in doubt...

Advice from colleagues to stand up and hook if bowlers were trying to corner him with bouncers was not really what an uncertain and unwilling player of the hook needed to hear. Sounder advice came from the former Pakistan batsman, Zaheer Abbas, who advocated a readjustment of his grip. By wrapping his right hand further round the handle, Azharuddin found he could stroke the ball with greater control and assurance. In the second innings of the Faisalabad Test, having been dismissed for 0 in the first innings, he made his first century away from home. In the course of it, he found his confidence and his true touch returning. Changes in selection were soon to thrust him further into the limelight, and although he had little experience of leading sides, he was made captain for the tour of New Zealand in early 1990.

Such is Azharuddin's nature, however, that he takes everything in his stride, not making a drama out of a crisis, or even a crisis out of the drama that is so often Indian cricket. He set about tackling his new responsibilities with the modesty that is a refreshing trait: the devout Muslim probably believed in just praying extra hard and leaving his young team to play to the best of their resources. Such a style was disastrous to begin with, but soon enough Azharuddin learned to assert himself as captain.

The Auckland Test, the last of the New Zealand series, brought a sensational twist to his career as a batsman, for it saw the fruition of his counter-attacking style. Suddenly, everything he did came right and a truly majestic innings of 192 unfolded. Marked by straight- and on-driving of a very high order, the innings was supreme also in that it was the highest by an Indian captain abroad. His match- and series-

winning half-century at Trent Bridge in the second of last summer's Texaco one-dayers was a further indication of how completely 'Azhar' had rediscovered himself.

Having made his name as a stylist who used the power of his wrists to create the mesmeric effect of strokes played late, he had often been struggling in his attempt to put percentages ahead of style. It was an index of his re-emerging batting personality that he should score the centuries which fascinated Englishmen so. He explained away the seeming desperation which sparked India's strokeplay in the defeat at Lord's as the need for aggression which has always acted as a tonic for him. 'It's not as if we were always hitting the ball as if we wanted to take the cover off it. But there was so much loose bowling, especially from Malcolm, that it was easy to send the ball speeding down the slope.' But at Old Trafford, and again at The Oval, where a century seemed his for the taking, Azharuddin reached the very heights of artistic batting. The Old Trafford hundred pleased him particularly. 'I always knew that the ball was going when I aimed to hit it.' Watching some of the power developed, especially off the back foot, it was hard to believe he was playing with one of the lightest bats in modern cricket.

Since childhood, Azharuddin has believed in turning out neatly at a cricket match, be it a hit in the park or a Test. Notice how he always goes out to toss in a blazer. By his manner, he also promises to re-establish sporting standards in the game as well as sartorial ones. Certainly, if India's tour of England was a resounding success for the game, Azharuddin can take pride in being a leading contributor to it... The future beckons brightly. His only regret is that his grandfather, who used to stand under the trees on the boundary line watching him, did not live to see him play Test cricket.

WISDEN — 1992

1990–91 was a quiet time for India internationally, with only a brief visit from the Sri Lankans and the usual participation in one-day competitions in Sharjah and elsewhere. Their domestic cricket, however, was by no means incident free.

THE SRI LANKANS IN INDIA, 1990–91, by R. Mohan

After a largely successful tour of the English counties in 1990, the Sri Lankans were keen for international cricket. But they were ill prepared for their single Test on a visit to India which was hastily arranged amid uncertainty about the series proposed for later in the season. For the Indians, it was their first home Test for two years, during which time they had played 14 Test matches on four overseas trips without a win. Eagerness to register the long-awaited victory was one factor blamed for the under-preparation of the pitch at Chandigarh, the 14th Indian city to host a Test, as was the late transfer from the proposed venue of Jullundur. Certainly the pitch was nowhere near standard at the start of the match.

The chief architect of India's win was the 21-year-old orthodox left-arm spinner from Hyderabad, Venkatapathy Raju. His nagging accuracy, genuine spin and even some bounce, on a pitch where the ball kept disturbingly low, brought him figures of 6-12 as Sri Lanka were dismissed for 82, their lowest Test score, and 8-37 in the match. It was a welcome return for Raju, who had missed most of India's 1990 tour of England after a knuckle on his bowling hand was broken by a ball from Courtney Walsh. Another Indian bowler with cause for celebration was Kapil Dev, who equalled I. T. Botham's return of 376 Test wickets, second only to Sir Richard Hadlee's record 431...

The one-day series was far more entertaining and better patronised, with the Sri Lankans proving a better match for the Indians in limited-overs cricket. After losing the first two games, they finished an otherwise unsuccessful tour on a winning note, doing well to pull off victory in Margao on a heavily watered pitch that baffled the home batsmen, who unwisely chose to go in first. Conditions were not very different when Sri Lanka batted, but the boldness of De Silva saw them home with more than 17 overs to spare. Thus honour was restored to a team so anxious to play that they offered to take part in any additional Test or one-day internationals that could be arranged. The Indian board, however, was unwilling to extend the 11th-hour exercise.

CRICKET IN INDIA 1990–91, by R. Mohan and Sudhir Vaidya

While modern batsmen may need more than a wand of willow to protect themselves on the field of play, a degree in law may become a prerequisite for informed cricket journalism in India. To see the game being dragged to the courts was not a unique experience, but the sight of a bowler uprooting a stump to assault a batsman certainly was. Such an extraordinary incident, in the final of the nation's premier tournament, the Duleep Trophy, was the worst instance of the deterioration in standards of behaviour.

The violent action, senseless yet far from unprovoked, of Rashid Patel of West Zone, who went after Raman Lamba of North Zone, stump in hand, will be remembered as the most shameful moment in the history of Indian cricket. It occurred on the final afternoon of the five-day match in Jamshedpur, after Patel had come down the pitch to aim a head-high full toss at the batsman, Lamba. Nor was it the only controversy in a game in which senior players questioned the umpires' decisions and berated officials. Yet in the end, the Board of Control for Cricket in India seemed to draw a veil over the acrimony which found its final expression in the beamer attack, for none of the players was disciplined except for Patel and Lamba, who were banned for 13 and ten months respectively. The sequel to the violence on the pitch was a riot in the crowd, which resulted in the covers and anything else suitable being set alight, bringing the match to a premature conclusion.

WISDEN – 1993

India as guinea-pigs: in 1992, India not only became South Africa's first international opponents for over 20 years, but they also took part in the first series to be overseen by match referees. What's more, they also became the first team to face Shane Warne in a Test. He made his debut in the Third Test, taking one wicket for 150 runs in 45 overs. Ravi Shastri was his first Test victim – caught by Dean Jones for 206.

THE SOUTH AFRICANS IN INDIA, 1991–92, by Matthew Engel

The South Africans arrived in Calcutta, four months after rejoining the International Cricket Council, at the insistence of the Board of Control for Cricket in India after Pakistan had called off a scheduled tour because of worsening Hindu–Muslim tensions. The visit was arranged almost as hurriedly as some of the rebel tours in which South Africa had lately specialised. But it was organised with the special blessing of the Marxist government of West Bengal. Thousands of people lined the route from the airport to the hotel to welcome the team, carrying banners with slogans that only a few months ago would have been politically unthinkable, 'South Africa–India friendship long live'. The tourists' plane was said to be the first from South Africa ever to land in India…

The Indians were surprised when, in South Africa's very first game back, Bacher made 'an informal protest' about the state of the ball, which had apparently been gouged while the Indians were fielding to help it swing. World-weary observers thought it was a little too soon for South Africa to switch from being cricket's pariah to its preacher. The Indians denied any wrongdoing and the South African board president, Geoff Dakin, was obliged to apologise to his hosts.

India v South Africa
First One-Day International, at Calcutta, November 10, 1991

South Africa's first officially blessed representative match in almost 22 years, first one-day international and first-ever game against India attracted a crowd widely claimed as beating the world record for a day's cricket of 90,800. However, Jagmohan Dalmiya, president of the Cricket Association of Bengal, said Eden Gardens now contained 90,452 seats and estimates putting the attendance higher included all the various officials, pressmen, policemen and peanut vendors.

The cricket was a disappointment and India's victory was easier than the margin suggested. South Africa were obliged to bat at 9am when the ball swung in the Calcutta smog and, understandably, the batting was nervy since 90,000 people, many of them throwing firecrackers, were able to create quite an atmosphere even if they did not break the record… Even in defeat, the South Africans were still overwhelmed by the occasion, 'I know how Neil Armstrong felt when he stood on the moon,' said their captain Rice.

India won by three wickets.

THE INDIANS IN AUSTRALIA 1991–92, by Dicky Rutnagur

India's 4–0 defeat in their first full series in Australia in 14 years betrayed serious shortcomings in the team, but it also highlighted the tourists' handicap of inadequate preparation for the Tests. On the insistence of their own board, India were allowed only one first-class match before the opening Test. While Australia won the First, Second and Fifth Tests by crushing margins, India were deprived by the weather of almost certain victory in the Third. In addition, they salvaged much glory from the Fourth…

The outstanding Indian batsman was Tendulkar, whose 148 not out in the Third Test was so largely responsible for giving India a glimpse of victory and whose 114 at Perth saved them from an even quicker rout in the Fifth…

The series was historic in that it was the first to be played under the ICC's new code of conduct and the first in which the restriction on short-pitched bowling applied. It also marked the inception of the office of referee – shared by former England captains Mike Smith and Peter May. Played in amicable spirit, the series was free of altercations… There were occasions when the Indians expressed dissatisfaction with the umpiring. As often as not, television showed their complaints to be justified. At one stage, India's cricket manager, Abbas Ali Baig, drew attention to the disparity in lbw decisions given against the two sides. 'Perhaps,' he noted drily, 'there are changes in the lbw of which we have not been made aware.'

THE BENSON AND HEDGES WORLD CUP 1991–92, by David Frith

India lost a tight opening match against England, beat Pakistan, who fell apart under the Sydney lights, but were themselves soon to fall by the wayside through poor fielding and an indecisiveness in all departments.

YORKSHIRE, by John Callaghan

Yorkshire's decision to break with treasured tradition and sign an overseas player brought some commercial success, checking the worrying decline in membership. However, the county endured a disastrous season on the field, emphasising that there are no easy or short-term answers to long-standing problems…

Australian fast bowler Craig McDermott, the original choice as Yorkshire's first officially recognised 'outsider', broke down during the winter and required an operation for groin trouble, so, with little room for manoeuvre, the club turned their attentions at the last minute to Sachin Tendulkar. The 19-year-old Indian's appearance on the scene at least silenced all those who, from a distance, accused Yorkshire of being racist, and he proved extremely popular with the public and fellow-players. Tendulkar collected his runs with a good deal of style, scoring quickly in the limited-overs competitions and being prepared to apply himself diligently in the Championship, but he lacked the experience to dominate.

OBITUARIES

Pandove, Dhruv Mahender, was killed in a car accident near New Delhi on January 31, 1992. He was an attractive left-handed batsman, full of promise, and at 18 was already being tipped for Test honours. The Indian team observed two minutes' silence for him before the start of play during the Fifth Test match against Australia in Perth. In November 1987, aged only 13, he made 94 for Punjab against Himachal Pradesh on his debut in the Ranji Trophy – an astonishing achievement – and a year later he hit 137 against Jammu and Kashmir in his third first-class match. He became the youngest player ever to have reached 1,000 runs in the Ranji Trophy when he scored 170, his second century, against Services a few weeks before his death.

Swaroop Kishen, who died on November 21, 1992, aged 62, was one of the best-known Indian Test umpires and undoubtedly the most distinctive. He was an exceptionally tubby man who looked like Alfred Hitchcock, chewed betel-nut and generally lent an air of jollity to some highly-charged cricket matches. He umpired in 17 Tests, equalling the Indian record held by B. Satyaji Rao, between 1978–79 and 1984–85, and acquired a reputation for exceptional fair-mindedness among touring players. This, however, was dissipated in his last Test, at Bombay in 1984–85, when, often after interminable pauses for thought, he gave out several England batsmen in bizarre circumstances.

WISDEN – 1994

England toured India and Sri Lanka in 1992–93 on what was probably their least successful overseas trip. Of course, it was never quite their fault that they lost...

India, meanwhile, continued on their ground-breaking adventures – this time in Zimbabwe and South Africa, while in his Notes, the editor, Matthew Engel paid tribute to a number of cricketers who had retired the previous year:

> I shall miss too Kris Srikkanth, whose practice of opening Test matches as if he were Gilbert Jessop on speed finally laid to rest the idea that Indian batsmanship was inherently boring.

ENGLAND IN INDIA AND SRI LANKA, 1992–93, by Peter Hayter

In fact, England did play terribly. They became the first team ever to lose all their matches in a Test series in India, going down 3–0, each time by a huge margin. They then lost a Test match to Sri Lanka for the first time....

The communal violence in the wake of the destruction of the temple of Ayodhya that resulted in hundreds of deaths all over India also created an unsettled atmosphere among the squad. Their fears were heightened when the first international match, due to be played in Ahmedabad, was cancelled because the safety of the players could not be guaranteed. As a result of this and crowd disturbances at games that did take place, some of the party simply gave up trying to come to terms with a country that, at the best of times, can be quite overwhelming.

They were also subjected to a bizarre itinerary, drawn up by the Indian board in the belief that the Test matches would be unpopular. India's successes proved this quite mistaken. The trip would have been exhausting even if Indian Airlines pilots had not been on strike…

Some suggested that, in future, any player fortunate enough to be selected for India should acclimatise by revving a car engine in a locked garage. Even the scorer, Clem Driver of Essex, collapsed during the First Test and returned home; Monica Reeve, mother of Dermot, took over the scorebook…

Kumble was the best of the spinners England met in all four Tests, taking 21 [wickets] at 19.80. His success set the seal on an unhappy first tour for new team manager Keith Fletcher. After having returned from a costly spying mission to watch India's Test in Johannesburg, Fletcher announced the following verdict on the bespectacled leg-spinner, 'I didn't see him turn a single ball from leg to off. I don't believe we will have much problem with him.'

INDIA'S FIRST TEST VICTORY AGAINST ZIMBABWE

After being on the wrong side of a draw in the inaugural Test between the two countries at Harare a few months earlier, India came back strongly to beat Zimbabwe in the only Test of this tour, part of the new Test nation's learning curve.

THE ZIMBABWEANS IN INDIA, 1992–93, by R. Mohan

The Zimbabweans came to India to learn. Though they lost the Test match by an innings and the limited-overs series 3–0, the newcomers to Test cricket gained valuable experience from their first overseas tour at this level. It was a useful step forward after a debut Test season at home, in which they had announced their arrival by dominating the one-off Test against India in Harare. The conditions were very different. The well-rolled turf of the Harare Sports Club had denied help to all the bowlers, fast and slow, while the Feroz Shah Kotla in New Delhi held out something for the spinners. The Indians, fresh from their rousing 3–0 triumph over England, were hot favourites to win a fourth consecutive Test, and duly did so.

Only Test, at Delhi, 13, 14, 15, 16, 17, March, 1993

The scoreboard read Zimbabwe 275-3, A. Flower 115, G. W. Flower 96. About half an hour after lunch on the fourth day a draw was written all over the one-off Test and Feroz Shah Kotla seemed destined to mark the end of India's sequence of stirring triumphs. A sudden rush of blood came to Andy Flower's head, like some African gust of wind. He charged Maninder Singh, the slow left-armer, to be stumped by the wicketkeeper Vijay Yadav. The complexion of the contest changed decisively. The Flowers had been well set to join Ian and Greg Chappell and Mushtaq and Sadiq Mohammad as the third pair of brothers to make centuries in the same Test innings, but Grant was lbw in Maninder's next over. Zimbabwe's defiance of Indian spin was at an end. By tea the visitors were batting again.

For India it had been a battle against time. Almost a day was lost thanks to the primitive covers, which a minor shower penetrated to reach the pitch and render the run-ups soggy. The momentum on the opening day, which saw successive century partnerships for the second and third wickets, was arrested. But in the brief play possible on the second day Kambli took part in a third stand that went over 100, for the fourth wicket, before running out his captain, Azharuddin, while in the nervous 190s. He went on to emulate Hammond and Bradman in making a second successive Test double-century, before he fell victim to the veteran off-spinner Traicos. Kambli came three runs closer than he did against England in Bombay to breaking the record score by an Indian in Test cricket, S. M. Gavaskar's 236 not out against West Indies at Madras nine years earlier. But he remained third, behind V. Mankad's 231 against New Zealand at Madras in 1955–56. The accuracy of Traicos was the only check on the rampaging Indian batsmen until India called a halt at lunch on the third day, with Amre's quick fifty having taken them to an imposing 536.

Zimbabwe would have left satisfied at the close that evening. The Flowers had steadied the innings after Arnott was leg-before first ball, with Campbell and Houghton dismissed by the 34th over. The left-handed Andy and the right-handed Grant formed an effective combination to counter the spinners, and held them at bay for 192 runs and nearly 82 overs. Andy, who scored his 115 in 289 minutes from 236 balls, was the more aggressive foil to Grant, who made his 96 in 425 minutes and 359 balls.

Once the brothers had gone the spinners shared the spoils. But it was the last wicket, that of Shah attempting a second run against Sidhu's throwing arm at long leg, which sealed Zimbabwe's fate. They were left 15 short of saving the follow-on and they struggled throughout their second innings after Grant Flower was lbw in the second over. A bright 61 from Campbell and his stand of 64 with fellow left-hander Andy Flower, after Houghton went early on the final day, represented the height of resistance. Andy Flower's second, more subdued, innings lasted 214 minutes and 191 balls; it was defence of a high calibre on a wearing pitch. In all, he spent more than eight hours at the crease and ensured that Zimbabwe were far from disgraced. But Maninder took 4-66 and Kumble, mixing top-spinners with the occasional genuine leg-break, finished with 5-70 and eight in the match, giving him 53 in ten Tests, the quickest any Indian bowler has reached 50 wickets.

India 536 for seven wickets declared (Kambli 227, Tendulkar 62, Sidhu 61, Amre 52*; Traicos 3-186). **Zimbabwe 322** (A. Flower 115, G. Flower 96; Maninder Singh 3-79, Kumble 3-90) and **201** (A. Flower 62*, Campbell 61; Kumble 5-70, Maninder Singh 4-66). India won by an innings and 13 runs.

THE INDIANS IN ZIMBABWE AND SOUTH AFRICA, 1992–93,
by Richard Streeton

A great deal of humdrum cricket failed to detract from the diplomatic and sporting history made when India embarked on a tour of Zimbabwe and South Africa late in 1992. Slow scoring and negative captaincy, coupled with moribund pitches, marred both Zimbabwe's inaugural Test and the first series staged in South Africa for 23 years. The continued failure of the Indians to do themselves justice away from home also militated against the representative games being worthy of these occasions.

OBITUARIES

Aggarwal, Vivek, was killed on April 26, 1993, when an Indian Airlines plane crashed just after take-off from Aurangabad. He was 31 and a flight purser with the airline. He played in one first-class match, in the Ranji Trophy for Haryana against Bengal at Faridabad in 1982–83.

Deodhar, Professor Dinakar Balwant, who died at Pune on August 24, 1993, aged 101, was the world's oldest living first-class cricketer. He not merely became a real-life centurion, he was the first Indian to score a hundred for a representative side against a visiting team: 148 for All-India against A. E. R. Gilligan's MCC team in 1926–27. This confirmed his reputation as one of the best batsmen in India, secured over several seasons playing for the Hindus in the Bombay Quadrangular. India's Test status came too late for him, since he was already 42 by 1932, but he remained a successful batsman for Maharashtra in the Ranji Trophy until 1946. He led them to the trophy in 1939–40 and 1940–41, having effectively founded the team as a breakaway from Bombay and recruited V. S. Hazare to play for him.

Deodhar was still scoring first-class centuries long after he was 50: two in a match against Nawanagar in 1944–45, the last in a charity match in 1946. He was almost 56 when he played his final first-class match in 1947–48. In 81 first-class matches he scored 4,522 runs, averaging 39.22 and hitting 12 centuries. He was a Professor of Sanskrit. He was also an Indian selector, first-class umpire, radio commentator and the author of three books in English and Marathi. When he was 97 he wrote an introduction to a book about C. K. Nayudu. The tribute included a rebuke about Nayudu's chain-smoking which, he said, led to his early death at the age of 72.

Patel, Jasubhai Motibhai, the Indian off-spinner, died on December 12, 1992, aged 68. Jasu Patel will always be remembered as the man who bowled India to their first-ever victory over Australia at Kanpur in 1959–60. He was already 35 with tinges of grey hair, but he was unexpectedly included at the insistence of Lala Amarnath, the chairman of selectors. Patel was known as a matting specialist but Amarnath thought the newly laid turf wicket might suit his unclassical whippy action.

Patel responded by taking the best-ever analysis for India, 9-69 in the first innings – McDonald, Harvey, Davidson, Benaud and Kline were all bowled – and 5-55 in the second. India won by 119 runs. He took 15 wickets in six other Tests, before and afterwards. Patel was the first cricketer to be awarded the Padma Shri, India's second-highest civilian award.

WISDEN – 1995

This edition was notable in that Mike Selvey wrote an appreciation to mark the retirement of Kapil Dev, the same accolade that Sunil Gavaskar had enjoyed a few years earlier.

THE RECORD-BREAKERS RETIRE

Perhaps the hardest thing to appreciate about Kapil Dev finally exchanging his cricket box for the TV commentary box is the fact that he was only 35 years old when he did so. Well, give or take a bit maybe: he might be a touch more geriatric than that; it is often suggested that at the time he was born, whenever that was, it was not necessarily the custom in northern India to register the year of birth. But that misses the point: however old he was, he seemed to have been around for a lot longer, prancing in to shore up the Indian attack and joyfully retrieving an innings with uninhibited squeaky-clean hitting. An Indian team without him will never seem quite the same.

With his departure comes the end of an era that has been blessed with a quartet of all-rounders unmatched in the history of the game, beginning in the early 1970s with Richard – later Sir Richard – Hadlee and Imran Khan, progressing to the laddo Botham, and finally, with his Test debut in October 1978, to the man who became known to his countrymen as the Haryana Hurricane.

What deeds from these four! Between them, they took 1,610 Test wickets and scored 17,379 runs. With the possible exception of Hadlee, each was equipped technically to play international cricket as a specialist in either role. But what a contrast: Hadlee the Inquisitor, with a surgeon's touch and an accountant's brain; Imran, the haughty, proud Pathan; Botham, the bull elephant who lived cricket and life on the edge; and Kapil, flamboyant and cavalier, charming but deadly. Today, Wasim Akram alone is left to carry a torch for the standards set by these four.

Kapil has perhaps been regarded as the most lightweight of the group. But with 434 wickets and 5,248 runs, he is the one who proved, in the end, to be the most prolific with both ball and bat. That has much to do with the fact that he played 131 Tests compared with Hadlee's 86, Imran's 88 and Botham's 102. And, as the last to survive, he was in a position to make sure that he finished top of the heap. But he laid out his credentials as soon as he entered Test cricket. His teeth may have flashed a disarming smile but this was a formidable competitor worthy of his fierce Punjabi ancestors.

Kapil has always regarded bowling as his primary role. And on February 8, 1994 he took the wicket of the Sri Lankan, Hashan Tillekeratne, to go past Hadlee's world record haul of 431 wickets. For the latter part of his career, it had been a hard slog, chipping away bit by bit at the target, like someone climbing a rock face and gradually running out of handholds with the top of the pitch in sight. Towards the end the years caught up and he was reduced to little more than medium-pace, with away-swing going invitingly early.

But it hadn't always been so. In his prime, he was much like the young, lithe Botham, with pace enough – goaded by the irrational Indian belief that their bowlers were born only to beguile – to render footwork leaden. This was accompanied by snaking late outswing, helped by a contortionist's action so far round that it presented his left shoulder-blade to the batsman, and a wicked break-back that struck with the speed of a cobra. Superficially, his bowling may have lacked Hadlee's relentlessly searching examination, or Imran's leaping, muscular pace, or Botham's bludgeon and willpower, but it was deceptively effective for all that.

Yet in the fullness of time, he may be remembered more for his carefree, hawk-eyed batting. He was helped by the fact that he was an all-rounder and so had the freedom to play as he did: one discipline fuelled the other. The rate at which he was capable of scoring was phenomenal. At Lord's in 1982, he brought the England bowling to its knees, hitting 13 fours and three sixes, an innings of 89 that came from just 55 balls, well on course then for what would have been the fastest Test century in history. And in his last Lord's Test, in 1990 – Gooch's match – he scored the 24 India required to save the follow-on by hitting Eddie Hemmings for four successive straight 6s while the last man, Hirwani, blinked myopically at the other end and got out next ball.

And yet perhaps his finest moment came not in a Test but in a limited-overs international against Zimbabwe, not even a Test-playing nation then, at, improbably enough, Tunbridge Wells. In 1983, it was Kapil's lot to lead India in the World Cup, and he found himself at the crease on a damp pitch, with the scoreboard reading 17-5. He was to play what he has described as the innings of a lifetime, scoring an unbeaten 175 as India reached 266-8 and went on to win the game.

Eventually, they progressed to the final at Lord's where, against all the odds, they beat West Indies, then arguably the most potent cricket force ever to set foot on the ground. Kapil and India showed they could be taken, and an illusion was shattered: West Indies have not won the World Cup since.

THE INDIANS IN SRI LANKA 1993–94, by R. Mohan

India's first victory in an overseas Test, let alone series, since the defeat of England in 1986 may have been a while coming, but beating their neighbours on Sri Lankan soil gave the players enormous satisfaction. However, success was accompanied by acrimony. Throughout the series, the referee, Peter Burge, was kept busy with complaints over the umpiring from the Indians, who believed they had to take many more than the 20 wickets usually required to win a Test.

The controversy was at its height during the Second Test, when the Indians accused umpires Ponnadurai and Anandappa of palpably biased decision-making. Burge could do little other than send his observations back to headquarters, but at the behest of ICC he did call for a meeting mid-Test between the contestants to cool them down. India's delight in their eventual victory helped to restore normal relations between the two sides, which had been bitterly strained by the midfield exchanges.

THE SRI LANKANS IN INDIA, 1993–94, by R. Mohan

For the second time the Sri Lankans came to the rescue when Pakistan cancelled their visit to India amid fears about security. The fact that they were soundly beaten in all three Tests, each time by an innings and inside four days, was somehow insignificant compared to the need to keep up these exchange tours in the Asian subcontinent.

The only real controversy, as in India's visit to Sri Lanka a few months earlier, was provoked by the umpiring. Sri Lankan manager Bandula Warnapura claimed the batting failures of the first two Tests owed as much to his players' nerves, waiting for the next bad decision, as to bad shots. But after the Third Test, in which the umpires avoided giving anyone lbw unless he was playing right back, captain Arjuna Ranatunga agreed that Sri Lanka had been beaten fair and square.

The Sri Lankans were not the first side to disparage home umpiring, and probably not the last, even though these were the last Tests played with two local umpires rather than one local and one overseas umpire from the ICC's panel.

THE HERO CUP 1993–94

The Hero Cup, staged to commemorate the diamond jubilee of the Cricket Association of Bengal, produced a repeat of the 1983 World Cup final. Once again, India unexpectedly defeated the favourites, West Indies, who had headed the table after the preliminary rounds with three wins in four matches.

India v West Indies
Hero Cup Final, at Calcutta, November 27, 1993

A crowd widely estimated at close to 100,000 watched with delight as West Indies' batting collapsed. From 57-1 they lost nine wickets for 66 and were all out with nearly ten overs remaining. Kumble took the last six for four runs in 26 balls. His full figures of six for 12 were the best for India in one-day internationals.

India 225 for 7 (50 overs) (V. G. Kambli 68). **West Indies 123** (40.1 overs) (A. Kumble 6-12). India won by 102 runs.

CRICKETERS OF THE YEAR 1996
A. KUMBLE, by Scyld Berry

The first Indian since Duleepsinhji to be chosen as a Cricketer of the Year for his efforts on behalf of an English county – in his case Northamptonshire – Anil Kumble was chosen before he matched Jim Laker by taking 10-74 in a Test against Pakistan in 1998–99.

The summer of 1995 saw a pleasing contrast between international cricket and the domestic game. The Test series between England and West Indies was so dominated by pace bowlers, on both sides, that spinners took less than a tenth of the wickets. In first-class cricket, on the other hand, the two leading wicket-takers were Asian leg-spinners: Mushtaq Ahmed with 95 wickets, and Anil Kumble with 105.

Kumble thus became the first bowler to take 100 wickets since 1991; the first spinner to do so since 1983; and the first leg-spinner since 1971. But only nominally can Kumble be classified as a leg-spinner, for he does not specialise in temptations that end in a stumping, or a catch at long-off, and a deceived bat slammed against pad. He is a bowler of his own kind: a brisk top-spin bowler, making the ball turn a little both ways; tall at 6ft 2in and dangerously bouncy on a hard pitch; and as persistently accurate in finding his target as a mosquito. Not one of his 105 victims was stumped. Twenty were leg-before and 21 bowled, most of them making the mistake of thinking they had time to play back to this leg-spinner. All the rest were caught, seldom in the deep, largely by Richard Montgomerie at short leg, David Capel at slip, Rob Bailey at silly point and Kevin Curran at gully. Kumble paid tribute to them all, and to Bob Carter who conducted their practices, for fulfilling such a demanding task without previous experience of such bowling.

Over the first-class season he conceded 2.3 runs per over, and then the bat's edge was frequently the scorer: at times a whole session would pass without Kumble conceding a boundary in front of the wicket. He bowled more overs than anyone else as well, except Mushtaq; and as his Indian compatriots at Gloucestershire and Durham, Javagal Srinath and Manoj Prabhakar, were equally hard-working, together they did much to change the perception of Indian players, hitherto not renowned for their stamina, in county cricket. After the NatWest Trophy final at Lord's when Kumble turned on what he thought was his best one-day bowling of the season, Warwickshire's captain Dermot Reeve summarised the impression of all English cricket when he declared that Kumble was 'a fabulous bowler'.

There is only one bowler of the last generation to whom he could be compared. But as Anil Kumble was born on October 17, 1970, in Bangalore, he was too young to have studied Bhagwath Chandrasekhar and did not take him as a model. However, the conditions which prompted Chandrasekhar to bowl medium-paced top-spinners and googlies were those that governed Kumble's development. Club cricket in Bangalore is played on matting spread over baked mud (Kumble still occasionally turns out for his club, Young Cricketers), and the springy rather than fast surface can make a top-spinner bounce exceptionally. Kumble smiles at the recollection of wicketkeepers who were apprehensive about standing up to him. As in the case of Chandra, the batsman can sometimes hear the ball fizz after leaving Kumble's hand – although it is no easier to play for being audible as well as visible.

Kumble's father, a management consultant, had not played the game formally. Anil began by playing tennis ball cricket in the streets outside his house, a form of the game which has organised tournaments there. He moved on to bowl medium-pace until his conversion at 15, when for one reason or another, his elder brother Dinesh persuaded him to try leg-spin as a novelty, even in southern India. 'There was no one to guide me or coach me or show me how to grip the ball,' Kumble remembers. But with a long and energetic arm-swing, and powerful shoulders, he could soon make it bounce like a tennis ball.

He was rapidly selected for Karnataka Schools Under-15, then for Karnataka in 1989–90, when Chandra was in his last year as a state selector. On the 1990 tour of England he made his Test debut at Old Trafford, aged 19, as a bespectacled No. 10 (he has since shed the glasses for lenses, and his lowly status in the order, making hundreds for Karnataka). His first Test wicket was Allan Lamb, caught at silly point, which had long-term consequences.

His 100th came in his 21st Test, on his home ground in Bangalore. In home Tests he often had turning pitches to bowl on, and large Tendulkar-fed totals to bowl at, but that is still a fine record: Shane Warne took two more Tests to reach his 100. His Indian captain, Mohammad Azharuddin, phoned Lamb to recommend Kumble when Northamptonshire wanted to replace Curtly Ambrose; and when the county contacted him at a Madras hotel, he accepted without even discussing terms.

Kumble's aim in undertaking county cricket was to develop his variety and to learn more about pitches, with a view to India's tour of England in 1996. This ambition he fulfilled. While he kept to his lower trajectory and faster speed for one-day matches, in the Championship he bowled more slowly than hitherto, and turned the ball sideways both further and more often, not just fizzing it through. He would bowl six googlies in an over against a left-hander.

His county did their best to make Northampton's pitches as similar as possible to Bangalore. He took 64 wickets at 16 runs apiece at Northampton, and 41 wickets at 27 elsewhere. If he sometimes had to come on before the seam bowlers had taken a wicket, he was always accurate, and calm, as native Kannada-speakers are reputed to be.

'I'm very satisfied with my season,' he declared afterwards, and so were the county, who failed to win that elusive Championship through no fault of their overseas signing. Unmarried, teetotal and vegetarian, a graduate in mechanical engineering and speaking excellent English, Kumble would join in with his team-mates at the bar, even if taking soft drinks. They would have him back any time he can get away from his public relations job for Triton Watches, his employers in Bangalore; and from the Test match game so dominated by seam.

WISDEN – 1996

West Indies toured India, but otherwise India merely participated in four one-day tournaments: The Singer World Series in Sri Lanka, the Wills World Series in India, the Pepsi Asia Cup in Sharjah, and the New Centenary Tournament in New Zealand. They won the first three and finished last in the fourth.

THE WEST INDIANS IN INDIA, 1994–95, by R. Mohan

An outbreak of pneumonic plague in the western state of Gujarat raised doubts about whether this tour would take place at all. Eventually, the West Indians arrived a week late – and they left the preservation of their reputation very late too. Having gone one down in the First Test at Bombay and drawn at Nagpur, they waited until the last day of the tour to hit back and level the series. West Indies had not lost a Test series since their 1–0 defeat in New Zealand in March

1980; the turnaround at Mohali near Chandigarh, was a great escape for Courtney Walsh and his party on a tour when little went right…

The hastily rearranged itinerary was heavily loaded with one-day cricket. Though West Indies began the bilateral series (reduced from six games to five) with an emphatic win, India made sure of it by winning the next four. And the Indians also dominated the fortnight of the triangular competition, which interrupted the main programme…

West Indies thus reached Bombay for the Test series in a downbeat mood. Still, they had every chance to win there, especially when Kenneth Benjamin had India on the run at 11-3 in the second innings. But a couple of vital chances went begging and Sachin Tendulkar – unexpectedly backed up by tailender Javagal Srinath – set up India's tenth successive home victory, which was also the tenth Test win for captain Mohammad Azharuddin, an Indian record…

On the final day Benjamin and Walsh swept aside the Indian batting. The pair had had to carry the pace attack throughout the series and finished it with 17 wickets apiece. Bouncing back to win by 243 runs did Walsh and his team great credit, and earned them the newly constituted Fatesinhrao Gaekwad Trophy (on the strength of their 3–0 series win the previous time the teams met). Meanwhile, India had to accept their first defeat in 15 Tests since they lost in South Africa in December 1992.

TRAGEDY AT NAGPUR – NINE PEOPLE KILLED WATCHING INDIA V NEW ZEALAND

Nine people were killed and 50 injured when a wall collapsed at the Vidarbha Cricket Association Ground at Nagpur during a one-day international between India and New Zealand on November 26, 1995.

The disaster happened during the lunch interval when, according to reports, spectators from the third tier of the East Stand were rushing down and those from the second tier were going up to try to get a better view. The staircase wall gave way under the pressure of people. Three youngsters were killed immediately when they plunged 15 metres to the ground. Six more died in hospital. Among the dead was a female engineering student. Some reports spoke of up to 12 dead and 70 injured but these figures were not confirmed. Four cricket fans had already been killed in a car crash while on their way to the ground.

The wall had only just been built as part of an extension constructed in preparation for the World Cup. It had been built without reinforcement and four people, including the architect and contractor, were charged with negligence. VCA officials decided to continue the match, despite protests from some members of the city council. The players were not told and New Zealand went on to win.

WISDEN – 1997

ENGLAND WOMEN IN INDIA 1995–96, by Carol Salmon

India v England
Second Test, at Jamshedpur, November 24, 25, 26, 27, 1995

A momentous finish transformed the game. India needed just 128 to win and recovered from a shaky 75-5 to 105 without further loss. Then Debbie Stock struck twice with successive balls and a run-out left them 106-8. Another run-out, when India were four short, brought in Neetu David, who must have thought she had won the match when she completed a Test record of eight wickets for 53 earlier in the day. She played the first ball of the penultimate over for a single; Laya Francis blocked the next delivery, but the third one hit her on the pads and ran to fine leg. The crowd shouted to the batsmen to run, England shouted to Metcalfe to throw the ball in, but Jo Chamberlain shouted an appeal to the umpire, who, after what seemed an age, raised his finger.

England 196 and **194** (N. David 8-53). **India 263** (S. Dabir 60, S. Shaw 54) and **125**. England won by two runs.

A WIND BLOWS FROM THE EAST, by Mihir Bose

Mihir Bose looked ahead and saw quite clearly how Indian money would change the game.

Napoleon's warning that the world should beware when China awakes has, in the last year, been translated into a wholly unexpected warning for the cricket world from another part of Asia – the Indian subcontinent. It has happened, not on the cricket field, but off it…

It is the money that the subcontinent can now generate through cricket that is posing a challenge to the established power centres. It is transforming the traditional image of the subcontinent as the land of magical spinners, wristy batsmen and (in Pakistan) devilish fast bowlers, into a place whose rich cricket administrators can dictate the future of the game…

A hint of this had come in 1993 when India, Pakistan and Sri Lanka, after the most fractious meeting ever of the International Cricket Council, won the right to stage the 1996 World Cup. The key to victory was the way the three countries got the ICC's Associate Members – hitherto treated much as the Soviet Union used to treat its eastern European satellites – on their side by promising them £100,000 each. England, who believed they had a gentleman's agreement guaranteeing them the 1996 tournament, had offered £60,000 each, and throughout the meeting seemed to assume this was yet another cosy old boys' gathering. The Asians wheeled in politicians and lawyers and treated the event as if it were an American presidential convention. They outflanked England and won a rich prize. How rich only became evident when the 1996 World Cup began...

As soon as they had won the competition the hosts set about selling it. Their biggest success was auctioning the television rights for a staggering $US14 million... The organisers loved the rivalry. They were aware that they could keep all the profits, once they had met their expenses, which included a fee of £250,000 to each of the competing Test countries. This amount did not even cover the expenses of some of the teams, but the hosts pocketed a profit of almost $50 million...

It could be argued that the cricket administrators of the rest of the world were naïve to agree to such an arrangement. But in five previous World Cups nobody had sought, let alone achieved, such commercial success. Not everyone on the subcontinent foresaw it. The Sri Lankans, co-hosts of the tournament along with India and Pakistan, clearly had doubts: they did not agree to underwrite the costs, so did not participate in any of the profits.

The man who drove the commercial juggernaut was Jagmohan Dalmiya, secretary of the Indian board. He hails from the Marwari community of India whose business skills are both feared and respected. The joke in India is that a Marwari can do business with a Scotsman and a Jew and still make money. The other joke, less flattering, is that if you should see a Marwari and a tiger together in the jungle, you should shoot the Marwari first...

Had the subcontinent been content with its World Cup killing, this would have been an interesting marketing story. What has made it an explosive cricketing one is the use the triumphant administrators made of their new-found financial power. They launched a two-pronged attack. The short-term aim was to make Dalmiya chairman of ICC. The long-term aim was to make sure that the subcontinent was at the centre of the cricket world.

The first battle came to a head during the annual ICC meeting at Lord's in July. With Sir Clyde Walcott coming to the end of his term, Dalmiya stood for the chairmanship, along with Malcolm Gray from Australia and Krish Mackerdhuj of South Africa. On the basis of a simple majority, Dalmiya, bolstered by the Associate countries, had the votes. But he did not command the majority of the Test-playing countries. The rules were less than clear, but the Indians, having taken the advice of a QC, contended that the election should be decided by a simple majority. Walcott argued that any successful chairman must have the backing of a two-thirds majority of the Test-playing countries: six out of nine. Underlying this was concern about what a Dalmiya chairmanship might do...

The meeting ended in stalemate... In the meantime Walcott carried on. The wider issue remains: how can ICC accommodate the new power? The Asians want to be at the top table. As one administrator put it, 'We do not want to come to

Lord's for ICC and just nod our heads like little schoolboys as we used to. Now we come with fully prepared plans and want to be heard as equals.'

It is interesting to note that on this issue the old racial solidarity displayed when ICC tackled apartheid in South Africa no longer holds. In subcontinental eyes the West Indies are part of the old power structure, marshalled by England and Australia. Cricket has evolved no mechanism to cope with a changing situation...

The ICC may no longer be a creature of the MCC, but its offices are still at Lord's. And the two men who have presided over it since the MCC president stopped being automatically head of ICC, Sir Colin Cowdrey and Sir Clyde Walcott, have been old-world figures. In such a setting, Dalmiya is seen as a parvenu out to wreck the game. As one (non-Asian) administrator put it, 'Dalmiya, personally, may not have been acceptable, and his tactics of trying to storm the citadel were probably wrong. But we have to realise that the subcontinent is a major power in world cricket. The television market there alone makes it very important.'

... In May 1997 the Indians are planning to hold a tournament to celebrate 50 years of their independence. Traditionally, the idea of playing in India in May was considered preposterous. But in order to avoid the worst of the intense heat, the Indians intend to start matches at about 3.30 in the afternoon and play until midnight. The Indians can contemplate this because the profits of the World Cup have helped them install lights in most of their grounds. And they know the TV rights will fetch large sums of money. Already, cricket in Sri Lanka from August has cut into the latter half of the northern summer, which used to be the exclusive cricket preserve of England. A tournament in May will be another dent.

The end result could be a far more powerful ICC – more like FIFA or the International Olympic Committee than the present small-scale set-up consisting of David Richards, the chief executive, a couple of assistants and a few phones. The subcontinent may not even want such an outcome: its bid for power should be seen as more akin to the barons at Runnymede extracting concessions from King John. But just as the Magna Carta led to consequences undreamt of by the barons, so this could make ICC the real powerhouse of cricket.

But is this what cricket wants, or needs? Does it really want to exchange the cosy club – admittedly biased in favour of the older cricketing countries – for an elective dictatorship at the mercy of the richest? In such a situation the subcontinent may even find that it has created an animal it cannot always control.

THE WILLS WORLD CUP 1996, by Alan Lee

Alan Lee did not mask his views on the Sixth World Cup.

The event was poorly conceived in its format and its logistics and suffered throughout from the threat – and ultimately the reality – of crowd disorder. The abandonment of the semi-final at Eden Gardens, Calcutta, following bottle throwing and firelighting on the terraces, was a shameful reflection on standards of sportsmanship in an area until recently renowned for its appreciation of all things good in the game of cricket.

Perhaps, however, we should not be too harsh on the individuals responsible for the riot in Calcutta. They were merely responding to the seductions created for them by the promoters of the Wills World Cup, an event that plainly, disastrously, put money-making above all the fundamentals of organising a global sporting competition. As the glamorising of the Indian and Pakistani cricketers reached new and absurd heights, so too did the unshakeable belief of the masses in their invincibility. Defeat, of the kind that came to India that night in Calcutta, was popularly unimaginable, with consequences for which many must share the blame.

It was all markedly at odds with the 1987 World Cup, also co-hosted by India and Pakistan and widely judged to be an organisational triumph… The opening ceremony was attended by more than 100,000 people, most of whom must have left wondering what on earth they had been watching. The laser show malfunctioned, the compere was embarrassing and the grand launch was a complete flop – so much so that there were subsequent calls at Calcuttan government level for the arrest of the Pilcom convenor, Jagmohan Dalmiya, on a charge of wasting public money…

Sri Lanka's victory was to the great approval and acclaim of much of the cricketing world. It was also a result that, to some degree, rescued this World Cup from an abiding image of bungling mediocrity.

The tournament achieved one aim in increasing the profile of cricket, through television coverage on an impressive but largely uncritical scale, and undoubtedly it satisfied the organisers in the amount of money accrued. But the impression was that the cricket was secondary to the commercialism. Even in a game newly awakened to its financial opportunities, that cannot be right.

India v Sri Lanka
Semi-final, at Calcutta, March 13, 1996 (day/night)

Sri Lanka played brilliantly after a disastrous first over to achieve an unbeatable advantage. But the headlines were devoted to the riot which ended the match. Enraged by an Indian collapse of seven wickets for 22, some home supporters threw bottles on to the outfield and set fire to the seating. Referee Clive Lloyd took the teams off for 15 minutes, attempted a restart and then awarded Sri Lanka the game by default. Nobody questioned the result; India needed a near-impossible 132 from 15.5 overs, with only two wickets standing. But the Indian board smarted at the word default and asked for Sri Lanka to be declared winners on run-rate.

Sri Lanka 251 for eight wickets (50 overs) (P. A. de Silva 66, R. S. Mahanama 58 not out). **India 120 for eight wickets** (34.1 overs) (S. R. Tendulkar 65).
Sri Lanka won by default after a crowd riot.

THE INDIANS IN ENGLAND, 1996, by John Etheridge

For Mohammad Azharuddin, a man of dignity and a fine batsman to boot, India's 13th tour of England could scarcely have been a more harrowing experience. He was burdened by problems before the team even arrived and they escalated during the next ten weeks. India were comprehensively outclassed in the one-day internationals, beaten in the Test series and failed to win a single first-class match.

There is more. One of the team's leading players, Navjot Singh Sidhu, flew home in a huff after a bitter disagreement with his captain before the Test matches started. Azharuddin was accused of poor communications and being distant from his players, and endured mutterings about his personal life. He had left his wife and two children a few months previously and his girlfriend, a glamorous product of the Bollywood film industry, was by his side for much of the tour. His form with the bat virtually evaporated: he scored just 42 runs in five Test innings.

Ultimately, though, it could have been worse... Sourav Ganguly emerged as a batsman of impressive technique and temperament, Rahul Dravid was not far behind him, Javagal Srinath and Venkatesh Prasad established themselves as one of the best new-ball attacks in the world and Sachin Tendulkar confirmed what most people already knew: he stands alongside Brian Lara as the world's premier batsman. So, although Azharuddin's personal star barely flickered, he could at least take satisfaction from some elements of his team's performance...

India made errors in selection, bringing four spinners and only three quicker bowlers. They recognized the mistake quickly enough, though, summoning seamer Salil Ankola from league cricket in Northumberland, rather than another batsman, to replace Sidhu. A team bulging with spinners needed warm and dry conditions. Such weather was denied them; they spent the early weeks of the tour swathed in sweaters and buttressed against the cold. They even suffered stomach upsets – Brummy tummy rather than Delhi belly perhaps. As Sanjay Manjrekar put it, 'You just can't trust this English food.'

The Arctic winds were crucial because India's slow men – and Anil Kumble in particular – failed to slip into an immediate rhythm, and were always below their best... If the slow bowlers were ineffective, Srinath and Prasad were magnificent. They were the best bowlers on either side and, with more fortune, could have inflicted greater damage on England's batting. Rarely can a bowler have endured worse luck than Srinath. He consistently moved the ball, beat the bat and showed unflagging stamina. But dropped catches, poor umpiring and endless playing and missing conspired against him. Eleven wickets at 39.36 did him no sort of justice. Prasad, playing in his first Test series, was only a fraction behind Srinath...

Which leaves Tendulkar. Ah, Tendulkar! For a man who had his 23rd birthday just days before arriving in England and whose country had been starved of Test cricket, it is astonishing to think he scored his tenth Test century at Trent Bridge. It was a masterpiece, although not as good as his hundred in a losing cause at

Edgbaston. Tendulkar's technical perfection, insatiable run-hunger and unwavering concentration would put him in the top bracket in any era of batsmanship. Anything remotely loose – and plenty that is not – is dispatched with power and precision generated by his muscular, 5ft 5in frame…

The problems in the Indian team became public after the third one-day international when Sidhu was omitted and then flew home. His parting shot brooked no debate, 'I promised my father on his death-bed that I would live my life with integrity and respect. As long as I stay on this tour, I cannot do that.'

CRICKETERS OF THE YEAR 1997

S. R. TENDULKAR, by Mike Selvey

Undoubtedly the greatest batsman of his generation, and quite possibly the greatest ever Indian batsman, Tendulkar is also one of the richest cricketers of all time, one of the most easily recognised and one of the most unspoiled by his huge success. In the years since he was selected as a Cricketer of the Year, he has gone on to become the world's most capped Test player, the greatest Test run-maker, the greatest ODI run-maker and the scorer of the most Test and ODI centuries.

It was one brief moment in time. The World Cup, India versus West Indies in Gwalior, and a single stroke of such exquisiteness that the old maharajah surely would have had it carved in ivory and placed on a plinth. In essence, it was no more than a leg-side flick to the boundary and, in a competition that gorged itself on hitting, might have been worth only transient acclaim. But this was a gem: a length ball from a high-class pace bowler met initially with a straight blade, and then, at the last nanosecond, turned away with a roll of the wrist and such an irresistible alliance of power, timing and placement that first of all it eluded the fingertips of a mid-wicket fielder diving to his right, and then it did the same to the boundary runner haring and plunging to his left. Skill, technique, confidence, awareness, vision: pure genius, and four more runs to Sachin Tendulkar.

The young man is probably the most famous and feted man in India, outglitzing even the stars of Bollywood movies. With endorsements over the next five years estimated to be worth at least US$75 million, he is also the highest earner in cricket. He has become public property in a country of enthusiasms that can spill over into the fanatical, but has managed to maintain a dignified, mature outlook, remaining aware of his responsibilities while protecting his privacy. When he married Anjali, a doctor and friend from his childhood, he rejected massive sums from satellite TV for live coverage, keeping the ceremony a family affair. He knows his worth, and is wealthy beyond the dreams of almost a billion Indians, but he is not a grabber. His father, a university professor, imparted a sense of perspective and a work ethic.

Tendulkar averages over 50 in Tests and is the supreme right-hander, if not quite the finest batsman on the planet. He is a focused technician, who offers a counterpoint to Brian Lara's more eye-catching destruction, fuelled on flair and ego. He has, it seems, been around forever. In the Third Test at Trent Bridge last summer, he scored 177, the tenth century of his Test career and his second of the series: yet remarkably, at 23, Tendulkar was younger than any member of the England team, with only Dominic Cork and Min Patel born even in the same decade. His figures have been achieved despite a lack of Test cricket, particularly at home. Seven of his centuries had been scored before his 21st birthday, a unique record... With time on his side and a return to a full Test programme, he could prove Sunil Gavaskar right and rewrite the records.

Sachin Ramesh Tendulkar was born in Bombay on April 24, 1973, and, since childhood, has trodden a steady, almost inevitable, path to greatness. He attended the city's Sharadashram Vidyamandir school, where the Harris Memorial Challenge Shield, a competition for under-17s, provided the chance to bat for hours. From the age of 12, when he scored his first century for the school and came to notice as a special talent, he indulged himself. When 14, he compiled not out scores of 207, 329 and 346 in the space of five innings, one of them contributing to an unbroken partnership of 664 with Vinod Kambli, a record in any form of cricket.

He was 16 years and 205 days old when he made his Test debut, in November 1989, in the National Stadium in Karachi – for a young Indian, perhaps the most fiery baptism of all. The following year, at Old Trafford, he hit his first Test century – not a scintillating innings, but an exercise in technique, concentration and application beyond his tender years, which saved a game that might have been lost. Had it come 31 days earlier, he would have been the youngest century-maker in Test history. During the winter of 1991–92, he went to Australia, where they still talk in awe of the centuries he scored in Sydney and in Perth.

A few days after his 19th birthday, Tendulkar came back to England: to Yorkshire, no less, as the county's first overseas player. It would have been a massive responsibility for anyone, let alone a teenager from India, and it did not quite work, Tendulkar assumed the mantle conscientiously, and posed with cloth cap and pint of bitter, impressing colleagues and supporters alike with his understanding of public relations. But, in the end, he failed to come to terms with the county game, scoring only one century and barely scraping past 1,000 runs in his only season. Hindsight would tell him that it was part of his education, but a mistake nonetheless.

In 1996 he returned to England, a teenage prodigy no longer, but a seasoned Test batsman fit to stand alongside his first hero, Gavaskar. The pair have much in common: Gavaskar was slight of build and, of necessity, a supreme judge of length. Tendulkar, too, is short. There is a lot of bottom hand, but he drives strongly, on the rise, such is his strength of wrist and the control in his hands, while he is devastating off his legs, pulls well and – given good bounce – can cut wide bowling to ribbons. If the delicate and unexpected talents of Sourav Ganguly provided a distraction last

season, then Tendulkar's two hundreds in three Tests were ample demonstration of the team's premier batsman leading from the front. The first of them – at Edgbaston, where he made 122 out of 219 – was a stunning display of virtuosity in adversity.

In August, aged 23, Tendulkar succeeded Mohammad Azharuddin as captain of his country. Had he craved it and pursued it with a passion, he would surely have got the job earlier, perhaps even while a teenager. Rather, it was a position that was being held in abeyance until the time was right. His leadership has a firm base of experience to it now. His first Test in charge was against Australia. He made ten and nought but India won, just as one almost assumed they would. Some things just seem part of a wider plan.

OBITUARY

Modi, Rusi Sheriyar, who died on May 17, 1996, aged 71, was an Indian Test batsman, writer and all-round enthusiast for the game. Modi made his reputation when he hit centuries in seven consecutive Ranji matches for Bombay in the Indian seasons of 1943–44 and 1944–45. He scored three double-centuries in 1944–45, when he became the first batsman to make 1,000 in a Ranji Trophy season, and a fourth the following year against the Australian Services team on their way back from England, which Modi regarded as his best-ever innings.

He was still only 21 when he came to England in 1946, and John Arlott was quick to notice the contrast between Modi off the field, tall, painfully thin, grey of face and huddled into an overcoat, tending to tremble, and the confident, controlled batsman. Modi made 57 not out on his Test debut, at Lord's, and went on to play ten Tests, contributing crucial innings in the two games at Brabourne Stadium, Bombay, against West Indies in 1948–49: 112, his only Test century, in the Second, and 86 in the Fifth, when India almost snatched victory.

WISDEN – 1998

In a trend that was picking up pace, the Editor's Notes in this edition were increasingly concerned with matters off the pitch rather than on it. The first intimations of match fixing and spot betting were also noticed.

NOTES BY THE EDITOR, by Matthew Engel

Mr Dalmiya goes to Lord's

In 1996, the possibility that the Indian businessman Jagmohan Dalmiya might take control of the International Cricket Council had caused such consternation that it was almost split asunder. In 1997 he assumed office as President of ICC for a three-year term without a murmur of dissent. And the first public utterance of a man previously painted as a sort of money-mad barbarian was to congratulate Colin Cowdrey on his elevation to the House of Lords. ('The most radical revolutionary will become a conservative on the day after the revolution' – Hannah Arendt.)

Dalmiya's job had never existed before. His predecessor, Sir Clyde Walcott, had been called Chairman. Dalmiya's title sounded grander, but the reality was less imposing. The work done by Sir John Anderson, head of New Zealand Cricket, in reconstructing ICC's decision-making processes had ensured a presidency with influence rather than power. There is now an 18-member executive board, with subsidiary committees covering cricket, finance and development. At long last, there are the glimmerings of a proper decision-making structure.

None the less, the game over which Dalmiya presided was one he had played a major part in creating, as Indian cricket's chief powerbroker. There were 110 one-day internationals played in 1997 (plus two washouts). Most blurred into each other… But sports politicians can get carried away by their own rhetoric. Dalmiya was quoted as saying this January that the game had to spread to all corners of the world to survive. That is nonsense. If cricket were to mutate into something different simply to try and sell itself to the American market, or anywhere else, it wouldn't be cricket and it wouldn't be worth having.

If You're Broke, Fix It

It might be healthier if cricket officials spent a little less time reaching for the sky and paid more attention to what was going on in the gutter. As 1998 began, the rumours that results in one-day internationals were being twisted to suit the interests of betting syndicates operating illegally, mainly in Mumbai and the Gulf, were moving from a murmur to something nearer a roar. Nobody now doubts that this gambling takes place, for large sums, and that cricketers are involved in the process.

This does not necessarily mean that players have deliberately thrown matches. It is possible that the substantial number who have made allegations – Tim May, Shane Warne, Manoj Prabhakar, Aamir Sohail and so on – are making mischief or a mistake. Possible, but increasingly implausible. ICC needs to set up a credible international investigation designed to discover the truth, not what everyone wants to hear.

Anyone with experience of gambling will feel that the amount of smoke billowing out of this story is a pretty reliable indicator of fire. The international programme, particularly as played by India and Pakistan, is a guaranteed recipe for jiggery-pokery. The one-day tournaments of which these countries are so fond have no real meaning. No one remembers who wins them, so honour can never overcome profit. And the actual rewards for victory are hardly exciting. England's success in the Sharjah Champions Trophy in December won them just £25,000 between a squad of 14. Champion golfers tip their waiters better than that, never mind their caddies…

Cricketers are not getting rich – not from cricket. A handful do manage to turn their fame to good commercial advantage, but that is not the same thing. It would be astonishing if some of the others had not been tempted by villainy.

THE AUSTRALIANS IN INDIA, 1996–97, by Mike Coward

Australia's tour of India in October 1996 was a disappointment and a setback. They lost the Test match and the five one-day games they contested with India and South Africa in the Titan Cup…

India's solid performance should not be devalued, but the result was probably inevitable. So unsympathetic was the tourists' itinerary that the one-off Test appeared to have more to do with Australian foreign policy than cricket: the Test, played for the new Border-Gavaskar Trophy, was arranged to coincide with a festival designed to strengthen links between the two countries.

Australia arrived seriously under-cooked for their first Test in India for almost ten years. It came after a winter lay-off, a visit to Sri Lanka for another inconsequential limited-overs quadrangular and just one first-class match, rain-affected…

The Australian Cricket Board had been in bad odour in India since it directed Mark Taylor's team not to play in Sri Lanka in the World Cup earlier in 1996 and then campaigned against Indian board secretary Jagmohan Dalmiya's bid for the chairmanship of the International Cricket Council. Suffering from subcontinental fatigue syndrome on their third visit within nine months, the Australians were unable to distance themselves from the politicking and it showed in their cricket.

THE SOUTH AFRICANS IN INDIA, 1996–97, by Colin Bryden

While Australia and West Indies embarked on a series grandiosely entitled 'The Decider', a Test series of some significance was being played in India.

The Indians had not lost a home series since 1986–87, and had won ten out of 14 Tests at home since 1992–93, the most recent being an emphatic win over Australia in a one-off match at Delhi. South Africa, meanwhile, had not lost any series, or a one-off, since their inaugural Test on rejoining the cricketing world, at Bridgetown in April 1992. They had played enough one-day cricket on the subcontinent not to worry unduly about the conditions. But they soon discovered that Tests were different: they lost the series 2–1, sandwiching a win in Calcutta between defeats in Ahmedabad and Kanpur.

Their cause was not helped by their build-up. Since the first week of 1996, South Africa had played 29 one-day internationals – and won 25. But when they arrived, many of their players had played no first-class cricket in ten months…

The Indians had the bonus of a late flowering from Mohammad Azharuddin. Relieved of the captaincy, he found sublime batting form: his hundred off 74 balls in Calcutta was extraordinary; his unbeaten 163 in Kanpur clinched the series,

Javagal Srinath, the First Test match-winner, and Venkatesh Prasad were an effective new-ball pair, while Anil Kumble had an outstanding series in an unexpected role. Showing a straight bat and good sense, he played vital innings in each Test, and there was no diminution either in his powers as a brisk-paced bowler of leg-spin and top-spin. Although his figures were not sensational, the South Africans never mastered him...

The South Africans were unhappy with conditions in both Ahmedabad and Kanpur, considering Ahmedabad, especially, an unsuitable Test venue – Cronje said the pitch was unsatisfactory and condemned the absence of suitable practice facilities.

INDIA'S FIRST TEST VICTORY AGAINST SOUTH AFRICA

Two strong teams met in 1996–97, but India proved to have the edge. For a change, it was an Indian pace bowler who made the difference in gaining India their first victory over South Africa.

First Test, at Ahmedabad, November 20, 21, 22, 23, 1996

Devastating pace bowling by Srinath gave India victory on a poor pitch. Though it seemed best suited to the spinners, Srinath's fast, accurate inswingers and off-cutters brought him career-best figures of 6-21. South Africa crashed for 105 after being set a modest 170 to win.

It was obvious that batting would not be easy on a brown, dusty pitch, and by winning the toss Tendulkar gave India a substantial advantage. But there were frequent changes of fortune and several questionable umpiring decisions. Although Mongia fell early to de Villiers, in the first of umpire Bansal's controversial lbw verdicts, India negotiated the first morning safely enough until Manjrekar misread a top-spinner from the unorthodox Adams. Thereafter, they struggled against accurate bowling and sharp fielding. Donald was superb, but the two most critical blows were struck by Rhodes. He held a dazzling diving catch at mid-wicket to dismiss Tendulkar and then ran out Azharuddin with a direct hit from cover.

Having restricted India to 223, South Africa needed to bat sensibly. Instead, they slumped to 119-7. Bansal gave Cronje out to a ball which pitched well outside leg stump and Cullinan when he was struck on the half-volley at full stretch, but the South Africans were always struggling against the spinners. De Villiers showed the application needed over three hours: with first Symcox, then Donald, he established a 21-run lead.

Donald struck twice before India erased the modest deficit, and they were 38-3 when Tendulkar sliced a slower delivery from McMillan to Rhodes – again – at backward point. It was to be Rhodes' last significant contribution: later he strained his hamstring badly. Donald had Azharuddin brilliantly caught at second slip by McMillan, and, when Dravid was trapped by Symcox, India were just 70 ahead with five down. The 22-year-old debutant Laxman showed a cool head during a 56-run partnership with Kumble.

Needing 170, with nearly two days to get them, South Africa looked to their openers for a solid start before the spinners came on. Instead, Srinath took centre stage. His fifth delivery swung in to Hudson and Bansal's fateful finger rose again (replays suggested it would have missed leg stump). Cullinan edged the next, and South Africa were two down without a run on the board. With Cronje the only batsman to last long, his team seldom looked like reaching the target. Srinath's pace and swing combined perfectly with Kumble's customary accuracy on a crumbling pitch which made driving through the line virtually impossible. From 96-4, South Africa lost their last six for nine runs. Tendulkar said he could not recall a Test with so many twists and turns.

The match was stopped for ten minutes on the third afternoon when Adams was struck by golf-ball-sized pieces of concrete thrown from the crowd. Azharuddin became the first cricketer to play against all eight other countries, both home and away.

India 223 (Donald 4-37) and **190** (Laxman 51; Adams 3-30, Donald 3-32).
South Africa 244 (de Villiers 67*; Joshi 4-43) and **105** (Srinath 6-21).
Toss: India. Test Debut: V. V. S. Laxman.
India won by 64 runs.

THE INDIANS IN SOUTH AFRICA 1996–97, by Dicky Rutnagur

The return fixture was less successful for the Indians.

The Indians arrived in South Africa in mid-December for the second leg of their back-to-back Test series. They had just won the home leg 2–1 on some characteristically Indian wickets. But now it was their turn to play on pitches vastly different from their own. The itinerary, including only two first-class matches outside the three Tests, militated against India, particularly their batsmen, and their difficulties in acclimatising were compounded when their only fixture before the First Test was badly disrupted by rain. Criticism of the itinerary should be aimed at the Indian authorities, however: the length of the tour, or rather its brevity, was their choice...

Even allowing for the handicap of inadequate preparation, India were poorly equipped to match South Africa, who won the first two Tests to clinch the rubber and avenge the defeat in the series completed in India only a fortnight earlier...

The potential strength of India's batting was not fully realised, largely because of a distressing weakness at the top of the order. Vikram Rathore made runs in the two provincial matches, but lacked the technique to play high-class fast bowling on a pitch of any pace, while Woorkeri Raman failed every time. Both were dropped, and Rahul Dravid and Nayan Mongia, the wicketkeeper, were pushed up the order to open. It was only in the final Test, in which the South Africans bowled below their best, that an Indian innings got off to a start worth the name.

Sachin Tendulkar, the captain on whom the Indians were so reliant, recovered from a barren season at home, yet played only one sizeable innings. Azharuddin, too, came good only once, together with Tendulkar at Cape Town when the pair produced a golden partnership, with bold and brilliant batting considered by many observers to be the best they had ever seen. But it could not avert defeat.

THE INDIANS IN THE WEST INDIES, 1996-97, by Tony Cozier

Both teams had just lost their preceding series – West Indies in Australia, India in South Africa – so both had plenty to play for on India's first tour of the Caribbean for eight years. In the event, they were thoroughly frustrated by the weather…

The exalted batsmen on both sides were seldom seen at their best. Sachin Tendulkar and Brian Lara had their moments, notably Tendulkar's dominant 92 in the first innings in Barbados, Lara's second-innings 78 off 83 balls in Jamaica and his more measured 103 in Antigua. More was expected of the world's two greatest batting stars. The unofficial contest within a contest, to determine the better player, was unresolved. But Lara earned more points for his handling of the team in Barbados, to win his first Test as captain when Courtney Walsh was injured…

At the end, the indelible images were less of dashing batting or incisive bowling than of groundstaff trying to dry swampy outfields by the antiquated method of sponges and buckets.

CRICKET IN INDIA 1996–97, by R. Mohan and Sudhir Vaidya

Mumbai won the Ranji Trophy for the 33rd time in its 63 years, but in an untraditional manner; the Indian board decided to stage the final under lights at a neutral venue. The players of Mumbai and fellow finalists Delhi were not best pleased by the change; after six months playing in daylight with red balls, they were required to switch to white balls, which had to be replaced every 50 overs, for the floodlit games.

OBITUARY

Kischenchand, Gogumal Harisinghani, who died on April 16, 1997, aged 72, was a small right-handed batsman, with an ungainly stance, who was a prolific scorer in Ranji Trophy cricket but had a disastrous record in Test cricket. He played five times for India, and on every occasion was out for a duck. In Australia in 1947–48 he was out for nought in each of his four second innings; recalled at Lucknow against Pakistan five years later, he got nought in the first innings. He did score some runs, including 44 in the low-scoring and rain-ruined Test at Sydney, but his Test average of 8.90 compares oddly with his overall average of just under 50.

WISDEN – 1999

The whiff of corruption in cricket has been wafting around for a number of years. By the late 1990s it arrived centre stage – and it will never really go away – and sadly at this point the centre stage appeared to be India.

THE CORRUPTION OF CRICKET, by Mihir Bose

The Australian Cricket Board was finally forced to admit something it had known, and covered up, since February 1995. Mark Waugh and Shane Warne, who had made the original allegations of attempted match-fixing against the former Pakistan captain Salim Malik, had themselves accepted thousands of dollars from an Indian bookmaker for providing apparently innocuous information...

Suddenly, the Australian board announced that it would hold an investigation. So did the International Cricket Council. Unfortunately, said ICC chairman Jagmohan Dalmiya, the very fabric of the great game is being damaged. Yet both bodies had known about Waugh and Warne for four years, since the ACB had informed ICC officials (but no one else) at the time. The fabric, apparently, was damaged only when the public found out.

Cricket-watchers have never had much faith in the game's administrators. But what they expect is incompetence, not cynicism. In fact, the ICC investigation never materialised as such. The national boards, obsessed by territorial imperative, refused to allow it...

It is not easy to understand the new world of cricket if you sit in London or even Melbourne. Go to Dalmiya's own patch, though, to a hotel room or a middle-class home with satellite TV, pretty well anywhere in South Asia. There nearly always seems to be a game being broadcast from somewhere, usually a one-day international (India played 48 in 1997–98), otherwise another one-day game. Yes, these matches do have some spectator appeal. But they have as much lasting resonance as the afternoon greyhound meetings staged in Britain for the benefit of betting shops. And since cricket goes on longer than a dog race, it makes better, more cost-effective, visual wallpaper without losing its power as a gambling medium...

I like a punt myself: I would be sorry if cricket betting had to end. But it is an ironclad rule that unregulated gambling leads to gangsterism, and, when that gets a grip on a game, then radical action is the only solution… Cricket's response so far has been pathetic, almost frivolous. Dalmiya almost split world cricket trying to take charge of ICC. Having succeeded, he has given the game no leadership whatever. He should resign and be replaced by someone capable of providing that leadership.

THE INDIANS IN SRI LANKA, 1997–98, by Sa'adi Thawfeeq

Records and bowlers took a beating in the mini-Test series between Sri Lanka and India, but two high-scoring draws led to stalemate. With both sides rich in batting and short of bowling the only hope of a decisive result would have been a sporting pitch, which neither ground provided.

The series proved that Sri Lanka had durable batsmen capable of batting long hours in the middle with unflagging concentration. No one made the point more emphatically than the indomitable left-handed opener Sanath Jayasuriya. His 799 minutes of unwavering concentration on a dead-as-a-dodo pitch at R. Premadasa Stadium brought him 340 runs, the fourth-highest innings in Tests and the first triple-hundred by a Sri Lankan in first-class cricket…

India could consider themselves lucky to save the Test series (they were white-washed in the one-day internationals). Although their bowlers were pulverised without mercy, their batsmen managed to keep some of their pride. Two of their most experienced cricketers, captain Sachin Tendulkar and Mohammad Azharuddin, scored a couple of hundreds apiece. The tourists' biggest weaknesses were the failure of their key bowlers, Venkatesh Prasad and Anil Kumble, to take wickets consistently, and the lack of guidance for Tendulkar. There were occasions when the 24-year-old captain seemed lost for advice; he was not getting any from his deputy Kumble, nor from his predecessor Azharuddin.

Sri Lanka v India
First Test, at R. Premadasa Stadium, Colombo, August 2, 3, 4, 5, 6, 1997

India 537 for eight wickets declared (S. R. Tendulkar 143, M. Azharuddin 126, N. S. Sidhu 111, R. Dravid 69). **Sri Lanka 952 for six wickets declared** (S. T. Jayasuriya 340, R. S. Mahanama 225, P. A. de Silva 126, A. Ranatunga 86, D. P. M. D. Jayawardene 66, Extras 58). Match drawn.

THE AUSTRALIANS IN INDIA, 1997–98, by Dicky Rutnagur

Australia's sequence of nine victorious Test series, starting with the 1994–95 Ashes, was ended by India, who had not lost a series on home soil for exactly 11 years. There had been one blip in Australia's record before this, also involving

India, when they lost a one-off Test in Delhi in October 1996. But India's 2–1 victory – the Australian win came in the dead last game – was only the second time they had had the better of Australia over a Test series. The last was in 1979–80, during the Packer era, when the Australian team was gravely weakened...

Pre-series hype concentrated on the head-to-head contest between India's batting champion, Sachin Tendulkar, and Warne, the greatest contemporary bowler. The two jousted five times during the Tests and only once was Warne the winner. Of the Indian bowlers savaged by Don Bradman in the first-ever series between the two countries, in 1947–48, a handful survive: watching Tendulkar blasting away at Warne et al might have left them with a sense that vengeance had come at last. The 446 runs Tendulkar scored in the series, at a strike-rate of 80.65 per hundred balls received and a Bradmanesque average 111.50, were the product of sheer genius. The Australians had been given a warning of the storm to come in their opening fixture against Mumbai, when Tendulkar made 204 not out from 192 balls. Warne's ten wickets in the series cost 54 runs apiece; his career average previously was 23.81. The Indians, using their feet, played him expertly...

The series was played in congenial spirit. However, the referee, Peter van der Merwe, twice took punitive action for dissent: against Mongia in the First Test, and Ganguly – suspended for one match – in the last. Crowds for the Chennai and Calcutta Tests were large and exuberant but well behaved, and the conspicuous camaraderie between the locals and a substantial group of visiting Australian supporters was most heart-warming.

OBITUARIES

Desai, Ramakant Bhikaji, died in a Mumbai hospital on April 27, 1998, aged 58, while awaiting heart surgery. Tiny Desai was only 5ft 4in tall but, from a supple run-up, generated sufficient pace to sustain the Indian attack in the 1960s, when it desperately needed sustenance, and usually got it only from spin bowlers. He was drafted into the side as a 19-year-old for the Delhi Test in 1958–59, and had to bowl 49 overs in West Indies' only innings, taking 4-169; he promptly took over the leadership of the attack for the 1959 tour of England. At Lord's he had England in deep trouble at 80-6, and finished with 5-89 in the innings. *Wisden* praised his rare ability, endless courage and his outswinger, though the team was hopelessly overmatched, and he was over-bowled. That was often the way: he was on the winning side in only four of his 28 Tests...

His finest hour arguably came in that series, at the Brabourne Stadium in the opening Test, when he scored 85, batting No. 10; his ninth-wicket stand of 149 with P. G. Joshi remains an Indian Test record. He also scored a crucial 32 not out at Dunedin in 1967–68, continuing to bat after his jaw was broken. India won, but he never played Test cricket again. In 53 Ranji matches for Bombay, he took 239 wickets at 15.61, and he retired completely in 1969, aged only 30. Desai returned to the front line in 1996 when he was appointed chairman of selectors, and he was responsible for the appointment – and the dismissal – of Sachin Tendulkar as captain. It was not a happy term of office, and his natural sense of loyalty and reticence, combined with increasing ill health, made it difficult for him both in committee and in his dealings with the media. He resigned the month before he died.

Ghulam Ahmed, who died on October 28, 1998, aged 76, was a harbinger of the great Indian spin-bowling tradition. He bowled off-breaks with a high, handsome action, sometimes compared to Jim Laker's, and on the right wicket could be just as effective. Ghulam made his Test debut at Calcutta in 1948–49, when Everton Weekes scored twin hundreds. But Ghulam dismissed him both times, and took four for 94 in the first innings. Against England in 1951–52 he was highly successful, and was instrumental in India's maiden victory at Madras, before becoming by far the most potent member of a weak attack on the 1952 tour of England. 'He had days when he looked in the highest world class,' said *Wisden*, 'but on other occasions he lacked bite.'

Later that year he helped Mankad bowl India to victory in Pakistan's first Test match, at Delhi, and – improbably – scored 50, sharing a last-wicket stand of 109 with H. R. Adhikari, still an Indian record. His subsequent career was deeply involved with shifts in local cricket politics. In 1955–56, Ghulam captained India against New Zealand in his home town of Hyderabad, then mysteriously resigned... In 1958–59, against West Indies, he was captain again but, after two hefty defeats, he stood down for reasons that never became clear.

'By his action,' wrote one Indian observer, 'he strengthened the belief of his critics that he was not a fighter'... Ghulam became a prominent administrator: he was secretary of the Indian board from 1975 to 1980, and served twice as a selector; when India won the 1983 World Cup he was chairman. Asif Iqbal, who played for Pakistan, is his nephew.

Lamba, Raman, the former Indian Test player, died in a Dhaka hospital on February 23, 1998, aged 38. Three days earlier he had been hit on the temple while fielding, without a helmet, at short leg in front of a substantial crowd at a big club match at the Bangabandhu Stadium. Lamba walked off the field and the injury appeared not to be serious, but he suffered an internal haemorrhage and his condition worsened dramatically. A neurosurgeon was flown in from Delhi but it was already too late. The news caused widespread grief in both India and Bangladesh. Lamba was a popular cricketer in India, but in Bangladesh he was a legend.

He first went there to play club cricket in 1991, and was a key figure in the revival of interest in the game there. 'I am the Don of Dhaka,' he would joke to his Indian friends. The tragedy happened in Dhaka's traditional local derby between Mohammedans and Abahani, when Maharab Hossain, the Mohammedans' opener, played a full-blooded pull shot. Lamba had only moved in from the outfield that delivery and it was reported that he had already signalled for a helmet. Lamba was known to be fearless, though, as well as an exceptionally committed and enthusiastic player. The commitment sometimes went too far: he was banned for ten months after provoking Rashid Patel, who charged after him brandishing a stump in the 1990–91 Duleep Trophy final.

Critics also pointed to his technical shortcomings, but he always hoped for a recall to the Indian team after his four indifferent Tests in the late 1980s: 'Runs I am going to make,' he would say, 'then we shall see.' And he did make runs. His career average was over 50: in 1996–97, his 19th season, he scored 1,034 runs in just 14 innings for Delhi in the Ranji Trophy. He was one of only two Indians (with Vijay Hazare) to score two triple-centuries: 320 for North Zone in the 1987–88 Duleep Trophy final, and 312 for Delhi against Himachal Pradesh in 1994–95. He had been chosen to tour England in 1986, but failed to make the Test team.

He did, however, establish a lasting rapport with Ulster: he played club cricket there for 12 years, appeared four times for Ireland, and married an Irish girl. They had two children.

WISDEN — 2000

THE PAKISTANIS IN INDIA, 1998–99, by Qamar Ahmed

In January 1999, Pakistan arrived for their first Test series with neighbours India for nine years, and the first on Indian soil since 1986–87. Though there were only two Tests (a third match at Calcutta, won by Pakistan, was regarded as part of the separate Asian Test Championship), it was probably the most exciting of the 11 series between the rivals. Pakistan won a narrow victory at Chennai, only for India to strike back with a massive win at Delhi. The star players were the spinners, Saqlain Mushtaq of Pakistan and Anil Kumble of India: Kumble provided the sensational conclusion to the series by taking all ten wickets in the final innings.

It was also probably the most important series between the teams from a political standpoint. Three previous attempts to organise a Pakistani tour of India in the 1990s had been aborted because of threats of disruption by right-wing Hindu fundamentalists. In 1998, both countries had tested nuclear weapons, adding a new dimension to their traditional tension. The Shiv Sena party, led by maverick politician Bal Thackeray, were the most prominent opponents of the visit. Early in January, activists dug up the Test pitch in Delhi, forcing the Indian board to move the First Test to Chennai. Shortly afterwards, the board's offices at Mumbai were ransacked and officials manhandled, though this time Shiv Sena denied responsibility. Supporters and opponents of the tour both held processions in the major Indian cities. But Prime Minister Atal Behari Vajpayee urged the Pakistanis to come, promising maximum security for both teams, and sent a senior minister to negotiate with Thackeray. Shiv Sena sensed that the mood was against them, and they were in danger of being alienated from the coalition government; the day before the tourists arrived, they withdrew the threat of further disruption.

Nevertheless, commandos and plain-clothes officers shadowed the Pakistani team everywhere. The board even engaged snake charmers, after rumours that extremists might release snakes in the crowds or on to the pitch. But the two Tests went off without any trouble: a victory for cricket and diplomacy (when crowd trouble came later, at Calcutta, it was of a less political nature). The tourists' team manager, former diplomat and foreign minister Shaharyar Khan (who subsequently became Ambassador to France), and captain Wasim Akram did much to contribute to the success of the series and the goodwill it created. The Chennai Test attracted an estimated 50,000 spectators a day, and the Delhi Test nearly 40,000 a day...

In retrospect, the series was an immense success, and was about far more than winning and losing. As one Indian writer put it, 'The doubting Thomases and the detractors who threatened to disrupt the series were silenced; the Indian government flexed its security muscle to put diplomacy in front, and give cricket the opportunity to defeat hatred, and hatred was soundly defeated.'

India v Pakistan
Second Test, at Delhi, February 4, 5, 6, 7, 1999

India won a massive victory, their first over Pakistan since 1979–80, to draw the series. But the headlines belonged to leg-spinner Anil Kumble. He claimed all ten wickets in Pakistan's second innings, becoming only the second man in history to take ten in a Test innings, following English off-spinner Jim Laker in 1956. Kumble's match figures of 14-149 were the third best by an Indian in Tests.

Kumble had bowled six overs without taking a wicket on the fourth morning, mostly from the Football Stand End. Pakistan had little hope of winning after being set a formidable target of 420, but needed only a draw to take the series, and had seemed well placed at 101 without loss. After lunch, Kumble operated from the Pavilion End: he bowled 20.3 overs and claimed ten for 47, aided by some brilliant fielding and a substandard pitch – hastily repaired after the fundamentalists' vandalism a month earlier. Pakistan were all out for 207.

Kumble started the slide when Shahid Afridi was given out caught behind dabbing outside off stump. Afridi lingered in protest at the decision by home umpire Jayaprakash, whose performance was much condemned by Pakistani observers. With his next ball, Kumble had Ijaz Ahmed lbw as he stretched forward. Inzamam-ul-Haq averted the hat-trick, but played on off an inside edge minutes later. Yousuf Youhana, pushing forward, was lbw; Moin Khan was caught low down in the slips; and Saeed Anwar, who had defended for two and a half hours, was caught bat and pad at short leg. Pakistan had slumped to 128-6, and Kumble had taken 6-15 in 44 balls. 'That was the moment when I thought all ten could be mine,' he said afterwards.

But he had to wait until after tea for number seven, as Salim Malik and Wasim Akram held firm in a stand of 58. Then Kumble resumed the demolition. He bowled Malik, trying to pull; Mushtaq Ahmed was caught at gully off an awkward bounce; and the next ball hit Saqlain Mushtaq on the toe and trapped him lbw. That ended Kumble's 26th over, with one wicket remaining. Azharuddin privately instructed Srinath to bowl a wayward line in his next over. Wasim, who had resisted for an hour and a half, then kept out the hat-trick ball, and the next one, but top-edged Kumble's third ball to Laxman at short leg.

Kumble was carried back to the pavilion on his colleagues' shoulders as the crowd rejoiced. 'My first reaction is that we have won,' he said. 'No one dreams of taking ten wickets in an innings, because you can't. The pitch was of variable bounce, and cutting and pulling were not easy. All I had to do was pitch in the right area, mix up my pace and spin, and trap the batsmen. The first wicket was the hardest to get – the openers were cruising.' He added that the match award should have gone to a batsman in those conditions…

The rest was history, for Kumble, and for Richard Stokes, a 53-year-old English businessman. As a schoolboy, he had seen Jim Laker take some of his ten wickets at Old Trafford in 1956, and he arrived at Feroz Shah Kotla – on his birthday – just in time to see Kumble repeat the feat.

OBITUARIES

Bhattacharya, S. K., who died on May 7, 1999, aged 79, umpired two Tests in India. Unfortunately, the second was the Hyderabad Test against New Zealand in 1969-70, which is remembered for the umpires' failure to get the pitch mown on the rest day. On an over-grassed pitch, India were shot out for 89.

Jaisimha, Motganhalli Laxmanarsu, died on July 6, 1999, aged 60, from lung cancer. Jai was one of India's best players and most endearing personalities of the era just before the country began to fight the established cricketing powers on equal terms. With a silk scarf around his neck, and equally elegant on- and off-drives to go with it, he made cricket seem chic, which had an impact on the then-young men who later took Indian cricket to greater heights.

Jaisimha played in the Ranji Trophy for 23 consecutive seasons, captaining Hyderabad for 14 of them, and in 39 Tests, though he was sometimes omitted mysteriously by selectors who seemed to think him showy. His first Test, at Lord's in 1959, was the 91st and last for Godfrey Evans, who died two months before him. Jaisimha, then 20, achieved nothing, and lost his place, but came back in the final Test of 1959–60 series against Australia, where he achieved an enduring footnote in history by becoming the first player ever to bat on all five days of a Test. He was not out overnight on both the first and third evenings, then batted throughout a slow fourth day. Playing for a side who were often in trouble, he was

India v Pakistan

Second Test, at Delhi, February 4, 5, 6, 7, 1999

INDIA	1st Innings		2nd Innings
S. Ramesh b Saqlain Mushtaq	60	– c & b Mushtaq Ahmed	96
V.V.S. Laxman b Wasim Akram	35	– b Wasim Akram	8
R. Dravid lbw b Saqlain Mushtaq	33	– c Ijaz Ahmed b Saqlain Mushtaq	29
S.R. Tendulkar lbw b Saqlain Mushtaq	6	– c Wasim Akram b Mushtaq Ahmed	29
*M. Azharuddin c Ijaz Ahmed b Mushtaq Ahmed	67	– b Wasim Akram	14
S.C. Ganguly lbw b Mushtaq Ahmed	13	– not out	62
†N.R. Mongia run out	10	– lbw b Wasim Akram	0
A. Kumble c Yousuf Youhana b Saqlain Mushtaq	0	– c Ijaz Ahmed b Saqlain Mushtaq	15
J. Srinath lbw b Saqlain Mushtaq	0	– c Ijaz Ahmed b Saqlain Mushtaq	49
B.K.V. Prasad not out	1	– b Saqlain Mushtaq	6
Harbhajan Singh run out	1	– b Saqlain Mushtaq	0
Extras (b 11, l-b 9, n-b 6)	26	Extras (b 13, l-b 9, n-b 9)	31

1-88 2-113 3-122 4-191 5-231 6-240   252   1-15 2-100 3-168 4-183 5-199 6-199   339
7-243 8-247 9-248 10-252   7-231 8-331 9-339 10-339

First innnings – Wasim Akram 13–3–23–1; Waqar Younis 13–5–37–0; Mushtaq Ahmed 26–5–64–2;
Saqlain Mushtaq 35.5–9–94–5; Shahid Afridi 4–1–14–0
Wasim Akram 21–3–43–3; Waqar Younis 12–2–42–0; Mushtaq Ahmed 25–4–86–2;
Saqlain Mushtaq 46.4–12–122–5; Shahid Afridi 9–1–24–0

PAKISTAN	1st Innings		2nd Innings
Saeed Anwar c Mongia b Prasad	1	– c Laxman b Kumble	69
Shahid Afridi b Harbhajan Singh	32	– c Mongia b Kumble	41
Ijaz Ahmed c Dravid b Kumble	17	– lbw b Kumble	0
Inzamam-ul-Haq b Kumble	26	– b Kumble	6
Yousuf Youhana c & b Kumble	3	– lbw b Kumble	0
Saleem Malik c Azharuddin b Prasad	31	– b Kumble	11
†Moin Khan lbw b Srinath	14	– c Ganguly b Kumble	3
*Wasim Akram lbw b Harbhajan Singh	15	– c Laxman b Kumble	43
Mushtaq Ahmed c Laxman b Harbhajan Singh	12	– c Dravid b Kumble	1
Saqlain Mushtaq lbw b Kumble	2	– lbw Kumble	0
Waqar Younis not out	1	– not out	6
Extras (b 1, l-b 8, n-b 9)	18	Extras (b 13, l-b 1, w 2, n-b 11)	27

1-1 2-54 3-54 4-60 5-114   172   1-101 2-101 3-115 4-115 5-127   207
6-130 7-139 8-167 9-168 10-172   6-128 7-186 8-198 9-198 10-207

First innnings – Srinath 12–1–38–1; Prasad 11–2–20–2; Harbhajan Singh 17–5–30–3;
Kumble 24.3–4–75–4
Second innings – Srinath 12–2–50–0; Prasad 4–1–15–0; Harbhajan Singh 18–5–51–0;
Kumble 26.3–9–74–10

India won by 212 runs.

willing and able to change his method and produce the long innings that his team required. He spent 500 minutes scoring 99 against Pakistan in Kanpur in 1960–61, which included a full session with just five scoring strokes, and was then run out going for his century.

But against England in 1961–62, he flowered, and scored a lovely 127 at Delhi, with a further century when England toured again two years later, and a third immediately after being flown out to Brisbane as a replacement in 1967–68. Jaisimha scored 74 and 101, which took India to the edge of victory. He was still in the team in the West Indies in 1970–71 when Sunil Gavaskar stormed on to the scene. But a new era in Indian cricket was beginning, Jaisimha was to remain as one of the midwives, playing on for Hyderabad until 1976–77. When he died he was state coach, a job he did with shrewdness and humour… There was a notable warmth to the tributes that poured in from across India after his death. 'He had style, elegance and grace not only as a batsman but also as a man', said the administrator Raj Singh. 'A gem of a person', said Lala Amarnath.

CRICKETERS OF THE YEAR 2000

R. DRAVID, by Alan Lee

The Indian batting line-up of Ganguly, Dravid, Tendulkar and Laxman (who appeared together in 79 Tests) was probably the strongest of recent times. Add Sehwag and Gambhir as openers (in 14 of those 79 Tests), and any opposing bowler was entitled to feel daunted at the prospect. Dravid, a quiet but hugely popular player, lay fourth in the list of all-time Test run-makers to the end of 2009.

Think of modern Indian batsmen, and the Englishman thinks of Tendulkar. Even regular cricket followers find it hard to recognise the other members of India's top order. This may be a comment on the enduring gulfs in culture, or more simply, gaps in fixtures; but after the summer of 1999 it is an unsustainable position. India supplied two of the outstanding batsmen of the World Cup, and neither of them was Tendulkar.

Sourav Ganguly and Rahul Dravid had introduced themselves three years earlier. They made their Test debuts together at Lord's, Ganguly scoring 131 and Dravid 95 from No. 7. David Lloyd, then England coach, had been told by his observers that Ganguly would open the face of his bat outside off stump, while Dravid's weakness was working the straight ball to leg. This dossier was quickly consigned to the out-tray.

Three years on, and the scene changes to Taunton, its bucolic traditions given over for a day to Asian exuberance. India are playing Sri Lanka in a World Cup group match. India lose a wicket in the opening over but they will not lose another until the total has reached 324. Ganguly and Dravid's stand of 318 is, by a distance,

a record for any wicket in international one-day cricket (until November, when Ganguly and Tendulkar raise it to 331). For Dravid, the day brings his second century in four days. Despite India's failure to qualify for the second round, he would complete the tournament as its leading run-scorer, and return home feted as a hero among perceived failures. To his embarrassment, Dravid fan clubs have sprung up, their membership loaded with teenage girls, and though his features may still be shamefully unfamiliar in England, they have attracted advertisers and film-makers in the land where star cricketers are national property.

Rahul Dravid was born in Indore on January 11, 1973. The son of a food scientist, he was firmly encouraged to complete his studies before branching into sport, and obtained a degree in commerce at Bangalore University. But he made his first-class debut at 18, for Karnataka, and scored 134 in his second match. He was soon identified as one of the meteors of Indian cricket. Shy and introspective, he did not seek attention, but it was to come his way naturally, through weight of runs and an impression of quiet authority that led him to captaining most of the teams he represented.

At first, his method was a painstaking one, his fierce determination to preserve his wicket matched by a desire to learn. In Toronto one year, he buttonholed Ian Chappell at a party and put searching questions to him for an hour. At Lord's he learned how to succeed and how to fail, all in the same innings. Had he made five more runs, it would have been the first time in the history of Test cricket that two debutants in the same team had made centuries. 'It hurt,' he recalls. 'But I realised it would not do me any good to keep thinking about it.' He went out in the next Test and made 84.

At the start of 1999, India, a team that had spent too long confining its talents to one-day cricket, played a sudden raft of Test matches. They were beaten 1–0 in New Zealand, but the third game of that series, at Hamilton, belonged to Dravid, who made an elegant, eight-hour 190 in the first innings and followed it with 103 not out in the second. In Colombo seven weeks later, he made his fifth Test century, against Sri Lanka. By now, he had a Test average of 54 and had cemented his preferred place at No. 3.

Next, though, came the World Cup and further evidence that this pleasing player is far more capable than most of his countrymen on alien pitches, reason enough for Kent to engage Dravid as their overseas player for 2000. He was also to demonstrate that his game had moved on and that he was resourceful enough to dominate.

In late November, as he waited in a Mumbai hotel for the flight to Australia and another challenging chapter in his development, Dravid reflected on his golden year. 'I have improved a lot since 1996,' he said earnestly, 'but my game can still progress further.' Taunton, he said, had been 'great fun, fantastic', but the World Cup, overall, had left him with mixed emotions. 'There are such expectations of us at home. We are followed very closely and people were disappointed. We had no excuses, although I thought we played well enough to reach the semi-finals.'

Dravid certainly did. His total of 461 runs, 63 more than his closest challenger Steve Waugh (Ganguly was third with 379), contained not only two successive centuries but also fifties under pressure against England and Pakistan. His batting was as undemonstrative as his personality, but as eloquent, too. It spoke of a man who has the time, both in technique and age, to graduate into the very highest company, and to do it with an understated, old-fashioned grace.

CHAPTER 6
THE 21ST CENTURY

In the past decade, India has become, as Wisden *predicted, the epicentre of world cricket. Whether this is a good thing or a bad thing,* Wisden, *like many cricket lovers, has yet to make up its mind. But now when it writes about India, it is as likely to be about the politics and administration of cricket as it is about the beauty and artistry of a Tendulkar, the sheer power of a Sehwag or the mercurial brilliance of a Laxman.*

Wisden *has dropped its condescending, paternal tone when writing about India, and it is noticeable that by far the most strident criticism of the Indian authorities, the Indian team or Indian umpires and pitches comes from Indian writers.*

The first edition of the new century centred on one sad story of a 'game in shame' as Mihir Bose called it.

WISDEN — 2001

There was really only one story in the 2001 Almanack.

NOTES BY THE EDITOR, by Graeme Wright

Hansie Cronje's reputation was peeled away, leaf by leaf, at the King Commission hearings last summer. It wasn't so much the facts themselves: the bribes from bookmakers, the attempts to fix matches and inveigle his team-mates into corrupting cricket's, indeed sport's, very ethos. It was the date when Cronje first crossed the line and accepted money from the Indian bookmaker, M. K. Gupta: 1996. We would learn later, through India's Central Bureau of Investigation, that Mohammad Azharuddin's involvement with Gupta began a year earlier. Still significant. It was in February 1995, you see, that Mark Waugh and Shane Warne admitted to the Australian Cricket Board that they had accepted money from another bookmaker. Admissions that the ACB, with the compliance of the International Cricket Council, whose chief executive was a former ACB employee, chose to keep under wraps. What I kept wondering was whether Azharuddin and Cronje would have become involved with Gupta had those two supposedly responsible organisations gone public immediately, and made an example of Waugh and Warne. As it was, the sound of silence rang out loud and clear both to bookmakers and cricketers. The game's administrators were not going to interfere in their activities. It took the Indian police to throw some light on cricket's darker side...

Of the three government-sponsored inquiries into match-fixing, in India, Pakistan and South Africa, India's CBI enjoyed much wider scope than the terms of reference that constricted both Qayyum and Justice Edwin King. As the title of their report implied, the CBI had freedom to investigate 'related malpractices', allowing them to be wonderfully critical of cricket administrators in a way the other two could not. In spite of much post-Cronje posturing, the CBI decided, the office-bearers of the Board of Control for Cricket in India (BCCI) had been negligent by not looking thoroughly into alleged malpractices in the past, even though there had been clear indications of the malaise in the game there. The primary reason behind this was 'the lack of accountability of the BCCI to anyone'. The BCCI, the report made clear for anyone who didn't know it, 'perpetuates a system of self-aggrandisement'. It is not only in India, either. The men in clover become so besotted by the opiate of their own importance that they lose the will to confront problems. The trappings of power become more important than the judicious exercise of the power.

A GAME IN SHAME, by Mihir Bose

Cricket corruption, like taxes and poverty, may always be with us. But after cricket's *annus horribilis* of 2000 we can, for the first time, understand how a combination of players' greed, dreadful impotence and infighting by cricket administrators, and a radical shift in cricketing power from England to the Indian subcontinent helped create cricket's darkest chapter.

Two incidents illustrate this, and both occurred in India. The first was in 1984, some months after India's unexpected victory in the 1983 World Cup. One evening a Delhi bank clerk, Mukesh Kumar Gupta, was walking near his home in the grimy bylanes of old Delhi when he saw some people betting small amounts on a cricket match. This, as he would later tell the Central Bureau of Investigation, India's top police investigators, caught his imagination. Having ascertained that the betters were neither well educated nor well informed about cricket, Gupta began to hone his cricket knowledge by listening to the BBC. And over the next decade he would travel the world, following cricket and meeting many of the world's top cricketers. Meeting and bribing.

Meanwhile, as Gupta was transforming himself from a lowly bank clerk to cricket's most notorious match-fixer, and enriching himself in the process, cricket was also being reinvented and enriched. By the mid-1990s, even the Ashes Tests, the bedrock of the international game for more than 100 years, had been – away from the insular focus of England – sidelined in favour of one-day internationals.

By 1996, and the heyday of Gupta the match-fixer, there had been an enormous spread of such matches, the greatest expansion in the history of the game, with series in 'non-cricketing' venues such as Sharjah, Singapore and Toronto. Sharjah had started by staging benefit matches for Indian and Pakistani cricketers, who had no recourse to an English-style system... Similar tournaments represented the commercial opportunities that limited-overs cricket provided to businessmen seeking to reach the emerging Indian middle-classes...

Television companies, in particular Rupert Murdoch's Star, were keen to reach this new economic group. It is estimated that every second person watching cricket in the world is an Indian, and their insatiable appetite for the one-day game since 1983 has created a market worth cultivating. As Justice Malik Mohammad Qayyum pointed out in his inquiry into match-fixing, submitted to the Pakistan government in 1999, 'with the massive influx of money and sheer increase in the number of matches played, cricket has become a business'. It was a business, however, that was run like a private members' club...

'There was, is, a power struggle in international cricket,' one highly placed ICC source admitted, 'and the Asian countries are resentful of England, the old colonial power, but then the subcontinent has not helped matters by being very defensive about match-fixing. We have known for years that match-fixing goes on, helped by the fact that betting is illegal and in the hands of criminals there. But in the past, whenever the matter has been raised, they have said we are cricket administrators, not cops. Then a clean-cut white South African, Hansie Cronje, was caught in the net, the game changed and everyone has had to come clean.'

... Before that moment, five and a half years after Shane Warne, Mark Waugh and Tim May had made allegations of match-fixing against the Pakistan captain, Salim Malik, there had been inquiries in India, Pakistan and Sri Lanka, as well as media investigations led by the Indian magazine *Outlook*. But apart from the fines on Waugh and Warne for receiving A\$6,000 and A\$5,000 respectively from an Indian bookmaker in return for information, which the Australian board and ICC had covered up, nothing had been done. It would subsequently emerge that Justice Qayyum had recommended a life ban on Salim Malik, but his report was still to be published...

At the beginning of November, the Indian government released the CBI's report of their investigation into match-fixing. By interviewing illegal bookmakers as well as players, this added a new dimension to the story. The result was that, for the first time, a cricketer, former Indian captain Mohammad Azharuddin, admitted to being involved in the fixing of one-day internationals. And drawing on the information from Gupta and other bookies, the CBI revealed how international cricketers had been lured and, in some instances, corrupted. What began as a scandal could be seen at last as a conspiracy. Match-fixing could no longer be shrugged off as an occasional isolated instance; there was now a history and a pattern of corruption.

Gupta's first cricket contact was Ajay Sharma, very much a bit-player in international cricket – one Test and 31 one-day internationals for India – but a useful conduit to other cricketers. They first met at a club tournament in Delhi in 1988 when Gupta, impressed by the way Sharma batted, gave him 2,000 rupees (£100 at the current rate of exchange) as a token of his appreciation. Gupta saw this as an investment for the future, and it was to prove a shrewd one. A fortnight later Sharma contacted him and soon the two men had formed a bond which, as the CBI report made clear, 'was to prove beneficial to both'. When Sharma toured New Zealand with India in 1990, Gupta claimed he provided him with information about the pitch, weather and the team which he used to make 'a good amount of money'. Sharma denies he provided any information, but he did later introduce Gupta to Manoj Prabhakar, who was keen to get a new car, 'a Maruti Gypsy with wide tyres'. On the 1990 tour of England, said Gupta, Prabhakar gave him information about the team and 'underperformed' in one of the drawn Tests. Prabhakar got his Maruti Gypsy – he told the CBI he paid for it himself – and Gupta got to know yet more cricketers.

The picture Gupta painted for the CBI, which was often backed in testimony from Sharma, Prabhakar, Azharuddin, Ajay Jadeja and even Cronje, shows how frighteningly casual the whole thing was. Gupta goes to Prabhakar's Delhi home for dinner (Prabhakar denies this); Prabhakar rings Gus Logie, who refuses to help (Prabhakar confirms this). When the Sri Lankans tour India in 1990, Prabhakar introduces Gupta to Aravinda de Silva (Prabhakar denies this). He in turn, and over the phone, introduces Gupta to Martin Crowe, and they get on so well that when Gupta visits New Zealand in 1991 – Sri Lanka toured there from January to March – he lunches with Crowe and his wife, Simone, at their home. At a Hong Kong six-a-side tournament, Prabhakar introduces Gupta to Mark Waugh; Gupta flies to Colombo during some festival matches there and, so he claims, meets Dean Jones, Arjuna Ranatunga and Brian Lara. When the winners of the Indian and Pakistani Wills one-day tournaments play in Delhi, Prabhakar introduces him to Salim Malik, and when England tour India in 1993 he introduces him to Alec Stewart. Gupta and Prabhakar agree on this.

Gupta's success with these cricketers varies. During the 1994 Sri Lankan tour of India, he claims, Ranatunga and de Silva agreed to 'underperform' – '[they] could manage it since they were the captain and vice-captain,' he told the CBI – and he profited when Sri Lanka lost the First Test. For this, he says, he paid de Silva US$15,000. There was talk of fixing other Tests, but the odds were too low. Gupta claims he paid Crowe US$20,000 for information, but he refused to fix matches. Jones was offered US$40,000, he says, but while Jones promised to think about it, he did nothing. In Hong Kong, says Gupta, Mark Waugh was paid US$20,000 to provide information 'whenever Australia played', but on another occasion, in Sharjah in 1994, he refused to help as did Salim Malik. Later that year, however, Gupta recalls making good money on Malik's information that Pakistan would lose to Australia in the Singer World Series in Sri Lanka, a match mentioned in both the CBI and Qayyum reports. When the West Indians toured India in 1994–95, Gupta says he paid Brian Lara US$40,000 to underperform in two one-day games. After the CBI report was released, de Silva and Ranatunga denied Gupta's allegations. Crowe said he thought he was dealing with a journalist and was duped. Waugh denied accepting Gupta's money and talked of taking legal action. So did Lara. The most robust denial came from Stewart. According to Gupta, Stewart was paid £5,000 for information but refused to fix matches for him. Stewart not only denied receiving any money but claimed he did not remember knowingly meeting Gupta…

However… there can be no doubt about his intense and close relationship with Azharuddin and Cronje. After Ajay Sharma had introduced Azharuddin to Gupta at the Taj Palace hotel in Delhi in 1995, the two had a relationship that lasted until 1997. During that period, says Gupta, Azhar's wife Sangeeta Bijlani was also involved. He claims he paid Azhar 90 lakh rupees (£150,000 – a lakh equals 100,000 rupees) but, finding some of Azhar's predictions 'proved incorrect', asked for his money back and was repaid 30 lakh rupees – in instalments from Azharuddin's locker at the Taj Palace.

It was Azhar's unreliability as a forecaster, Gupta told the CBI, that made him seek out Cronje late in 1996… Gupta quickly told Cronje that he was a match-fixer who wanted to be sure that South Africa would lose. He asked Cronje to obtain the players' co-operation. Cronje would later tell the King Commission, 'I led him to believe I would. This seemed an easy way to make money, but I had no intention of doing anything.' He accepted US$30,000 from Gupta, hid it in his kit bag and smuggled it out of India, into and out of South Africa, and finally to a bank account in England, so violating the foreign exchange laws of both India and South Africa.

That established the Cronje-Gupta relationship. Cronje says he lied to Gupta about match-fixing but took his money nevertheless. And during the last match of the Indian tour, the entire South African team debated whether to accept Gupta's bribe, variously said to be US$200,000 and US$250,000, to play badly in the one-day international at Mumbai, intended as a benefit match for Mohinder Amarnath. Pat Symcox told the King Commission, 'Some guys including myself said it was a lot of money and we should look at it. Some guys were for it, some against.' In the end the offer was rejected, but it remains the only known instance of a whole team discussing match-fixing… According to Gupta, Cronje had promised that, during the one-day tournament, South Africa would lose some matches against India. When they didn't, he told Gupta that India had played so badly and missed so many chances that he couldn't do anything about the result. Poor Gupta: he had invested in both camps and still couldn't get the result he wanted. Could it be that other players were in hock to other bookies seeking a different fix?

The age of Gupta the match-fixer ended in May 1998, and there is some evidence to suggest that the high tide of cricket match-fixing ended then, although Majid Khan, former chief executive of the Pakistan board, remains convinced that Pakistan's two World Cup losses to India and Bangladesh in 1999 were fixed...

The ICC has taken tentative steps with the setting up of an investigation unit under former London Metropolitan Police commissioner Sir Paul Condon. But, as Sir Paul himself has admitted, he has no legal powers; if he discovers anything, it will be reported to the ICC. He can do nothing to administer justice, he can only react, and what co-ordination he can achieve is through persuasion.

Since its initial report, the CBI has begun looking into links between cricketers, bookmakers and the Indian underworld, and could discover more secrets. The King Commission wants to go back to the beginning of 1992, when South Africa re-emerged into international cricket. It has high hopes of unlocking more secrets, but others in South Africa would prefer to see a line drawn under the whole sorry business. This would be a mistake. The high tide of match-fixing in cricket may have ebbed, but the full story of what happened throughout the 1990s has not yet been told.

THE INDIANS IN AUSTRALIA, 1999–2000, by Dicky Rutnagur

The Indians failed to live up to having top billing in a season of twin tours. Never before in almost 68 years as a Test nation had an Indian national team been so completely overwhelmed. It wasn't just that they were outclassed in all three Tests. They lost to Queensland on the fourth morning, were soundly beaten by 164 runs in a one-day fixture against the Prime Minister's XI, a team of young aspirants, and lost seven of their eight games in the Carlton & United series. Their only win, other than beating Pakistan once in the one-day series, was against New South Wales, who fielded a depleted side.

Apart from Sachin Tendulkar and Sourav Ganguly, India's batsmen could not come to terms with the pace and bounce of Australia's pitches. Tendulkar, despite being the victim of dubious umpiring decisions in both innings of the First Test, averaged 46.33, scoring a splendid 116 in the Second and two half-centuries. However, V. V. S. Laxman, with some substantial innings early on the tour and a gloriously elegant 167 in the final innings of the rubber, showed that he could have made a bigger impact batting lower down the order. Not yet an established Test player, he was pitchforked by circumstances into opening the innings in the Second and Third Tests. The big disappointment was Rahul Dravid who, to date, had an impressive overseas record. He made a hundred on a lifeless pitch in the drawn game against Tasmania but gathered just 93 runs in six Test innings.

Javagal Srinath was India's best bowler, and his new-ball partner, Ajit Agarkar, toiled hard and bowled at a rapid pace for one who is small of build and whose career had been blighted by frequent injury. Between them they claimed 21 of the 38 Australian wickets in the series, whereas Anil Kumble, who was expected to be a big force on resilient Australian pitches, obtained no more than five. India took early wickets in every innings of the Test matches – Australia's highest opening stand was nine – but never managed to restrict the home side's first innings to under 400, which was a clear reflection of their meagre bowling resources.

OBITUARY

Amarnath, Nanik Bhardwaj, died on August 5, 2000, aged 88. 'Lala' Amarnath scored India's first Test century and went on to become Indian cricket's patriarchal figure: as selector, manager, coach and broadcaster, as well as in a literal sense – his three sons became first-class cricketers and two played in Tests. Amarnath, a Punjabi, was also the first to kick against the stifling domination of Indian cricket by the local princes and their imperial backers. It severely damaged his career. Amarnath's figures in his 24 Tests are nothing special, but they do no justice to either his spasmodic brilliance or his enduring influence.

From a poor background in Lahore, when it was still part of India, he rose to prominence by scoring 109 ('a brilliant display,' said *Wisden*) for Southern Punjab against MCC in 1933–34, and a few weeks later became a star with a century on his Test debut, India's first Test at home, at the genteel old Gymkhana ground in Bombay. With India facing an innings defeat, he took on the England attack and played, so he said later, 'as if possessed by a mysterious power.' He hit 83 in 78 minutes, hooking Nichols and Clark with confidence and going down the pitch to hit Hedley Verity. Slowing just a fraction, he reached his century in 117 minutes. According to Mihir Bose, 'Amarnath was engulfed with spectators, garlanded and congratulated while the band played "God Save the King"... As the day's play ended, women tore off their jewellery to present it to him, Maharajahs made gifts of money, and India hailed a hero.' England's eventual easy win was almost forgotten in the hysteria.

Though he did little in the remaining two Tests of that series, Amarnath was by far the best player – with bat and ball – in the early stages of the unhappy Indian tour of 1936, captained by the Maharaj Kumar of Vizianagram ('Vizzy'). Furthermore, Amarnath knew he was the best player and, having waited, padded up, during an unusually big partnership in the match against Minor Counties at Lord's, he was infuriated to be told that other batsmen would be promoted ahead of him. He swore at the captain and tour treasurer, and was sensationally sent home. The team's subsequent failures, a commission of inquiry, and history as written by people with a more egalitarian world-view than Vizzy have all combined to exonerate him. But it meant a 12-year gap between his third Test and his fourth.

He remained a force in Indian cricket, however, scoring 241 for Hindus v The Rest in 1938–39. But when he visited England with the 1946 team, by then rehabilitated, his bowling was more potent than his batting, most dramatically in the first post-war Test, at Lord's, when he reduced England's first innings to 70 for four by dismissing Hutton, Washbrook, Compton and Hammond. 'After a shuffling run of only three paces, he bowled off the wrong foot,' said *Wisden* with slightly shocked admiration, 'but he kept an almost impeccable length, moved his inswingers probably more than any bowler in England, and mixed these with a cut leg-break of some venom.'

The following year he was appointed India's captain for their first tour of Australia when Vijay Merchant withdrew. But with Bradman at his most merciless, India were understandably overwhelmed. Amarnath did little himself in the five Tests, averaging 14 with the bat, and taking 13 wickets, although he was magnificent against state sides. His 228 against Victoria contained, Neil Harvey said, the best cover driving he ever saw. He remained captain against West Indies in 1948–49 and in Bombay narrowly failed to lead India to their first Test victory. Then cricket politics again turned against him. There were arguments about money and second-class treatment (the visitors were treated royally; Indian players were dumped in second-class hotels). Amarnath fell foul of the powerful board secretary, Anthony De Mello, who was furious with the man he had dragged 'out of the gutter and made captain of India' and had him suspended for 'continuous misbehaviour and breach of discipline'.

Amarnath sought refuge in the Lancashire League. But he was buoyed by support from Bradman, who called him 'a splendid ambassador', and by De Mello's subsequent fall from power. He was restored, though reduced to the ranks, in 1951–52 and took part when India at last won a Test, against England in Madras; passed over for the humiliating 1952 tour of England; and then given back the captaincy against Pakistan in 1952–53, apparently at the insistence of – of all people – Vizzy. Although India won their first series, Amarnath's contributions as a player were minor, and yet more internal machinations meant he left the job in anger. However, the wheel keeps spinning in Indian cricket and Amarnath's reputation grew with the years. He became chairman of selectors, most famously insisting on the inclusion of off-spinner Jasu Patel at Kanpur in 1959–60, which led to a historic win over Australia. Lala also supervised the development of his sons: Surinder, too, made a century on debut; Mohinder ('Jimmy') played 69 Tests. He was a well-informed and humorous commentator, and in old age he acquired widespread affection as the nation's leading source of cricket anecdotes. But he never lost his habit of speaking his mind. 'He was an impetuous man,' said his contemporary, Mushtaq Ali, 'quick to love and quick to fight'. The Indian Prime Minister, A. B. Vajpayee, called him an icon.

WISDEN – 2002

India's role in international cricket, behind the scenes more than on the field, continued to expand, and the 'old guard' needed to take note.

NOTES BY THE EDITOR, by Graeme Wright

The word 'anarchy' appeared in cricket headlines a few times in 2001; not something anyone should be proud of. An atmosphere of lawlessness hung over the first two Tests between Sri Lanka and England in March; by November, India and South Africa had taken the law into their own hands. In Sri Lanka, the umpires were under siege – psychologically if not physically; in South Africa it was the match referee, Mike Denness.

Denness was officiating at the Second Test between South Africa and India at Port Elizabeth when he imposed penalties on six Indian players and incurred the wrath of a nation. It would be unfair to say he brought the game to the brink of schism; others did that, among them Jagmohan Dalmiya, former president of the ICC and, since September 2001, president of the Indian board. When India took umbrage at Denness's penalties and insisted he be removed as referee for the final Test – otherwise the team would go home and take their lucrative television purse with them – the South African board buckled under the threat of lost revenue. Denness was denied access to the Third Test, at Centurion, and the ICC withdrew their imprimatur. For the time being anyway: past experience warns that one should never take any ICC ruling for granted. But as things stand, the match at Centurion does not count as an official Test.

Viewed dispassionately, it was difficult to gauge what grieved the Indians more: the fact that prime among the penalised was Tendulkar, accorded god-like status by his millions of adoring fans, or that Denness, white and British, a former England captain, was a representative of the old colonial power. Accusations of racism, because he took no action against the South Africans' appeals and sledging, muddied the waters further...

In another year, the matter might have ended with the unofficial Test. But Denness, as well as fining captain Sourav Ganguly, Virender Sehwag, Harbhajan Singh, Deep Dasgupta and Shiv Sunder Das for other breaches of the Code of Conduct, also handed out a one-Test suspension to Sehwag, who had earlier hit a hundred on debut at Bloemfontein. In happier circumstances, that would have been the Centurion match. Now, however, India's next Test, as far as the ICC were concerned, was against England at Mohali in December. India, who had not played Sehwag at Centurion, argued otherwise and a period of brinkmanship followed. The Indian selectors included Sehwag in their squad; the ICC's new chief executive, Malcolm Speed, warned in no uncertain manner that the council would not give the Test official status if he played; the ECB said England would not take part in an unofficial match. For a day or two there was the threat of an international split. One deadline passed but eventually, perhaps inevitably, India accepted Speed's offer to set up a 'referees commission' to investigate whether Denness had acted in accordance with the Code of Conduct, the role of referees generally and whether players should have a right of appeal. Given that the ICC executive board had already agreed to strengthen the disciplinary power of referees from April 2002, the commission looked like being about as sabre-toothed as its name.

ICC Call the shots

A year or two earlier, the Indians would have headed off the ICC well before the impasse. What this eyeballing emphasised was the confidence with which the new administration had grasped authority, following universal acceptance of recommendations in the Condon Report on cricket corruption… But the stand-off also reminded the cricket world that India, through her cricket-crazy population and television's immense marketing potential, has an economic clout no other country can match. Cricket's old establishment may be undecided whether Dalmiya is a smoking gun or a loose cannon, but he epitomises the progressive, post-imperial, nuclear India. He is both poker player and politician. At the 11th hour, he knew he couldn't trust his hand against Speed's, but he knew he held the better cards when he wagered an extra India-England one-day international against this summer's Oval Test. It may not have been a gentleman's bet; the ECB had, after all, agreed terms with the pre-Dalmiya administration. But such is the precarious nature of their finances that they could not afford to lose the income the Oval Test would generate. They agreed to the extra one-day game in India (the Indians had initially wanted two), which ironically allowed England to draw the series 3–3.

It is as great an irony that Dalmiya's business acumen, when ICC president, provided the council with the financial muscle to stand up to India. Through television rights to the World Cup and interim knockout tournaments, he showed how cricket could be enriched beyond previous imagination. He may not always have won friends, but he knew how to influence people. He knew, too, how to nurse a grudge; for he had been sorely hurt by the peremptory way the ICC had dropped their pilot once they were in secure waters. When the opportunity came to rock their boat, he was hardly likely to resist it. Dalmiya aside, old attitudes towards India will have to change.

INDIA'S FIRST TEST VICTORY AGAINST BANGLADESH

Perhaps not surprisingly, Bangladesh opted to play their inaugural Test against India. After a bright start by Bangladesh, it did not prove to be a very close contest.

THE INDIANS IN BANGLADESH, 2000–01, by Richard Hobson

Saber Chowdhury, the president of the Bangladesh Cricket Board, described his country's elevation to Test status as the third most historic event in their national life, behind independence and the adoption of a United Nations mother-tongue day commemorating the suppression of the Bengali language under Pakistani rule. Certainly, the five days of celebrations leading up to the inaugural Test against India reflected its perceived importance to the national well-being. Events included a ceremonial dinner, a vivid firework display, school activities and the recording of a song written by a local journalist. Among the gestures of goodwill from the existing Test nations was the donation of ten corneas from the Board of Control for Cricket in Sri Lanka to help visually impaired Bangladeshis. Two of them were fitted in time for the beneficiaries to see the game.

A near-capacity crowd of around 40,000 watched the first day's play, which began after a simple but poignant opening ceremony in which parachutists carried flags from each of the ten Test-playing countries into the Bangabandhu Stadium. During the tea interval, Naimur Rahman, the Bangladesh captain, and Yuvraj Singh, a member of the Indian squad, injected four children with a polio vaccine to promote a new immunisation programme. The Bangladesh team delighted supporters as they advanced to 400 over the first two days. Their performance then gradually dropped off; so did attendances, as the later stages coincided with the Muslim festival of Shab-e-Barat, during which Allah is said to write the destiny of all men. Bangladesh's destiny, on this occasion, was defeat.

Inaugural Test, at Dhaka, November 10, 11, 12, 13, 2000

Bangladesh 400 (Aminul Islam 145, Habibul Bashar 71; Joshi 5-142) and **91** (Srinath 3-19, Joshi 3-27). **India 429** (Joshi 92, Ganguly 84, Ramesh 58; Naimur Rahman 6-132, Mohammad Rafique 3-117) and **64 for one wicket**.
India won by nine wickets.

THE AUSTRALIANS IN INDIA, 2000–01, by Dicky Rutnagur

Although the Australians began the tour with the awesome achievement of 15 consecutive Test wins, they deemed victory in the series against India as absolutely essential if they were to stand comparison with the greatest teams Australia had fielded. Winning in India was, in their eyes, a conquest of the 'final frontier', not least because 31 years and four tours had passed since Australia last left there triumphant.

Steve Waugh's team seemed to be on the point of emulating Bill Lawry's when they won the First Test at Mumbai, by ten wickets in three days, and then made India follow on 274 behind in the Second at Kolkata (formerly Calcutta). However, India not only denied them a winning 2–0 lead there, but rallied strongly enough to achieve one of the most remarkable victories in the history of Test cricket. They went on to win the deciding Test in a gripping finish.

The chief architects of the epic win at Eden Gardens were V. V. S. Laxman and Rahul Dravid, whose partnership of 376, one of several records in this match, was the basis of the recovery, and the 20-year-old Sikh off-spinner, Harbhajan Singh. His hat-trick in the first innings – the first for India in Tests – was only the precursor to taking 13 wickets in the match. In the next match, he topped that with 15. Harbhajan's and Laxman's glory was the greater for the fact that neither was hitherto established in the side...

India were without Anil Kumble for the whole series and Javagal Srinath for the last two Tests. The bonus that went with victory was the maturity achieved by Laxman and Harbhajan. A batsman of stately style, Laxman scored 503 runs at 83.83 in the Tests and should be an adornment to the game for many a year. It took much strength of character for Harbhajan to retain his poise and confidence after the ferocious battering he took from Gilchrist and Hayden in the First Test, but he went on to claim 32 wickets in the series at an average of 17.03. Only three bowlers – George Lohmann, Sydney Barnes and Richard Hadlee – had collected more in a three-Test series; Harbhajan was the first spinner to take so many.

India v Australia
Second Test, at Kolkata, March 11, 12, 13, 14, 15, 2001

An astonishing Indian recovery provided several records and culminated in only the third victory in Test history for a side who had followed on. Australia were the victims in the previous instances also, losing to England at Sydney in 1894–95 and Leeds in 1981. Laxman amassed 281, the highest Test score for India, while his partnership of 376 with Dravid was an Indian fifth-wicket record. Their feats almost overshadowed the outstanding performance of off-spinner Harbhajan Singh, who claimed India's first Test hat-trick while capturing a career-best seven wickets in the first innings, and followed up with a match-winning six in the second.

Fortune had already swayed quite vigorously before Australia achieved their formidable first-innings total of 445. Their early prosperity was based on large partnerships for the first two wickets, with Hayden the common factor... He was dismissed immediately after tea, and the decline that followed was expedited by Harbhajan's hat-trick, which claimed Ponting and Gilchrist lbw, both playing back, before Warne glanced a full toss to short leg. When Kasprowicz soon followed, Australia had lost seven wickets in the space of 26 overs and 76 runs, and were 269-8. But India were kept in the field until an hour after lunch on the second day as Steve Waugh batted more than five hours to orchestrate the revival. Tailenders Gillespie, who shared a stand of 133, an Australian ninth-wicket record against India, and McGrath lent noble support until Waugh was last out for 110. It was his 25th Test century, during which passed 20,000 first-class runs.

The fact that Australia's last two batted for 222 minutes between them was proof enough that the pitch was playing easily. Yet India somehow contrived to get themselves in a terrible mess. All four bowlers succeeded but, predictably, McGrath dominated with 4-18 in 14 overs. If there was a silver lining to the debacle, it was that Laxman's swashbuckling 59 from 83 balls prompted his promotion from No. 6 to No. 3 when India followed on 274 behind. The tall, elegant, Hyderabad batsman responded to the responsibility with a flawless display that stretched over ten hours 31 minutes, during which he faced 452 balls, picked up 44 fours with a wide range of exciting shots, and comfortably surpassed India's previous best, 236 not out by Sunil Gavaskar against West Indies at Madras in 1983–84. India lost four wickets before the first-innings deficit of 274 was cleared, but as Dravid's batting recovered its sparkle in Laxman's company, the game was transformed.

They batted together for 104 overs, including the whole of the fourth day, when they added 335 in 90 overs. Their stand of 376 overtook India's fifth-wicket record, a mere 214 between Mohammad Azharuddin and Ravi Shastri against England on this ground in 1984–85, and then India's all-wicket record against Australia, an unbroken 298 for the sixth wicket between Dilip Vengsarkar and Shastri at Bombay in 1986–87. By the time Laxman was out, it was the second-highest partnership for any Indian wicket, behind the opening stand of 413 between Vinoo Mankad and Pankaj Roy against New Zealand at Madras in 1955–56, and the third best by any country for the fifth wicket. Their efforts not only dispelled India's troubles, but opened up an avenue to a momentous victory. Dravid was eventually run out for a chanceless 180 from 353 balls in seven hours 24 minutes, with 21 fours.

When Ganguly declared with a lead of 383, India had equalled the second-highest Test total by a side batting second, 657 for eight by Pakistan at Bridgetown in 1957–58; only New Zealand, with 671 for four against Sri Lanka at Wellington in 1990–91, had scored more. It meant Australia had to bat out 75 overs for a draw, on a pitch affording turn without being devilish. Their prospects looked good when Hayden, given an early life, and Slater stayed together for 23 overs. But once they were separated, wickets fell at regular intervals... Harbhajan again did the major damage, and Tendulkar, bowling leg-spin, took three wickets, including the crucial ones of Hayden and Gilchrist – for a king pair. Australia were all out in the 69th over and their record run of Test wins had come to an abrupt and spectacular halt.

AUSTRALIA

	1st Innings		2nd Innings	
M. J. Slater c Mongia b Khan	42	– c Ganguly b Harbhajan Singh	43
M. L. Hayden c sub b Harbhajan Singh	97	– lbw b Tendulkar	67
J. L. Langer c Mongia b Khan	58	– c Ramesh b Harbhajan Singh	28
M. E. Waugh c Mongia b Harbhajan Singh	22	– lbw b Raju	0
*S. R. Waugh lbw b Harbhajan Singh	110	– c sub b Harbhajan Singh	24
R. T. Ponting lbw b Harbhajan Singh	6	– c Das b Harbhajan Singh	0
†A. C. Gilchrist lbw b Harbhajan Singh	0	– lbw b Tendulkar	0
S. K. Warne c Ramesh b Harbhajan Singh	0	– lbw b Tendulkar	0
M. S. Kasprowicz lbw b Ganguly	7	– not out	13
J. N. Gillespie c Ramesh b Harbhajan Singh	46	– c Das b Harbhajan Singh	8
G. D. McGrath not out	21	– lbw b Harbhajan Singh	12
Extras (b 19, l-b 10, n-b 7)	36	Extras (b 6, n-b 8, pen 5)	19

1-103 2-193 3-214 4-236 (all out, 131.5 overs) 445   1-74 2-106 3-116 4-166 (all out; 68.3 overs) 212
5-252 6-252 7-252 8-269 9-402 10-445   5-166 6-167 7-173-174 9-191 10-212

First innings – Khan 28.4–6–89–2; Prasad 30–5–95–0; Raju 13.2–3–44–1; Harbhajan Singh 37.5–7–123–7; Tendulkar 2–0–7–0; Ganguly 1–0–2–0
Second innings – ZKhan 8–4–30–0; Prasad 3–1–7–0; S. Raju 15–3–58–1; Harbhajan Singh 30.3–8–73–6; Tendulkar 11–3–31–3

INDIA

	1st Innings		2nd Innings (following on)	
S. S. Das c Gilchrist b McGrath	20	– hit wicket b Gillespie	39
S. Ramesh c Ponting b Gillespie	0	– c M. E. Waugh b Warne	30
R. Dravid b Warne	25	– run out	180
S. R. Tendulkar lbw McGrath	10	– c Gilchrist b Gillespie	10
*S. C. Ganguly c S. R. Waugh b Kasprowicz	23	– c Gilchrist b McGrath	48
V. V. S. Laxman c Hayden b Warne	59	– c Ponting b McGrath	281
†N. R. Mongia c Gilchrist b Kasprowicz	2	– b McGrath	4
Harbhajan Singh c Ponting b Gillespie	4	– not out	8
Z. Khan b McGrath	3	– not out	23
S. L. V. Raju lbw b McGrath	4		
P. K. V. Prasad not out	7		
Extras (l-b 2, n-b 12)	14	Extras (b 6, l-b 12, w 2, n-b 14)	34

1-0 2-34 3-48 4-88 Total (all out; 58.1 overs) 171   1-52 2-97 3-115 (7 wickets dec; 178 overs) 657
5-88 6-92 7-97 8-113 9-129 10-171   4-232 5-608 6-624 7-629

First innings – McGrath 14–8–18–4; Gillespie 11–0–47–2; Kasprowicz 13–2–39–2; Warne 20.1–3–65–2
Second innings – McGrath 39–12–103–3; Gillespie 31–6–115–2; Kasprowicz 35–6–139–0; Warne 34–3–152–1; M. E. Waugh 18–1–58–0; Ponting 12–1–41–0; Hayden 6–0–24–0; Slater 2–1–4–0; Langer 1–0–3–0

India won by 171 runs.

CRICKETERS OF THE YEAR 2002

V. V. S. LAXMAN, by Dicky Rutnagur

V. V. S. Laxman is one of only four players who did not play any cricket in England in the year they were chosen, the others being Sanath Jayasuriya, Matthew Hayden and Andy Flower. It was one innings that secured for him his honour – 281 for India against Australia in the Second Test at Kolkata to turn a likely innings defeat into an Indian victory.

For two reasons at least, the second Test of the 2000–01 series between India and Australia, at Eden Gardens, will stand out among the most prominent landmarks in the game's history. India's win brought to an end Australia's awesome run of 16 wins, the longest ever, and no side following on as far behind as 274 runs had previously come back to win a Test match.

Victory against such heavy odds was too large a feat to be accomplished by just one man. Indeed, three architects went into shaping it: off-spinner Harbhajan Singh, whose 13 wickets included a first-innings hat-trick, V. V. S. Laxman and Rahul Dravid. To weigh importance of the roles played by each of them might seem unfair, but in truth India owed the largest debt to Laxman. First, he kept the jaws of defeat wrenched apart until they ached and became too weak to snap; and secondly, he scored his epic 281 in the second innings at a rate that left enough time for Harbhajan and his fellow-bowlers to finish the job.

The First Test at Mumbai had been won by Australia in three days. And when India were 317 behind with only two wickets standing at the end of the second day in Kolkata, the prospects of another premature finish were writ large. Laxman was 26 not out that evening. He was unbeaten also – albeit now in the second innings – on the following evening, and again on the one after, this time with 275, the highest Test score by an Indian. By then, it was India whose nostrils were filled with the scent of victory. Haste required by the impending declaration deprived Laxman of further personal glory, but his partnership of 376 with Dravid was India's largest for any wicket against Australia, and their second highest ever.

Vangipurappu Venkata Sai Laxman was born on November 1, 1974 in Hyderabad, to parents who are both doctors – his father a general practitioner and his mother a radiologist. It was taken for granted that Laxman, like almost all members of his near family, would take up a profession that required academic excellence, and he was therefore sent to an appropriate school, Little Flower. His father was Laxman's role model and he always assumed he would become a doctor as well. But medicine receded into stand-by mode once he fell under cricket's spell.

Yet with sport not figuring in Little Flower's curriculum, Laxman's talent could easily have remained latent. It was spotted by a cricket-playing uncle during family games in his grandparents' back yard. Having learnt the basics from this uncle, he then went to St John's Coaching Foundation for more advanced tutoring,

and from there graduated to playing age-group cricket for Hyderabad, beginning with the Under-13s.

As Laxman approached his 18th birthday, his head and his heart were both telling him that his future lay in cricket. The defining moment arrived when he had to choose between exams for entrance to medical school, or a place at an Under-19 national coaching camp. Looking back to that fateful day, he said, 'I decided to give myself four years to make it in cricket, knowing that if I didn't, I could always go for medicine. My parents must have had many misgivings about my decision, but they gave me their fullest support.'

He did not have to wait long to reassure his parents that he had chosen wisely. Already a full state player, he was picked for India in an Under-19 Test series against Australia, who had Jason Gillespie, Brett Lee, Matthew Nicholson and Andrew Symonds in their ranks. He made four big scores against them, with 151 not out his best, giving early evidence of his taste for Australian bowling (his average against Australia is currently 56.00). A call to full colours was only a matter of time, and while he waited he had an extremely successful Under-19 tour of England. He began the 'Test' series with a century on a blissful Taunton pitch.

As Laxman grew to full strength, tall and elegant, and big scores became more frequent, his batting acquired a captivating splendour. His driving possessed a Dexterian majesty and his flicked drive through mid-wicket stirred the senses. He was capped in 1996–97, a winter in which India played home-and-away series against South Africa, followed by five Tests in the West Indies. Laxman played eight Tests during this span and passed 50 three times. Indeed, he was given a fair run, but without being allowed a secure place in the batting order; in the Caribbean, he found himself opening, a role for which he had no taste.

His Test career went into a trough and might well have ended on the Australian tour of 1999–2000, when India were whitewashed 0-3. But in his final innings there, at Sydney, he hit a sumptuous 167 out of a total of 261, from only 198 balls. It was, one thought at the time, the sort of innings a batsman plays once in a lifetime. And so it seemed it would be when he was dropped after India's Mumbai defeat by South Africa not quite two months later. His volume of runs in that season's Ranji Trophy, a record 1,415 with a record eight hundreds, might almost have been mocking him. In Hyderabad's semi-final against Karnataka, he made 353, his fourth score at the time over 200.

Laxman achieved little in his one Test when Zimbabwe visited, or for that matter in the First Test against the Australians. That Sydney century seemed a long time ago. But promoted to his favourite No. 3 position for the second innings at Eden Gardens, he bettered it handsomely, sustaining his brilliance for ten and a half hours, during which he faced 452 balls. Half-centuries in both innings of the final Test helped India take the series 2–1; they also took his aggregate for the three matches to 503 at an average of 83.83. Medicine would just have to wait a while longer for V. V. S. Laxman.

CRICKET IN INDIA, 2000–01,
by R. Mohan and Mohandas Menon

Cricket is known to have existed in India since 1721, when British sailors played on a beach on the western coast. But for much of the past 280 years, the game has been an elitist pursuit, generally confined to the major cities, such as Calcutta, Bombay, Madras (now known as Kolkata, Mumbai, and Chennai) and Delhi. It also took root, however, in the princely states of the hinterland, such as Holkar and Patiala, whose royal house commissioned the handsome Ranji Trophy... In the glory days of the Raj, cricket thrived in the palace grounds of Baroda, and continued to do so in the decade after independence...

There could have been no greater confirmation that the game has permeated the length and breadth of India than the semi-finals of the 2000–01 Ranji Trophy, in which Baroda and the Indian Railways overcame Orissa and Punjab respectively. Punjab, the modern heirs of Patiala... reached the semi-final having won all seven of their Ranji matches, five by an innings. But Orissa, a state more often in the news for bearing the brunt of natural calamities, were playing in the semi-finals for the first time...

Railways, in the final for only the second time, had first joined the Ranji tournament in 1958–59, with Lala Amarnath, towards the end of his playing career, at the helm. They were a product of government patronage in the early days of independent India, when national institutions were asked to take on the Maharajahs' role in sponsoring sport...

The desperation with which both teams sought to win brought the contest an intensity quite different from that of a clash between the traditional giants of Indian cricket. They had won through to the final despite the huge imbalance in resources between the haves and have-nots of Indian cricket. The facilities at the Gujarat State Fertiliser Corporation ground in Baroda were far removed from what Steve Waugh's Australians found at the major Test venues, and the success of the have-nots should have sent a message to the selectors.

OBITUARY

Roy, Pankaj, died in Calcutta on February 4, 2001, aged 72. He had suffered from cardiovascular problems. His son Pranab and nephew Ambar each played a few Tests for India, but Pankaj Roy had 43 to his credit; once, in 1959 at Lord's when Datta Gaekwad was poorly with bronchitis, he captained India. Cricket buffs recall him easily and affectionately for his great opening partnership with Vinoo Mankad when, against New Zealand at the Corporation Stadium, Madras in January 1956, they raised the world Test record for the first wicket to 413 runs. Mankad made 231 and Roy 173. They were the first Indians to bat together through a whole day's play in Test cricket – and only the third pair at the time.

This was the highest, and also the last, of Roy's five Test centuries that went towards a Test aggregate of 2,442 runs at 32.56. The first two had been made against England in 1951–52 in his debut series. However, Roy found the pace of English bowlers and pitches too lively for him when he toured in 1952 – he managed just 54 in the four Tests – and as vice-captain in 1959. He had a happier time in the West Indies in 1952–53, averaging 47.87 in his four Tests and finishing with 150 at Kingston as he and Vijay Manjrekar put on an Indian-record 237 for the second wicket to save the match.

From 1946–47, when he hit a hundred on debut, to 1967–68, the stockily built, patient Roy was the anchor of the Bengal side in the Ranji Trophy. His highest score was 202 not out for Bengal against Orissa at Cuttack in 1963–64, and in all first-class matches he made 11,868 runs at an average of 42.38. Pankaj Roy's business life was occupied with the fisher-trawler trade and he was a figure of considerable prestige in Calcutta. He played a vital role in the development of cricket in Bengal and India, when both were coping with the political and social fall-out of the Second World War and the country's independence. Although he never forgot the humiliation, as he saw it, of his failures in England, he was well entitled to enjoy the compensation of that important opening partnership, still the world record at the time of his death.

WISDEN – 2003

In 2001 and 2002 England provided the opposition for two tours, one home and one away.

ENGLAND IN INDIA, 2001–02, by David Hopps

England's first Test tour of India for nine years should have been a delight, an overdue opportunity to sample the cricketing and cultural pleasures of a land seething with life and unpredictability. Instead, it came close to being blighted before a ball was bowled – first by no-shows from three regular players, then by the prickly politics of two countries still carrying plenty of colonial baggage. The cricket might have been incidental, but turned out to be much more interesting than that. Nasser Hussain rose to the challenge of returning to the land of his birth with an inexperienced team and made sure that the Test series, although lost, was close and competitive. The one-day series was even closer, culminating in a dramatic denouement at Mumbai: the abiding image of the tour was of Andrew Flintoff, transformed from a Test reject to a fast-bowling all-rounder, careering round the Wankhede Stadium with his shirt off after clinching a hard-earned 3–3 draw...

The Test series was only three weeks from start to finish, but was absorbing enough to catch the imagination. England were heavily beaten at Mohali, but fought back to have the better of a draw at Ahmedabad, and were well on top when rain ruined the finale at Bangalore. Hussain proved a shrewd and diplomatic leader, tactically astute, imaginative, yet realistic about his team's limitations. He was a polite, intelligent spin doctor with the media, and immensely loyal to what he never tired of reminding everybody was a young side, largely untutored in Asian conditions...

England's batsmen were caught cold by India's spinners, Harbhajan Singh and Anil Kumble, at Mohali, where the seamers had been expected to dominate. England played the turning ball with increasing confidence thereafter, pushing Harbhajan and Kumble's joint strike-rate from 36 in the First Test to 58 in the Second and 340 in the Third...

Winning the series gained a little respite for India's captain Sourav Ganguly and coach John Wright after their troubles in South Africa. The selectors dealt them a curious hand for the First Test, supplying a seam attack that was even greener than England's. If Ganguly lost most of the tactical battles, he won the war. He himself was a weak link in the batting, which leant heavily on Tendulkar, but there were runs at different times from all the other big guns plus Deep Dasgupta, the wicketkeeper and makeshift opener, who batted a great deal better than he kept. Sehwag joined Adam Gilchrist as a Test No. 7 with the ability to take the breath away... After starting the series by fielding three seamers on a turning pitch, India ended up playing three spinners on a surface that seamed. Ganguly took the new ball himself with his little dobbers, awakening memories of Eknath Solkar...

England carried on the good work in January, when they returned to India – reinforced by Thorpe, the refuseniks Gough and Caddick, and a handful of limited-overs specialists – for a six-match one-day series. Few gave them much hope, and when India's openers ran riot at Kanpur to go into a 3–1 lead, a thrashing was on the cards. But England held their nerve, won the last two games by a whisker and nearly reduced Ganguly to tears as he faced the wrath of the Mumbai crowd at the presentation ceremony. For India, a drawn series felt more like a defeat.

Typically, the cricket had been preceded by politicking behind the scenes. Dalmiya's predecessors had agreed to a five-match series, but he demanded six and also wanted to expand England's next tour, in 2005–06, from three Tests to five. If his demands were denied, he threatened that India would play three Tests, not four, in England later in the year. Negotiations carried on until the end of December, when it was agreed that England would play a sixth international, at Cuttack, in a reshuffled schedule, but they offered no concession on the future tour.

The cricket, played in six different cities and in front of packed houses, was vibrant and enthralling... England were no longer one-day pushovers.

BATTING FOR A BILLION, by Rohit Brijnath

Modern cricket heros are feted and analysed as never before, and the bigger the hero, the greater the analysis.

Sachin Ramesh Tendulkar is now 30, he has a wife and two children, his face is wreathed in a goatee and faintly lined by time and travel, but to the world, and to India in particular, he is still a boy wonder. Thirteen years and 105 Tests have passed since he first took guard at Karachi in November 1989, but the poet's son with the almost-falsetto voice and the supremely dignified manner continues to write an elegant, belligerent and unprecedented history. When he walks to the crease – one eye occasionally turning to the sun, one hand hitching up his box – it is cricket's equivalent of Michelangelo ascending a ladder towards the ceiling of the Sistine Chapel. He is short, 5ft 4in, and his stance is a study in stillness, his body finely balanced, his muscles relaxed. His mind has already mapped the geography of the field: as the ball is bowled, rarely does tension or indecision impede the instructions from brain to body. Only sometimes, so it seems, will he silently struggle within, caught between the responsibility he carries for his team and the force of his natural attacking instincts.

Then he plays. He is both tyrant and technician, batting with a thug's ferocity and a sculptor's finesse, though sometimes he fails to strike the necessary balance between the two. In his room, he occasionally takes one last look at his technique in front of the mirror; on the field, most days, we see that genius reflected…

Many things are unique to Tendulkar, and most of all the fact that the man has stayed faithful to the gifts he was given as a boy. Once, according to a possibly apocryphal story, a junior Indian team on tour was awakened by a thumping on the roof. On investigation, it was Tendulkar lost in some midnight practice.

Later, too, he took little for granted. When Shane Warne toured India, Tendulkar went into the nets, scuffed the pitch on the leg side and had a spinner pitch it there; before India toured Australia, Tendulkar had the seamers deliver the ball from closer to his end, artificially manufacturing the pace and bounce he expected to face. The net has remained his temple. Asked about this once, he was gently annoyed that people felt it all came so naturally to him, thus discounting how disciplined his journey had been: his gifts, he explained, were oiled with sweat.

He will never be the greatest batsman in history: that seat is taken. But as much as Donald Bradman's Test average (99.94) outstrips Tendulkar's (57.58), the gap diminishes substantially when other factors are taken into account. Tendulkar travels more in a year than Bradman did in a decade; he has had to manage the varying conditions of 49 Test grounds, to Bradman's ten; he has already played twice as many Tests as Bradman, and over 300 one-day games, nearly all of them under the unrelenting scrutiny of television. And whereas Bradman had to cope with the expectations of a small populace, not given to idolatry, in an age of restraint, Tendulkar must play god to one billion expectant worshippers.

Steve Waugh has said, 'You take Bradman away and he is next up, I reckon,'... Wasim Akram once suggested that when Tendulkar is out, heads droop in the Indian dressing-room. Rarely has Tendulkar had the comfort of knowing that the men who follow him are as certain in rising to a challenge.

More demanding is his nation, for when Tendulkar plays, India stills, it quietens, till it is almost possible to hear a collective exhalation with every shot. In a land where governments stutter, the economy stagnates and life itself is an enduring struggle against failure, he is deliverance. For most of a billion people, unmoved by any other sport, he is escape as much as he is hope, standing like some solitary national advertisement of success. Tendulkar is not allowed to fail...

If Tendulkar is India's escape, it may well be that the crease is his escape, the place where he finds his full expression. Only once, under persistent interrogation, did he admit, 'People expect too much of me, a hundred every innings. They call and say, "you scored a hundred in Kanpur, so why not in Delhi?" They must accept my failures.'

He stands now, closer to the end of his career than the beginning, with 8,811 Test runs, sixth on the all-time list. The only current player ahead of him is Steve Waugh, who is nearing retirement. Barring catastrophe, Tendulkar will surpass Allan Border's 11,174 with some ease; Sunil Gavaskar's record 34 centuries will be outstripped as well. In the one-day game, Tendulkar already stands alone and untouchable at the summit – Border and Gavaskar rolled into one, with more than 12,000 runs, while nobody else has 10,000, and 34 centuries. He even has a hundred wickets.

In the Test arena, Bradman will never be equalled. In Tests and one-dayers together, the reality of international cricket today, Sachin Ramesh Tendulkar will take some catching, too.

THE INDIANS IN ENGLAND 2002, by Rahul Bhattacharya

A series of more than three Tests is a rare thing these days. Its shifting dynamics embrace such abstractions as momentum, luck, form, intensity – karma, even – as if it were a universe in itself. India's tour of England in 2002 captured the ebb and flow, the up and down, of this strange and enchanting realm. The series was played out by sides that were evenly matched at the start, became absurdly superior to one another at different points, and ended exactly level as if to reconcile themselves to the truth of the original equation. Life, it appeared, had come a complete circle within the space of four Tests.

The scoreline, 1–1, was frustrating but fair. Michael Vaughan, who came of age with three princely hundreds, did not deserve to be on the losing side; nor did Rahul Dravid, who matched him for excellence if not for excitement. The series was India's first of more than three Tests in England since 1979, and in those 23 years Indian ready-meals had sprung up in Marks & Spencer, chicken tikka masala had overtaken fish and chips as the national dish and Britain had become more multicultural, or more comfortable in its multi-culturalism. On hoardings and TV screens, the summer was branded as Indian: there were more Indian movie festivals than anyone could possibly attend, plus the opening season of Andrew Lloyd Webber's musical *Bombay Dreams*. And the lasting flavour of the cricket was Indian.

It was India who made the larger gains, and did so in more valiant fashion. This may seem harsh on England, who at different times were without three, four, even six of their first-choice players. But that must be weighed against India's entire cricket history, which reveals that winning a single Test outside the subcontinent, let alone drawing a series of four matches, is a less frequent occurrence than national elections. India had never drawn a series in England, and although they had won two, in 1971 and 1986, they had lost the other 11 for a combined tally of 41 Tests played, three won and 22 lost…

In the second over of India's second innings in the Second Test, when they lost their second wicket with the total barely into double figures, India were in danger of losing the match by an innings, putting a series win beyond their reach. Dravid and Tendulkar came together. A spectacular sun came angling out through the clouds late on the fourth evening. Trent Bridge looked beautiful. Now was the time.

By the next evening, the Test had been saved. Tendulkar made 92 runs of bona-fide brilliance, Ganguly scraped an equally crucial 99, and Dravid's 115 occupied almost as many deliveries as both put together, which was a fair indication of its value. Even little Parthiv Patel, the 17-year-old debutant wicketkeeper with bright wide eyes and chubby cheeks, hung around for an hour and a half at the end, a performance stirring enough for the battle-hardened Alec Stewart, 22 years his elder, to put a fatherly arm around him as the players made their way off the pitch. Like an alcoholic who had hit rock bottom, Team India had risen and reformed themselves.

They took this self-belief to Headingley where, given usual conditions, it was all but written in stone that they must lose… Every piece fell into place: defensive batting and then attacking batting, seam bowling and then spin bowling, close catching and outfield catching. Dravid and Bangar guarded their wickets on the opening day as if the hopes of a billion hinged on them, then Tendulkar and Ganguly steamed to a tantalising 249-run partnership at more than four an over…

When it was time to bowl, Anil Kumble produced his greatest performance away from home, and for the first time in a 12-year international career, reaped the rewards. India won by an innings and 46 runs, their largest overseas win. Such was the power of belief…

The last-day Indian presence indicated a general preference among Asians for one-day cricket over Tests. They book their one-day games in advance, as they did during the NatWest tri-series, but prefer to wait and watch before buying Test tickets. This means their time comes on Monday, when tickets are reasonably priced – and available at the gate.

On each fifth day, the Indian team responded to their support. At Lord's came a great revival in a losing cause, at Trent Bridge a great escape, at Headingley a great victory. And at The Oval it rained great showers, which coincided almost perfectly with the end of the monsoon season back home. It was like some grand, cosmic levelling – with a whiff of India. It went well with the series.

OBITUARY

Gupte, Subhash Pandharinath, died in Port-of-Spain on May 31, 2002, aged 72. He had suffered from diabetes and was unable to get about without a wheelchair or walking frame. Sir Everton Weekes had recently said Gupte was 'easily the best leg-spin bowler of all time', and certainly between 1953 and 1956 he was peerless. In 15 successive Tests for India he beguiled his way to 82 wickets at 23.57, averaging a wicket every 70 balls. At a comparable stage in his Test career, Shane Warne's strike-rate was 75.

In contrast to his burly younger brother Baloo, who also bowled leggies and won three caps in the 1960s, Subhash Gupte was small and slight. But he had a high arm action and the wrist-spinner's predilection for experimenting with flight and rotation. Unlike some, he possessed the control and patience to afford his variations. His leg-spinner, nicely looped, turned on the flattest pitches, while a scurrying top-spinner and two googlies provided sufficient chicanery. The googly he bowled with a lower trajectory was for batsmen to read; the other, from his customary high trajectory, came laced with overspin and dipped and bounced deceptively. Unhappily, his close catchers struggled to pick his repertoire almost as much as the batsmen, so chances often went begging. He would have taken all ten wickets, instead of nine for 102, against West Indies on jute matting at Kanpur in 1958–59 had the wicketkeeper Naren Tamhane not dropped Lance Gibbs. It was the first time an Indian bowler had taken nine wickets in a Test innings – and still India lost by a large margin...

After a debut Test against England in 1951–52 and two the next season against Pakistan, Gupte won his spurs – and a nickname, 'Fergie', after the Trinidad leg-spinner Wilf Ferguson – in the Caribbean in 1952–53. He also met his future wife, Carol. Though few of the pitches helped bowlers and Weekes was rampant, averaging over 100, Gupte took 27 wickets at 29.22 in the five Tests, including seven for 162 at Port-of-Spain, and ended the tour with 50 at 23.64...

Gupte was considered the best of his kind when India went to England in 1959, but the strain of carrying India's attack was beginning to tell. Gerry Alexander's

West Indians had recently made him pay 42.13 apiece for his 22 wickets; India's next highest wicket-taker claimed only five and Gupte's workload of 312 overs was almost three times that of anyone else. Though he remained India's leading wicket-taker, he did not always come up to expectation on the hard pitches of that sun-baked English summer. And the Indians' slothful fielding didn't help; he was patently dispirited by the poor standard...

The old familiar flight and fizz were much in evidence when he was recalled for the Kanpur Test against Ted Dexter's MCC side in December 1961. He took the first five wickets and, for the first time, India made England follow on. But the comeback did not last long. During the next Test his roommate, Kripal Singh, phoned the hotel receptionist to ask her for a date. She complained to the Indian management who, claiming they did not know who made the call, suspended both players. Even worse, the Indian board president, himself an acquaintance of the lady, told the selectors not to pick Gupte for the forthcoming tour of the West Indies. Bitter and disillusioned, Gupte quit India for good at 33 and emigrated to Trinidad, where he worked in the sugar refinery and as a sports officer within the industry.

WISDEN — 2004

There were mixed results for India in 2002–03. In the winter West Indies toured India, then, following the World Cup in South Africa, India toured New Zealand before returning home to face the Kiwis again.

A new concept was introduced in Wisden *in 2004 – The* Wisden *Forty, the top world cricketers of the year, in the opinion of the editor, 'made in consultation with many of the game's most experienced writers and commentators'. Five Indians made the first list – Dravid, Kumble, Laxman, Sehwag and Tendulkar.*

For the first time, too, a locally printed edition of Wisden *was produced, an exact replica of the UK edition.*

RAHUL DRAVID

Just when it looked like the man nicknamed 'the Wall' could not scale any greater heights after a run-laden 2002, Dravid took his batting to another level. It is not easy to stand out in the Indian top six – who by the end of the year were established as cricket's answer to Real Madrid's footballing *galacticos* – but Dravid began India's unusually light Test year with 222 and 73 against New Zealand at Ahmedabad, and finished with a man of the series performance in Australia, where his tally of 305 for once out at Adelaide was one of the all-time great performances. Few batsmen anywhere could match his blend of patience, elegance, strokeplay and modesty. Through it all, he remained the backbone of the Indian line-up, as five unbeaten innings out of ten plus an average of over 63 at the World Cup – despite the burden of keeping wicket – confirmed.

2003: 5 Tests: 803 runs @ 100.37. 23 ODI (19 as wicketkeeper): 623 runs @ 41.53. 19 catches as keeper, 2 stumpings.

THE WORLD CUP 2003, by Simon Wilde

The hosts of the eighth World Cup wanted it to be the greatest yet. In financial terms, it was – profits of US$194 million represented a huge increase on the US$51 million made in 1999 – but in other respects, it fell short. Indeed, this traditional organisers' boast rather came back to haunt the South Africans, who headed a pan-African triumvirate also including Zimbabwe and Kenya. A great tournament needs dramatic tension, and the brilliance of the Australians never allowed it. In winning all their 11 matches, the champions repeatedly displayed talent, audacity – and a superiority over all rivals…

Ganguly's side… emerged from the tournament in credit. Not fancied to do well in the conditions, they steadily grew in confidence after a shaky batting performance in their opener with Holland and put together a winning streak of eight matches – including one in their first meeting with Pakistan for almost three years – with some of the most entertaining cricket on show. An 11th-hour decision to restore Tendulkar to the opener's role he favoured proved inspired. He ran up a record run aggregate of 673, more than 200 ahead of his nearest challengers – his own captain, Ganguly, and Australia's captain, Ponting…

The run-up to the tournament was fraught with problems, with countries courting damages claims from the ICC for failing to fulfil contractual commitments. An intractable dispute between the Indian board and their players, over product endorsement, threatened their participation… In the end, India took part, with the ICC withholding their share of revenue until the contracts problem was resolved.

World Cup Final: Australia v India
At Johannesburg, March 23, 2003, by John Stern

Ricky Ponting played a captain's innings to deliver Australia their third title. His 140, the highest individual score in a World Cup final, and his leadership through the tournament completed his ascent from under-achieving Tasmanian devil to cornerstone of Australian dominance…

Ganguly raised eyebrows by putting Australia in. He was acting from fear of Australia's bowlers rather than on aggressive intent: against any other opponents, he would surely have batted first. Yet it had been 71 matches and three years since Australia last failed to defend a total of 200 or more.

Ganguly was right to think that the pitch would offer movement and bounce, but his in-form seamers were now under pressure to perform. They buckled. The first over from Zaheer Khan contained ten deliveries and 15 runs, and there was no coming back. Gilchrist and Hayden chanced their arms, as they do: after nine overs, Australia were 74 without loss. 'Intent and intimidate – that has been our motto,' said Ponting afterwards. The grammar was dubious; the effectiveness beyond question.

Ganguly turned to spin in the tenth over, and Harbhajan Singh did send back both openers. But Australia were not reined in for long. The partnership of 234 between Ponting and Martyn was Australia's highest for any wicket in one-day internationals. So was their total...

The gear-change occurred when Harbhajan returned in the 39th over. Ponting completed his fifty with a single – then hit him out of the attack with two successive sixes over mid-wicket. Harbhajan was replaced by Nehra; Ponting responded with a remarkable one-handed slog-sweep off a low full toss that also disappeared over mid-wicket. Off the penultimate ball of the innings, he drove Srinath for six over long-on into the second deck of the stand at the Golf Course End. Australia's acceleration had been breathtaking: 109 off the last ten overs, 64 off the last five. Srinath conceded 87 runs, the most in a final.

The army of Indian supporters – many from the UK – had been bemused when Ganguly asked Australia to bat. By the interval, they had all but given up hope. The dream was shattered entirely when Tendulkar tried to pull McGrath's fifth ball and was caught by the bowler off a top edge. Sehwag, who was caught off a Lee no-ball on four, did his best to keep India in it with a bullish run-a-ball 82, including ten fours and three sixes. But he was run out by a direct hit from Lehmann at deep mid-off, ending a promising stand of 88 with Dravid.

Rain had briefly threatened the unsatisfactory prospect of a replay the following day, with Australia's record-breaking performances consigned to history – so every sign of precipitation was greeted uproariously by India's fans. Knowing his side had to bowl 25 overs to ensure a result, Ponting brought on his spinners: there was a surreal period where Hogg and Lehmann were being thrashed to all parts as Indian supporters cheered and the fielders, running to their positions to speed up the over-rate, got wet. Then the umpires called a drinks break. After drinks, Bichel and McGrath returned, the lights came on, and the rain became heavy enough for the players to leave the field, with India on 103-3. They returned 25 minutes later – no overs were deducted – and the formality of Australia's third World Cup (and 17th consecutive one-day victory) was completed under darkening skies to the sound of frequent thunderclaps.

Australia 359 for two wickets (50 overs) (R. T. Ponting 140 not out, D. R. Martyn 88 not out, A. C. Gilchrist 57). **India 234** (39.2 overs) (V. Sehwag 82). Australia won by 125 runs.

WEST INDIES IN INDIA, 2002–03, by Amit Varma

How absurd it would have been, two decades ago, to imagine that West Indies could be relieved to lose a three-Test series against India 2–0. Yet that is how it was. Their decline of the 1990s had accelerated into an alarming freefall. Of their last 27 overseas Tests, West Indies had lost 23, and they had just suffered a humiliating home defeat by New Zealand. In India, they began with more of the same, as they were drubbed in the first two Tests. But they salvaged some pride at Kolkata, where they might have won until Sachin Tendulkar and V. V. S. Laxman saved the day…

THE INDIANS IN NEW ZEALAND, 2002–03, by Lawrence Booth

India's tour of New Zealand was an unmitigated disaster for them. The Tests were surrendered in the blink of an eye, and the seven-match limited-overs series was decided almost as quickly… India's trip ended as it began: in total disarray…

New Zealand's cricket fraternity wondered whether this was the worst side ever to visit; Bangladesh had been guests the previous year, so that was stretching a point. But on some measures India were indeed worse: they averaged 13.37 runs per wicket against the Bangladeshis' 14.50. A fairer contention was that, for sustained misery, the tour ranked alongside India's disastrous visits to Australia in 1991–92 and 1999–2000, when they lost 4–0 and 3–0 respectively. It worsened an already awful record outside India – just six wins in 65 Tests since beating England in 1986.

THE NEW ZEALANDERS IN INDIA, 2003–04, by Richard Boock

New Zealand's preparations for their tour of India included practising on custom-made dirt pitches, having music blasted through earphones as they batted, and hiring people to shout abuse and rattle the sides of the nets. The Kiwis, who had risen to third in the ICC Test Championship, were desperate to consolidate their position with a strong performance on the subcontinent, a region in which they had previously struggled to be competitive…

For India, the series was billed as a chance to exact revenge on the New Zealanders, who had prepared unplayable greentops in the previous summer's series in a move designed to nullify the Indians' batting strength. As it happened, the pitches for both Tests were more durable than most Indian roads, and neither India at Ahmedabad nor New Zealand at Mohali could capitalise on their hard-earned advantage to deliver a telling blow.

OBITUARIES

Adhikari, Lieut-Col. Hemchandra Ramachandra, died on October 25, 2003, aged 84. Hemu Adhikari played in 21 Tests for India, bringing a military man's stay-at-your-post sense of duty to Indian cricket of the late 1940s and 1950s when the national team was frequently on the brink of rout and flight. His finest hour came in one of the darkest times of all, when India's batsmen were frightened by Wes Hall and Roy Gilchrist in the 1958–59 home series against West Indies and, at 39, he became the fourth captain in the five Tests. He was not even the obvious choice for this role – the selectors almost went for G. S. Ramchand – and Adhikari only accepted after prompting from his wife and his commanding officer. But he led by example with innings of 63 and 40, took three wickets with leg-breaks scarcely seen in Test cricket, and secured a draw to halt West Indies' three-match winning sequence.

Despite his success, he did not make himself available for the 1959 tour of England which turned out even more disastrously. Adhikari had played only two Tests in the previous six years, partly because of army commitments, but his leadership qualities had been much in evidence as he guided Services to two successive Ranji Trophy finals. In his early days, he had won three Ranji Trophies with Baroda. At that stage he was renowned for his strokeplay, but in Test cricket he usually had to concentrate on crisis management: his only Test century came at Delhi in the maiden Test between India and West Indies in 1948–49 when his 114 not out just failed to save the follow-on…

After retiring from the army, Adhikari became national coach and was manager of the triumphant 1971 tour of England. His style involved strict discipline, an emphasis on fielding and, in the words of Bapu Nadkarni, 'not bothering about what anybody else thought'. He was also occasionally heard as a radio summariser in a style the *Daily Telegraph* described as 'somewhat Delphic'.

Divecha, Ramesh Vithaldas, died on February 19, 2003, aged 75, having suffered from Alzheimer's disease. 'Buck' Divecha played in India's first Test victory, against England at Madras in 1951–52, and 11 different first-class sides in all, but his golden days were spent at Oxford. He could swing the ball both ways at a brisk but accurate medium-pace, which had been honed under Alf Gover's tuition, and was an enthusiastic middle-order bat. Later, he added off-breaks to his repertoire, and used both bowling methods to remarkable effect in the 1950 and 1951 Varsity matches, culminating in 1951 when he took seven for 62 in the second innings and spun Oxford to a thrilling 21-run victory. Barely a week later he was back at Lord's taking 5-81 (including Compton and Hutton) for the Gentlemen against the Players. Divecha played four Tests against England over the next 13 months to less effect, but he took a hat-trick on the 1952 tour in a surprising win over the ultimate champions Surrey, swiftly followed by 8-74 against Glamorgan. He was called up the following winter against Pakistan at Madras, where he trapped 18-year-old Hanif Mohammad lbw. Thereafter, his work as an oil company executive limited Divecha to a handful of Ranji Trophy appearances. 'He was a cheerful and amusing character who loved to bowl,' recalled his Oxford contemporary, Donald Carr.

Gopalan, Morappakam Joysam, his first name being his place of birth, died on December 21, 2003, aged 94 years and 198 days. M. J. Gopalan had been regarded as the oldest surviving Test cricketer since Lindsay Weir's death in October, although Gopalan and his family believed he was three years older than records show. 'I don't know how the school where I studied listed my year of birth as 1909, but that stuck,' M. J. told *Cricinfo* on his birthday in 2001. 'I can confirm that I am 95 today.'

His Test career comprised just one match against England at Calcutta in 1933–34. And by touring England in 1936 he missed out on a hockey gold medal at the Berlin Olympics that summer, for he was already established as India's centre-half. But he was little more than a bystander on the tour and then returned home on the same ship as the victorious Olympians. Gopalan had 25 years of first-class cricket during which he captained Madras and South India. In taking ten wickets on debut, opening the Indians' bowling against the Europeans in 1926–27, he so impressed the former Kent and Cambridge batsman, C. P. Johnstone, that he found M. J. a job with Burmah Shell that allowed him to concentrate on cricket. In November 1934 Gopalan bowled the first ball in the inaugural Ranji Trophy match.

Ramchand, Gulabrai Sipahimalani, died on September 8, 2003, aged 76. 'Ram' Ramchand captained India to their first Test win over Australia, at Kanpur in December 1959. Off-spinner Jasu Patel took 14-124 on a newly laid pitch and Ramchand 'led us brilliantly to victory', Chandu Borde recalled, 'always giving us the self-belief that we could beat them.' Australia's captain, Richie Benaud, went to the Indian dressing-room afterwards and presented his counterpart with his Australian blazer. Born in Karachi, Ramchand played his first Ranji Trophy cricket for Sind and moved south to Bombay after partition, helping them win six Ranji finals between 1948–49 and 1962–63…

He proved himself a useful utility player around the counties on India's 1952 tour but was less successful in the four Tests, spun out for a pair on debut and capturing only four wickets in the series. Given the new ball at Headingley and Lord's, he 'looked every inch a fast bowler until he actually bowled,' as Sujit Mukherjee put it… In 1975, by now an executive at Air India, he was India's manager at the first World Cup.

Sarwate, Chandrasekhar Trimbak, died on December 23, 2003, aged 83. A diminutive spin-bowling all-rounder in the legendary Holkar team that contested ten Ranji Trophy finals in 11 seasons, Chandu Sarwate played nine Tests for India between 1946 and 1951–52. He is perhaps best remembered for his last wicket partnership of 249 with Shute Banerjee against Surrey in 1946. As Banerjee walked out to join Sarwate, Oval groundsman Bert Lock went with him to ask the Surrey captain what roller he wanted between innings. Three hours ten minutes later both batsmen had hundreds, the only time the No. 10 and No. 11 have achieved this in the same innings. When Surrey followed on, Sarwate spun the Indians to victory… A week later he took a hat-trick against Scotland, but he was seen at his best only occasionally after that… Shortly before going to England in 1946 he hit 101 when opening Holkar's innings against Mysore – one of six centuries in their 912-8 declared – and followed up with a career-best 9-91 in Mysore's first innings. Sarwate's small stature and boyish smile led to him being called the Peter Pan of Indian cricket. His cricketing longevity made it even more appropriate. Having made his debut at 16 in 1936–37, he continued playing Ranji Trophy cricket until he was 48.

WISDEN – 2005

This edition included the Test averages for 2004. The top five batsmen were:

S. R. Tendulkar	915 runs at	91.50
J. H. Kallis	1288 runs at	80.50
G. P. Thorpe	951 runs at	73.15
V. Sehwag	1141 runs at	63.38
R. Dravid	946 runs at	63.06

In the bowling averages, Australia claimed three of the top five places (McGrath, Kasprowicz and Warne) but then came:

I. K. Pathan	38 wickets at	24.18
A. Kumble	74 wickets at	24.83

Kumble's total made him the year's leading Test wicket-taker.

Six Indians were included in the Wisden *Forty – Dravid, Harbhajan Singh, Kumble, Laxman, Sehwag and Tendulkar.*

HARBHAJAN SINGH

Until his doosra was queried by the match referee Chris Broad, Harbhajan was well on the way to making up for the various disappointments of 2003. Not for the first time his opposition of choice were the Australians, who provided him with 11 wickets at Bangalore and a match-winning analysis of 5-29 on a Mumbai minefield.

There was also 7-87 against South Africa at Kolkata, just to prove that Harbhajan could beguile others too. His one-day success was limited to two meaner-than-mean performances against England. And he was left with a serious problem: the ICC had mooted a limit of 15 degrees of permissible straightening for bowlers of all types; his off-spinner's wrong 'un was believed to have been measured at 22.

2004: 7 Tests: 155 runs @ 17.22; 38 wickets @ 25.68.
11 ODI: 62 runs @ 20.66; 13 wickets @ 32.00.

THE INDIANS IN AUSTRALIA 2003–04, by Sambit Bal

India's international year had included a quick trip to England to play a one-day series, tours to Australia, Bangladesh and Pakistan as well as visits from the Australians and South Africans. The trip to Australia was the high point.

Every once in a while comes a special sporting contest that leaves behind a whiff of glory and magic. Australia and India played one such Test series in 2000–01; Kolkata was a match for the ages and Chennai not far behind. But ever so rarely comes a series that marks a turning point in history. It may be years or decades before the significance of India's tour of Australia in 2003–04 can be truly assessed, but in this series they announced themselves as a force in Test cricket, after years of living on promise and vain dazzle. They didn't quite end Australia's reign, but how close they came.

To expect anything to match Kolkata was a tough ask. Yet Adelaide, where India came back from the dead to win, was almost a replica. The quality of cricket was admittedly superior in 2000–01, because bowling was a factor then. This was a series decided by batsmen's rare mistakes; injury kept out leading bowlers from both sides, and the rest were blunted by the flatness of the pitches and a galaxy of batting talent. But throughout, the cricket was captivating, grand and redolent with meaning. It ended with a realignment of the world order: the Ashes and the Frank Worrell Trophy could keep their tradition, but the Border-Gavaskar Trophy had emerged as the worthiest in contemporary cricket. And yes, India kept it.

The 1–1 scoreline did not fully reveal India's gains. These have to be viewed through the prism of their wretched past. The last time they had won a Test series outside the subcontinent was in England in 1986, and not since 1980–81 had they won a Test in Australia (where they had lost seven of their last eight). Their previous tour had left deep scars, for they had come boasting a strong middle order and had sunk without a murmur…

It was one hell of a series.

Australia v India

Second Test, at Adelaide, December 12, 13, 14, 15, 16, 2003, by Sambit Bal

After five breathless days it was difficult to decide what was more confounding. Just how had Australia managed to lose after scoring 556 by the second afternoon? Or how had India managed to win after being 85 for four in reply? Only once had a team scored more runs in the first innings of a Test and yet lost, and that 109-year-old record too belonged to Australia: they made 586 at Sydney in the Ashes opener of 1894–95, enforced the follow-on, and fell 11 short of the 177 needed to win.

So, did India win the match or did Australia lose it? The truth was somewhere in between. It was inevitable that a game yielding more than 1,500 runs would be decided by batting mistakes. Australia's inability to stick to their guns on the fourth day cost them the match. But it was as much a triumph of the Indian spirit, exemplified by none better than Dravid, who was on the field for most of the five days, batting 835 minutes and scoring 305 runs. He was last out in the first innings and there at the end to secure victory. It was a monumental effort, the finest performance by an Indian batsman in an overseas Test, because he made the difference.

The victory was all the more incredible because India had not won a Test in Australia in 23 years, and Australia had not lost a home Test of consequence in five – and because Australia had scored 400 runs on the first day, a record for any day on this ground…

Ponting was an exception on a day of breezy cameos, though he was hardly sedate… He hit 31 fours in all, and batted for eight hours 28 minutes, pausing to blow a kiss to his wife when he reached 200. No one had ever made as much as his 242 in a Test and gone on to lose…

Bichel, a controversial selection after a poor game in Brisbane, struck three vital blows. He bowled straight to a canny, defensive field set by Waugh (to Sehwag, there were no slips, only a gully) and India slumped from 66 without loss to 85-4 when Ganguly was run out. Laxman joined Dravid. It took Australia 94 overs to separate them. It was not quite Kolkata; there, they had added 376 for the fifth wicket, here it was a mere 303. That made them only the third pair to share two triple-century stands in Tests, after Bradman and Ponsford and, more recently, the South Africans Gibbs and Smith…

The Test took a decisive turn on the fourth day when a combination of weariness, tight bowling and a fatal urge to dominate the bowlers caused a dramatic Australian collapse. Agarkar bowled his best spell of the series, swinging the ball both ways, to account for Langer and Ponting, and thereafter every top-order batsman fell trying an aggressive stroke on a pitch that had slowed down. India were left to make 230 in 100 overs; Dravid redeemed a pledge to himself by being there to score the winning runs.

Australia 556 (R. T. Ponting 242, S. M. Katich 75, J. L. Langer 58; A. Kumble 5-154) **and 196** (A. B. Agarkar 6-41). **India 523** (R. Dravid 233, V. V. S. Laxman 148) **and 233 for six wickets** (R. Dravid 72 not out). India won by four wickets.

THE INDIANS IN PAKISTAN 2003–04, by Rahul Bhattacharya

India's tour of Pakistan, their first full one in 14 years, was extraordinary even before a ball was bowled. Two years earlier the two countries had appeared on the brink of nuclear war, but the tour gained impetus from what was popularly described as the 'wind of brotherhood' blowing at long last between the nations, and also became an agent of change in itself. Sport, far from being an agent of division, turned out to be the centrepiece for something resembling a peace march. For India, there was another dimension. Their rising cricket team shone as never before in Pakistan, winning the Tests 2–1 and the one-day series 3–2. They had never won even a single Test there in 20 previous attempts…

It was a strange Test series, and not as absorbing as it might have been. While results fluctuated wildly – India romping to innings victories in the first and third matches, and Pakistan winning the second by nine wickets – within the life of each Test there were few surprises. They started out on one road and never departed from it. The last two were mirrors of one another: the side batting first was seamed out on the opening day, before the opposition built a lead too heavy to counter. In the First Test, this form of bullying by runs happened in the very first innings. Virender Sehwag flogged 309 in only 375 balls, India's first triple-century in Tests, while Sachin Tendulkar controversially missed a double-hundred when Dravid declared.

Four of the six highest scores ever made for India in Tests were made in 2003–04, as Wisden *listed:*

Highest Test Scores for India

309	V. Sehwag	v Pakistan at Multan	2003–04
281	V. V. S. Laxman	v Australia at Kolkata	2000–01
270	R. Dravid	v Pakistan at Rawalpindi	2003–04
241*	S. R. Tendulkar	v Australia at Sydney	2003–04
236*	S. M. Gavaskar	v West Indies at Madras	1983–84
233	R. Dravid	v Australia at Adelaide	2003–04

OBITUARY

Hazare, Vijay Samuel, died on December 18, 2004, aged 89. Vijay Hazare was one of the few Indian batsmen of his time who could translate prolific domestic form into success at Test level, and who could perform equally well on turf and on matting pitches. Despite coming late to international cricket because of the war – he was 31 when he made a subdued debut in England in 1946 – Hazare went on to play 30 Tests and score seven centuries and, above all, skipper India to their first Test victory, over England at Madras in 1951–52.

Hazare was one of eight children of a Maharashtra schoolteacher and, unusually in India, was not merely Christian but Protestant. He was picked for the first unofficial Test at Lahore against the very strong touring team brought over by Lord Tennyson in 1937–38, mainly for his medium-paced bowling, but was only allowed two overs, and batted No. 9…

In January 1940, Hazare became the first Indian (excluding Duleepsinhji, who was playing as an Englishman) to hit a triple-century: 316 not out for Maharashtra against Baroda at Poona. He made 619 runs in five Ranji Trophy innings that season, and Indians proclaimed that the great Vijay Merchant had a rival. It was the age of the two Vs, unlike the silky, stylish Merchant, Hazare was a functional batsman with few flourishes, and his habit of tucking the bat between his pads in the stance worried the purists. But he liked to hook and cut, and in an age of formidably high scores in Indian domestic cricket vied with Merchant on the topmost peaks. They exchanged the batting record in the Bombay Pentangular tournament – then as important as the Ranji Trophy – four times in the early 1940s, including three times in a week late in 1943. Hazare was helped by a move to Baroda, where princely patronage enabled him to devote himself to cricket. This paid off when he put together an extraordinary sequence from March 1943 to February 1944 of 264, 81, 97, 248, 59, 309, 101, 223 and 87.

That 309, in the Bombay Pentangular final, was an extraordinary innings, made out of a total of only 387 as the Rest followed on against the Hindus. He shared (if that is the word) a stand of 300 with his brother Vivek, who scored just 21. The Hindus still won by an innings. Three years later, playing for Baroda in the Ranji final against Holkar, Hazare made 288, and put on 577 for the fourth wicket with Gul Mahomed, the highest partnership in all first-class cricket.

When Test cricket returned to England in 1946, Hazare made his debut in front of a packed Lord's; his first real flourish as a Test batsman came at Adelaide in 1947–48 when he scored two centuries in the match. These also came in an understandably losing cause: Bradman had made 201, and Hazare's second-innings 145 was more than half the total. But this made him a member of what was then a very exclusive club, and the feat enhanced both his own reputation and India's. A century at Bombay against West Indies a year later left India six runs short of their maiden Test victory…

Merchant later observed, 'Hazare was always a disciplined soldier, never a commander. Captaincy affected his otherwise unflagging concentration and he was never the same batsman again. It was a tragedy of Indian cricket.'… But he will be remembered above all for his batting. 'He had an impregnable defence and a wide array of strokes,' said the Indian cricket eminence Raj Singh. 'The manner in which he held the bat, hands spread slightly apart, made him different. He had great hands, and could move them up or down the handle, like a flute player.'

WISDEN – 2006

The same six Indians were included in Wisden's *Forty for the second year running, but this year there were no Indians in the top six Test batting averages (Sehwag was highest placed, in eighth place) and no bowlers in the top ten (Pathan was highest placed, in 11th place).*

THE AMAZING STORY OF THE RUNAWAY TRAIN,
by Siddhartha Vaidyanathan

For a 17-year-old boy from Orissa, 1994 was a very tough year. His daily routine involved waking before sunrise and travelling 15 kilometres by bus from Cuttack to work on the railway at the small town of Kandarpur. Hardly any trains stop in this forgotten corner of eastern India, but someone still had to walk six kilometres along the line, oil the tracks, check for faults and climb dangerous heights to check the wiring.

The boy would return home limp and sapped. But nothing could stop him from spending the rest of the day trying to master the routine he loved best – picking up a cricket ball, hopping in from an angular run-up and ripping off-breaks. These were Kulamani Parida's struggles as a Class IV employee in his first two years of working for the Indian Railways.

Across the vast reaches of the world's most complex railway system, other young men were doing much the same. For them, there was no elite support system, no pre-season tour, no sponsors' car. The reward was a place in the Railways team that competes with India's state sides in the Ranji Trophy. Not many successful first-class cricketers face as severe an initiation as Parida. And surely no successful first-class team has as frail a support system as Railways.

From a purely cricketing angle, Railways' journey from the brink of relegation to the national championship makes a fantastic tale. Bearing in mind the background, it is the stuff of legend…

The Railways Sports Control Board had acquired a first-class team in 1958. Like Services, representing the armed forces, the sheer size of the organisation meant they had a pool of sportsmen big enough to make them competitive. With a staff of about one and a half million, Indian Railways are said to rank behind the Chinese Army and ahead of the British National Health Service in the list of the world's largest employers.

Lala Amarnath, the former Indian captain, worked for the Railways (though no one asked him to oil the tracks), and he played a major role in building the side, recruiting well-known names like Dattu Phadkar, Budhi Kunderan and Mushtaq

Ali. But at first, Railways were regularly thwarted by Delhi and Services in the North Zone league. Things improved when they transferred to the weaker Central Zone in 1975, but still they struggled to be contenders.

Part of the problem was always money. In contrast to the airlines and banks who have run well-funded teams in Pakistani domestic cricket for many years, Indian Railways could not easily divert funds from oiling the tracks at Kandarpur to running a prestige cricket team. But in the 1990s the side threw up a nucleus of talented young players like Bangar and Murali Kartik. And once Railways began doing well, players who were struggling to find a place in rival first teams – and were also looking for jobs – began to make themselves available. They gained men like Amit Pagnis, who moved from Mumbai in 2000. 'I wasn't making it to the Mumbai XI too often,' he explained. 'It's better to play every game for a slightly weaker side than carry the drinks for a strong team.' Pagnis's 98 sealed Railways' victory over Hyderabad in the 2005 semi-final.

The next day Punjab stunned Mumbai in the other semi-final. The Punjab Cricket Association showered their team with 1.5 million rupees (about £19,000), and Intikhab Alam, their coach, was awarded the same amount. In Delhi, the Railways coach, Sharma, waited for his salary, 11 months overdue, before the team travelled to Mohali for the final.

Comparing the facilities at Mohali to those at Karnail Singh Stadium is like comparing a Mercedes to a cycle rickshaw… Players like Jai P. Yadav have been around long enough to know that it is futile to complain. 'No point saying they have this and we have that,' he said. 'We made the choice to play for Railways and we have to ultimately win.'

Yadav and his namesake, the left-arm spinner Madan Yadav, did the damage in Mohali that gained Railways first-innings lead; in a drawn game, that was enough to secure the title. Parida, the poor boy from Orissa, was also an established member of the side. But Madan had to spend 2004 undergoing the experience Parida had ten years earlier. For most of the year he was in Bhopal repairing train wheels with massive pliers and monitoring electrical connections – and, between whiles, working on his flight, spin and angle of delivery. When asked about the importance of the title, Jai P. Yadav said, 'Class IV employees like Madan will get a promotion and his quality of life will improve. If we win, it will be like our gift for those players and their families.'

And they did win. Madan Yadav's days with the pliers should now be behind him. He was said to be earning just 5,000 rupees a month (about £60), nowhere near enough to support a family properly. That should be tripled now, which will at least be enough to supply the necessities, if not luxuries like a car or a computer.

These are the champions of India. Yet for them, the lifestyle of Sachin Tendulkar and Sourav Ganguly is just a rumour. The rumour now is a little less distant than it once was.

THE DHONI FAMILY AND THEIR STRUGGLE AGAINST THE EUNUCHS

India took part in three Test series in 2005 – against Pakistan at home, against Sri Lanka at home and drew against Zimbabwe away. They won by two Tests to nil against both Zimbabwe and Sri Lanka, and drew the series with Pakistan at home, one game all.

Against Pakistan, India won the second one-day international, at Visakhapatnam, largely thanks to a brilliant 148 off 123 balls by M. S. Dhoni. Wisden reported the aftermath…

The morning after Dhoni's triumph, his parents had a set of unwelcome visitors at their home when a group of eunuchs barged in, showered them with traditional blessings and demanded 50,000 rupees (about £600) for doing so. Dhoni's father, Pan Singh, slipped away to a neighbour's flat and phoned for help. His mother plied the eunuchs with sweets until the police arrived. It is customary in India to give money to eunuchs on auspicious occasions – but of late their demands have become regarded as a nuisance, and the police are regularly called.

ZIMBABWE V INDIA, 2005–06, by a Special Correspondent

It was a pleasant but uncompetitive series. India did not really miss Sachin Tendulkar, recovering from surgery on his elbow. Virender Sehwag and Gautam Gambhir gave their innings two good starts, with Gambhir almost as fluent as the more celebrated Sehwag and also fielding well at short leg. Indeed, with the exception of the final innings of the series, India's close catching was their most brilliant in years, especially that of Rahul Dravid and V. V. S. Laxman, who also regained their form with the bat.

But the player who did most to make the series one-sided was Irfan Pathan. His fierce, controlled swing bowling, on pitches doing little to encourage pace, brought him 21 wickets, equalling Johnny Briggs' record for a two-Test series, for England in South Africa in 1888–89.

INDIA V SRI LANKA, 2005–06, by Ramakrishnan Kaushik

Nothing boosted morale more than the return of Sachin Tendulkar. He had gone under the knife in May for surgery on persistent tennis elbow in his left arm, but looked none the worse for wear and tear. He was not always consistent, but there was no suggestion that 16 years at the top had done anything to diminish his enthusiasm or his skills. He passed Sunil Gavaskar's record of 34 centuries in the Second Test, which was a monkey off his back, and he looked determined to press on.

OBITUARIES

Mushtaq Ali, Syed, died on June 18, 2005, aged 90. Tall and debonair, often with a kerchief knotted jauntily round his neck, Mushtaq Ali – the son of an Indore police inspector – was a prototype for India's modern cricket heroes. In his foreword to Mushtaq's autobiography, *Cricket Delightful*, Keith Miller called him 'the Errol Flynn of cricket – dashing, flamboyant, swashbuckling and immensely popular wherever he played'. He was the first Indian to score a Test century overseas, with 112 at Old Trafford in 1936, when he beat Vijay Merchant to the mark during an opening stand of 203. He reached his hundred inside the final session on the second day, entrancing Neville Cardus, who enthused, 'He transforms the bat into a conjuror's wand.' There was one other Test century, 106 against West Indies at Calcutta in 1948–49.

Mushtaq had a long career, starting in 1930 and continuing until 1963–64... In between there were numerous Ranji Trophy finals for Holkar, but just 11 Test appearances. These were spread over almost 20 years and finished with India's first victory, by an innings, over England at Madras in 1951–52... He should have played more Test cricket, but the authorities were suspicious of him... He pulled out of the 1947–48 trip to Australia after one of his brothers died, and was not selected for the disastrous England tour of 1952. Even at 37 he might have been useful because, unlike most who toured that year, he relished fast bowling. Later, he was a slim, graceful, elder statesman at many of the multifarious awards nights that punctuate India's cricket seasons.

Solkar, Eknath Dhondu, died on June 26, 2005. He was 57, and suffered from diabetes. Statistically, Solkar remains Test cricket's most successful fielder, with 53 catches in just 27 matches – of those who played at least ten, the next best is Bob Simpson's 110 in 62 Tests, or 1.77 per match to Solkar's 1.96. The top catchers are usually firmly camped in the slip cordon, but most of Solkar's came at forward short leg, where he lurked uncomfortably up close and personal to the batsman. Bishan Bedi, one of the great Indian spinners of the time whose menace was greatly enhanced by this, confirmed, 'His close-in catching was really intimidating. We would not have been the same bowlers without him.' Tony Greig, an opponent in the 1972–73 series in India, said, 'Ekki was the best forward short leg I have ever seen.' His catching was often preceded by some very idiosyncratic sledging. 'I'll get you, bloody,' he advised Geoff Boycott, and he told Garry Sobers to mind his own business.

Solkar rose from humble roots. His father was the groundsman at the Hindu Gymkhana in Bombay, and he grew up in a one-room hut on the ground... He impressed the Bombay players with his bowling in the nets, and turned himself into a handy all-rounder, allying adhesive batting to his enthusiastic left-arm seamers... Some affectionately called him 'the poor man's Sobers', but he outdid even him in India's victory in the West Indies in 1970–71, with six catches and a crucial 55 in the only definite result, India's win at Port-of-Spain. Later in 1971, he played an equally vital role in India's first Test and series victory in England, with 44 and three wickets in a famous triumph at The Oval. There were also three catches, one – in England's second-innings collapse to dispose of Alan Knott, who had made 90 first time around – as fine as any, when Solkar was stationed even closer than usual.

WISDEN – 2007

Only four Indians made it into Wisden's *Forty for 2007: Rahul Dravid, Anil Kumble, Shantakumaran Sreesanth and Sachin Tendulkar.*

S. SREESANTH

Competition for places in the Indian fast-bowling pantheon has never been particularly fierce, but Sreesanth showed enough promise to suggest that, one day, he might take a seat alongside Kapil Dev and Javagal Srinath. In his first year as a Test player his control, interrogatory seam movement and chippy attitude troubled many a good batsman: he inflicted a pair on Chris Gayle in the series decider in Jamaica, and then took eight for 99 during an even more improbable victory, over South Africa at Johannesburg. India had the bad cop of their new bowling pair; if they found a good cop to go with him they could be really dangerous.

2006: 7 Tests: 119 runs @ 17.00; 35 wickets @ 24.37
18 ODI: 6 runs @ 1.50; 25 wickets @ 32.08

INDIA V ENGLAND, 2005–06, by Simon Wilde

The tour highlighted a new phenomenon – the emergence of high-class cricketers from families of modest means outside the major cities that had traditionally produced the sport's stars. Patel was a farmer's son from Gujarat, Raina hailed from once-unfashionable Uttar Pradesh (now the Ranji Trophy champions) and Mahendra Singh Dhoni, the flamboyant wicketkeeper-batsman, came from Ranchi, in Bihar. 'Dhoni represents the new mindset of small-town India – aggressive, uncomplicated, unabashedly consumerist and ready to take on the world,' said the *Times of India*.

Dhoni's feats in one-day cricket had quickly turned him into a nationwide star and a very wealthy young man. Startlingly, he walked to the wicket to bigger cheers than were accorded the struggling hero, Tendulkar, who was booed by some during the Test in Mumbai, his home city.

PAKISTAN V INDIA 2006, by Osman Samiuddin

For purists, the tour represented a chance to concentrate on cricket rather than the broader cultural exchange. Pakistan had just defeated England, India had overwhelmed Sri Lanka, and a quality contest was awaited. It was fitting, in the context of the peace process, that both sides finished happy about something: Pakistan took the Test series by winning the final match, while India came from behind to win the one-day games 4–1. It was just a shame that, for the first half of the tour, the contest was almost non-existent…

WEST INDIES V INDIA, 2005–06, by Siddhartha Vaidyanathan

Until the penultimate day, India's tour of the West Indies bore an uncanny resemblance to the previous two: high on expectation but low on productivity. This time, though, they ended it differently, scrapping to a victory that removed several monkeys from Indian backs. It was their first series win in the Caribbean for 35 years, since Sunil Gavaskar's triumphant maiden series, and also their first major triumph outside the subcontinent since they won in England in 1986.

And so India made history – but only just… They won largely thanks to one man, their captain Rahul Dravid who, on a dodgy surface, produced two great innings… Conditions rarely perturb Dravid, who towered over the rest with 496 runs. He had made winning contributions in victories in every country apart from South Africa (where India did not win a Test until December 2006) and New Zealand (where they last won one in 1975–76). In terms of getting his side results, Rahul Dravid is, unarguably, India's greatest-ever batsman.

SOUTH AFRICA V INDIA 2006–07, by Neil Manthorp

India arrived for their fourth tour of South Africa with low expectations, and lived down to them at first by struggling throughout the one-day series, losing all four completed matches by wide margins. A win in the one-off Twenty20 match was not much consolation – but then came the First Test, when they confounded expectations by gliding to their first victory ever in South Africa, at the tenth attempt.

That was the end of the good news for them, though: a determined South Africa bounced back, winning well at Durban, then capitalising on a timid batting display to take the series at Cape Town – a match India should never have lost after making 414 in their first innings.

OBITUARIES

Hanumant Singh, died on November 29, 2006, aged 67, after suffering from hepatitis and dengue fever. Of princely blood (his father was the Maharajah of Banswara), he was regarded as a batsman of appropriate style to stand comparison to his uncle Duleepsinhji and Duleep's uncle Ranjitsinhji. Hanumant made a silky century on his Test debut, against England at Delhi in February 1964. It was 'delightful and delicately composed', *The Times* correspondent reported. 'For someone so quiet and fresh of face, the maturity was remarkable.'

Hanumant was the fifth Indian to score a hundred in his first Test and, like the previous four, never made another, winning only 13 more caps, although he did manage a fine attacking 94 against Australia, with Graham McKenzie at the peak of his form, at Madras in 1964–65. He went down with the ship on India's grim tour of England in 1967, despite a fighting, unavailing, 73 at Headingley. But he was left out of the tour of Australia that followed on grounds of fitness – although this was a puzzle, and the captain, the Nawab of Pataudi, wanted him in the side, 'He should have made the trip. I asked for him. But they did not want him. It was very unfair.'...
He became one of Indian cricket's father figures, as a tour manager, selector, ICC referee (England's scores-level draw at Bulawayo in 1996–97 was one of his nine Tests) and coach. In 2000, he became the first director of India's national academy, and then coached players from India and abroad at the World Cricket Academy in Mumbai. At his funeral, he was cremated with a bat on his chest.

Kunderan, Budhisagar Krishnappa, died of cancer on June 23, 2006, aged 66. Budhi Kunderan was an attacking batsman and a solid wicketkeeper, whose appearances for India were restricted by the presence of a similar livewire in Farokh Engineer. Kunderan played only 18 Tests to Engineer's 46, but Kunderan liked to point out, in a spirit of friendly rivalry, that his batting average was higher (32.70 to 31.08). His first Test, against Australia at Bombay in 1959–60, came even before he had played a Ranji Trophy match, and he had to borrow some wicket-keeping gloves from Naren Tamhane, the man he had displaced. Even so, he acquitted himself well, hitting 71 in his second match after opening, 'I scored about 16 runs in the first over,' he recalled, 'and later the Australian commentator Michael Charlton came to me and said "Do you realise you're playing Test cricket?"'...

After spanking 79 from No. 9 against a mighty West Indian attack at Bombay in December 1966, Kunderan came to England the following year, and played two Tests as a batsman while Engineer kept wicket. In what turned out to be his final Test, Kunderan even opened the bowling after a series of injuries (when asked what sort of bowling to expect, he told reporters, 'I don't know')... Disillusioned with Indian cricket, in 1970 he moved to Scotland, where he proved a popular professional with the Coatbridge club Drumpellier, staying with them until he was 55, and inspiring them to four Western Union titles in the 1970s... At birth his name was 'Kunderam', but he changed the spelling in 1964.

Umrigar, Pahlanji Ratanji, died on November 7, 2006, aged 80. When his international career was ended by back problems in 1962, Polly Umrigar had played in more Tests (59) and scored more runs (3,631) and centuries (12) than any other Indian. Big and burly, Umrigar liked to pummel the ball, hooking and pulling savagely as well as driving with rare panache. His maiden century, an unbeaten 130, helped set up India's first Test victory, over England at Madras early in 1952, and he was expected to be one of the middle-order stars of the return tour of England later that year. He scored freely in the county games, piling up 1,688 runs all told, but was a miserable failure in the Tests, often found backing away against the raw pace of the young Fred Trueman. Tony Lock, fielding at short leg, is supposed to have complained that he couldn't see properly as Umrigar, who managed only 43 runs in the four Tests, was retreating into him.

It was only a temporary blip, though: the following winter Umrigar was happily tucking into some quick bowling in the West Indies, and he continued to do so – in his penultimate Test, in Trinidad in 1962, he flogged Wes Hall, Charlie Stayers and Garry Sobers for a rapid unbeaten 172, smashing four fours off Hall's first over with the second new ball. Umrigar's highest Test score was a boundary-studded 223, India's first double-century, against New Zealand at Hyderabad in 1955–56...

Umrigar won seven Ranji Trophy finals with Bombay, captaining in three of them, and also played in the Lancashire League. After retirement, he moved into administration, chairing the selection committee, managing three overseas tours, and eventually becoming executive secretary of the Indian board. He was popular with the players: Ravi Shastri, a later Indian all-rounder, said, 'He was the finest human being among cricketers I've known. Like a doctor to patients, he was one to the game of cricket. You could go to him any time you needed advice.' Umrigar was also responsible for pitch preparation at Mumbai's Wankhede Stadium, and there is a restaurant named after him down the road at the Brabourne Stadium, whose guiding light, Raj Singh Dungarpur, remembered Umrigar as 'the most complete cricketer'.

WISDEN – 2008

By some reckoning, the Indian team was becoming stronger. Eight members of that side made it onto the Wisden *Forty list – M. S. Dhoni, S. Ganguly, A. Kumble, V. V. S. Laxman, R. P. Singh, S. R. Tendulkar, Yuvraj Singh and Zaheer Khan.*

R. P. SINGH

Zaheer stole the show, but he would not have been the same without his left-hand man. Especially during the tour of England, Singh's ability to swing the ball both ways, and late, confounded the batsmen. He also exhibited plenty of the mongrel so integral to the identity of the new breed of Indian fast bowler. If the statistical returns were sometimes modest, closer inspection showed a penchant for snaring the big wickets: of his 20 Test victims, 19 were in the top seven, and he nailed Pietersen twice in the decisive victory over England at Trent Bridge. Some splendid work at the World Twenty20 – four for 13 against South Africa and three for 26 against Pakistan in the final – confirmed a taste for the big occasion. And when Zaheer went lame during the Australia tour, he fearlessly took on the role of attack leader. At 22, he was a real prospect.

2007: 6 Tests: 34 runs @ 6.80; 20 wickets @ 30.45.
      18 ODI: 26 runs @ 13.00; 24 wickets @ 32.83.
      8 T20I: 1 run without being dismissed; 13 wickets @ 14.69.

NOTES BY THE EDITOR, by Scyld Berry

As the Indian public began to fall out of love with the 50-over game, a ready replacement was available, and the love affair was even more passionate.

Twenty-over cricket in India is shifting the tectonic plates of the professional game as never before. In the late 1970s Kerry Packer's World Series Cricket, while reshaping the international scene, left the domestic game untouched. Until now, the best cricketers have earned most of their money by representing their country, whether in an official eleven or a rebel team in World Series or apartheid South Africa. This period in the game's history, of primarily representing countries, seems to be ending, suddenly.

Leading cricketers can now earn more by representing an Indian city, whether in Zee TV's Indian Cricket League or the officially sanctioned Indian Premier League. City-based cricket has arrived and will surely spread, annulling the player's traditional relationship with his county, state or province. The day has lurched closer when England's best cricketers, in addition to representing England, will play for an English region in a first-class tournament at the start of each season; for an English city in the 20-over competition in midsummer; and for an Indian city. County cricket will then become a relic at amateur level, like the county championship of English rugby.

Cricket administrators in Test-playing countries around the world should be prepared to ride this Indian tiger, to keep the 20-over game in proportion and not let it swamp all other forms. I am not convinced they are ready, because the standard of administrators is not high enough. For a start, they took ages to understand what baseball discovered in the United States several generations ago: that the majority of people want to watch their sport in a package of about three hours. Twenty20 cricket is making up for a lot of lost time...

The inaugural ICC World Twenty20 in South Africa later in the year caught the public imagination, precisely because the 50-over World Cup had not. The game in its longer versions laid itself open to a takeover by the shortest format.

I am not against Twenty20 cricket. Some matches in South Africa, notably the semi-final between Australia and India, had most of the ingredients that any cricket match with a time limit could offer. (Australia had no spin bowler worthy of the name, and they lost because of it.) The ICC has stacked its tournaments with one-sided matches; the IPL has realised that drama depends on competitive games and has shared out the stars. But, in the course of time, what 20-over cricket lacks – if only a change of tempo – will become ever more apparent, by comparison with Test cricket.

ICC WORLD TWENTY20, 2007–08, by Hugh Chevallier

1. India
2. Pakistan
3. = Australia and New Zealand

This tournament was a dream. It just got things right. In utter contrast to the fiasco of the 50-over World Cup in March and April, this competition, a Twenty20 World Cup in all but name, enjoyed outrageous success. The final typified it: the biggest draw in world cricket, India v Pakistan, went to the last over in a compelling game of shifting fortunes. India eventually triumphed, sending a billion people Twenty20 crazy.

Yet success brought its own problems, even if the ICC was glad to have them. How, for example, should the huge demand for Twenty20 internationals be handled? As the temptation to lift the lid of Pandora's box grew stronger, the ICC stuck to its limit of three home and four away matches for each team. Yet that raised the question of how they could be played in a meaningful context. And in an indication of the strength of the product, even below international level, the ICC announced during the tournament that a Twenty20 version of European football's Champions League would start in 2008. Initially, eight teams from four nations would compete for a winner's purse of $2 million (almost £1 million). A county's finances would be transformed...

This was a tournament brimming with *joie de vivre*. Intense, in-your-face, incessant. Most days saw two games, some three; planned as a tournament at speed, sometimes it felt more like a tournament on speed, punctuated by blasts of music and countless dance-sets. Yuvraj Singh epitomised the frenetic pace when he achieved cricketing nirvana by hitting England's Stuart Broad for six sixes in an over. His fifty came from 12 balls: scarcely credible...

It was symbolic of the contrasting fortunes of the two tournaments that in the World Cup proper the predicted India v Pakistan became the low-key Bangladesh v Ireland, while here it was the showcase final.

ICC World Twenty20 final: India v Pakistan
Johannesburg, September 24, 2007, by Hugh Chevallier

India won the inaugural Twenty20 World Cup when Misbah-ul-Haq's attempted scoop landed in the hands of Sreesanth at short fine leg. Pakistan started the final over needing a manageable 13, though with their last pair at the crease. That became 12 from six after Joginder Sharma bowled the widest of wides, then 12 from five after Misbah played and missed. He played and hit next time, launching Sharma's nervy full toss down the ground. Six from four – one stroke would do it. But the Indian juggernaut – they had defended totals in their last three games – had just enough momentum: Misbah's shot proved too ambitious against a bowler of Sharma's modest pace. The tension released, the Wanderers erupted in deafening ecstasy. Hundreds of Indian tricolours waved in late-afternoon sun as the victory lap began.

Dhoni opting to bat after winning his fifth successive toss was expected; Gambhir's opening partner was not. Yusuf Pathan, half-brother of Irfan, replaced the injured Sehwag to make his international debut. But it was Gambhir, unfurling classical cover-drives and regularly splitting the off-side field, who kept the Indian innings afloat as wickets fell. After astounding performances against England and Australia, Yuvraj Singh was seen as the threat, but he radiated tiredness, not terror, and his bat had the power of a sherbet fountain, but with rather less fizz. The disciplined Pakistani bowlers made life awkward too, and the acceleration barely materialised. Umar Gul, searing in yorkers, led the way with three wickets.

On a reliable, if slowish, pitch India's total felt distinctly below par – and Pakistan felt in control. Even though R. P. Singh whipped out Mohammad Hafeez in the first over and cleaned up Kamran Akmal, heaving across the line, in the third, it was surely Pakistan's game. After all, Imran Nazir had plundered 21 from Sreesanth's skew-whiff first over and was going like a train. Sreesanth's second was a maiden, and the pivotal moment came in his third, thanks to an inspired piece of fielding from Uthappa. His stop, gather and throw formed one sinuous movement – and the rampant Nazir was a fraction short. Pakistan needed to rebuild, but the middle order perished in a rash of mistimed shots. Bowling with intelligent variation of pace, Irfan Pathan grabbed two in an over as Pakistan slumped to 77-6. Now India seemed in control.

However, the levelheaded Misbah set about rescuing Pakistan, just as he had in the group game against India (when he had overseen 41 from the last 18 to level the scores) and against Australia. Until the seventh wicket fell with 54 required from four overs, he was in no hurry. He promptly hit three sixes off Harbhajan Singh to restore parity, and in no time 35 from 18 balls became a realistic 20 from 12. Pakistan now looked better placed, though by the end of R. P. Singh's tight over, the 19th, no one could tell who was in the ascendancy – 13 needed with nine down was too close to call. Dhoni plumped for the seam of Joginder Sharma rather than the chastened Harbhajan for the last over, and the engrossing conclusion to an enthralling competition had one final twist.

India won by 5 runs.

ENGLAND V INDIA 2007, by Nasser Hussain

This was a series that had it all. Brilliant, competitive cricket, incidents aplenty, controversy and even childish behaviour. England felt hard done by, losing it 1–0, but the bottom line was that it provided a fitting finale for some of the great names of Indian cricket: Sachin Tendulkar, Sourav Ganguly, Rahul Dravid and Anil Kumble, none of them expected to tour England again...

Dravid's first job as India's captain was to win the series, his second job to win the match, his third to entertain... Here was a man carrying the weight of India's expectations on his shoulders without the support of a team coach. He was to stand down a month later, but he did so as only the third Indian captain to win a Test series in England after Ajit Wadekar (1971) and Kapil Dev (1986).

AUSTRALIA V INDIA 2007–08, by Greg Baum

'Bollyline' in Sydney will go down in history as a kind of cricketing six-day war. It was all too real and nasty while it was happening, but it was over almost as soon as it had begun. By the start of the next Test in Perth ten days later, there was such peace and harmony on the surface it was as if nothing had ever happened...

There were casualties, not least among them the game's dignity. Harbhajan Singh was given a three-Test ban (later rescinded). Posturing Indian authorities threatened to abandon the tour. Commentator Peter Roebuck called for the sacking of Ricky Ponting. Steve Bucknor lost his umpiring commission, and seemed unlikely ever to regain it. India's captain Anil Kumble dramatically invoked the spirit of a previous cricket war when he declared that, 'only one team was playing in the spirit of the game.'

An animus had been brewing for months, since the World Twenty20 championship in South Africa. Some of the Australians thought India's victory celebrations in that tournament were disproportionate to the achievement... The Australians alleged that Harbhajan also taunted Symonds on the field. Publicly, Harbhajan said the Australians were in no position to complain; they were as vulgar as ever. Behind-the-scenes manoeuvres to broker a peace between Symonds and Harbhajan evidently failed...

A slanging match erupted. Principally, it was between Harbhajan and Symonds, whose mutual dislike was now well known. Ponting reported to the umpires that Harbhajan had uttered a racist epithet, perhaps 'monkey' or 'big monkey'. Some said Ponting acted preciously, even provocatively, given Australia's history of waging so-called 'mental disintegration'. Unsustainably, some even alleged that Ponting seized on the race card in an effort to rid himself of Harbhajan, whose bunny he had become (he fell to him twice more in this match). Others, including Ponting, said he did only what he had been enjoined to do by the ICC in its anti-racism campaign...

This contretemps led to another between Ponting and Indian journalists after the match. Victory, gained in long shadows with nine minutes to spare, prompted unbridled jubilation among the Australians, leaving Kumble, who had played a gallant unbeaten innings, to cool his heels. 'That's about as good a win as I've been in,' chortled Ponting. But at a press conference soon afterwards, Kumble charged Australia with a lack of sportsmanship as grievous as Douglas Jardine's in 1932–33. It was an overwrought claim: though Australia had behaved less than nobly, India were also guilty of breaches of the game's spirit. Indians objected to Australia's triumphalism at the end, but forgot the exuberance of Harbhajan upon dismissing Ponting in the second innings, when he ran almost to the pavilion and performed two inelegant forward rolls on the turf before team-mates caught him.

In the small hours of the next morning, after a long hearing, Procter suspended Harbhajan for three Tests. Meantime, India brought a countercharge against Brad Hogg for referring to them as 'bastards'. The next few days were inglorious. India's authorities claimed, bizarrely, that it was impossible for an Indian to be racist. They threatened to call off the tour unless Harbhajan's ban was overturned, and the team, instead of travelling to Canberra as scheduled, took refuge in their Sydney hotel. The ICC called in their chief referee Ranjan Madugalle to broker a truce between Ponting and Kumble. They also replaced Bucknor with Billy Bowden for the next Test, saying they were acting in the best interests of the umpire and the game, but – absurdly – denying that they had yielded to pressure from India…

At length, cooler heads prevailed. Harbhajan was given leave to enter an appeal, which – conveniently – would not be heard until after the series. The Indian board's threat to abandon the tour had always been fatuous anyway, given the television interests involved…

Indian board vice-president Lalit Modi was reported to have said that, unless Harbhajan was cleared, the tour would be cancelled and India would reconsider future engagements with Australia. He also said that an adverse finding would affect the prospects of Australians in the new Indian Premier League. Australian players muttered anonymously about how India's money was now ruling the game, which was a bit rich – pun intended – since many of them were greedily eyeing the vast spoils available for the new Twenty20 tournament in India. Justice Hansen indignantly denied media reports about a deal between the two countries, or that he had been under pressure to reprieve Harbhajan for the sake of future series, and rebuked the Indian authorities for even allowing that impression to form. He had, he said, reached his decision independently. But Hansen regretted the ICC's incomplete data about Harbhajan's disciplinary record, which might have affected his sentence.

So ended Bollyline – for now. Three things were clear. Hypocrisy still drags the game down. The ICC remains toothless. And India, failing to learn lessons from long periods of powerlessness, are intent on throwing their newly acquired weight around at every opportunity.

NEVER A CRICKETER OF THE YEAR –
FIVE WHO SOMEHOW MISSED OUT

BISHAN BEDI, by Michael Brearley

In 2008, Wisden's editor, Scyld Berry took pity on five great cricketers who had somehow never been chosen as one of the Five Cricketers of the Year. One of those five men was Bishan Bedi.

The first epithet that comes to mind for Bishan Bedi's bowling is 'beautiful'. More than with any other slow bowler, this is the word that stays. He prepared to bowl with remarkably supple stretches for a man who was not slim: he must have practised yoga. His fingers were wonderfully supple too, and part of his theatricality was fizzing the ball from one hand to the other before starting his run-up. He was also striking in his choice of patkas, often pink or bright blue.

He was not an elegant mover with the bat, or in the field. In both departments he could be clumsy. Like Colin Cowdrey among batsmen, Bedi was one of those athletes whose athleticism was expressed almost exclusively in what he did best. A few easy rhythmic steps, perfectly balanced, and he moved smoothly into the delivery stride. There was no sense of striving, nothing rushed or snatched, no hiccoughs, just an easy flow. He bowled at the slower end of the spin bowler's range, though not dead slow.

Like most great bowlers, his variation was subtle. Of all the slow bowlers of Bedi's time, none forced you to commit yourself later than he did. With tiny, last-second adjustments of wrist and hand-angle, he could bowl successive balls that looked identical, perhaps as if each would land on a length just outside off stump. But with the first he would cock his wrist more, deliver the ball slightly higher – it would spin sharply, stay wider of off, and be shorter than you anticipated. The next ball, ever so slightly undercut and a little quicker, would pitch further up and come in towards middle and leg stumps. To the first ball you were likely to play inside the line, and away from the body; to the second, outside the line, and round your front leg, so that there was a risk of inside edge on to the pad. The error of judgement induced in the batsman could be as much as a yard in length and a foot in width. And he could make these changes according to what he sensed the batsman was trying to do, in the moment of delivery, so firm and balanced were his action and rhythm.

Bishan Singh Bedi, born on September 25, 1946, in the Sikh capital of Amritsar, was a gentlemanly cricketer. If you hit him through the covers for four he would say, 'Well played'. When David Hughes of Lancashire hit him for 26 in an over in a Gillette Cup final, Bedi applauded each of the three sixes. He didn't approve of the lap or sweep; being a purist he felt these were unworthy shots. He did not

readily bowl defensively – flat and directed to middle and leg – though he could also do this. He liked to defeat the batsman in the flight, and have him stumped or caught off a skyer.

Having watched the England players being mesmerised by him in India in 1972–73, and written about them not using their feet, the author batted at Northampton for Middlesex a few months later. The outcome: Brearley st Sharp b Bedi 18 (though 57 in the second innings!). Of his 1,560 first-class wickets, he took 434 in six seasons for Northamptonshire, and 266 in 67 Tests for India.

Besides being a gentlemanly cricketer, Bedi was also a terrific competitor. Tony Lewis, who captained England in 1972–73, said he was a Dennis Lillee among slow bowlers. If he liked you, he would be extremely friendly (I greeted him with a *namaste* – the Indian greeting with hands together – when I came in to bat at Lord's, and he enjoyed that). But if he took against you, he could be a fierce antagonist.

Bedi is an extremely generous man. Being of a rare blood group, he gave blood in Karachi on a Cavaliers tour in response to a newspaper appeal; Benazir Bhutto sent him two carpets and a tea-set, while shopkeepers invited Bedi to help himself. A forthright man too. He is not diplomatic. He can be choleric. He declared in Jamaica in 1976 when he believed the umpires had been too weak to put a stop to intimidatory and dangerous bowling by West Indies. Recently he has not minced words about Muttiah Muralitharan or Shoaib Akhtar. He is worried for future generations, who will copy these actions. He has no faith in cricket's administrators. In retirement Bedi has run a cricket school in Delhi. He also writes and speaks on television about cricket, outspokenly.

GANDHI: DID HE SPIN MORE THAN KHADI?
by Ramachandra Guha

It was in, of all places, the New York Public Library that I came across a connection between the greatest of modern Indians and the greatest of modern Indian sports. This was in the papers of Louis Fischer, who wrote what, in the West, remains the best-known biography of Gandhi. Through an Indian friend Fischer had sent a list of questions for the Mahatma's only surviving sister. In answer to 'What does she remember about her brother Mohandas as a child and as a boy? Did he play games?' she replied, 'When Mahatmaji was young he used to play with rubber balloons, tennis, cricket and such other games. He used to have such great interest for those games that he would not remember even his meals... He would not stay at home in the evenings as he would get engrossed in playing.'

The interview was conducted in December 1948. Ten years later, an Indian journalist met an old classmate of Gandhi's, who remembered a 'dashing cricketer' who 'evinced a keen interest in the game as a school student.' If these oral testimonies are reliable, Gandhi spun a cricket ball long before he spun khadi, the hand-woven cloth he argued should be worn by all Indians in preference to machine-made textiles.

The thought is appealing, even if the evidence of the printed record runs in the other direction. In his autobiography, which deals extensively with his childhood and schooldays, Gandhi does not mention cricket. In his 90-volume *Collected Works* there is only one reference, in the context of Hindu–Muslim relations. While other Indian nationalists such as Jawaharlal Nehru and C. Rajagopalachari keenly followed cricket, there is no record of Gandhi, in adult life, ever having attended a match. (Nor did he favour India's other great popular passion: he saw only one Hindi film, and that not in full.)

There is, however, an example of the famed Gandhian humour being applied to cricket. When Laxmi Merchant, the sister of the legendary Indian opening batsman Vijay Merchant, went to get the Mahatma's autograph, he scanned through her book for a suitable page, eventually settling upon one containing the names of the 1933–34 MCC touring party. Captained by Douglas Jardine, the team included the Yorkshire slow left-armer Hedley Verity and the Essex all-rounder Stan Nichols. The party had 16 members. To their list of numbered signatures was now appended, '17. M. K. Gandhi'.

CRICKETERS OF THE YEAR 2008

ZAHEER KHAN by Pradeep Vijayakar

The first Indian fast bowler since Kapil Dev to be chosen, Zaheer Khan proved that the phrase 'Indian fast bowler' was not oxymoronic. For a team used to winning games through brilliant batting and unplayable spin bowling, a fast bowling hero is always something of an anomaly.

England = India minus Zaheer – this is the equation that summed up the three-Test series of 2007. Zaheer Khan was adjudged India's player of the series for his 18 wickets at 20 each. He swung the ball into and away from right-handed batsmen from over and round the wicket, and stopped them pushing forward by using a sharp, accurate bouncer. His round-the-wicket approach, along with that of Rudra Pratap Singh, took England completely by surprise: they had seen video analysis of the two Indian left-armers bowling round the wicket on their preceding tour of Bangladesh, but nothing in county cricket had prepared them except the occasional old-ball spell by Sussex's Jason Lewry. Only English batsmen old enough to have faced Wasim Akram were familiar with the ball coming from such an angle.

Zaheer, moreover, disguised his deliveries masterfully. He swung the ball conventionally far more than he reverse-swung it last summer, but whether the ball was going to come into them or leave them England's batsmen could not predict. Andrew Strauss, who made a fifty in England's second innings of the Trent Bridge Test, said that when he was batting with Michael Vaughan, who made a century, neither the striker nor the non-striker could work out which way Zaheer was going to swing. All the normal cues were unavailable because he ran up and delivered in the same way, with his right hand covering the ball until the last second. It took exceptional skill to deprive England of their six-year unbeaten run of Test series at home.

So how was it that Zaheer clicked after a chequered career, including nine months out of India's side when Greg Chappell was coach? 'County cricket in 2006' is Zaheer's ready answer. 'Playing for Worcestershire meant playing in different conditions, pitch and weather for five months. You had to innovate, use your thinking power. There were some experiments that I couldn't carry out when playing for India. I carried them out in county cricket. I went through the range of left-arm fast bowling... I am a rhythm bowler. When I get it right, I get into the zone and there's no stopping me. One of the things I did after coming back from injury was cutting down my run-up... The functional exercises I did were the key. Above all the Dukes ball was a boon for me. I adapted well to it and claimed 78 wickets.'

... Zaheer Khan, often known as Zak, was born on October 7, 1978, in Shrirampur in Maharashtra... His father Bakhtiyar recalls, 'I was also a left-hander. Seeing Zaheer bowling left-handed thrilled me. There was a college near our residence. Zaheer's love for cricket developed watching the college lads. Soon he was playing with them – a willing young kid happy to just field and retrieve the ball hit by the collegians.'

At 17, Zaheer was taken to Mumbai by his father to play cricket. The fees for the Gymkhana clubs were too high. The father observed net practice at the National Cricket Club on the *maidan* and was impressed by the discipline. 'For the first two seasons I played every tournament there was,' Zaheer says...

National's assistant coach, Vidya Paradkar, recalls, 'He was regular and sincere. He would be there at seven in the morning, again sharp at 2.30 in the afternoon.' A seven-wicket haul in a final against Shivaji Park Gymkhana had people talking about Zaheer. He got into the Under-19 sides of Mumbai and West Zone in 1998–99. He joined the MRF Pace Foundation in Chennai. The co-ordinator T. A. Sekhar remembers, 'He had most of the things needed for bowling fast, strength and technique and a good build. I called up Dennis Lillee, our coach. Lillee right away made the prognosis that he would bowl for India.'

When Zaheer could not get into Mumbai's Ranji Trophy side, Sekhar arranged for him to join Baroda. He helped them win their first title for 43 years in 2000–01, taking eight wickets in the final against Railways. By then he had made his

international debut in the ICC Champions Trophy in Kenya: he was India's best bowler as they knocked out Australia. But ups and downs followed as he neglected his gym work. Lillee and Sekhar took time to persuade him that his jump before delivery was too high. And he was not one of Chappell's favourite players.

When Zaheer was picked for the tour of England, there were still doubts. 'When I got wickets in the second innings at Lord's, I got the confidence that I would do well on tour. The best spell was at Trent Bridge in the second innings. The pitch was settling down, both teams had a good score. I got rid of Michael Vaughan and the slide began.'

OBITUARY

Ibrahim, Khanmohammad Cassumbhoy, who died on November 12, 2007, aged 88, was India's oldest living Test player. A correct top-order batsman who sometimes opened, in 1947–48 Ibrahim established a first-class record that still stands, scoring 709 runs between dismissals. He made 218, 36, 234 and 77, all not out, for his own XI in the Bombay Festival, before being out for 144 in his first Ranji Trophy innings of the season. Not surprisingly, he forced his way into the Test side for the 1948–49 series against West Indies. He started well, with 85 and 44 at Delhi, but fell away after that, managing only 40 more runs in six innings, although he did make 219 in more than ten hours in that season's Ranji Trophy final, while captaining Bombay to victory over Baroda.

Madhav Mantri, a Bombay team-mate and the uncle of Sunil Gavaskar, recalled, 'He was a solid player, one who believed in staying at the wicket for as long as possible. He had a good range of strokes – a fierce cut, drive and glance – but was known to be one who hung in there to grind out runs. In the 1950s and 1960s young boys used to be told, 'Bat like KC – stay at the wicket and the runs will definitely come'. Ibrahim extended five of his 14 centuries past 200 and finished with a first-class batting average of 61.24. He later went to live in Pakistan, and died there.

WISDEN – 2009

The IPL was beginning to change the way international cricketers play, and manage their careers. In his Notes, the editor saw the way the wind was blowing.

NOTES BY THE EDITOR, by Scyld Berry

It was a *son et lumière* worthy of the Sphinx or Grand Canyon. The opening ceremony of the Indian Premier League, on a shirtsleeve evening in mid-April in Bangalore, was the most spectacular that cricket has seen. I sensed the same ingredients of success at the first official day/night international, between Australia and West Indies, at Sydney in 1979: people hurrying to a ground to see the cricket they wanted, of the duration they wanted, at the time they wanted.

Brendon McCullum lit up the night sky as brilliantly as the fireworks by hitting 158 from 73 balls, and most of the major talents in world cricket joined in over the next six weeks. While there were initial doubts about whether Indian crowds and television audiences would identify with an Australian or South African, and a sizeable proportion of each crowd was admitted free, city-based cricket soon became as popular in India as soap operas. In spite of the poor television camerawork, and advertisements that shaved many overs to five balls, tens of millions – perhaps hundreds of millions – watched, for evening after evening, live cricket.

The IPL is a clever mixture of ingredients because its administrators have understood their market – their mass market. Although it is impossible to be sure from such a recent perspective, it looks as though the supranational IPL is the single biggest change in cricket not merely since the advent of the limited-overs game in the 1960s but of fixtures between countries in the 19th century: that is, since the invention of international or Test cricket...

India went ahead with organising their multimillion-dollar Champions League – before the recession every 20-over league was 'multimillion-dollar' – with Australia and South Africa as their junior partners. To make room in the schedule, the First Test in Perth between these junior partners was put back five days: thus 20-over cricket was established as the priority, even though the launch of the Champions League was later postponed a year. Then Sri Lanka's 13 best players refused to tour England for a Test series in May 2009 because they had already pledged themselves to the IPL. In the New Year, England's star cricketers decided they were going to India for half of the second IPL season, even if they returned home only four days before the First Test in May. Christopher Martin-Jenkins observed that Twenty20 was a 'Frankenstein which could devour everything unless rationally controlled'.

NOTES BY THE EDITOR, by Scyld Berry

England's tour of India was notorious for all the wrong reasons.

The terrorists who attacked Mumbai on November 26 were reported to be from Pakistan. One of their main targets was the Taj Mahal Hotel, beside the Gateway of India. If anywhere in the world could have been called 'the cricket hotel', it was the Taj. Two South African security officers, who had arrived to protect officials drawing up regulations for the new Champions League, organised a large part of the defence of the Taj from within. Faisul Nagel, an England security officer on more than one tour, and Bob Nicholls should be remembered for helping to save approximately 150 lives.

If a terrorist attack can have a silver lining, it was that the Indian board and the ECB came closer together. Not alone, I took angry exception to the IPL chief commissioner Lalit Modi proclaiming that England's Test series in India would go ahead while the siege of the Taj was still going on. A far better statement of propriety and human decency came simultaneously from India's captain, the highly impressive Mahendra Singh Dhoni, who said, 'We are entertainers, and now is not the time to entertain'. It was obvious that Modi's prime concern was to ensure that the second IPL went ahead.

Ideally, England would not have gone back to India so quickly: playing 12 days after the Mumbai attacks must have been insensitively soon for some of the bereaved. By then it was also apparent that India's tour of Pakistan would be cancelled, and most of January would have been free for both countries. But better that the tour went ahead when it did than not at all. And, in the aftermath, the English and Indian boards realised that what united them was greater than what divided them, especially in a major economic crisis.

THE IPL, by Lawrence Booth

The IPL itself required a feature article in this edition – not quite Indian domestic cricket, and not quite international cricket.

Such was the impact of the Indian Premier League on world cricket that it created major headlines two months before the second tournament was due to start. When Andrew Flintoff and Kevin Pietersen were both sold for $1.55 million (well over £1 million) in Goa's Hermitage Hall on February 6, 2009, they became 'Cricket's Most Expensive Players' and 'Richest Cricketers Ever'. Much to their chagrin, England players had missed out on the inaugural IPL, apart from Dimitri Mascarenhas. While most of the most famous names in the contemporary game flocked to India in April 2008 – drawn by unprecedented sums of money and, also, by unprecedented glamour for a cricket event – England's Test players had to represent their counties and play against New Zealand. Never again: such was the collective determination of Flintoff, Pietersen and several others to go east, and fulfil the wishes of the IPL chief commissioner Lalit Modi, that they forced major concessions out of the England and Wales Cricket Board. A three-week window, from the start of the second IPL tournament on April 10, 2009, until May 1, only five days before the Lord's Test against West Indies, was eventually agreed. For the first time English cricketers were going to play outside England during the English season other than on national service. Such was the shift in the game's balance of power...

The IPL's second auction appeared able to defy the worldwide recession thanks to the success of its inaugural tournament, which at times suggested a soap opera on fast forward. In the space of just over seven weeks, there were petty rows and even physical ones, dolled-up women in short skirts, gratuitous sackings, walk-on parts for celebrities, the occasional cliffhanger and an implausible main storyline – all of it underpinned by the bottom line. But it was hard to escape the conclusion that much of the sporting drama was pretty good too – from the moment Brendon McCullum spectacularly raised the curtain on a heady night in Bangalore, to Rajasthan Royals' last-ball victory over Chennai Super Kings in the final in Mumbai 44 evenings later. The subsequent rush by rival national boards to establish their own Twenty20 leagues spoke volumes for a tournament which some had feared would drown in a sea of hype...

More fortunate for the tournament organisers was the identity of the eventual winners. Warne's Rajasthan Royals charmed through their sheer improbability. None of the other seven franchises had spent as little at the first auction, in Mumbai, and none had been so written off in advance. But Warne's ability to get the best out of a motley crew of Indian youngsters and overseas imports was the story of the tournament. And by embodying one of sport's most enduring themes – the triumph of the underdog – it reminded observers that the IPL really could be about more than just money.

Tony Cozier, the respected veteran West Indian broadcaster and journalist, expressed the fears that many shared.

I am fearful for Test cricket... It's difficult to see where it's going, although I don't think Twenty20 would exist without Test cricket. It could all change in the next 30–40 years, long after I've gone. Perhaps people won't regard their national sides with as much fondness as they do now – look at the way things are going with football, where the Champions League is so important. So-called English clubs don't have any English players in them. It might well happen in cricket too.

The Wisden *Forty was quietly dropped, to be replaced by the* Wisden *Test XI of 2008. There were five Indians in the XI – Sehwag, Tendulkar, Dhoni, Harbhajan Singh and Zaheer Khan. The Leading Cricketer in the World was Virender Sehwag.*

INDIA V ENGLAND 2008–09, by David Hopps

England's 2008 tour of India was one of the most politically significant in cricket history. From the moment that the vibrant Indian city of Mumbai fell prey to Islamist extremism, and a shaken touring party flew home without playing the last two one-day matches because of safety fears, arguments resounded about whether they should return to fulfil the two Tests before Christmas. That they did go back was a decision that did them great credit. The prime minister, Gordon Brown, called them 'brave and courageous'.

From the time that the first TV pictures of the Mumbai atrocities were seen, and England's cricketers – then staying in Bhubaneshwar – looked in disbelief at rolling news footage of fires, gunfights, explosions and bloodied bodies being pulled from the Taj Mahal Hotel, where they had stayed only a fortnight earlier, the two scheduled Tests took on a magnitude far beyond a sporting contest. After much agonising, England did fly back to play – and their choice was widely praised for the defiant message that normal life must proceed, however wicked the terrorism...

The most resonant image throughout the Chennai Test had been that of Tendulkar, looking drawn and suppressing his emotions as he perched on an armchair for a TV advert that felt more like an address to the nation. He ended it by vowing, 'I play for India. Now more than ever.' And play he most certainly did. It was the first time he had scored a match-winning century in the fourth innings of a Test. He called afterwards for perspective, acknowledging that he could not assuage the hurt of those who had lost loved ones, but the symbolism was powerful...

Not just the Second Test in Mumbai, but the First Test in Ahmedabad, one of India's more volatile cities, was switched, while the three-day warm-up in Vadodara was cancelled. The new venues of Chennai and Mohali were chosen because the ECB had confidence that the Indian board could deliver its promises in those regions. N. Srinivasan, the BCCI secretary, was also president of the Tamil Nadu Cricket Association; I. S. Bindra, one of the most influential figures in the board's history, was the Punjab president. The commitment with which the authorities delivered the ECB's security demands, which cool analysis might have judged excessive, encapsulated cricket's importance in India's social fabric.

THE LEADING CRICKETER IN THE WORLD IN 2008

In order to overcome the perceived injustice of some men, such as Bishan Bedi, were never chosen as one of the Five Cricketers of the Year, in 2004 Wisden *instituted the new award of Leading Cricketer in the World, the player chosen for his efforts anywhere and everywhere in the world during the previous year.*

VIRENDER SEHWAG, by Ravi Shastri

It would be such a shame if Virender Sehwag needed to be buttressed with figures, hugely impressive as they are. They don't convey an iota of what the stocky figure of this Delhi dasher implies at the crease for bowlers. Fours and sixes come off his bat in rapid-fire succession, as if from a machine gun, and bowlers are out of their

wits before long. A certain numbness overtakes them as they run up to bowl. And then there is mayhem.

Any coach of a rival team is at risk of slipping down in the eyes of his wards as soon as he floats a plan to curb Sehwag. In eight years and 66 Tests, there have been plans aplenty. Bowl him short-pitched deliveries – he doesn't have an on-side stroke except the thrust off his pads, and his straight drives aren't his strongest point. Don't give him room on his off stump, and tuck him up with big inswingers, are other suggestions. Yet nothing works. Sehwag somehow always creates room to free his arms. The overwhelming impression is that he wants every delivery to yield him a four or six.

Yet it would be folly to view Sehwag as no more than a rampaging bull in a cricketing arena. He is a masterful judge of a single, and it doesn't matter if the ball goes no more than a few feet away. He gets off the block quickly and has the confidence to take on the world's best. He isn't just a threat to those patrolling the boundaries; he is as much a menace to those who are marking the square. The opening pair of Sehwag and Gautam Gambhir are as exasperating with their running between wickets as with their inventive strokeplay.

Reputations don't matter to this most amazing of all modern cricketers, whose way of thinking is unlike any I have seen. He made a return to Test cricket in Perth at the start of 2008 and, despite being a borderline selection for the Australian tour and having been in hibernation for the best part of a year, he was as nonchalant as ever. Australia had packed their attack with four genuine fast bowlers on a track billed to be the WACA at its liveliest. No less a factor was the scorching hot and humid conditions. Sehwag's response? 'Well, heat is welcome. It would mean the bowlers won't have long spells.'

His mind is always working overtime on how to make bowlers lose their bearings. It was the same when, after almost two days in the field in the humidity of Chennai, he squared up to Dale Steyn, arguably the bowler of the year, and scored 319 off only 304 balls, judged by the ICC rankings as among the top ten Test innings of all time. Off his own bat Sehwag scored 257 runs on the third day, the most in modern times, against a high-class fielding side. Or when he smashed that double-hundred against Muttiah Muralitharan and freakish Ajantha Mendis, tipped to be the one who would redefine the art of spinning in years to come, and carried his bat for 201 out of India's total of 329 at Galle in July.

Sehwag is no mean off-spinner either, and has a five-for against Australia to prove it. Ego doesn't have any part in his mental make-up, and he rejoices as much in the success of a young mate as he applauds the milestones of a master like Sachin Tendulkar. He isn't the kind to hold grudges. And he only turned 30 in October 2008.

Sehwag is unorthodox, yet his batting skills vouch for the soundness of the time-tested art of batsmanship. Head completely still and movement of feet only once the ball is delivered. The only other player in the last decade who can be compared to him is Sanath Jayasuriya, but Sehwag is tighter and plays straighter, and hence is more consistent in all conditions, as shown by the fact that he has extended the last 11 of his 15 Test centuries to date past 150. His hand-eye co-ordination, grooved on the smooth concrete driveway beside the family home on the outskirts of Delhi, is freakish, and it allows him to predetermine his strokes. Virender Sehwag is a marvel of modern times, a genius who has confounded conventional wisdom, whose daring is now a part of cricket's folklore.

OBITUARY

Mankad, Ashok Vinoo, who died on August 1, 2008, aged 61, won 22 Test caps for India but constantly struggled to live up to the reputation of his father, the great all-rounder Vinoo. He was also frequently forced to play as an opener, which he did not enjoy. Promoted to open in his fourth Test appearance, he started brilliantly, scoring 64, 68 and 97 in successive innings against the 1969–70 Australians at Kanpur and Delhi, but never went on to make a Test century, and struggled on faster pitches overseas. He did quite well opening with Sunil Gavaskar in the Caribbean in early 1971, but later that year his scores in the (ultimately triumphant) three-Test series against England were 1, 5, 8, 7, 10 and 11.

Gavaskar recalled that Mankad kept his sense of humour and told the England players they were lucky it was not a five-Test series because he was obviously improving and would have got to 25 by the end… 'He was a wonderful batsman, but he was not allowed to fulfil his potential because he was converted into an opener for which he was not well equipped,' said one contemporary, Bapu Nadkarni… After retirement Mankad turned to coaching, taking charge of four Indian state sides including Bombay (by now Mumbai) and inspiring them to the Ranji title in 1999–2000. He married an Indian tennis champion, and one of their sons, Harsh, played in the Davis Cup.

WISDEN – 2010

The Wisden *Test XI included Sehwag, Gambhir, Tendulkar and Dhoni, and its Leading Cricketer in the World was Virender Sehwag – again. Still, all was not sweetness and light. However, Twenty20 was still at the forefront of the editor's thoughts.*

NOTES BY THE EDITOR, by Scyld Berry

An Indian businessman arrived at the India Office in London more than a century ago, seeking permission to start the first steel industry in his own country. Jamshedji Tata was graciously given permission, but only after the Viceroy of India had declared that he would eat his hat if Tata succeeded in producing one ingot of steel. As the Allied war effort in Asia was later to depend on the steel made in the city named after its founder, Jamshedpur, it was just as well for most of us – if not for the vice-regal digestion – that Tata did succeed.

Indian businessmen have now taken over the English invention of Twenty20 cricket, just as Jamshedji's descendants, the Tata Steel Group, have bought up what was British Steel. Last year the second Indian Premier League was staged in South Africa, relocated there with a speed and efficiency previously unknown to cricket, and the inaugural Champions League – the first tournament for domestic Twenty20 winners, and some runners-up – was staged in India. While the International Cricket Council repeatedly stated that Test cricket is the highest form of the sport, they organised a second World Twenty20, and seem to be turning it into an almost annual event.

The England and Wales Cricket Board announced before the start of last season that the 2009 Pro40 would be the final 40-over competition, and that it would be replaced by an all-singing and all-dancing Twenty20, so that county cricket would have not one but two 20-over tournaments per summer. Later, the ECB worked out that the sums did not add up, reverted to one 20-over tournament, and abolished the domestic 50-over competition instead. There was no catching the Twenty20 boat once it had sailed east.

INDIAN CRICKET 2009: THE VIEW FROM THE SUMMIT,
by Anand Vasu

Despite this apparent obsession with Twenty20, India rose to the top of the ICC Test rankings for the first time.

For years – no, decades – the complaint India's players endured from their overseas peers was that the country produced brilliant individuals but few world-beating teams. In the meantime, Indian cricket administrators were traditionally never accused of brilliance, but it was said they were worried only about votes or money. Against that backdrop, 2009 was a crucial year for Indian cricket. The team rose to the top of the ICC's Test rankings for the first time – yet this only sharpened the criticism of the administrators.

If cricket's biggest challenge is asserting the primacy of Test matches, three specific areas require addressing: the need for a careful balance between bat and ball, only ensured by sporting pitches; thoughtful scheduling of matches in all formats; and a quality experience at grounds for the paying public.

On all of these counts, the Board of Control for Cricket in India abdicated its substantial responsibility. The board's attitude to pitches was exposed when the final one-day international of the year, against Sri Lanka at Delhi on December 27, was called off after just 23.3 overs. Alan Hurst, the match referee, called the pitch 'unfit' and 'totally unsuitable for one-day international cricket' in his report following the abandonment...

While there was hope that India's No. 1 ranking would force administrators to schedule more Test matches, this was balanced by the fact that Lalit Modi headed the board's tour programmes and fixtures committee. Modi's involvement with franchise-based Twenty20 cricket, its expansion, and the desire for a long and international 'natural window' for the IPL, led to scepticism over whether he would actually try to schedule more Tests...

The year was also marked by the board's directive to state associations to acquire land and build cricket grounds of their own rather than use stadiums that belonged to the municipal corporation or trusts on long leases. The board's sizeable annual infrastructure subsidy (in the region of 30 million rupees, or more than £400,000) to states led some of them – notably Vidarbha, the home of BCCI president Shashank Manohar – following through on developing their own facilities. The new stadium at Jamtha, outside Nagpur, seats 50,000 and boasts state-of-the-art facilities that prompted ICC to call it 'a blueprint for all future grounds internationally' after a routine inspection ahead of the World Cup. The problem was that it lies more than 12 miles outside Nagpur, with no reliable public transport, making it excessively expensive for spectators to attend. The Vidarbha Cricket Association made matters worse by selling only season tickets for the Test against Australia, further deterring spectators from making the trip. In the end approximately 50,000 people – a fifth of the total capacity – watched the game over its five days...

If anything, 2009 was a year when cricket, in all forms, thrived in India, despite what the administrators did.

THE LEADING CRICKETER IN THE WORLD IN 2009

The title of Leading Cricketer in the World can be awarded to the same player more than once. The first person to win the title twice was Virender Sehwag, in 2008 and 2009, even though he has not yet been chosen as a Cricketer of the Year. Perhaps after the 2011 tour of England he will put that right.

VIRENDER SEHWAG, by Scyld Berry

Several strong candidates advanced their case to be the Leading Cricketer in the World in 2009. None, however, made such an impact as to displace the incumbent, Virender Sehwag, India's 31-year-old opening batsman, who extended the sport's traditional boundaries further still. He scored more quickly than any specialist batsman in Tests or one-day internationals. Last year he broke Test cricket's

sound barrier by scoring at more than a run a ball. Australia's former captain Ian Chappell, in as good a position to judge as anybody alive, directly compared Sehwag to Sir Donald Bradman: they have the fastest scoring-rate among players of their generation, and are the only men to have exceeded 290 three times in Tests. Chappell called Sehwag 'the greatest destroyer since the U-boat', and dismissed the accusation that he prospered only in home conditions by pointing out that he averaged almost 50 abroad.

Sehwag raised the bar even higher than in 2008, when he had scored at a strike-rate of 85 runs per 100 balls in Tests, and 120 in one-day internationals.

In 2009 he did not play so much, after injuring his right shoulder during the second IPL, and for much of the year the giant rested. It was no coincidence that, in his absence, India were knocked out in the early stages of both the World Twenty20 and the Champions Trophy. He still played in all of India's Test matches in 2009 – a three-Test series in New Zealand and another at home to Sri Lanka – and, in steering them to No. 1 in the Test rankings for the first time, Sehwag averaged 70, with a strike-rate of 108.9.

Adam Gilchrist had set a new standard with his strike-rate of 81.9 while averaging 47 in Tests, but he did so almost entirely from the relative comfort of No. 7 in one of the greatest Test teams of all. Sehwag has taken on the opposition from the first ball of India's innings, shredding their confidence with his strokeplay, demoralising them as no Test batsman has done since Bradman, who scored at 61.2 per 100 balls. In one-day internationals in 2009 Sehwag had a strike-rate of 136.5 – again, far higher than any batsman of substance has achieved over a lengthy period – while averaging 45.

'The feat of the year', as Chappell called it, came when Test cricket returned to the Brabourne Stadium in Mumbai last December. Sri Lanka scored 366 for eight on the opening day as they attempted, in the last match of the series, to overturn India's 1–0 lead. Next morning they continued to 393 all out; 79 overs remained in the day. Few would have thought of winning the game from this position, rather than settling for a draw. Sehwag did. By the close of the second day he had scored 284 not out from 239 balls with 40 fours and seven sixes – and Sri Lanka are Asia's best fielding side.

By dispiriting bowlers Sehwag has made batting so much easier for team-mates. Rangana Herath made a fine comeback last year as Sri Lanka's left-arm spinner, yet, when he came on to bowl, Sehwag went down the pitch to drive his second ball for six. Herath's fellow spinner was Muttiah Muralitharan, his captain Kumar Sangakkara – a candidate himself to be the Leading Cricketer in the World. But Sehwag still surged to the second-fastest Test double-hundred ever recorded, from only 168 balls. Those of us who saw the fastest – Nathan Astle's from 153 balls against England – would vouch that Christchurch's drop-in pitch played as flawlessly as an artificial one.

Sehwag, not surprisingly, could not continue in the same vein next morning and was dismissed for 293 from 254 balls. But by then India had taken a first-innings lead, and Sehwag had given his team so much time that even though Sri Lanka made more than 300 in their second innings as well, India won by an innings early on the fifth day, and took the series 2–0 to claim top spot.

… One definition of genius is doing what nobody else can: and in 2009 Sehwag batted like nobody else has ever done for any length of time… If he had an identical twin, who batted at the same rate as Viru in 2009, India would score 600 in a day of 90 overs. Test cricket has been threatened by the greater excitement that is perceived in 50-over and 20-over cricket; it will not be if more batsmen emulate Sehwag, as he pushes back the parameters and scores at the same rate in Tests as others do in Twenty20.

… Sehwag has to be first on the team-sheet to represent the World, whatever the game's format. He would take on the Martians, however hostile and alien their attack, disrupting their lines and wavelengths; and, if he succeeded, as he normally does, he would make life so much easier for those who followed.

OBITUARY

Raj Singh Dungapur, who died on September 12, 2009, aged 73, was a significant figure in Indian cricket for half a century: as a player, administrator, selector, commentator and centre of attention. Raj Singh was the son of a prince and had a long-standing relationship with 'India's Nightingale', Lata Mangeshkar, which made him doubly glamorous in Indian eyes. He was also tall, voluble and very sociable, with an anecdote for every occasion, which made him popular with those around him. And with no urgent need to make a living, he put his energies into the game.

His father was the last Maharawal of Dungarpur, a 15-gun state in Rajasthan. At Daly College in Indore, Raj learned to swing the ball, and he had a long career in the Ranji Trophy, mainly with Rajasthan, playing 86 first-class matches without making the Indian team. But he soon established himself as a power off the field, firstly in the Cricket Club of India, the national equivalent of MCC, where his aristocratic lineage, bearing and reputation for integrity enabled him to establish some authority in a body full of warring factions. He became a regular tour manager… and a selector with a penchant for youth. Raj propelled a reluctant Mohammad Azharuddin into the captaincy and quickly recognised the talent of the young Sachin Tendulkar, getting the CCI rules changed so he could enter the dressing rooms at 14, and picking him for the Test team at 16. In 1996 he achieved Indian cricket's highest office, the presidency of the Board of Control, serving three years… Raj Singh was a man who loved the game more than he loved himself, which has not been true of every modern Indian administrator.

MISCELLANY

Note: *Although* Wisden's *Chronicles of the Year began in 1994, the first Indian stories were not printed until the 1996 edition.*

An Indian MP complained in parliament that the Communication Department had refused to provide Sunil Gavaskar with an immediate telephone connection unless he produced a certificate proving his claim that he was a well-known sportsman.
Indian Express, August 23, 1995

The North Zone players, on the way to play their Duleep Trophy fixture against Central Zone in Lucknow, had to bed down in the corridor of their sleeper train owing to a mix-up over bookings. Passengers were said to be angry because their kit was blocking all the gangways.
Times of India, November 26, 1995

A toast was drunk at Ballynahinch Castle, a hotel in County Galway, to mark the centenary of the Test debut of Ranjitsinhji, who bought the castle and the estate in 1927, six years before his death.
Daily Telegraph, July 27, 1996

A local cricketer shot dead an opponent during a match in Kashmir, after an umpire's decision went against his team. The player pulled out a revolver and fired at the opposition, killing Ghulam Hassan and wounding two others, before fleeing.
Asian Age, November 21, 1996

Deepak Choughale, a 12-year-old schoolboy, scored 400 not out in Karnataka's 589 for four against Goa in a two-day match in the Sportstar Under-13 tournament in Madras. He batted 316 minutes and was given a bicycle as a reward.
The Hindu, December 25, 1996

Hundreds of cricket lovers threw stones at the cable TV office in Jammu, northern India, after the company failed to relay an India–Pakistan one-day international from Toronto. Police charged the crowd to restore order.
Times of India, September 15, 1997

Nizanjan Sarkar, a tailor from Gauhati, Assam, died from heart failure, apparently overcome by excitement while watching the close one-day game between India and Pakistan in Dhaka.
The Hindu, January 19, 1998

A leading Hindu sage has called on India to give up cricket because the manufacture of balls involves the slaughter of nine cows, which are sacred to Hindus, every day. Swami Nischalananda Saraswati Maharaj, custodian of the temple at Puri, said an alternative to cowhide should be found if the game was to continue.
Daily Telegraph, November 5, 1998

A batsman clubbed a bowler to death in a club match in Pune, India, after he appealed for lbw. Amit Shinde (19) rushed down the field and hammered Arul Awachat (23) on the head with his bat before the umpire could give his verdict. Awachat died in hospital before doctors could operate to remove a blood clot. Shinde was batting for Modern against Golden on the Fergusson College ground.
Times of India, May 4, 1999

A 26-year-old man was killed at Kallipparra in the Indian state of Kerala when the power failed while he was watching the World Cup. He climbed up a nearby electrical pole to try to solve the problem, and was electrocuted.
Times of India, May 17, 1999

A Muslim terrorist group, the al-Umar Mujahideen, said it tried to kidnap the former Indian captain, Kapil Dev, in 1996 to try to secure the release of the group's leader from an Indian jail. 'Our plans didn't work out,' said a spokesman.
The Hindu, January 8, 2000

A Calcutta schoolteacher, Tejesh Adhikary, has invented a new game called 'Reading Cricket' to help cricket-crazy students to improve their literacy. Two teams are given separate unseen texts. The batting side has to read out a passage, and the fielding side appeals to an umpire if it feels a word is mispronounced or omitted. The batsman gets one run for reading a column correctly, and a boundary for pronouncing correctly any word in a foreign language. 'This is a unique method for developing a flair for reading among school students,' Mr Adhikary said.
Asian Age, February 28, 2000

The Hizbul, a militant anti-government group in Kashmir, played a friendly game against the Indian Army in the normally tense border area of Kupwara. A large crowd saw the Hizbul beat the Army by 25 runs. However, their commander left immediately the game was over for fear of being arrested by the soldiers.
Gujarat Samachar, August 6, 2000

Tom Gueterbock approached the *wisden.com* website to help publicise the sale of his £495,000 home in Battersea, south London, which he thought might particularly appeal to Indian cricket fans. The address was 10 Dulka Road.
Daily Telegraph, January 25, 2001

Asia's largest prison has removed the name of Manoj Prabhakar from one of its jail blocks. Cited during his heyday as a role model for inmates at Tibar Jail in New Delhi, the former Indian Test all-rounder had been embroiled in the match-fixing scandal.
Asian Age, July 9, 2001

India's National Commission on Population used the one-day international against England to launch a birth control campaign, complete with the slogan, 'Little bouncers – no more please', 'No slips please, population control is not a laughing matter' and 'China stumped – India produced more babies in the last hour!'
Times of India, January 20, 2002

The original Ranji Trophy is to be returned to the Saurashtra Cricket Association by Wiltshire Queries CC, whose members discovered it at a clearance sale in London last year.
Wisden Asia Cricket, March 2002

The Sachin Tendulkar lookalike, Bulvirchand, who had already co-starred with Tendulkar in an advert for Visa cards, has been chosen to play him in the movie *Kaisi Mohabbat*, in which the heroine fulfils her dream by meeting the great man.
The Observer, August 11, 2002

Ashok Ohri, the manager of the India Under-19 cricket team in England, denied allegations that he had 'misbehaved' with a female guest in a swimming pool at the team's hotel in Leicestershire. It was alleged that he had 'by design bumped into a lady swimmer which the latter did not like.' Mr Ohri said he was not in the pool and could not swim.
The Tribune, September 19, 2002

Muslim militants arrested in Jammu, northern India, were found to have concealed cash, a wireless handset and 120 bullets inside cricket bats.
Associated Press, February 2, 2003

Ramanlal Pathak, a Sanskrit scholar from Valodara, India, has spent seven years assembling a cricket vocabulary to freshen the appeal of 'a dying language'. A batsman is *bat-dhar*, runs translate to *gaccha* or *dhavan*. *Pashya pashya chowka*

means 'another glorious shot for four', whereas 'another four: the crowd is ecstatic' is *sahatu chowkra – sarvatra prekshaka mandalie anandasya vatavaranam.*
Times of India, March 22, 2003

Parthiv Patel's uncle, Jagat Patel, has sworn to marry only after the wicketkeeper is performing consistently for India's Test XI, a tactic once tried, successfully, by Sachin Tendulkar's brother, Ajit.
Rajasthan Patrika, October 7, 2003

A group of young cricketers playing in Naroda, Ahmedabad, stumbled across 23 signal rockets, which are normally used by ships in distress. One was inadvertently launched, the ensuing explosion triggering panic in the streets, bringing a bomb disposal unit rushing to the field. Police are mystified as to how the rockets found their way 100 miles inland.
Times of India, April 15, 2004

All India's 174 retired Test players and umpires are to receive a pension of 5,000 rupees a month.
Times of India, April 22, 2004

Research by zoologists at St Joseph's College, Bangalore, showed that many professional cricketers exhibit the same fingerprint patterns. Almost all those they surveyed had the 'ulnar loop' pattern on the right little finger. Their study was hindered because many Indian players refused to co-operate.
Times of India, May 2, 2004

The Indian government has reversed a ruling that barred Sachin Tendulkar from displaying the national flag on his helmet. The cabinet said it will amend the Prevention of Insults to National Honour Act, and will allow the flag to be used on sporting uniforms – but not below the belt or on underwear.
Mid Day, July 4, 2005

India's top golfer Arjun Atwal complained of his country's indifference despite unprecedented success on the USPGA tour. 'I have gone to every possible sponsor. But they say, "You don't play cricket."'
Times of India, July 20, 2005

Nandu Patel, 29, scored 403 not out for PD Hinduja Hospital against Central Excise in the *Times of India* Shield. Patil had intended to bat on and beat the 72-year-old tournament record of 515, but the opposition quit at the tea interval.
Times of India, December 6, 2005

Disaster was narrowly averted when a pilot trying to make an emergency landing at Solapur Airport, Maharashtra, suddenly noticed more than 500 people playing cricket matches on the runway. The Air Deccan aircraft, carrying oil workers, had developed a technical fault and flew over the landing strip twice as a warning. 'In the third approach, I landed the aircraft but to save the people I put on the emergency brakes,' said pilot Thomas Lynn. 'The craft began skidding at full speed and it stopped when both the rear tyres burst.' Bhima Kola, resident of a nearby slum, said they regularly played on the airstrip, and had ignored the plane because there were no regular landings there.
Indian Express, March 22, 2006

The family of Mushtaq Ali, India's first Test match centurion who died in 2005, are living in a cramped, derelict house in Indore because their father was never able to move into a modern bungalow allotted to him by the state government. When the family tried to get the keys in 1995, they found a judge living there and he never moved out, Mushtaq's son Gulrez said.
Hindustan Times, April 19, 2006

Istabraque Shaikh, a 15-year-old fan of Rahul Dravid, scored 36 in four hours 12 minutes in a three-day schools match in Mumbai. He was lbw just before close of play on the first day. 'Take it from me, we haven't shouted that loud an appeal in a long, long time,' said bowler Salman Charolia. Two years earlier, Istabraque spent 12 and a half hours making 69 in a similar fixture.
Mumbai Mirror, January 23, 2007

Cricket fan Sarun Sharma, 23, from Mango near Jamshedpur, offered one of his kidneys for sale so that he could go to watch the World Cup in the Caribbean. 'Anybody can survive with one kidney,' he said, 'but you will never get the opportunity to watch India win the cup in the West Indies.' Police said his offer was illegal.
Financial Express, March 14, 2007

Ho-Sen-Hing, a Mumbai resident of Chinese origin, hanged himself after losing a large sum betting on India to beat Bangladesh at the World Cup.
Hindustan Times, March 27, 2007

An American company that failed to get the rights for India's neutral-venue international matches has bought a cricket ground on the moon in protest. *Dreamcricket.com* paid $25 to the Lunar registry for a patch of moonscape near the Crater Manilius. Venu Palaparthi, co-founder of the company, said the Dreamcricket Lunar Cricket Field was the perfect venue for Indian cricketers as

the low gravity would enable out-of-form batsmen to recover their touch. The legal standing of the purchase is dubious.
Sunday Times of India, July 1, 2007

Officials at Headingley and the Melbourne Cricket Ground turned down Indian film star Emraan Hashmi and director Kunal Deshmukh when they sought permission to make a film about match-fixing. The cricketing scenes for the film, *Jannat*, were eventually shot at Newlands in Cape Town.
Ahmedabad Mirror, March 15, 2008

Indian Prime Minister Manmohan Singh said after the conclusion of the inaugural Indian Premier League that he was not a cricket fan. 'I do believe that to the ordinary people of this country games like hockey and football have far greater significance,' he added.
Hindustan Times, June 2, 2008

Groundstaff at Eden Gardens in Calcutta have threatened suicide unless they get a pay rise.
Daily Telegraph, July 10, 2008

In Mahendra Singh Dhoni's hometown of Ranchi, kite-maker Mohammad Talib said he was unable to meet demand from children wanting kites carrying the Indian captain's image, 'Every day I prepare around 1,500 kites with photos of Dhoni, but I get over 2,000 young customers daily asking for them.'
Indo-Asian News Service, January 9, 2009

Play in a one-day match between Himachal Pradesh and Punjab at Una was halted when a helicopter landed on the field by mistake. The pilot thought the H for Himachal painted on the pitch was a landing pad.
Reuters, February 23, 2009

Three former Test cricketers have been elected to the new 543-member Indian parliament at the 2009 election, all supporters of the victorious Congress Party: Navjot Singh Sidhu, Kirti Azad and Mohammad Azharuddin.
Asian Tribune, May 18, 2009

Note: *Sidhu and Azad are actually members of the BJP party – even* Wisden *nods occasionally.*

A 12-year-old has scored 439 in the tournament that propelled Sachin Tendulkar to fame. Twenty-one years after Tendulkar (as a 15-year-old) scored 329 in the Harris Shield, Sarfaraz Khan surpassed him, playing for Springfield Rizvi School against the Indian Education Society. Sarfaraz enjoyed hitting 12 sixes and 56 fours in 421 balls, but disliked the fuss afterwards. 'I swear I will never hit another 400 in my life,' he was quoted as saying.

Agence France-Presse, November 6, 2009

INDEX

ALSO AVAILABLE FROM WISDEN

www.wisden.com

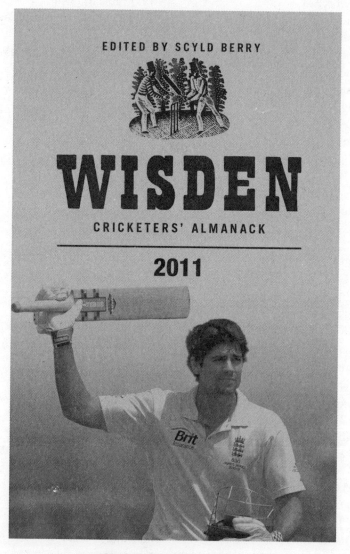

EDITED BY SCYLD BERRY

WISDEN

CRICKETERS' ALMANACK

2011

ISBN 978-1-4081-3130-5

ALSO AVAILABLE FROM WISDEN

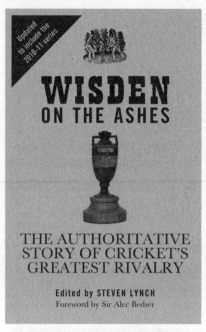

ISBN 978-1-4081-5239-3

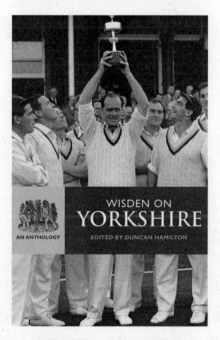

ISBN 978-1-4081-2462-8

ALSO AVAILABLE FROM WISDEN

ISBN 978-1-4081-2756-8

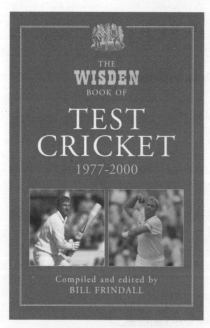

ISBN 978-1-4081-2758-2

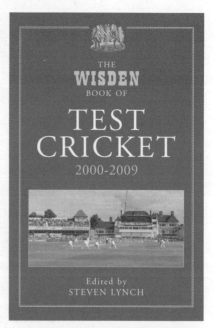

ISBN 978-1-4081-2335-5

ALSO AVAILABLE FROM WISDEN

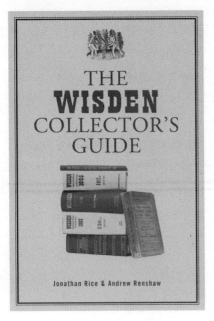

ISBN 978-1-4081-2673-8

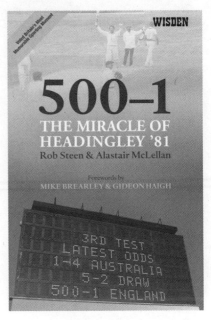

ISBN 978-1-4081-4085-7

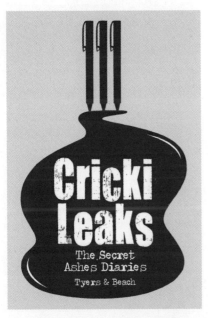

ISBN 978-1-4081-5240-9

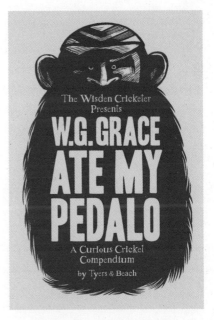

ISBN 978-1-4081-3042-1